A REVOLUTI   ᴐNSCIENCE

Theodore Parker and Antebellum America

Paul E. Teed

University Press of America,® Inc.
Lanham · Boulder · New York · Toronto · Plymouth, UK

Library of Congress Control Number: 2012941409
ISBN: 978-0-7618-5963-5 (paperback : alk. paper)
eISBN: 978-0-7618-5964-2

Portions of chapter 9 previously appeared in "'A Brave Man's Child':
Theodore Parker and the Memory of the American Revolution, 1845-1860,"
Historical Journal of Massachusetts 29 (Summer 2001) and is reprinted by
permission of the *Historical Journal of Massachusetts*.

Portions of chapter 10 previously appeared in "The Politics of Sectional
Memory: Theodore Parker and the *Massachusetts Quarterly Review*,
1847-1850," *Journal of the Early Republic* 21 (Summer 2001) and is
reprinted by permission of University of Pennsylvania Press.

Portions of chapters 13 and 17 appeared in "Racial Nationalism and Its
Challengers: Theodore Parker, John Rock and the Antislavery Movement,"
Civil War History 49 (June 1995) and is reprinted by permission of
The Kent State University Press.

⊖™ The paper used in this publication meets the minimum
requirements of American National Standard for Information
Sciences—Permanence of Paper for Printed Library Materials,
ANSI Z39.48-1992

FOR
MELISSA, EMILIA AND LUCY

TABLE OF CONTENTS

Acknowledgements vii

Introduction ix

1   "Bred Up Amid the Memories" 1

2   Divinity School and Beyond 15

3   Spiritual Indifference 29

4   The Transcendentalist Controversy 39

5   The Making of a Public Radical 49

6   A Reckoning with Ministers 63

7   Church and Society 71

8   Classes, Families and Reform 83

9   Slavery, Politics and the Revolution 95

10   Making Antislavery Culture 107

11   Conscience and the Fugitive Slave Act 119

12   Continual Alarms 133

13   Race, Politics and Antislavery Violence 147

14   Conscience, Politics and Religion 159

15   The Anthony Burns Crisis 171

16   The Politics of Confrontation 185

17   The Idea That Blood Must Flow 197

18   Principles, Parties and Partings 213

19   The Final Journey 223

20   Conclusion 237

Notes 241

Selected Bibliography 273

Index 285

ACKNOWLEDGEMENTS

Like all authors, I have benefitted from the encouragement and assistance of many people. R. Kent Newmyer, my dissertation advisor at the University of Connecticut, was an outstanding model for an aspiring historian. His vast knowledge and devotion to scholarship, as well as his deep commitment to teaching, continued to inspire me as I worked on this project. Richard D. Brown, Lawrence Goodheart and Harlow Sheidley read all or part of the manuscripts at various stages in its development as well. I am very grateful to them for their insights. I have also benefitted from the support, both intellectual and personal, of Richard Francis Crane, Brad Jarvis, Jeff Koperski, Tom Renna, and Don Bachand. David Kiracofe is owed special thanks for his meticulous reading of the manuscript and his friendship.

This book would not have been possible without the aid of librarians and archivists who helped to locate and identify sources. The Zahnow Library staff at Saginaw Valley State University obtained materials for me and recommended new electronic resources. Archivists at the Massachusetts Historical Society, the Houghton Library, Boston Public Library, and the Harvard-Andover Theological Library were helpful as well. I am also grateful to these repositories for granting me permission to quote from their rich collections. In addition, I am grateful to the *Journal of the Early Republic*, *Civil War History*, and the *Historical Journal of Massachusetts* for permission to reprint portions of my articles in those journals as part of chapters 9, 10, 13, and 17.

The faculty, staff, and administrators at Saginaw Valley State University have made important contributions to my work as well. Two faculty research grants and a sabbatical leave gave me the time and resources needed to develop the project. Ann Garcia in the Technical Publications Office read the manuscript and provided critical assistance in formatting the final product. She cheerfully responded to my many requests for changes. Pat Latty took time to proof the manuscript as well.

My family has provided constant support and inspiration. David Teed's passion for history is deep and abiding, and I look forward each week to discussing my work with him. My daughters, Emilia and Lucy, have filled my life with joy and laughter throughout this project. They are constant reminders of what matters most. But it is to Melissa Ladd Teed that I owe my deepest gratitude. She believed in the project when I did not, and gave me the confidence and the time to see it through. In the midst of her own work, she read the manuscript multiple times, listened to my ideas, and offered her own. Her insights, suggestions and questions have contributed to this book in so many ways.

INTRODUCTION

On the evening of May 26, 1854, a thin, wiry man with intense blue eyes and nervous movements stood on the stage at Faneuil Hall in Boston to deliver a speech against the recent capture and imprisonment of an escaped slave. The already seething audience knew the man immediately as Theodore Parker, the fiery Unitarian minister of the Twenty-Eighth Congregational Society of Boston, and one of the city's most militant abolitionists. As he approached the podium amidst shouts of approval and anticipation, the forty-three year old minister soaked in inspiration from the symbols of American revolutionary heroism that adorned the walls of Faneuil Hall, and he marshaled his prodigious intellectual and rhetorical powers for the speech to come. Parker intended to provoke his audience into rescuing the fugitive slave, Anthony Burns, from his jail cell in the Boston Courthouse just a short distance away.

Telling the crowd that corrupt laws were not binding on the consciences of human beings, he pleaded with them to act in defense of the principles for which their revolutionary ancestors had sacrificed. He reminded them that during the Stamp Act resistance, their "brave fathers" had defied a "wicked law" and had transformed "absolute justice into common justice, making it common law." He confessed that though he was a clergyman and "a man of peace," the preservation of liberty sometimes required the use of force. Patriotic words were no longer enough, the time had come for "deeds as well as words." Only a few minutes later, the Hall emptied as the crowd rushed madly toward the Courthouse where the largest civil disturbance in Boston since the Revolution ensued.[1]

In his dramatic appeals to conscience and revolutionary memory at Faneuil Hall, Theodore Parker combined the two basic themes that shaped his life as one of antebellum America's most controversial religious and social reformers. Placing his faith in the ability of human beings to discern moral principles directly, Parker reaffirmed his life-long belief that an unfettered conscience was the essential building block of a just society. The power to end "wickedness" he believed, lay within the self, placed there by a loving and just God. Beginning in the 1830s, with his immersion in the culture of American Transcendentalism, he waged unremitting war against the ideas and institutions that claimed special authority over conscience. His devastating critiques of biblical inerrancy, the church, and unjust law were often dismissed by his contemporaries as "destructive," but they were not meant to be. In breaking down traditional or institutional sources of moral authority, he sought to foster moral self-reliance and to build a society in which moral duty could be known directly and chosen freely. At its core, Parker's belief in conscience amounted to a soaring optimism about human nature and confidence in the ultimate direction of human history.

This book argues, however, that the explosive power of Theodore Parker's conscience cannot be understood apart from his commitment to the American Revolutionary tradition. Steeped in the memories of the American Revolution that defined the cultural world of his childhood, Parker carried with him a highly dramatic narrative of personal courage and integrity that shaped his understanding of conscience. The grandson of a Revolutionary war hero, he was thrilled by confrontations in which conscience could be displayed at personal cost or physical peril. It was in such moments, he believed, when abstract political and moral ideals became concrete realities and when the forces of human progress were fully unleashed.

Parker's deep personal need to display his own revolutionary conscience propelled him into the great conflicts of his life and shaped the kind of leader he became. His antislavery activism was built upon a skillful deployment of the revolutionary symbols, monuments and memories that dotted the physical and cultural landscape of antebellum New England. Monuments were visible manifestations of deeper truths about human rights and human freedom. If they had any purpose, it was to promote action against slavery, an institution that nullified God's purpose for the enslaved, numbed the conscience of the slaveholders, and perverted the American idea of liberty. Just as his grandfather had committed treason against his King in the name of freedom and conscience, so Parker was ready to break the laws of the American Republic to defeat human bondage.

This book examines the personal, intellectual and political dimensions of Parker's revolutionary conscience. Beginning with his youth in post-revolutionary Lexington, Massachusetts, it follows Parker's largely self-made path to Harvard Divinity School and into the Unitarian clergy. A brilliant student with an astounding facility for the acquisition of languages, Parker was drawn into the circle of young ministers and intellectuals whose fascination with European romantic literature and philosophy was called "transcendentalism" by their critics. Quickly emerging as the most skilled theologian among these unorthodox thinkers, he scrutinized the claims of traditional Christianity in light of romantic philosophy and German biblical criticism. His blunt rejections of biblical inspiration and the divinity of Christ placed him not only in direct opposition to the dominant evangelical Christianity of the day, but also shocked members of his own liberal denomination. Fearing that their orthodox opponents would use Parker's heresies to label all Unitarians as Deists or Atheists, Unitarian leaders ostracized him and hoped that he would leave the ministry.

But as we shall see, the plans of Parker's detractors backfired on them. Marginalized by his former colleagues, he nevertheless reemerged as a symbol of conscientious dissent and religious liberty. After leaving his small church in West Roxbury, Massachusetts, he founded a new religious society in Boston where he preached to huge audiences and became a trenchant critic of the city's religious and mercantile establishment. He also sought out national audiences for his views through the lyceum lecture circuit and the periodical press. By the 1850s, his sins against the Massachusetts establishment also included militant abolitionism. He denounced the Fugitive Slave Act of 1850 from his pulpit and played a leading role in obstructing attempts by state and federal officials to enforce the law. In the years before his death in 1860, moreover, Parker came to believe that the slavery issue was the central problem of his generation and he predicted that the conflict would end in a violent, sectional confrontation. As a partial fulfillment of that prophecy, he joined the Secret Six conspiracy that helped to fund John Brown's ill-fated 1859 raid on the federal armory at Harpers Ferry.

As may be inferred from the foregoing sketch, Theodore Parker's short life of less than fifty years was packed with ideas and experiences. So much so, in fact, that he has seemed an unapproachable subject for biographers. The sheer size of his correspondence, his voluminous published work, and his well-deserved reputation for profound scholarship has made scholars wary of writing his life. But historians' lack of attention to Parker has also stemmed from problems of categorization. After several biographies by Unitarian authors in the nineteenth century, twentieth century writers struggled to make sense of Parker's unusual combination of values. He was deeply religious, for example, yet intensely critical of both the Bible and the Church. Although a member of the Transcendentalist circle, he criticized Ralph Waldo Emerson's philosophy and disliked both Bronson Alcott and Margaret Fuller. A committed antislavery activist, he was nevertheless influenced by the "scientific racism" of his era.

Without resolving these tensions, Henry Steele Commager's 1936 book *Theodore Parker: Yankee Crusader* attempted to build a case for Parker as a quintessential scholar-activist, and Daniel Aaron's 1951 work *Men of Good Hope* linked his social criticism with the larger Progressive tradition. Both Commager and Aaron were inspired by the sympathetic portrait of Parker in Vernon Parrington's *Main Currents in American Thought*, but none of these works led to a full-scale Parker revival. During the 1960s and 70s, he resurfaced briefly in the surge of writing on the American antislavery movement. Yet again, however, Parker's anomalous place in that movement meant that his career was not the focus of systematic analysis. He was something of an "interstitial" figure among the abolitionists, positioned between the various ideological factions that historians were interested in exploring; and so, he fell through the cracks of most studies. The study that follows here attempts to demonstrate the distinctiveness of Parker's ideas about conscience and revolutionary memory in

uniting an otherwise fragmented antislavery movement around a shared moral
and historical vision.[2]

Works on American Transcendentalism, the movement with which Parker
was most closely associated in his early career, have given him greater consideration. William Hutchison's 1959 study of church reform, for example, contains a lengthy section on the creation of Parker's Boston church, the Twenty-
Eighth Congregational Society. Two edited collections of Transcendentalism's
key documents, one by Perry Miller and the other by Joel Myerson, include se-
lections from Parker's sermons and essays. Both editors see Parker's 1841 sermon "The Transient and Permanent in Christianity" as one of the movement's
defining texts. Yet historians have sometimes been confused about Parker's
place in the Transcendentalist movement and some have even argued that his
criticisms of Emerson place him outside it altogether. Ann Rose's 1981 book
Transcendentalism as a Social Movement cited Parker's "quite conventional
private life" as a reason to exclude him from her study of the movement's social
reform culture. Parker fares better in Phillip Gura's recent overview of Transcendentalism, emerging as a central figure in what Gura sees as the more socially-engaged wing of the group that understood conscience as more than simply "self-culture." Building on Gura's insight, this study makes the case that
Parker's idea of conscience was nurtured by his association with Transcendentalism, but that it took mature shape only after his personal detachment from
others in the movement. By the 1850s, Parker had become more an observer of
Transcendentalism than a participant. He valued its intellectual and spiritual
contributions while forging much stronger relationships with abolitionists whose
own understanding of conscience and revolutionary memory mirrored his own.[3]

Most recently, the return of intellectual biography as a legitimate historical
genre has borne enormous fruit in Parker's case. The 2002 publication of Dean
Grodzins' *American Heretic: Theodore Parker and American Transcendentalism*, has done much to restore Parker's reputation as the finest scholar and theologian of his generation. Painstakingly reconstructing Parker's intellectual and
personal world to 1846, Grodzins has amply demonstrated his subject's immersion in a trans-Atlantic world of ideas. In uncovering new details about the conflicted nature of Parker's marriage, moreover, Grodzins has dispelled the view
that the fiery minister led a flat, one-dimensional domestic existence. The Parker
who emerges from the book is a brilliant and intensely ambitious man, but one
who is often frustrated and beset with feelings of inadequacy and disappointment.[4]

The more positive assessments by Gura and Grodzins suggest that Parker's
distinctive combination of religiosity and skepticism, intellect and activism, are
relevant once again. Larger cultural trends have helped as well. The resurgence
of evangelical religion as a force in American political and cultural life, it
seems, has led American progressives to re-examine religion as a force for social change, and to reclaim the spiritual roots of their social vision. Although
more theologically orthodox than Parker was, the Christian progressive *Soj*

ers movement has explicitly claimed kinship with his generation's crusades against poverty, slavery, and war. Similar attitudes can be found in what is called the "emerging church" movement which, along with a commitment to social justice, shares Parker's skepticism about traditional religious forms and institutions. As many American faith communities carry out intense debates over sexuality, poverty and violence, moreover, Parker's insistence that biblical precepts yield to the authority of conscience seems increasingly germane. And finally, at a time when biblical scholarship has undergone a revolution in methodology and gained an increasingly large popular audience, Parker's early contributions to the historical and critical study of the scriptures can now be appreciated more fully. Perhaps after a century and a half of neglect, Parker has finally come into his own.[5]

This study contributes to the revival of interest in Parker in two important ways. First, it places the concept of conscience at the very core of his self-conception and his public ideology. Above all, Parker desired to see himself, and to have others see him, as a man of conscience. So deeply rooted was this personal imperative that it constituted the most basic stance by which he related to the world and the people around him. Many contemporaries noted this characteristic and observed that it manifested itself as an unwillingness to moderate the force and tone of his attacks upon the theological, social, or political systems he opposed. Accused by friends and foes alike of transgressing the boundaries of public decorum, he expressed either bewilderment at such criticisms or rejected them. What others regarded as arrogance or unwarranted self-assertion, Parker regarded as necessary truth telling and he interpreted condemnation and personal ostracism as signs of his own moral independence. If such a self-conception often produced a grandiose sense of personal importance, it also helped to protect him from the inevitable self-doubts resulting from the sustained criticism of powerful and often self-interested enemies. Parker often wept when confronted personally by his critics, but his positions remained unchanged.

In his insistence upon subjecting the claims of institutions to the unrelenting scrutiny of conscience, Parker contributed to the emergence of what scholar T. Gregory Garvey calls "discursive democracy" in nineteenth-century America. Pursuing a ministerial career at a time when New England's religious Standing Order was adjusting to the twin shocks of disestablishment and intense sectarian division, Parker insisted that ecclesiastical and clerical authority of the church and of its ministers could no longer rest upon traditions of deference or biblical sanction. Liberal religious leaders would have to compete for public attention with their orthodox rivals as well as with politicians, reformers, lyceum lecturers and commercial leaders. It was this realization that led him to embrace new, more democratic styles of communication, including church reform, lyceum lectures and various forms of print media. Parker represented himself in this public discourse as a sincere man of conscience for whom failure to speak bluntly was a far greater moral lapse than any violation of decorum. He rejected claims that he was propelled by ambition to seek public attention, instead regarding himself as a conscientious and unrestrained critic of flawed institutions.

From this foundation, he helped to shape a new, more unruly public culture with expanded access to the public square. As his frustrated conservative detractors could attest, Theodore Parker was a master of finding new and larger audiences when old ones were closed off.[6]

But if conscience constituted a personal and professional ethic for Parker, it was also an intellectual commitment that placed him at one end of a spectrum of thought on individual moral capacities. As historians D.H. Meyer and Daniel Walker Howe have argued, the idea of conscience was central to the developing moral philosophy of the antebellum period. As geographical mobility, disestablishment, and democratic politics weakened the authority of family, church and state over the moral life of the individual, American moralists stressed the importance of internal restraint. Drawing upon the "common sense" philosophy of the Scottish Enlightenment, neo-Calvinist intellectuals and liberal Unitarian thinkers alike agreed on the existence of an innate mental faculty which they called the "moral sense." Human beings, in this view, were innately moral and accountable to a God who had provided them with the means to discern their duty. Although this view was a major departure from earlier Calvinist belief in man's natural depravity, mainstream moralists did not believe that the individual conscience was *infallible,* or that it cancelled the claims of institutions. The natural conscience, they insisted, required instruction from outside the self, either from divine grace, biblical revelation, ministerial authority, or secular law. Without such instruction, the natural conscience could misfire and lead the individual toward sin and society toward anarchy.[7]

Parker rejected such caution about authority of conscience and his mature conception of it verged on a belief in the complete moral autonomy of the individual. Like other Transcendentalists, he drew on German idealist philosophy to construct a romantic conception of the self as the source of knowledge. Moral discernment, like other key components of human reason, he believed, was rooted in the deepest structures of consciousness. It required no instruction or check from external sources of authority. Experience triggered the action of conscience, but did not significantly shape its content. This belief was a key component of Parker's larger theological system. Convinced that divine providence was carried out not through miracles or supernatural intervention but through the natural powers implanted in human nature, he was certain that conscience was more than adequate for the purpose it was intended to serve. God had given human beings a reliable conscience and merely asked them to apply it in discerning the moral law. To deprecate or deny the authority of conscience was therefore tantamount to a denial of God's benevolent purpose for human history. During the 1850s, he used the term "practical atheism" to describe those, like Daniel Webster, who demanded that obedience to human laws and institutions outweighed individual moral preferences.[8]

Even casual readers of Ralph Waldo Emerson's famous essay "Self-Reliance" will recognize similarities between Parker's idea of conscience and that of the Concord philosopher. They drew on many of the same philosophical sources and embraced a protean conception of the self that left many contemporaries gasping for breath. But the distinctive role that conscience played in Parker's assertive self-conception meant that he deployed it in ways that were quite different from other Transcendentalists. For Emerson, conscience was the primary tool in the art of "self-culture" which essentially began and ended with the individual. As one historian has argued, Emerson valorized the "the empowered individual, the self-reliant genius for whom conscience was the highest law." But for Parker, conscience was the common property of all who chose to use it, and it functioned best in direct response to concrete injustice. At times he argued that God had created conscience for the express purpose of preventing injustice from becoming a permanent part of human society. Progress therefore depended upon the willingness of individuals to actualize the moral intuitions revealed in conscience, not simply to accumulate and nurture them in the isolated cultivation of the self. It is hardly a coincidence that Parker and Emerson saw less and less of one another in the 1850s. As the conflict over slavery intensified, Parker's position demanded an assertive and confrontational deployment of conscience in ways that Emerson's did not.[9]

The dramatic conflicts of conscience that thrilled Parker were reinforced by his deep commitment to American Revolutionary memory, the second major theme of this book. As the grandson of Captain John Parker, the commanding officer of the Lexington, Massachusetts Minutemen on April 19, 1775, he felt a deep personal connection to the nation's founding events and ideas. Stories of his ancestor's bravery in the face of British firepower not only grounded his dramatic concept of conscience in family lore, but also gave him a personal stake in the culture of remembrance that saturated his region's identity. This book argues that American Revolutionary memory played a central role in Parker's emergence as an antislavery activist and defined his identity in the movement. Unlike many abolitionists who joined the movement in the 1830s out of evangelical convictions, Parker came to abolitionism in the 1840s in response to what he called the "slave power" conspiracy. In southern slaveholders and their northern allies, he perceived a dire threat to the natural rights principles that his grandfather and the larger revolutionary generation had fought to establish. Consistently reminding his fellow New Englanders that revolutionary monuments stood in their midst, he called for a reassertion of the principles their ancestors had sacrificed to establish. As the conflict over fugitive slaves drew antislavery activists into direct conflict with city, state and federal authorities, moreover, he called for forcible resistance to unjust laws in the tradition of Lexington and Concord. Along with black abolitionists, whose tradition of resistance rested upon revolutionary memories of their own, Parker became an important advocate of aggressive opposition to tyranny.

If other Massachusetts abolitionists drew inspiration from the American past, this study argues that Parker was a key player in the larger cultural struggle to redefine the meaning of the Revolution for a new generation of New Englanders. Historians have long been aware of the politicized nature of New England's antebellum memorial culture and the conservatism of its leading architects. Beginning in the 1820s, Massachusetts orators like Rufus Choate and Edward Everett used commemorative occasions to shape a conservative public understanding of their region's revolutionary past. At Fourth of July and Forefather's Day celebrations, they consciously downplayed the role of popular resistance in the events leading to Independence and insisted that the people had acted in orderly deference to New England's "natural leaders." In the words of historian Harlow Sheidley, they described a "conservative Revolution, undertaken to preserve law and order, and not in defiance of existing social relationships." This interpretation of the past was, of course, loaded with contemporary political meaning. Using history as an ally in preserving traditional authority, conservatives denied any connection between their "orderly" Revolution and unruly social movements like abolitionism. Parker and other abolitionists who sought to mobilize resistance to federal law in the fugitive slave crises faced a conservative historical tradition that equated revolutionary memory with obedience to authority.[10]

Having established an activist identity based on the memory of the Revolution, Parker was perhaps more sensitive than other abolitionists to the power that conservatives wielded over New England's revolutionary symbols. Consequently, his antislavery rhetoric in the 1850s is also distinctive in its explicit references to Boston's commemorative traditions and in its provocative use of monuments and historic landmarks. In ways that both mimicked and inverted conservative memorial performances, Parker's speeches against the enforcement of the Fugitive Slave Act warned Boston audiences that subservience to the South would profane the sacred relics of revolutionary heroism that surrounded them. "The American Republic is the child of Rebellion," he once argued. "The national lullaby was Treason." At stake in the conflict over the meaning of the Revolution, he argued, was New England's fidelity to those who had broken unjust laws in order to make liberty possible, including the African American martyr Crispus Attucks. Despite his attraction to theories of innate racial difference, Parker's commitment to revolutionary memory was surprisingly biracial. He saw attempts to erase the memory of any popular participation in the Revolution as a threat to the ongoing tradition of liberty and natural rights. As his activism matured, revolutionary memory became a central means by which Theodore Parker connected his own identity to the larger and sometimes fragmented community of New England antislavery activists.[11]

In making the case that conscience and revolutionary memory are central to a full understanding of Parker's life, this study will also explore various problems and contradictions that emerged in his public activism. One of the most significant was the issue of moral evil. Confident that human moral intuitions were both true and universal, Parker found it difficult to account for the fact that many of his contemporaries regarded the capture and return of fugitive slaves as their civic and moral duty. This was especially shocking in Boston where the monuments to revolutionary heroism and natural rights should have generated different responses. How had conscience failed to point the way to higher ground? Why did others fail to see the clear meaning of revolutionary symbols? Parker had theological explanations for moral evil, but they simply did not prepare him for the pitched battles with conservatives over issues like abolition and fugitive slaves. Like other passionate idealists whose expectations for the world are unfulfilled, he sometimes responded with frustration, anger and disillusionment. As the power of slaveholders and conservative Unionists appeared to grow during the 1850s, Parker's optimism about conscience as an engine of progress often gave way to darker visions of change. By the eve of the Civil War, his revolutionary conscience had become blisteringly anti-Southern, explicitly political, and overtly violent.

A second major challenge to Parker's revolutionary conscience was the issue of race. Many commentators have noted the glaring contradiction between Parker's militant abolitionism and his publicly stated belief in the innate "docility" of African Americans. Although Parker never doubted that blacks possessed a conscience, he was nevertheless deeply immersed in what historian George Frederickson has called a "racialist" worldview, assigning distinct qualities to the various races of the world. Veering dangerously close to the views of southern proslavery thinkers, he repeatedly expressed doubts about the intelligence and physical courage of enslaved people. Without attempting to resolve this paradoxical position, this study argues that Parker's racialism existed in constant tension with the more biracial vision that his revolutionary conscience implied. It also locates Parker's views in an ongoing public discourse about race in which black abolitionists were important participants. Though they valued Parker's endorsement of forcible resistance to slavery, black activists persistently chided him for his positions on race and offered him myriad reasons to revise them. Men like John Rock and William Nell patiently reminded him that black participation in the American Revolution, among many other examples, disproved his racial assumptions. Their partial success is demonstrated by his increasing interest in the history of black soldiers in the War of Independence, and in his endorsement of John Brown's plan to spark a servile insurrection in the South. Parker's relatively collegial association with men like Rock and Nell, moreover, provides insights into the ways in which white and black abolitionists forged effective alliances despite the persistence of racism among white reformers.[12]

Ultimately, the book that follows makes that case that Theodore Parker, like many in America's long dissenting tradition, used key structures of his culture to formulate a powerful reform ideology. Along with most of his contemporaries in antebellum America, he believed deeply in the importance of religion, morality, economic liberalism, and the republican tradition. But unlike others of his generation, he believed passionately that the concrete reality shaped by these values had somehow become an end in itself, rather than the beginning of a fairer, more just society. Whether in theology or in social relations, the progress of America required constant self-criticism, a persistent measuring of the gap between the ideal and the actual. For him, the witness of conscience and the ideals of the American Revolutionary tradition became the standards by which to judge that gap.

   In this emphasis upon natural rights, the universality of conscience, and the need for relentless self-criticism, moreover, Parker made an important contribution to the dissenting tradition in America. As historian Staughton Lynd once argued, Anglo-American radicals built their resistance to authoritarian institutions on the premise that ordinary people possessed an innate moral capacity which validated their claims to liberty and their right to criticize the state. In his personal and intellectual defense of conscience, therefore, Parker joins a tradition stretching back to Anne Hutchinson in the seventeenth century and forward to Daniel Berrigan in the twentieth. He told his fellow citizens to see their moral instincts as divine and to break unjust laws in the name of their revolutionary ancestors. Those ideas speak not only to the great struggles of the antebellum generation, but to ours as well.[13]

I
"BRED UP AMID THE MEMORIES"
1810–1834

Engaged in the cut and thrust of conflicts over religion and slavery, Theodore Parker liked to explain his confrontational public style as an outgrowth of his childhood in Lexington, Massachusetts. "I drew my first breath in a poor little town where the farmers and mechanics first unsheathed that Revolutionary sword," he once wrote. Using the romantic rhetoric that flowed so easily from his adult sensibilities, he declared that the "Spirit of Liberty, the Love of Justice was early fanned into a flame in my boyish heart" by the example of a grandfather's heroism on the fateful nineteenth of April 1775. To those who wondered at the relentlessness of his attacks upon falsehood and oppression, he delighted in pointing out that they came naturally to one "bred up amid the memories" of the American Revolution.[1]

Parker's self-conscious emphasis upon the revolutionary memory might easily be dismissed as an older man's longing for a glorious patrimony. After all, Captain John Parker's men had been outnumbered and outgunned by the British that morning, and they had done little more than retreat in the face of heavy British fire. But mythic versions of the encounter at Lexington had been woven into the town's cultural fabric by the 1820s. At Nathan Dudley's tavern, where the Parker children often spent the interlude between Sunday services at the Congregational meetinghouse, elderly revolutionary war veterans were often found swapping stories about their experiences while passing around mugs of the landlord's famous flip. These men were determined to counter neighboring Concord's insistence that the first "forcible resistance" to British tyranny had occurred at the town's North Bridge. In 1825, the old soldiers had convinced the Lexington town meeting to appoint a committee to set the record straight and uphold local honor. The town's chosen standard bearer was Elias Phinney, a lawyer and amateur historian whose account of the battle left no doubt of his town's transcendent importance to the cause of liberty. Blending the language of political liberty with that of sacred sacrifice, Phinney wrote that those who fell on April 19th were martyrs, "the first offerings upon the altar of their country's freedom." Such rhetoric would become Parker's stock in trade during his career as a social reformer.[2]

Theodore Parker's childhood in Lexington took place during a period of renewed fervor for matters revolutionary. As a ten-year-old, he attended a re-enactment of the battle in which his grandfather's part was played by a man who had served as his orderly sergeant on the fateful day. Yet as the ranks of living veterans thinned out in the 1820s, it became apparent that they could no longer serve as living monuments of the battle and the community looked for other ways to preserve its memory. The board of selectmen spared no expense to host the Marquis de Lafayette during his triumphant 1824 return to America and they organized a celebration that symbolically passed the mantle of revolutionary valor through three generations of townspeople. Escorted to Lexington common by a "troop of horse" and a "cavalcade of citizens", the old general met an assembly that included aged veterans of the battle and the town's school children. Fourteen-year-old Theodore Parker heard Elias Phinney fervently pray that when the "earthly labors" of the revolutionary generation ceased, "may their children rise up to bless your memory, and emulate your virtues." This concept of generational continuity in the struggle for liberty was therefore deeply rooted in the culture of Parker's childhood. It instilled a readiness to fight and re-fight the American Revolution if necessary.[3]

Of course the wells of memory to which the people of Lexington turned again and again during this period had special meaning for the Parkers who claimed the illustrious hero, Captain John Parker, as one of their own. They still had the musket he captured from the British on the day of the battle and they carefully preserved his words and actions in family lore. Dead within weeks of the battle of Lexington, Captain Parker had become more myth than man. But he loomed large in local tradition as a resolute man of action. Orators described him as a man of "intrepid spirit," and always "true to his convictions." To Theodore Parker he was always "the tall Captain who marshaled his fellow farmers and mechanics" and who dared to speak the "brave and dangerous words" that had begun the American Revolution. Some in Lexington claimed that Theodore resembled his grandfather physically, but Theodore was content with inheriting the spirit of the captain's defiance in the face of oppression and mortal peril. "I learned to read out of his Bible," he said of his grandfather. "[W]ith a musket that he captured from the foe I learned that 'rebellion to tyrants is obedience to God.'"[4]

In Theodore Parker, these early associations and experiences instilled both sensitivity to history and a tendency to understand contemporary experience in light of revolutionary events. Others of his generation also possessed these qualities, but in Parker's case the Revolution remained very much a living event. If much of the conservative oratory that Parker heard as a child in Lexington was designed to contain the radical potential of the Revolution by locating it firmly in the past, Parker's memory-soaked youth demanded that its principles and standards of action be applied in the present. As a child walking to church on Sundays, he and his family passed the granite monument to the fallen minutemen erected near the common only a decade before his birth. His personal standards of manhood and moral action were shaped by a tangible awareness that "it is my own name which stands chiseled in that stone."[5]

The Parker Family

The Parker family's illustrious place in Lexington history helped to compensate for a more difficult present and an uncertain future. As it had for many families in post-revolutionary New England, life for the Parkers involved shrinking land resources, rising indebtedness and limited prospects of inheritance. Located in the southern part of the town, an area the locals called "Kite End", the family property had been respectable enough in the eighteenth century to qualify the Parker men for important town offices. The modest family home, constructed in the central-chimney saltbox style, had been built on the family's original plot of sixty hilly acres by an ancestral John Parker who had migrated to the town from nearby Reading.[6]

But the Revolution was a turning point. The famous Captain's death from tuberculosis in 1775 left his widow Lydia with five young children. Her remarriage three years later to Ephraim Pierce of Waltham proved disastrous to the family's fortunes. In 1790, when Pierce himself died, his debts were so substantial that Lydia was left with nothing but the "widow's thirds" to support herself. Her eldest son John, already married with three children of his own, became the head of what was now an impoverished rural family. Consistently in debt and wringing the most they could out of a few worn out acres, the family lived with "rigid economy". Theodore Parker's nephew, Columbus Greene, said that when he came to live with the family in 1819, "the farm had been running down" for several years and was unable to produce enough corn to feed what was now a very large extended family.[7]

Theodore Parker was born on the "hot, sweltering morning" of August 24, 1810, and his five-year-old sister Emily squeezed his name into a recently completed family tree which already included seven sisters and three brothers. At the ages of forty-six and fifty respectively, Hannah and John Parker had produced eleven children and were fortunate to see all but three of them reach maturity. John was not a successful farmer but he provided for his family by maintaining a profitable peach orchard and using his prodigious woodworking skills to serve the needs of local farmers. Theodore remembered his father constructing "saw mills, cider mills, pumps and flax spinning wheels" and "turning bread bowls out of maple stumps" while his older brothers John, Isaac, and Hiram tended to the needs of the family farm. The Parker farm was never worth more than $300, a figure which placed them in the bottom third of Lexington society, and it required unremitting labor to keep it afloat. With little money to spare, it was impossible to hire labor and Theodore learned early in life the "discipline and habit of bodily toil."[8]

Theodore Parker's early life was shaped by dramatic revolutionary legacies and hard economic realities, but it was also influenced by the modernizing religious culture of eastern Massachusetts. Unlike neighboring Concord, the Lexington church had not experienced the religious divisions that plagued so many towns during the religious revivals of the 1740s. Its ministers had successfully insulated the community from emotional revivalism while at the same time softening orthodox conceptions of innate human depravity. Liberal ministers like the Rev. Charles Briggs, who took over the Lexington pulpit when Parker was nine years old, replaced the stern, wrathful God of the Puritans with a more benign creator. This rational God revealed himself to mankind through the beauty of nature and the moral message found in scripture. Though outright controversy between liberal and orthodox Protestants broke out all over eastern Massachusetts during Theodore Parker's youth, the long history of liberalism in Lexington left the community nearly untouched by the crisis. With the exception of a brief encounter with a stray Westminster Catechism at the age of eight, Parker grew up outside the influence of Calvinist orthodoxy.[9]

The religious values that John and Hannah Parker taught at home reenforced this rational theology. John Parker had very little formal education, but he possessed a self-reliant intellect and his share in the town's social library gave him access to moderate Enlightenment works on history, theology, and philosophy. John's unusual interest in books gained him a reputation for being "somewhat peculiar in his views on religious subjects." He was an admirer of the English theologian William Paley, whose 1802 work *Natural Theology* had proved the existence and benevolence of God through the evidence found in the natural creation. Though it departed somewhat from theological orthodoxy, Paley's powerful fusion of religion with Enlightenment thought appealed to men like John Parker who demanded empirical evidence for their faith. In his father, Theodore Parker found a man whose religion generated large and important questions whose answers could not be found solely within the sacred texts of his tradition. During "the long winter evenings, sometimes in the winter mornings before it was light, and other intervals of toil," he sought those answers in other books as his youngest son looked on.[10]

John Parker's rationalism and intellectual curiosity provided a life-long model for his eleventh child, but it was Hannah Parker's natural piety and gentle moralism that Theodore credited with forming his deepest religious sensibilities. She died of tuberculosis in 1823, when he was thirteen years old, but Theodore retained a vivid image of his mother as a "woman of slight form, flaxen hair, blue eyes and a singularly fresh and delicate complexion." Others described her as "mild-tempered and kindly," and "a quiet home woman" whose life was dominated by the endless work of the rural household economy. But to Theodore Parker, Hannah's simple, uncluttered faith had insulated him from both skepticism and "the dark theology of the times." As he remembered it, her views of God were devoid of traditional theological language, composed instead of natural and aesthetic analogies arising in the course of life. "She saw Him in the rainbow and in the drops of rain which helped compose it as they fell into the muddy ground to come up grass and trees, corn and flowers." Hannah's reading was more devotional than her husband's, centering on the Bible, the Puritan hymn book, and narratives of New England captives among the Indians. Her love of religious poetry and silent prayer injected a pietistic element into the religious culture of the family and balanced the rationalism of her husband. [11]

In rejecting the negative view of human nature that still informed the authoritarian child-rearing practices of more orthodox Calvinist families, moreover, Parker's parents laid the basis for his abiding belief in the reliability of human conscience. According to Columbus Greene, they used little or no physical discipline. Instead, they "taught their children to speak the truth" and "governed easily in the family." Some Calvinist parents continued to believe that "the autonomous will and self-assertiveness of the child must be reduced to impotency, be utterly suppressed and contained, or the child would be damned for eternity." But liberal families like the Parkers emphasized less the breaking of their children's wills than the control of sinful impulses through voluntary obedience to conscience. "The children of moderates grew to maturity with the sense that their own wills were free and within their power to control," writes historian Phillip Greven. "[T]hey also developed consciences which ensured that they would prefer to choose ways set forth for them rather than counter their parents' wills and wishes."[12]

Even within the parameters of liberal childrearing, however, Parker's parents operated with a remarkably strong notion of conscience. He recalled that at the age of four he had been walking along a small stream and encountered "a little spotted tortoise sunning himself in the shallow water." Following the example of neighborhood boys, he lifted up a stick to strike the vulnerable reptile when "all at once something checked my little arm and a voice inside me said clear and loud, 'It is wrong!'" Leaving the stick by the river, Parker ran home to his mother, related the incident, and asked her the identity of the voice. In Parker's telling, his mother wiped a tear from her eye and said "some men call it conscience, but I prefer to call it the voice of God in the soul of man." "If you listen and obey it, then it will speak clearer and clearer, and always guide you right," she continued, "but if you turn a deaf ear and disobey it will fade out little by little, and leave you all in the dark and without a guide." Rejecting the orthodox belief that moral action was impossible without the regeneration of divine grace, Hannah trained her son to trust his natural conscience. By identifying the voice of conscience with the will of God, moreover, she taught him to follow his convictions and to avoid moral compromise as a matter of duty.[13]

The self-control that John and Hannah Parker instilled in their children sometimes took the form of moderate attention-seeking and self-assertion in Theodore. As the youngest, and most intellectually gifted in a large family, his privileged position left him less concerned than others about the boundaries of individual autonomy and self-expression. "As the youngest child I was treated with uncommon indulgence and probably received more than a tenth part of the affection distributed," he confessed in his brief autobiography. So doting were his parents that neighbors warned them that they were raising a permanent dependent. He remembered neighbors saying, "Why, Miss Parker, you're spilin [sic] your boy!—he never can take care of himself when he grows up," to which she replied; "'she hoped not' and kissed my flaxen curls anew." But the effect of parental indulgence was to have very different effects. Those who knew him during these years describe a child who struggled to control his temper, who often indulged his considerable talent for mimicry, and who sometimes gave in to the impulse to make "sport of what others might do and say." Whether firing off pop-guns in school or entertaining the family with imaginary dialogues between the farm animals, he performed for others often, willingly and well.[14]

'No One Could Keep Up With Theodore'

In a small New England town like Lexington, it was not long before most people knew that the youngest son of John Parker was uncommonly clever. At eight years old, he astonished the village school-masters with his nearly effortless ability to commit prodigious quantities of material to memory. "I began to write verse at eight, and could repeat a poem of 500 or 1000 lines after a single reading, or a song from hearing it once," Parker remembered with perhaps only mild exaggeration. "I used to commit the hymns which the minister was reading before the choir had begun to sing." According to his nephew, it was generally agreed that "no one could keep up with Theodore." Parker's passion for intellectual distinction, which all of his biographers have noted, began at an early age.[15]

Lexington was not an especially wealthy community in the early nineteenth century, but young Parker benefited from the town's growing provision for education. The town's schoolhouses were plain, but well maintained, and they were usually staffed with intelligent young graduates of New England's colleges. Along with as many as forty other students whose ages ranged from five to eighteen, Parker attended three-month terms each winter beginning in December 1818. His enthusiasm for learning and phenomenal talent for languages, however, did not become apparent until 1820 when William Hoar White, a gentle but energetic young scholar, took over the Lexington schools. Recognizing his young pupil's ability, White encouraged Parker to begin learning Latin and Greek as well as elementary algebra and geometry. With the aid of a Latin grammar that White lent him, the young scholar spent every spare moment plowing through Virgil, Cicero, Sallust, and other classical authors. White's decision to teach Parker ancient languages, which were not on the curriculum of the rural district schools, indicates his belief in the boy's potential for a career in the law or the ministry. "I shall never cease to be grateful to him for all the kindness he showed me, for it was no duty of his to teach a boy Latin," Parker later wrote of White.[16]

By the age of seventeen, Parker's precocious childhood reading habits had translated into the insatiable appetite for knowledge, especially the knowledge of languages that became one of his most distinguishing features later in life. Like the young Abraham Lincoln, Parker was an obsessive reader who used books to escape the drudgery of farm work and to create "a world of my own, an ideal creation, where I could roam and luxuriate at random." During summer "noonings" when farm families usually rested or napped, young Parker would "take his book and read it," and he often remained at his books late into the night. But unlike Lincoln, whose access to books on the frontier was severely limited, Parker read his way through Lexington's small lending library and his teachers were sources of additional reading material. In addition to the classical languages that dominated his formal training, he studied French and Spanish, and explored historical and philosophical works whenever he could find them.[17]

Parker recognized quite early that learning was the most valuable asset he could acquire in youth, and the enormous value he placed on books required that he master their contents. "What was read at all, was also studied and not laid aside till well understood," he recalled of his early work habits. He had not yet decided on a career, but his expectations for the future were becoming more grandiose by the day and he found it difficult to restrain his growing passion for distinction. "How many times has my plough run upon a rock while I was expounding law, making speeches in the Senate, or astonishing men with a display of intellectual power," he wrote only a year after entering Divinity School. "Many a time have I strayed from the right path and gone far beyond my stopping place, while I was brooding over some scheme not yet accomplished."[18]

But these dreams would require higher education and the money for college was not available on the Lexington farm. As he considered the narrow options confronting him, he asked his older sister Mary if she thought he might survive at college eating only "two crackers per day." Perhaps indicating her answer, Theodore began trading upon his local reputation for brilliance to secure paid teaching positions in the area. In 1827, he was appointed head of the district school in nearby Quincy, and over the next two years he taught in the North Lexington, Concord, and Waltham schools.[19]

According to those who knew him at the time, Parker was his own closest adviser on matters pertaining to his future life and career. The death of his mother in 1823 had deprived him of his closest emotional support, and his father knew very little of the world that Theodore now dreamed of entering. "He knew his father couldn't help him," wrote his nephew and childhood friend Columbus Greene. "[H]e laid his own plans and carried them out." Though he possessed little experience of the world outside his own small corner of eastern Massachusetts, Parker was familiar enough with the history of the state to know that distinguished careers in politics, law, or theology were more often than not connected to a Harvard education.[20]

On the day before his twentieth birthday in 1830, and without a word to his father, Parker walked the twenty miles from Lexington to Cambridge where he easily passed the Harvard entrance exam and enrolled for the fall term. He could not afford tuition toward a degree at Harvard, but he obtained reading lists, attended lectures, and took periodic examinations in Cambridge while pursuing the bulk of his studies at home. The six-month freshman course required the mastery of many Greek and Latin works which Parker had already read, and he quickly outstripped his class despite the renewed demands of the farm. The ease with which he completed the course and passed the college examinations fueled a growing self-importance and intellectual pride. "I have read all the Greek and Roman authors named at Cambridge and many more in Algebra and Geometry," he told a correspondent. "This has been pursued in private and alone, *without the assistance of any teacher.*" The lack of a formal degree notwithstanding, his completion of the "Cambridge Course" in 1831 meant better paid teaching positions, a final break from the farm, and liberation from what he now saw as the narrow cultural world of Lexington. Boston, "the Athens of America," seemed the next step for a young man of intellect and ambition.[21]

Boston and Watertown

Later in life, Parker recognized how unprepared he had been for his first experience in "the hub of the universe" as Oliver Wendell Holmes once called antebellum Boston. He was "a raw boy with clothes made by country tailors," whose "coarse shoes, great hands, red lips and blue eyes" were better suited to guiding ploughs or clearing fields than to the genteel world of patrician scholars. Boston's men of letters were expected to possess refined manners, but Parker had little beside his astounding memory and his endless capacity for work to recommend him. Harvard had offered him its reading lists, but he had learned very little about the elite culture that it cultivated in its graduates. Still, his talent and energy opened doors and he found a position as an assistant teacher in one of the city's many private schools. The school demanded six or seven hours of teaching per day, but he was determined not to neglect his own private study. Devoting ten to twelve hours out of each day to reading and the study of language and mathematics, he found little time for exercise and pushed himself to the brink of physical and mental collapse. Although they reflected a commonly held belief that worldly success stemmed from self-mastery, Parker's work habits assumed a self-destructive character from this early point in his life. "[I]t makes my flesh creep to think how I used to work," he remembered of his first year in the city.[22]

Ambition drove Parker to test the limits of his physical and mental stamina. But his lack of a clearly defined vocational goal led to a great deal of soul searching and anxiety. A distinguished career in the law had often quickened his Lexington daydreams, but he was apprehensive about the moral costs of success in the legal profession. Parker doubted whether he could "defend a cause that I knew to be wrong," or, "use all my efforts to lead judge or jury to a decision I thought unjust." In searching for a profession, he had to balance the imperatives of conscience his parents had so deeply ingrained in his character with his equally strong desire for distinction. The "honors, judicial and political," that "eminent" Massachusetts lawyers like Joseph Story, Daniel Webster, and Rufus Choate had achieved were attractive to the ambitious young man, but were they consistent with the demands of conscience? "I saw men of large talents yielding to this temptation, and counting as great success what to me even then seemed only great ruin," he claimed later with clerical detachment. "I could not decide to set up a law mill by the public road to rob innocent men of their property, liberty, life."[23]

If the legal profession offered fame and success at the price of integrity, Parker worried that the ministry might not challenge him. Such worries reflected an important reality. The New England clergy were experiencing a profound transformation during the first third of the nineteenth century in ways that diluted their traditional authority. Eighteenth-century ministers had enjoyed an elevated status in the small communities where they usually settled for life. But the new, more mobile clergy of the antebellum period often served at the pleasure of church members. The disestablishment of the churches and the rise of sectarianism had also destroyed the ability of the old clerical "Standing Order" to speak with a unified, authoritative voice. As a boy in Lexington, Parker was exposed to a fair degree of anti-clericalism among his neighbors and he was aware of the high turnover rate among the town's ministers. "My friends advised me against the ministry," Parker wrote with amusement later in life. "It was a 'narrow place, affording no opportunity to do much!'" His ultimate choice of the ministry as a vocation always carried with it a determination to revitalize and transform its social influence.[24]

If the memory of tepid sermons from the Lexington pulpit haunted Parker's thoughts about a ministerial career, Boston provided him with a sharp counterpoint. There, the intellectual stars of the New England clergy were in the midst of a high stakes war of ideas that demanded innovation. First, there was William Ellery Channing, the great liberal preacher of the Federal Street Church who stoutly defended the rational faith of Boston Unitarianism against orthodox charges of infidelity. Pale, small in stature and emaciated by chronic illness, the fifty-one-year-old Channing was nevertheless a man of deep intellect and personal charm. A young disciple of Channing's once said that his vocal cadences contained "a strain of soft but irresistibly persuasive music," and that he possessed an "irresistible something" that captivated audiences both large and small. Parker was intrigued by the contrast between the older man's frail appearance and his ability to mesmerize his listeners. "When closely viewed he seemed a soul very lightly clad in a body," he once said of Channing. "His conscience and faith went into the audience till he left them breathless."[25]

Most important to Parker was Channing's expansive and reformist view of the ministry. If the clergy were to regain the social influence they had lost through disestablishment and internal division, he argued, ministers would have to seek out innovative ways to shape public culture. "Shall the minister linger behind his age, and be dragged along, as he often has been, in the last ranks of improvement?" Channing had asked at the dedication of Harvard's Divinity Hall in 1826. "Let those who are to assume the ministry be taught that they have something more to do than handle old topics in old ways, and to walk in beaten and long-worn paths." Theodore Parker would one day test the limits of Channing's call for innovation, but in the meantime his example helped to allay the young man's concerns about the irrelevance of the clergy. "Dr. Channing was the only man in the New England pulpit who seemed great," he later wrote.[26]

Channing's liberal theology formed one side of the city's most significant culture war. Emphasizing human reason and divine benevolence, Channing argued for a thorough reformation of traditional New England theology. He believed that the central principles of Christianity were consistent with modern philosophy and science, and complained that sectarian "bigotry" too often distorted its message. He deplored overheated revival enthusiasm. While there was a legitimate place for the "affections" in religious life, he was suspicious of the "feverish, forced, fluctuating zeal" of the evangelical churches. He also rejected the doctrine of the Trinity as mystical and unscriptural. But the most basic tenet of Channing's liberalism was a belief in the human capacity to overcome sin by persistent cultivation of morality and piety. The educated merchants and professionals of Boston responded enthusiastically to this message. Successful and cosmopolitan, such families found little satisfaction in the doctrines of human depravity and divine wrath which remained part of New England's Calvinist heritage.[27]

Ironically, given the ways in which Channing's theology coincided with his upbringing and religious education in Lexington, most of Parker's Sundays in Boston were spent under the preaching of "the most powerful orthodox minister in New England." The Rev. Lyman Beecher had left his Litchfield, Connecticut congregation five years earlier to battle "Unitarians, Universalists, Papists and Infidels" at the Hanover Street Church in Boston. A spectacularly successful revivalist, Beecher preached a revised Calvinism that retained the traditional emphasis on human sinfulness and the literal truth of scripture, but balanced God's sovereignty with human agency in the process of salvation.[28]

Beecher's attacks on Channing and the Unitarians went beyond issues of creedal orthodoxy. Since arriving in Boston, the great revivalist had led other orthodox ministers in denouncing the State Supreme Court's 1819 decision in *Baker* v. *Fales*. In that decision, the Unitarian-dominated court gave liberal parish committees in eastern Massachusetts a decisive advantage over orthodox church members in the choice of ministers and in the use of church property. The result was the near collapse of orthodoxy in eastern Massachusetts. To men like Beecher, this was nothing less than an elite conspiracy to wrest control of the churches away from true believers. He condemned Unitarians for using their wealth and political influence to undermine the faith. Reflecting the social and political tensions simmering just below the surface of the controversy between orthodoxy and Unitarianism, he argued that the "worldly grandeur, the wit, the learning, the wealth and power of the world are leagued against the friends of evangelical truth."[29]

Beecher's social critique of the Massachusetts elite resurfaced later in Parker's career as a reformer, but the revivalist's neo-Calvinism found no purchase in the young teacher's mind. His insistence on the sinfulness of human nature and the possibility of eternal damnation clashed with the moral optimism of Parker's youth. "I heard the most frightful doctrines set forth in sermon song and prayer," Parker remembered of Beecher's revival. "I came away with no confidence in his theology; the more I understood it, the more self-contradictory, unnatural, and hateful did it seem." Yet despite his rejection of Beecher's theology, Parker was impressed with the revivalist's "polemic zeal" and his eagerness to wage public war with his critics. In both Channing and Beecher, Parker found religious leaders who had taken their conflicting ideas into the public square. No longer able to close ranks behind a unified conception of orthodox thought or practice, these men performed for the public in a competitive marketplace of religious thought. This was an exciting prospect for a talented young man who sometimes worried that a career in the ministry would narrow the scope of his ambition.[30]

With Channing's theology and Beecher's style to inspire him, Parker decided to pursue a formal theological education at Harvard Divinity School. But in making this choice, he confronted two serious problems. The first was the familiar issue of finances. Tuition at Divinity Hall was more than sixty dollars a year, plus two dollars per week for living expenses. On top of this, he would have to find money to purchase suitable clothes and supplies. As a teacher in Boston, he could not save more than two or three dollars a month, and he was spending most of that on books. The second problem was a lack of academic preparation. His solitary study in Boston had not been systematically geared toward admission to the Divinity School, and he had found no mentor to direct and monitor his progress.

A solution to the first problem presented itself when a number of Parker's relatives who lived west of Boston suggested the idea of opening a private school in Watertown. Teaching in a school of his own would help him finance a divinity degree while affording him the time to prepare systematically for the difficult entrance exams. With this in mind, he left Boston in April 1832, and set up his school on the second floor of an old abandoned bakery where he presided over a small but successful academy for the next two years. Many children attended his school for free, but most parents paid five dollars per quarter, enabling the teacher to increase his library and to save one hundred and fifty dollars toward his tuition at Harvard.[31]

The intellectual friendship and vocational advice Parker needed was found in the Rev. Convers Francis of Watertown, a graduate of Harvard Divinity School and one of the most promising young scholars in the liberal ministry. Fifteen years Parker's senior, Francis's early life bore many similarities to his younger protégé's. He was born into an obscure, rural family, but possessed extraordinary intellectual gifts which he developed through intense self-discipline. By 1832, he had begun a distinguished career as a preacher and theologian. His commentaries on French, German, and British theologians would soon be published in the leading Unitarian journals, and he was rumored to possess one of the richest private libraries in New England. Perhaps seeing something of himself in the eager young man who called on him in April, 1832, Francis quickly agreed to help and he placed the riches of his library at Parker's disposal.[32]

Parker had, without knowing it, made an important intellectual and theological choice in approaching Francis. The minister's mastery of Continental philosophy and German biblical criticism placed him at the cutting edge of New England intellectual life. His library contained books that were not on the approved reading list at Harvard. Along with works by William Paley and other English natural theologians which formed the core of the Harvard curriculum, he urged Parker to read edgier texts that introduced him to the new, romantic trends in European letters. One was Samuel Taylor Coleridge's accounts of Immanuel Kant's philosophy which had come to dominate German universities. It would take several years for these ideas to mature in Parker's mind, but the intellectual road to his later theological radicalism undoubtedly began in the Watertown parsonage library.[33]

Amidst a grueling round of teaching, Hebrew lessons and voracious reading, Parker also fell in love with Lydia Dodge Cabot of Newton. Lydia was a fair-haired, blue-eyed nineteen-year-old who was staying at the same Watertown boardinghouse where Parker's own rooms were located. A member of one of eastern Massachusetts' most prominent and wealthy families, Lydia's background contrasted sharply with that of her future husband. Her father, John Cabot, was not among the most successful of the clan, but Lydia had spent much of her childhood with her unmarried aunt Lucy Cabot in Boston where she had been educated at the finest Boston ladies' academies. She possessed the grace, manners, and dress that were expected among genteel Bostonians. She liked to read novels, especially those of Sir Walter Scott, but had little interest in intellectual pursuits and was shy and retiring with strangers. "Her mild countenance, compared with his, suggested even more than the usual contrast between husband and wife" remembered the reformer Julia Ward Howe who knew the couple well. "Her complexion was fair, her features were regular, and the expression of her face was naif and gentle."[34]

For Parker, whose rustic appearance and rough manners were liabilities in the society that he now hoped to enter, Lydia's charm, good breeding and social connections were real assets and he pursued her vigorously. Finding that she taught Sunday school at Francis's church, he volunteered to teach a class himself and the two frequently took long, slow walks along the Charles River on their way back to the boardinghouse after church. Despite the differences in their backgrounds, Lydia knew that the polished, erudite minister of the Watertown church was optimistic about the prospects of the talkative young school teacher and she could not help but be attracted by Parker's boundless energy and sharp, handsome features. In October 1833, she accepted his proposal of marriage, but the couple agreed that they would not wed until Parker had established himself in a settled ministry. "I walked to father's...and informed him of the 'fatal' affair," he wrote her after a visit to the Lexington farm. John Parker, now in his early seventies, had become used to life-changing announcements from his youngest son and quickly consented to the match. But he could not help a last bit of paternal guidance. 'Theodore,' said he, and the words sank deep into my heart, 'you must be a good man and a good husband, which is a great undertaking."[35]

Marriage plans now adding to his already relentless drive for success, Parker sought his mentor's advice about admission to Harvard Divinity School. Francis approved of the plan and wrote a letter of introduction to Henry Ware, Jr., Professor of Pastoral Theology and Pulpit Eloquence at the school. In February 1834, Parker walked to Cambridge, interviewed successfully and enrolled in the junior class at Divinity Hall. The youngest child of a struggling Lexington farmer, Parker was about to enter the intellectual and cultural world of the New England elite. His mind bubbled over with excitement and expectations of success. "Nothing is too much for young ambition to hope, no eminence too lofty for his vision, no obstacle too difficult for his exertions, and no excellence unattainable," he exulted in a letter to Lydia. "Sincere desires are never neglected and real endeavors [are] never unassisted." Convinced that a life of moral leadership and scholarly achievement lay ahead of him, Captain Parker's grandson confidently sought his own path to greatness.[36]

II
DIVINITY SCHOOL AND BEYOND
1834–1837

Harvard Divinity School represented a major step toward the fulfillment of Parker's youthful dreams. "I found excellent opportunities for study," he wrote of his two years in Cambridge. "There were able and earnest professors who laid no yoke on any neck but left each man free to think for himself." The school was formally nonsectarian, but the founding of Divinity Hall in 1826, along with the creation of the American Unitarian Association the year before, clearly signaled the emergence of denominational Unitarianism in America. The organizers were all key figures in the liberal establishment of eastern Massachusetts and the school was the recognized training ground for those who aspired to fill Unitarian pulpits. But for New England liberals, who still nursed bruises from their theological battles with orthodoxy, denominationalism did not mean creedalism and they required no overt profession of faith from students.[1]

Parker also attended the Divinity School at a time when younger scholars like John Gorham Palfrey and Henry Ware Jr. were overseeing "a complete revolution in the intellectual atmosphere." During these years, discussion, disagreement with the professor, and openness to innovation modified an earlier elitism and emphasis on authority. Despite the Transcendentalists' later criticism of the school, its commitment to intellectual freedom was remarkable by nineteenth-century standards. But in Parker's case, even the wide boundaries of the Cambridge environment were too small to contain the ferment of his thought.[2]

Cambridge Theology and Harvard Moralism

Theodore Parker went to Cambridge in 1834 with a restless energy that was astonishing and sometimes troubling to his friends. Most of his classmates came from genteel families, and they found him both intense and rough around the edges. Christopher Pearse Cranch, whose father was a federal judge, described Parker as "charged full of electricity," and Cyrus Bartol, who later differed with Parker over theological issues, remembered his "exuberant life," and his "restless ambition to excel." Now twenty four, Parker retained his childhood penchant for mimicry and satire. The pressurized environment of the Divinity School only intensified his need to display the sharp edge of his wit. "He was literally *snapping* at times with sparks of fun and satire," Cranch recalled. And he often found ways to indulge his "appreciation for the humorous and ludicrous," indulging in "boyish and playful rebounds."[3]

One evening, when Cranch and another classmate, John Sullivan Dwight were "in full musical blast at something—fluting or singing," Parker protested against the interruption of his studies by loudly and rhythmically sawing wood just outside the door of their chamber. Dwight tried later to soothe Parker's irritation by giving him a singing lesson, but it turned out that the young scholar from Lexington was nearly tone deaf and was advised "to give up the hopeless task of cultivating his voice." At a university where many scholars had suffered depression or debilitating illness from overwork and lack of exercise, Parker's stamina, independence, and youthful high spirits were as striking as the tall stacks of books from the library that piled up on his desk in No. 29 Divinity Hall.[4]

Despite his capacious energy, Parker found student life very strenuous. He received financial assistance from the Divinity School "beneficence fund," but he was forced to take in several students and to follow an austere personal regimen. The "genteel poverty" that characterized the lives of many students was a bit more extreme in his case. Subsisting on a diet of bread and water for weeks at a time, he routinely worked fourteen hour days, often reading until the oil in his lamp ran out at night. Along with the translations, recitations, and practice sermons which his classes demanded, he also participated fully in a vibrant student culture. Divinity students formed a philanthropic society in 1831, organizing debates on controversial social issues like slavery, urban poverty and temperance reform. Taking William Ellery Channing's call for a socially engaged ministry seriously, he also taught a Sunday school class to inmates at the state prison in Charlestown.[5]

But it was theology that kept Theodore Parker up while his classmates slept, and theology that engaged his intellect to the point of preoccupation. When he entered Divinity School, he was a fairly conventional liberal Christian who remained comfortable with the language, if not all of the doctrines, of traditional Christianity. Just after enrolling in the spring of 1834, he explained to a family member that in Jesus he saw the "Son of God, conceived and born in a miraculous manner," but whose central importance lay not in sacrificing his life for human sin but rather in having preached a "better religion by which man may be saved." He accepted that the Bible revealed the will of God, but rejected the belief that all parts of the text were equally inspired. Some of what had been written was aimed at specific audiences rather than setting down universal rules of belief or conduct. "I believe the books of the Old and New Testament to have been written by men inspired by God for certain purposes, but I do not think of them as inspired *at all times*," he wrote. He was as convinced of human immortality as any orthodox Christian, but he joined most liberals in rejecting the idea that the "rewards or punishments of a future state are corporal." And as for punishment, Parker saw the consequences of sin not as eternal damnation or torment, but rather as the lashings of an outraged conscience. "May God preserve us from a worse punishment than one's own conscience" he declared in words that would have pleased his mother. These ideas were in line with liberal preaching in eastern Massachusetts, but they would have elicited a wry smile from the mature Theodore Parker.[6]

There were just three faculty members at Harvard Divinity School in 1834, but they offered students a finely tuned intellectual system. In broad outlines, it constituted an equal rejection of skepticism, revival "enthusiasm", and the dogmas of traditional Calvinism. Unitarian divines taught that Christian truths were rational truths, proved by nature as well as by miracle. Harvard's theological influences were English and Scottish, including the rational theology of John Tillotson, the empirical philosophy of John Locke and the moral philosophy of Richard Price. Parker would later challenge elements of this theology using the very tools it had given him, and he would join other reformers in demanding a religion that spoke to the heart as well as to the head. But his deepest intellectual foundations, even those he self-consciously rejected, were first encountered systematically in Cambridge. By first confirming his basic religious instincts, the Divinity School allowed him to move in a more original, and ultimately transgressive direction.

At the core of the Divinity School curriculum was Henry Ware Senior's class on the "Evidences of Christianity." For the seventy-year-old Hollis Professor of Divinity, modern philosophy had provided an inductive method by which central Christian doctrines could be proved conclusively at the bar of reason. In Newton's elegant and ordered physical universe, and in William Paley's ecology of perfect biological adaptation, Ware saw irrefutable proof of God's existence, rationality, and infinite love. But that did not mean discarding the Bible. Ware was careful to note that the religious truths found in nature did not supplant the need for special divine revelation. He insisted that the central principles of Christ's Gospel could not have been known through natural reason alone. A merciful God had therefore supplied that knowledge through the preaching of Jesus, a special messenger whose divine authority was proved by his miraculous interruptions of natural law. William Ellery Channing put it best in an 1821 lecture. "When Jesus Christ came into the world," he had argued, "nature had failed to communicate instructions to men in which they had the deepest concern." Reason required "additional supernatural lights" to grasp the deepest truths of religion and morality.[7]

This argument, often called "supernatural rationalism," holds that while the laws of nature testify to the existence of a rational God, Christ's miraculous interruptions of those laws was required in order to prove the authority of his more specific redemptive message to man. Clever though it was, its attempt to blend modern philosophy with the requirements of faith amounted to a perilous intellectual balancing act between biblical literalism on the one hand, and deistic natural religion on the other. It placed a great theological burden on the authenticity of miracles and raised potentially troubling questions. Was revelation really necessary for human knowledge of God? Could the all-important biblical miracles withstand the intense scrutiny of modern knowledge? Parker would soon answer both questions in the negative.[8]

A close examination of the biblical record was, of course, a central element in the education of a minister. On Mondays and Fridays, therefore, Parker attended John Gorham Palfrey's lectures on the textual criticism of the Old and New Testaments. Replacing the venerable Andrews Norton as Dexter Professor of Sacred Literature in 1831, Palfrey conveyed liberal exegetical techniques to a new generation of Unitarian ministers. Palfrey held that the Bible was a flawless revelation of God's truth, but he taught students to be cautious in approaching biblical texts. The notion that every word of the Bible was equally inspired, he argued, allowed texts to be taken out of context and used as proof of "almost any preconceived system of doctrine" including the Trinity. Interpreters should be carefully trained to "look beyond the letter to the spirit, to seek in the nature of the subject, and the aims of the writer, his true meaning." Liberal ministers, in other words, had to be steeped in history, language, and ancient culture if they were to guide their people effectively through the knotty problems of understanding revealed truth.[9]

In Palfrey's class on the New Testament, Parker translated Gospel texts from their original Greek and then decided on appropriate meaning in light of the text's probable authorship, audience and context. It is important to remember that in employing this method, liberals saw themselves not as attacking the authority of the Bible, but rather rescuing it from the "self-contradictory, unnatural, and hateful doctrines" of dogmatic Calvinism. Like Ware's presentation of Christian evidences, however, Palfrey's biblical criticism was a delicate balance between the old and new. What was essential about the Bible could be revered because it no longer carried the burden of the irrational or inessential doctrine. But it would be difficult to maintain consensus on just where to establish the line between the transient and the permanent in the scriptures. The New Testament miracles, for example, upon which Unitarian rationalists had staked so much of their theology, were off limits to public criticism. Men like Palfrey, whose positions in the college depended upon their pragmatism as well as their scholarship, understood and accepted the boundaries of the enterprise.[10]

Ware and Palfrey provided a systematic basis for theological study, but Parker also found a philosophical environment at Harvard that confirmed his family's belief in the reliability of human conscience. So popular among both students and faculty at Harvard that Parker referred to them as "the common books of philosophy," the Scottish writers Thomas Reid and Dugald Stewart supported the liberals' belief that moral knowledge was within the grasp of natural reason. As God had equipped the mind with "common sense," or basic tools to organize and judge experience of the physical world, they argued, so had he also provided an analogous "moral sense" for making reliable ethical judgments. "Men are moral beings because they have a moral nature, that is, a conscience, an innate inextinguishable sense of right," wrote one-time Harvard President James Walker. Men like Walker were convinced that this innate "moral sense" or conscience supplied human beings with a basic knowledge of a pure morality distinct from self-interest and independent of cultural conditioning. Because it linked human beings to God's larger moral purpose in creation, the conscience occupied the very highest place in the hierarchy of mental faculties. In this philosophical exposition of conscience, Parker found a sophisticated version of his mother's simple exhortation to heed "the voice of God in the soul of man."[11]

But as in his other subjects, Parker did not find the most radical elements of his idea of conscience in the curriculum or culture of Harvard Divinity School. For all their emphasis on the supremacy of conscience, the Unitarians described it in ways that emphasized harmony, balance and stability over "uninhibited self-expression." Prudence and affection were important allies of conscience, ensuring that the personality remained moderate in its expression of moral truth. Rejecting the revivalists' concept of an emotional "new birth", Harvard's elite, genteel liberals described human redemption as a life-long process of "cultivating" the higher virtues over baser passions like "violence or self-indulgence." During his tenure as Professor of Pulpit Eloquence and Pastoral Theology at the Divinity School, Henry Ware Jr. taught that the "complete" man was "wise, watchful, self-governed, self-sustaining, every part of him is in its right place, and of its right proportion, and every faculty is obedient to his will." To ensure that students were living up to these ideals of character, Ware visited their rooms in Divinity Hall and assessed their progress in building an ideal character. He encouraged students to perform works of personal and collective benevolence, but counseled against acts of conscience that threatened the smooth functioning of the college. As in questions of theology and biblical scholarship, the expression of conscience was placed within broad but very real limits. Although he strove mightily for this ideal, Parker strove in vain.[12]

Part of the problem was social. The Unitarian ideal of a balanced, cultivated human personality was the product of self-conscious, socially-conservative elites. Parker's obscure social origins provided no training in decorum. A young man of astounding physical energy, intellectual ambition and emotional intensity, he found it difficult to project the inner self-assurance and outward serenity required of members in this select group. Henry Adams's satirical description of the Unitarian clergy as men whose "mental calm" conveyed the impression that "Boston had solved the universe" certainly did not describe Theodore Parker. To his more tranquil classmate J.S. Dwight, Parker appeared "anything but calm." Dwight thought his friend had "too much will" and that his life was "a succession of convulsive efforts and the only wonder to me is that they do not exhaust you." Parker was well aware of this aspect of his personality and he confessed to Lydia that "stormy, violent passions" sometimes swept "tornado-like through my heart."[13]

To combat his deficiencies and meet the standard of Christian self-control that grounded Harvard moral philosophy, Parker imposed a code of discipline on himself throughout his first year in Divinity School. He labored "to be more constant in prayer, more exact in self-watchfulness, more perfect in outward conduct." In his private journal, he prepared specific rules by which his thought and conduct might be regulated, balanced and channeled in positive directions. He avoided excess consumption of "meat and drink," and resolved to exercise three hours per day. Having been scolded several times by Lydia for "*over-studying*," he resolved to get at least six hours sleep each night and admitted that "more is better." Betraying the hold that traditional piety still exerted on his daily life, he actively cultivated "devoutness" by meditating on nature, the "attributes of God" and "my own dependence." He prayed at least twice a day and vowed to remain "independent of external affairs" and to "restrain licentiousness of imagination." Parker never explained the meaning of the latter exhortation, but he admitted that it "comprehends many particulars that must not be committed to paper, lest the paper blush."[14]

Yet for all his good intentions, there was one front in the battle for self-control that Theodore Parker never engaged at all. "[Y]our love of learning is a passion," warned his classmate Dwight. "Have you not too much of a mania for all printed things?" Parker had long ago concluded that intellectual achievement was the foundation upon which his future success would be built, and despite Dwight's concerns, he immersed himself in books, passionately. Initially, his interests were fairly conventional if somewhat eclectic. His charging list from the Harvard College library shows that during his first year, he consumed a fairly high dose of ancient history and moral philosophy along with modern scientific texts, travel literature, and numerous works by Sir Edward Gibbon. Acquiring languages at a stupendous rate, there were few works in the library whose contents were off limits to him for very long. In early September 1834, for example, he took out a work on Arabic Grammar and just over a month later was ready to tackle an Arabic version of the Gospels. Determined not to allow the fruits of such vast reading to slip through his fingers, he divided his work into discreet subjects, kept notes of his reading and continually tested his knowledge and memory by repeated questioning.[15]

Testing the Boundaries of Thought

It was through this self-directed course of study that Theodore Parker marched his way past the relatively wide borders of the Unitarian frame of reference. By his second year at Divinity Hall, he was reading fewer of the English authors that Harvard professors admired, and more of the German ones they did not. An older generation of Unitarians found German writing full of "crabbed and disgusting obscurity," but Parker's generation of younger thinkers looked to Germany as the land of cutting edge scholarship, a place where romantic philosophy and rationalist biblical criticism were pursued "fearlessly, following out principles wherever they may lead, careless of the consequences." To Parker, German thought was always exciting, even if, or perhaps because, it was a little danger-ous. It was innovative in ways that suited his scholarly ambition and it combined the rational and the spiritual in ways that suited his temperament and his intel-lect.[16]

Just then, in fact, glowing reviews of German literature were appearing in the pages of the *Christian Examiner*, Unitarianism's chief theological journal. In 1833, Frederick Henry Hedge, a recent graduate of the Divinity School and a West Cambridge minister, surprised the anglophile readers of the *Examiner* by proclaiming that German preeminence in "intellectual culture" was a "univer-sally acknowledged" fact. He argued that the philosophy of Immanuel Kant, with its emphasis on "free intuition" and the innate creativity of the human mind, had done much to "establish and to extend the spiritual in man." Even more striking were George Ripley's 1835 essays on Johann Gottfried von Herder, the East Prussian poet and theologian who found the truth of Christian-ity not in "tradition and authority" but in the "individual consciousness of man." Ripley was an 1826 graduate of the Divinity School and the minister of Boston's Purchase Street Church. He risked the censure of older colleagues by reporting Herder's view that "the truth of any religion" could not be established "merely on the ground of miracles." Men like Hedge and Ripley did not yet declare open war on the English enlightenment theology of Harvard Unitarianism, but they used German writers to prioritize intuition over observation, spontaneity over authority.[17]

Parker was drawn to German romantic culture and his library records show that he read more and more books by German authors after 1835. The dynamism and turbulence of his inner world found sustenance in the works of poets like Goethe and Schiller who celebrated the creative power of human feeling. But it was Germany's leadership in the field of biblical criticism that drew his most intense focus. During his final year at the Divinity School, in fact, he prepared a special report for his fellow students that painstakingly described the emergence of what was to be known as the "higher criticism" of the Bible. Critics like Heinrich Paulus and Wilhelm De Wette, he reported, aimed at a fully historical approach to biblical texts, discarding traditional notions of inspiration. Such men either rejected miracles entirely or explained them as misreported versions of natural occurrences. Parker was entranced by the willingness of such learned Germans to discard ancient verities in conscientious service to the truth. After reading De Wette's *Commentaries on the Psalms*, for example, he noted that the author viewed "the Messianic interpretation of the Psalms as a mere chimera; which it is in my humble opinion." This readiness, even eagerness, to discard centuries of authority in favor of modern critical method indicates the kind of theologian he would soon become. As for De Wette, he was simply "a fearless critic; and a critic should fear only one thing—a falsehood."[18]

Like Ripley and Hedge in the pages of the *Christian Examiner*, Parker's student report presented the views of German biblical rationalists without openly endorsing them. But even a casual observer could not have mistaken his orienta-tion. "There is among them a love of truth, a depth of religious feeling, and an eagerness of purpose which is abundantly sufficient to keep them from falling," he declared near the end of the study. In using modern philosophical tools, Parker insisted, Germany's leading theologians had taken the necessary leap beyond the shaky historical basis for Christianity. They relocated the origins of true religion in human intuition, or what they sometimes called "the feelings." Perhaps most important, the new critical methods were generating a scientific understanding of the Bible that could pass the tests of reason and answer the taunts of skeptics. But such progress depended upon a meticulous truth telling that was "careless of the consequences." The Germans "trust to the Truth," he proclaimed, "for they know it is God's and fear nothing but falsehood." [19]

As his graduation neared in the spring of 1836, he found his elders less and less happy with the direction of his thought. Among those who knit their brows at him was the Rev. Andrews Norton, a former Divinity School Professor who now served a dual role as Unitarianism's leading biblical scholar and its chief polemicist. In May 1836, when Parker visited the fifty-two-year-old Norton's large, wooded estate in Cambridge, he found a man who was "gentlemanlike in his deportment" but "a bigot in his opinions," especially when it came to German literature. As far as Norton was concerned, Germans should give up philosophy and biblical studies and confine their activities to making "good dictionaries and grammars." Their language, he blustered to his young caller, was inherently inaccurate and it made them "unfit for metaphysics."[20]

Norton was disgusted by the German tendency to root religious truth in the "feelings," a view which he correctly associated with the Berlin professor Friedrich Schleiermacher but which he inaccurately called pantheism. Norton warned Parker against reading such books because they gave up "all that renders Christianity valuable" and denied the immortality of the soul. Two years earlier, Parker might have been cowed by such warnings, but he now approached the world with almost irrepressible self-confidence. He was as unconvinced by Norton's attack as he was unconcerned about its implications for his own career in the Unitarian ministry. "There is an infinite distance between myself and such men," he wrote in his journal, "but what of that?" He saw the examples of Convers Francis, George Ripley and Frederick Hedge as evidence that scholarly experimentation was permitted, even rewarded in the liberal ministry. "My little light may still burn on," he told himself.[21]

Parker's light was about to burn a little brighter. In September 1836, he purchased a small book which had left many in the city's religious and literary community perplexed. Ralph Waldo Emerson, a Divinity School graduate and former minister of the Second Church in Boston, had written an ecstatic celebration of natural beauty and the awakening of the soul to its own divinity. Unlike the work of Ripley or Hedge, Emerson's *Nature* was not a review or a report on German books. It was a highly original, and therefore much more personal statement and it demonstrated the vast changes that romantic ideas were generating in American letters. *Nature* proclaimed that profound spiritual insight was within the grasp of every thinking person willing to seek it. "Build therefore your own world," its author demanded in the chanting phrases near the end of his book. "As fast as you conform your life to the pure idea in your mind, that will unfold its great proportions" and a "revolution in things will attend the influx of spirit."[22]

Emerson had lost faith in the logical, outward proofs that grounded so much of American Christianity and he drew new waters from the bubbling wells of Christian Neo-Platonism, romantic philosophy, Quakerism and various forms of European mysticism. Parker was reading many of the books that had inspired *Nature*, and he was captivated by the spiritual energy of the writer's vision. Emerson's philosophical idealism was both more mature and more thoroughgoing than Parker's, but the book made an indelible impression on the younger man. He told a friend that *Nature* was brimming over with the waters of human inspiration. "Blessed is he who stoops and drinks of them, he erects himself in new vigor and freshness and becomes a man divine." The "beauty and truth" that Parker found in Emerson drew him closer to the startling way of seeing that many Unitarians were very soon to call "transcendentalism."[23]

Transcendentalism

With Emerson's euphoric prose to inspire him, Parker plunged into the work of finding a congregation. A settled pastorate would provide him a living and give him the time to pursue the theological work he craved. It would also allow him to marry Lydia Cabot after a long, three-year engagement. But this was a period of real anxiety because of emerging vocational doubts that would plague him for the next several years. After one sermon, which Lydia and her aunt Lucy attended, he confessed to feeling "much embarrassed" by his effort and hoped that "it did not show forth." Fortunately he received help and encouragement from Convers Francis who made his Watertown church available for the young candidate's first sermon at the end of July 1836. He tried to control his nerves by walking pleasant old paths with "my own" Lydia, but as the time grew near he began to experience "painful visitations" in the "deep watches of the night." As Parker fought his fears the day before, he received a short but encouraging note from Francis wishing him well and expressing "not the slightest doubt" about his success the following morning.[24]

Francis's confidence in Parker's ability proved well-placed, but the candidate still experienced reservations about the ministry. Did he have the temperament for a pastoral life? Perhaps he had "missed it capitally in becoming a minister" and that as "a lawyer or in other departments of thought and action I might have been more useful." As he stood in the pulpits of Massachusetts churches burning with romantic ideas and radical theology, he struggled to fit his intellectual and emotional dynamism into a reserved, dignified, clerical package. He had suddenly become aware of "a restraining bond --- invincible, but strong as fate," by which clerical convention "tied up every minister." Though not always blessed by perfect self-awareness, Parker had hit upon a problem that was to plague him for the next several years as he struggled to speak his conscience fully while remaining in the ministry.[25]

These worries about the ministry also stemmed from the feeling that the intellectual training he had received at Divinity Hall had not prepared him for pastoral duties. After so many years of intense study he felt disqualified for contact "with the real world." He even told his fellow candidate William Silsbee that with the exception of the "beards on our chins" the curriculum of the Divinity School had left its graduates "with no other signs of manhood." The work of conducting funerals, counseling the sick and bereaved, and responding to the religious doubts of ordinary people were new and daunting responsibilities. The news of his father's death in November made him even more sympathetic to the personal losses suffered by the people he met in the churches. He said very little outwardly about his father, but the funerals he performed as a candidate brought his suppressed emotions to the surface. "I wept," he confessed after performing a funeral on Cape Cod. "Who could see so many weep and not join them at such a time?"[26]

The search for a settled pastorate was also a difficult one for Theodore Parker because he had requirements of his own, not the least of which was his desire to remain close to the libraries of Cambridge and Boston and their collections of German books. While he admired the "generous and truehearted" fishermen and farmers of Barnstable on Cape Cod, he turned down their offer of a position because it would involve "an entire exclusion from books and literary society." In November 1836, just after turning down the job, he told Convers Francis that he was more interested in the vacant Spring Street Church in West Roxbury near Boston. The congregation there was smaller and somewhat better educated. Settling there, he wrote, meant that he could be near "you...and the College Library" to say nothing of Lydia who was still in nearby Watertown.[27]

Settling near Boston would also satisfy Parker's thirst to display his combative intellect as the conflict over German ideas broke into the press. Ralph Waldo Emerson's *Nature*, which Parker read with so much pleasure the previous September, was generating heated controversy among liberal divines. In Francis Bowen's scathing review of the book in the January 1837 issue of the *Christian Examiner*, Parker undoubtedly heard echoes of his conversation with Andrews Norton eight months earlier. Bowen was a philosophy tutor at Harvard and an admirer of all things English and Scottish. He spoke for many in Norton's generation of liberal theologians in declaring that religious truths, like scientific ones, must rest upon observation and rigorous logic. In Emerson's apparent endorsement of an intuitive basis for religious and moral knowledge, Bowen argued, the writer had quite simply exchanged reason for mysticism. In the hands of men like Emerson, Bowen warned, "the handlamp of logic is to be broken."[28]

Using the polemical language that would become a staple in this debate, Bowen accused the "transcendentalists" of teaching the absurd notion that "the truths which are *felt* are more satisfactory that those which are to be *proved*." Whatever claims could be made for innate knowledge, conservatives like Bowen insisted that intuition, like the allied notion of conscience, had to be balanced with "humble research" and "the observation of sensible phenomena." In an overt appeal to older notions of social order and deference that lay near the core of this conflict, he castigated the "new school" for seeing "novelty as a mark of truth" and for undermining the "objects which the wise and good have endeavored to attain."[29]

Bowen's attack on Emerson came at a time when Transcendentalism was taking on a social as well as intellectual shape. As Parker was preparing to leave for his four-week stay in Barnstable, for example, his friend Convers Francis attended a meeting of what became known as the "transcendental club" at George Ripley's home in Boston. Among the other participants was the brilliant and eccentric educator Amos Bronson Alcott whose ground-breaking pedagogy as Boston's Temple School was under fire from conservatives who wanted less open dialogue between teachers and students and more discipline. There was also the fiery young religious reformer, Orestes Brownson, whose vision of spiritual and social democracy had led him to create an experimental church in Boston. And then, of course, there was Emerson himself. Quiet, dignified and almost preternaturally well read, Emerson's personality was a unique combination of warmth and detachment.[30]

Parker's "deep, organ-like voice" would not be heard in the group for another eight months, but he was well-aware of the commonalties between his own emerging ideas about the Bible and religious authority and those of the Transcendentalists. Orestes Brownson's belief in a new theology based on "the broad ground of Christian truth common to all sects," for example, closely resembled Parker's evolving notion that religious authority rested on a single foundation rooted in human nature. Brownson represented a compelling personal model for Parker as well. Over six feet tall, hardened from physical labor and totally self-educated, he displayed a logical acuity and a command of European philosophy that Parker found intimidating. He too had wielded the weapons of intellect in his struggle against social obscurity and lacked a full immersion in elite class decorum. "I deem Brownson a noble man," Parker wrote after meeting him for the first time. "I was so ashamed of my ignorance after hearing Mr. Brownson converse that I have not held my head up since."[31]

The creativity and intellectual power Parker found in men like Brownson and Emerson made Francis Bowen seem petty, even ridiculous. It also brought out the young minister's ever-present disinclination to suffer those he deemed fools. In a remarkably unrestrained letter to his friend Silsbee, he declared that Bowen was "not fit to teach philosophy to cats." It was laughable that the offensive tutor was being considered for a position as Professor of Moral Philosophy and Metaphysics at Harvard. Perhaps "he ought to be Professor of Procrusteanism" instead. Sarcastically proclaiming Bowen the victor in the matter, he told his friend Sam Andrews that

He has given Transcendentalism 'sich a lick' that it is almost dead. Kant, Fichte and Schelling appeared to me in a vision of the night and deplored their sad estate. 'Transcendentalism is clean gone,' said Kant. "Verdammt! said Fichte. 'What shall we do?' exclaimed Schelling. They could not be appeased.[32]

As the controversy over Transcendentalism heated up in the spring of 1837, Parker finally landed the pastorate at Spring Street in West Roxbury he had coveted the previous autumn. Located just outside of Boston, the parish consisted of only sixty families, and its light pastoral requirements would leave the young minister ample time to pursue his theological work. It was not one of the prestigious city pulpits, but it was close enough to the action to satisfy Parker's ambition for intellectual distinction. "If I cannot preach to many, I can study at home and accomplish many schemes which are near to my heart," he told a friend after accepting the position. The annual salary of six hundred dollars was half of what Ralph Waldo Emerson had received in 1829 at the West Church in Boston, but Parker felt that the town's proximity to books and society more than compensated for the financial sacrifice. West Roxbury was also a good choice for Parker because of the make-up of the congregation. Its leading lights, including men like Francis George Shaw, George Russell, Charles Mayo Ellis, and Cornelius Cowing were educated, reform-minded people. "The people are good, quiet, sober, church going," he told Silsbee. "What is wanted in preaching they make up in listening."[33]

With a living secure, Parker married Lydia Cabot in Salem, where he had been preaching a final set of candidate sermons. Theodore and Lydia had seen surprisingly little of each other since their engagement in 1833, but there had been no slackening in their feelings for one another. While his letters to his fiancé were consistently formal and restrained, Parker often referred to her as "my Skyborn" and received her letters with "unspeakable pleasure and satisfaction." At the same time, he was clearly apprehensive about the effect of the marriage on his intellectual ambitions. "I dreamed last night of being at a bookstore," he told Lydia a few months before their wedding. "[W]hen the clerk showed me some book which I had long been seeking, and at a price most villainously cheap, 'Oh no,' said I; 'I shall never buy more books, I am a-going to be married!' and down went the corners of my mouth." Intellectual achievement had been the means of Parker's success at every stage of his young life, so he understandably feared that new domestic demands might interfere with his future eminence.[34]

Parker's determination that "a wife do not beggar the soul of the means of growth and nobleness" was also a response to Lydia's attempts to moderate his work habits. Since their engagement in 1833, she had frequently admonished her fiancé for his fourteen-hour workdays and the couple wrangled a bit over the issue. Parker outwardly denied his penchant for overwork, but his defensiveness suggests a deeper recognition that it might indeed be a vice. "I pray, for the future, that you would urge me to study than dissuade me from it," he told Lydia with obvious annoyance in January 1836. "[M]y conscience would as little permit me to *study* too much as to *drink* too much." Just as he had responded to the social and intellectual rigors of Divinity School with canons of self-discipline, Parker translated his anxiety about marriage into a list of "rules and laws" to govern his behavior toward his wife. He promised never to "oppose my wife's will…except for the best of causes," "never to scold," "never to look cross at her," "never to weary her with commands," "to overlook her foibles," and to "promote her piety." Parker entered marriage, as he entered each new stage of his life, with renewed but often conflicted efforts at self-control.[35]

On a cloudy June 21, 1837, Parker was ordained as minister of the small white church on Spring Street in West Roxbury. Henry Ware Sr. attended the service for Harvard College Chapel as did former president John Quincy Adams for the people of neighboring Quincy. The ordination prayer included a hope that the young minister's "fondness for peculiar studies never divert him from doing Thy work!" In the ordination service, however, it was younger ministers who predominated. Expressing admiration for Parker's scholastic achievements, Convers Francis delivered the ordination sermon and George Ripley welcomed him into the ministry with the right hand of fellowship. Ten years later, Parker mused that the only signs of his coming fate were in the sky. "I little knew what a destiny lay before me in the clouds of that day," he wrote. "A remarkably unexpected ministry it has been to me and the men who laid hands on me."[36]

III
SPIRITUAL INDIFFERENCE
1838–1840

Though Parker would look back on his nine-year ministry in West Roxbury with great fondness, it began in dissatisfaction and doubt. "I often ask myself what I am doing with my one talent, and can only reply that I deem myself well nigh wasting it," he wrote in his journal in January 1838. The quotidian duties of his life as a young parish clergyman mocked the grandiose dreams that had sustained his herculean intellectual preparation. His early life now seemed "a dull waste" in retrospect and days passed when he found little to "freshen my eye." Instead of revolutionizing the religious culture of New England, he now found himself "preaching to an audience of 70 or 120 souls, going about and talking tattle to old women, giving good advice to hypocrites, and scattering love here and there."[1]

The West Roxbury flock often complimented their energetic young minister on the power and skill of his preaching, but he took little satisfaction from such praise. "I would rather see one man practicing one of my sermons than hear all men praise them," he wrote. In choosing the ministry as a vocation, he had hoped to transform the religious and moral life of his parishioners, but now he was forced to confront the limits of his power. After only seven months as minister at West Roxbury, a tired and disillusioned Parker had reached the point of despair. "I have lost many things," he confessed, "the greatest was Hope." [2]

Parker's quest to energize the spiritual life of his congregation was a crucial dimension of his commitment to Transcendentalism. Like Emerson, Ripley, and Brownson, Parker came to the conclusion that the language and doctrines of traditional Christianity had lost their ability to transform the lives of believers. Unless the churches could find "new truths in the gospel, new meaning in life," religion would become nothing but an "empty form." Like many religious innovators in the antebellum generation, he longed for new manifestations of truth in which Christianity could be "apprehended in all its power."[3]

But, if spiritual vitality were to replace "spiritual indifference," a great deal of baggage would have to be cleared away first. The Bible presented the most serious problem of all. Many in Parker's congregation understood the scriptures as central to their faith, but they balked at miracles and recoiled from descriptions of God's anger and vengeance. One elderly congregant whom Parker had encouraged to reread the early books of the Old Testament returned to his young pastor saying that he was "sorry he had read it" because he now realized that "he could not believe it, [and] before he thought he believed all." As long as a belief in the historicity of the Bible hung "like a millstone" around the necks of those who sought an enlightened faith, he complained to Convers Francis, the church would lose the brightest and most educated part of its flock. Its social influence would plummet accordingly. Transcendentalism offered a way to shed traditional religious forms without losing the central Christian messages of divine and human love written in the human heart. As one historian has put it, Parker and the "[Transcendentalists] hoped to save Christianity from historical oblivion and give it personal immediacy by pointing out the identity of Gospel truth and intuition."[4]

Domestic and Parish Life

The frustration and disappointment that appeared in the first years of Parker's settlement in West Roxbury stemmed in part from the domestic tension that marked his marriage to Lydia Cabot. The source of the problem is not entirely clear from the record, but there are important hints. The first relates to the powerful financial and emotional position that Lydia's aunt, Lucy Cabot, assumed in the young couple's lives. Aunt Lucy was a wealthy woman and she provided the newlywed Parkers with a spacious first home in West Roxbury, a structure the locals called the "old 'Rain-water-Doctor's place" that was situated in a pine grove near the Spring Street church. Lucy not only moved to the new house with at least one servant, but she was also determined not to allow her niece's marriage to displace her as Lydia's emotional confidante.[5]

Lydia's relationship with Aunt Lucy made for a complicated emotional situation and Parker found it difficult to forge a complete bond with his wife. In contrast to the exciting world of his study, where ideas came with electrifying speed, he frequently complained of the "tomb-like" atmosphere of the house— even going so far as to call it "a dark hole" from which his view of the world was obscured. Careful of etiquette and respectability, Lydia and Aunt Lucy had little interest in the intellectual life that propelled the intense young man who had entered their lives. In June 1838 he wrote bitterly that "the most stupefying draught would [be] a stimulant, compared to the conversation in our (I should say—) family." There may have been a good deal of truth in this, but Parker could also be self-righteous and petulant in response to those who did not measure up to his expectations. "I expected and asked but little—a happy home," he complained the following summer. "Since it is the will of God that I should have none of this, so let it be."[6]

The problems inherent in this situation quickly became acute as Theodore and Lydia also confronted the possibility that their marriage would be childless. Emotional conflict over Aunt Lucy's presence certainly played a role in these troubles, but Parker's letters a few months after his marriage hint at some kind of physical incompatibility between the couple. When a friend inquired about the dejected tone of his correspondence, Parker responded in an uncharacteristically enigmatic fashion. "I admit its existence in a greater sense than you imagine, but of the cause, not a word!" he wrote, "let rumor tell you: *I shall not*, not even to you." A year later he complained that although neither he nor Lydia had experienced a single day of bad health for months at a time, he could not bring himself to thank God for their blessings. "Oh that our hearts had filled with Love in the same proportion," he lamented.[7]

During the next several years, he periodically described his life with Lydia and Aunt Lucy as "cheerless, loveless," "forlorn," and totally lacking in "fellow feeling." Yet other emotions competed with these feelings, suggesting that the relationship had another side to it, one in which Lydia accepted her husband's affection and sustained his sense of manhood. In a diary entry made only a few weeks after complaining of her coldness, he complained that her trip to visit relatives had left him unable to concentrate on his work. "I miss her absence— wicked woman—most exceedingly," he wrote. "It is not so much the affection she bestows as that she receives by which I am blessed—I want someone always in the corner of my heart to caress and comfort." Yet it must be said that these sentiments were rare in Parker's journals, and the prospect of a childless, loveless marriage made his bitter public struggles over religion and reform even more difficult to bear.[8]

Yet all was not darkness during these early years in West Roxbury. If Lydia and Aunt Lucy were uninterested in his world of ideas, there were "some intellectual young men and women" in the surrounding neighborhood who encouraged Parker's unorthodox religious and philosophical vision. His closest neighbor, George Robert Russell, was a retired East India merchant whose commitment to romantic causes had led him to participate in the Latin American independence movements during the 1820s. Parker once described him as "full of poetry" and "big with life." Russell wore his wealth and social position lightly, and, along with his wife Sarah, turned his home into a magnet for unconventional young people. The Russell children, who would soon enroll in the schools of the Brook Farm community, held informal events called "Olympiks" or extended discussions of the latest literary, philosophical and religious works. Parker encouraged the "fair damsels of the next house" in their literary endeavors and clearly reveled in the conversation of their learned father and mother.[9]

When Sarah Russell's brother Francis Shaw moved his own family to a house near the West Roxbury parsonage, the town's intellectual culture gained yet another degree of sophistication and unconventionality. Like George Russell, Frank Shaw came from a wealthy background, but his commitment to abolitionism and Transcendentalism led him to repudiate commerce and devote himself to social reform. Forsaking the urbane world of Boston for rural West Roxbury, Shaw anticipated both the Brook Farmers and Henry David Thoreau in seeking "in nature a 'real' existence in tune with the divine." His wife, Sarah Sturgis Shaw, and his younger sister, Anna Blake Shaw, were among Parker's closest friends and most ardent supporters in the Spring Street Church. They provided spirited conversation and playful diversion for their minister.[10]

If Parker sometimes found that the life of a parish clergyman did not live up to his ideals, he does not seem to have communicated that frustration to his congregation. He studied early in the mornings and late into the night, but he walked or rode on horseback through the community each afternoon. Parishioners remembered him rambling along woody paths "with his long awkward strides, hat on the back of his head." For all of his erudition and yearning for intellectual companionship, Parker avoided artifice or ceremony with his parishioners and was not afraid to indulge his characteristic penchant for "merrymaking." Among his favorite activities were the regular meetings with young Sunday school teachers eager for guidance in preparing their lessons. These discussions lacked the formality that so often undermined the effectiveness of preaching and Parker found them rewarding opportunities for spiritual growth and nurture. "I aim at the heart and the conscience not the less directly then in the pulpit," he told a friend.[11]

Although still a young man, experience had made Parker a sympathetic and compassionate pastor. His own family's heartbreaking experience with tuberculosis gave him an unusually deep sympathy with those who experienced personal loss. By 1840 only his brothers John, Isaac and Hiram remained from a family of eleven children. Yet rather than producing despair or bitterness, this ongoing tragedy had deepened his faith in the existence of a benign afterlife where the soul remained in the immediate and perpetual presence of God. He comforted himself and his parishioners in the belief that death was "always a blessing to him who dies" because it represented the end of physical pain and the beginning of a new, immortal life of spirit. Death itself was only a moment of transition like a child's "change from 'baby clothes' to the boy's dress" and, though it produced grief in those who remained behind, "it is a change which is always made for the better." [12]

In using such metaphorical language to soothe the sick and grieving, Parker struggled against an older New England Calvinist tradition that understood physical affliction as divine chastisement. Visiting the bedside of an indigent woman suffering from pulmonary consumption, he was disgusted to find that she had been made "almost insane" by an orthodox minister's wife who had warned her against dying in an unregenerate state. The patient, who was well known among the poor of West Roxbury for personal acts of compassion, had become distraught about her spiritual state and experienced "frightful visions," that left her distraught and sleepless. Parker's confrontation with Calvinism, and its continued influence on the liberal religious culture in Massachusetts, stemmed as much from real pastoral experiences as from abstract intellectual convictions.[13]

De Wette and the Bible

Some of Parker's dissatisfaction with his lot as a rural parson undoubtedly stemmed from the sheer exhaustion that came from a life that combined the practical business of ministry with a relentless devotion to scholarship. He was determined not to slight the pastoral demands of his flock, but remained utterly committed to biblical studies. "Old studies go on," he told Silsbee in September. "[A]ll that used so much to delight and instruct us flourishes and grows apace in my new situation." There would be no readjustment of priorities, only new responsibilities. [14]

In August 1836 he had begun translating Wilhelm De Wette's *Critical and Historical Introduction to the Old Testament*, a work whose publication in Germany in 1805 represented a stunning new direction in biblical scholarship. De Wette had argued that modern readers of the Hebrew Scriptures made a serious mistake in assuming that the authors of these texts intended to convey historical narratives. Historical consciousness, he insisted, was a recent phenomenon and had been unknown in the cultural world of the biblical authors. He labored to prove that the stories of the Pentateuch were written centuries after the events they described and should be compared with the *Iliad*, the *Aeneid*, or other epics of the ancient world. These stories had provided a mythic foundation for later Jewish life and reflected the creativity of "the Hebrew imagination" rather than a modern concern for historical accuracy. In using the term "myth," De Wette was not seeking to discredit the Bible as a religious source, but rather to turn the attention of scholars away from the historical elements of the scriptures toward the larger cultural worldview of the authors.[15]

Parker considered De Wette to be "the ablest writer in the world" on the Old Testament and he was thoroughly convinced by the German's description of the Pentateuch as Israel's "great national poem." He was determined to build his own scholarly reputation by introducing De Wette's work to American students of the Bible. But Parker's motivations in translating and annotating his work were not wholly ambitious, nor were they entirely separate from his pastoral role. De Wette's notion that ancient cultural assumptions, rather than divine inspiration, had shaped the basic message of the Old Testament, empowered the young minister to discard the troubling aspects of the scriptural tradition in favor of reason and conscience.[16]

While working on De Wette in 1839, he told the congregation at West Roxbury to think of the Hebrew Scriptures as "old garments which were fine in their day" but which "are laid aside when their end is answered." Understood as "an Epic" rather than "a history", in other words, the Old Testament lost much of its sacred authority and allowed Parker to dispense with its angry, punishing God in favor of a more benign, loving father. He begged his flock not to subordinate their own rational and moral judgments to the "myths" of ancient writers. His own conscience, he confessed, shuddered at "the Jehovah of the Jews, a God jealous and revengeful, partial and unlovely" whose law was used to justify "war, capital punishment, slavery, and other nameless sins." If some in the congregation balked at the radicalism of such statements, social activists like Frank Shaw found them useful arguments against those who cited the Mosaic law to support slavery and war. Parker acknowledged the Bible's sacred power and importance in religious life, but he told men like Shaw that the Bible was not greater than the conscience.[17]

Since his German was excellent, Parker quickly completed a "word for word" translation of De Wette's book. But he ultimately decided to use the work to introduce New England readers to the larger implications of German biblical criticism. Rather than stopping with a simple translation, he included detailed annotations of De Wette's text in which the entire history of critical studies was brought to bear on key points in order to establish the novelty and importance of the book's contributions. This turned out to be a monumental task. In addition to translating all of the Latin, Greek, and Hebrew quotations left in the original by De Wette, Parker read every Old Testament introduction published over the previous two centuries, all of the applicable early Christian writings, and an exhaustive list of modern critical works.[18]

The monumental project took him nearly six years to complete. It occupied every moment he could spare from writing weekly sermons, visiting the sick, and serving the larger needs of his parish. It was also expensive as his library began to swell with volumes imported from European booksellers. As his old friend John Sullivan Dwight had recognized several years earlier, Parker's bibliophilic impulses verged on obsession and his new project provided ample justification to indulge them. "I have got lots of new books—upwards of one hundred Germans!" he exulted to his friend Silsbee. "Some of them are old friends, others new, all sorts of creatures." It is likely that one of these "new creatures" was David Strauss's *Life of Jesus,* a work which took the radical step of applying De Wette's concept of "myth" to the New Testament miracles. Reason and conscience would soon outstrip all other forms of authority including those most precious to traditional Christianity.[19]

Joining the Transcendental Circle

The depression resulting from Parker's grueling work habits and domestic conflicts led him to seek sympathetic intellectual companionship. He began attending a "little society of good fellows" at Ralph Waldo Emerson's house in nearby Concord in the summer of 1837, and he rarely missed thereafter. Each session of this "transcendental club" revolved around a central question relevant to the theological, philosophical, and reform interests of its members. One evening they considered the question "Is Mysticism an element of Christianity?" The "character and genius of Goethe" dominated the conversation of another. Amidst the powerful minds gathered in the Old Manse for these discussions, the young West Roxbury minister soon demonstrated his powerful grasp of German biblical studies and developed the reputation as a "calm and accurate thinker."[20]

Parker was not intimidated by the other intellects in the group, and it appears that he paid little deference to age or experience in expressing his opinions. A. Bronson Alcott, whose rather mystical modes of expression grated on Parker's more muscular rationalism, was often the target of the younger man's barbs. During one session dealing with the topic of "Pantheism," Parker noted that Alcott described God as "progressively unfolding Himself...going forward to his own infinity." Whether he found this image of God too mystical or just self-contradictory, he felt no compunction about calling it "revolting." Parker's natural independence and his bedrock confidence in his own intuitions ensured that he would never be simply a cheerleader for the movement.[21]

Even in the midst of intellectual disagreements, however, the club provided Parker with a support network that included experienced ministers like George Ripley and Convers Francis as well as "young striplings" who struggled with the same vocational doubts and problems that plagued him. Caleb Stetson, John Sullivan Dwight, George Putnam, and Chandler Robbins were recent Divinity School graduates and they shared his interest in applying German theology and biblical criticism to preaching and pastoral life. Along with these male clergymen and reformers, Parker also met a group of well-educated, highly talented women. Elizabeth Palmer Peabody and Margaret Fuller were among the two most prominent, and they possessed the broad learning and intellectual curiosity that he found lacking in Lydia and Aunt Lucy.[22]

In Emerson, the group possessed a quietly inspirational leader whose example and consistent vision drew out the best from his friends. In outward, personal terms, Parker and Emerson were very different. Parker's penchant for impulsive, even theatrical display contrasted so sharply with Emerson's quietism that the older man once said that "our minds and methods were unlike—few people more unlike." But Parker deeply admired the sage of Concord and later remembered that his "brilliant genius...rose on those winter nights drawing the eyes of ingenious young people to look up to that great, new star."[23]

The new hope that Emerson offered to Parker and the other eager young liberal ministers who crowded into his home in the late 1830s was the promise of a revitalized and reinvented Christianity, a dynamic new faith rooted in human consciousness. Traditional Unitarianism had revised the orthodox Protestant doctrines of innate human depravity, eternal damnation, and the Trinity, but it still insisted on the divinity of Jesus, and the genuineness of the Gospel miracles as a proof of Christ's message. Like Parker and other young liberals who struggled to make Christianity relevant to the lives of indifferent parishioners, Emerson saw these doctrines as the worn out remnants of a theological system that looked to history for proof rather than to the soul for inspiration. The error of "historical Christianity," he wrote in 1838 was its "exaggeration of the personal, the positive, the ritual." He insisted that religion and morality, truth and conscience, were innate and required no outward authority to validate or check them. To Parker, whose belief in the power of an autonomous, awakened con-

science had been a dominant principle since childhood, Emerson's philosophy
of self-trust represented an intellectual challenge and a call to action. "Speak the
truth," Emerson once declared, "and the very roots of the grass underground
there, do seem to stir and move and bear you witness."[24]

Drawing confidence from his new associations, Parker thought more deeply
about the relationship between his intellectual life and his ministry in West Roxbury. Was there a way to bring the excitement and inspiration he received from
discussions in Concord to the people who filled the pews on Spring Street?
Could he break through the "restraining bond" of convention that had generated
his vocational doubts? How far should he go in preaching the new gospel to
parishioners who might not be prepared for it? Convention said that learned
criticism of the Bible was fine for the pastor's study or for the pages of scholarly
journals, but it had no place in Sunday sermons. It might undermine the faith of
simple people and confuse them in the midst of life's struggles. Parker's mentor
Convers Francis held just this view despite his otherwise progressive position.
"[A]s long as there is a great gulf between the wise and the foolish," he once
wrote to his young friend, "there would always be...the Bible for our study, &
the Bible for our public assembly." But Parker was uncomfortable with such
accommodations, and he wondered out loud whether they amounted to a failure
of nerve among the liberal clergy. Would not the people be "better, wiser, and
holier if they were emancipated from this stupid superstition" of biblical inerrancy, he asked Francis.[25]

Parker's break with the caution and elitism of men like Francis became apparent quickly. In early 1839, he preached a daring sermon on "The Relation of
the Bible to the Soul" to his West Roxbury flock. In clarity, boldness and radicalism, the sermon went much further than any of his earlier efforts. "The Bible
or the New Testament is not the sole and exclusive foundation of Christianity,"
he insisted. "Its truths are laid in human nature; they live with the Soul. They are
the soul's law." Critical to his thinking at this point was the notion that God
equipped human consciousness to see beyond the temporary world of the senses
to permanent spiritual and moral laws. These purely internal capacities, which
Parker identified by the classic terms reason and conscience, were the standards
by which all external truth claims were to be judged. The Bible was not the
judge of the soul, but rather the reverse. "Nothing arbitrary and capricious can
ever become binding on Reason and Conscience, let it be taught on what authority it may," he argued.[26]

Perhaps equally novel was Parker's insistence that reason and conscience
could arrive at truths not contained in scripture at all. If God worked in history
through reason and conscience, he asked, "then how do we know that the time
will not come when man on earth shall not need the New Testament, having
outgrown even that teacher also?" Progress could occur in religious life as well
as in science or politics. These were radical statements indeed. What Parker proposed in this sermon was an entire reorientation of the traditional premises upon
which all Christian truth was established. Despite their disagreement over specific doctrines, events, and methods of interpretation, Unitarians and orthodox

Protestants at least shared the basic assumption that the Bible contained an accurate and complete record of God's revelation to human beings. Parker's argument was revolutionary in suggesting that such revelation was secondary to the innate religious and moral imperatives contained in human nature.[27]

Parker's sermon on the Bible and the Soul, which was published under his initials in the Unitarian periodical the *Western Messenger* in 1840, represents not only a greater boldness of thought, but also a growing impatience with a religious culture in which restraint and decorum had become obstacles to the full expressions of reason and conscience. For example, in November 1837, he had published an anonymous article in the weekly *Christian Register* which lightly satirized the reverence with which some clergyman approached the scriptures. Seizing the readers' attention by lightly offending their sensibilities, he compiled a list of "reasons why a clergyman should *not* study the scriptures carefully and critically." Incensed subscribers wrote angry letters criticizing the article for using "sarcasm and levity...on a subject of so serious a nature." But Parker was determined to provoke a public discussion of ideas he believed were at the very root of New England's spiritual indifference. "I might have drained a Black Sea full of ink in scribbling about the importance of the Bible," he told William Silsbee. "[W]ho would have read my lucubrations?"[28]

Tact in expressing the truth was also at issue in Parker's anonymous review of John Gorham Palfrey's recent work on the Old Testament. Appearing in the pages of the *Boston Quarterly Review*, a new journal edited by fellow Transcendentalist Orestes Brownson, Parker showed little deference to his former professor and leveled a merciless attack on the whole tradition of liberal biblical criticism. In the vein of Herder and De Wette, he argued that attempts to prove the truth of the Christian message by historical methods were doomed to failure. Miracles were too shaky a foundation for Christian faith. "It is no relief to explain away ninety and nine miracles, while the hundredth is permitted to remain," he stated. "[I]f one camel may go through the eye of the needle all may." In place of the painstaking historical techniques employed by men like Palfrey and Norton, Parker suggested that the Bible be evaluated according to universal principles of religion and morality, which all men shared in common. "Is there not a sentiment in human nature which impels us to worship the Infinite God?" he asked. "Must knowledge of God, Duty, Religion be imparted to us from without, and sanctioned by miracles?" Palfrey went farther than other Unitarian critics in his rejection of Old Testament miracles, but Parker could find little inspiration in any critical method which derived the truth of religion from history.[29]

Many of Parker's friends felt that the tone of his attack on Palfrey was unwarranted and several expressed regret at his use of sarcasm and flippancy. "You think I indulge the ludicrous vein too much, such is my propensity no doubt," he responded to a critical letter from William Silsbee. "I wished to indulge in a little harmless pleasantry, but I fear that Dean [Palfrey] would not share the mirth he so excited." With a self-confidence that had rebounded from the doubts of the previous winter, Parker was now bristling under the restrictions of polite decorum. "How ought things to be treated?" he asked Silsbee. "Light things lightly, grave things gravely, ridiculous things ridiculously; ...I must think ridicule has its place in criticism."[30]

If his willingness to use satire and light mockery is one of the distinguishing features of Parker's role in the Transcendentalist controversy, it also demonstrates his self-conscious reliance on internal notions of moral duty over all external standards. When fellow Transcendentalist Elizabeth Peabody warned him that he was in danger of becoming a martyr, he was flattered. In a fleeting moment of modesty he denied having the "spirit" of martyrs like John Knox, but he professed to have "no fear of persecution." "Having settled the matter that an opinion is true and an action perfectly right," he wrote, "what have you and I to do with the consequences that may follow?"[31]

IV
THE TRANSCENDENTALIST CONTROVERSY
1838–1840

The open public debate over theological reform that Parker longed for began in earnest in the summer of 1838. On July 15, he walked the familiar paths to Cambridge to hear Ralph Waldo Emerson deliver the commencement address at the Harvard Divinity School. Though he had often been awed by Emerson's powerful intellect and the beauty of his prose, Parker was not prepared for the boldness and power of the speech he heard that afternoon. The explosive reaction to it would soon force him to make critical decisions about the direction of his ministry.

To an audience which included some of Harvard's most respected graduates, scholars, and financial supporters, Emerson launched an assault upon the theological foundations of Boston Unitarianism. The weight of his attack was directed against "historic Christianity" or the attempt to prove the truth of religion from the events of scripture. "[Historical Christianity]," Emerson argued, "has dwelt, with noxious exaggeration, about the person of Jesus." "The soul knows no persons, [but] invites every man to expand to the full circle of the universe." Traditional Christianity, he insisted, failed to give legitimacy to the revelation in the soul of the individual. "To aim to convert a man by miracles is a profanation of the soul," he flatly stated, "men have come to speak of the revelation as somewhat long ago and given and done, as if God were dead." These sentiments were not new to Parker, but the context of the address, and Emerson's prophetic style of delivery, was little short of intoxicating. "So beautiful, so just, so true, and terribly sublime was his picture of the faults of the Church in its present position," he wrote in his journal. "My soul is roused."[1]

But if Parker's soul was roused, so were the tempers of Massachusetts' religious leaders. Liberal Protestants had always claimed a catholic temper in spiritual matters, but Emerson's "Divinity School Address" tested the very limits of their toleration. After the publication of *Nature* in 1836, conservatives like Francis Bowen and Andrews Norton became increasingly fearful that orthodox Protestants would tar all Unitarians with Emerson's radicalism. Rather than expose themselves to the charge of apostasy, they had vigorously disavowed any association with his "new views." Emerson refused to take up the cudgels of public controversy, but his position was ably defended by George Ripley who accused Norton and company of conducting a theological witch-hunt. Ripley implied that the liberal establishment was betraying its own traditions and reverting to the repressive creedalism once used against them by the Calvinists. "There is a tone in your remarks, slightly suppressed, of the *odium theologicum*," Ripley complained after one of Andrews Norton's attacks. "I thought we had all breathed the air of freedom too long."[2]

Ripley's call for toleration had held the conservatives in check until 1838, but the "Divinity School Address" tore the controversy open. However beautiful its language, the address contained a stinging indictment of the clergy. Emerson complained that religious life in New England was ossified, tied to a language and a theology no longer able to inspire. Ministers, even liberal ones, failed to link religion to human life and substituted formal theology for direct experience. "Whenever the pulpit is usurped by a formalist, then is the worshiper defrauded and disconsolate," Emerson had bluntly charged. "We shrink as soon as the prayers begin, which do not uplift, but smite and offend us." The sharp tone of Emerson's address delighted radicals like Parker who were struggling against formalism in their own preaching, but it struck others as "a personal insult to the highly respectable officers of the [Divinity School]."[3]

As a co-founder of the Harvard Divinity School, and the author of a new book on the authenticity of the New Testament miracles, Andrews Norton felt compelled to respond both to Emerson's theology and to his damaging criticisms of the clergy. Breaking with elite tradition, he bypassed the scholarly or religious press and published a direct attack on the Transcendentalists in the pages of the *Boston Daily Advertiser*. Norton condemned Emerson and his friends for using "an over-excited and convulsionary style" designed to appeal to "silly young women" and "silly young men." Their theology was meaningless prattle made to sound impressive by the use of vague German philosophical terminology. "To produce a striking effect, our common language is abused; antic tricks are played on it," he fumed, "and withal a fresh infusion of German barbarisms." Dire warnings for the fate of society followed. "Should such teachers abound and grow confident in their folly," he prophesied, "we can hardly overestimate the disastrous effect upon the religious and moral state of the community."[4]

Parker was both amused and disgusted by these shrill attacks on Emerson. The address had "caused a great outcry," he told a friend in his usual satirical style. "One shouted, 'The Philistines be upon us!' another, 'We all be dead men!' while the majority called out 'Atheism!'" He refused to take conservative predictions of social disintegration seriously, and dismissed Norton's warnings as reactionary hysteria. "It is thought chaos is coming back; the world is coming to an end, some seem to think that Christianity will not be able to weather this gale," he wrote sarcastically. "[F]or my part, I have great doubts whether Emerson will overthrow Christianity this time."[5]

It was not that Parker slavishly followed Emerson on every point. He often complained about what he regarded as Emerson's overly mystical state of mind. God and man were alike, but not identical, and Parker thought Emerson sometimes mistook "Similarity for Identity." But Parker simply could not fathom the statements of men like John Gorham Palfrey who said that those parts of Emerson's address that were not "folly" would "be found to be Atheism." To one who believed that conscience and intuition were reliable guides to human behavior, conservative fears of social disorder were hard to credit. Instead, it was the establishment's continual reliance on the crumbling foundations of biblical authority that constituted the greatest threat to church and society.[6]

Parker's idea of conscience played an important role in shaping his response to the Transcendentalist controversy. As the conflict unfolded, he returned again and again to the inherent moral foundations of human nature as a better guide to spiritual and moral truth than either the Bible or elite opinion. During a conversation with William Ellery Channing a few months after the controversy began, he asked the great preacher "if conscience were not an *infallible* guide." The liberal and pious Channing, whose views of human nature were as positive as any Unitarian of his generation, "hesitated to assent." He compared the conscience to the eye, which "might be dim, or might see wrong." The conscience, he felt, was like other faculties of the mind, requiring careful instruction to function properly. Parker confessed that he "rather ridiculed" the notion that the conscience needed education. Channing's analogy of the eye missed the mark because it failed to describe the direct manner by which the conscience discerned the moral law. "It is not the eye which sees, but the soul which looks out at the eye," he insisted. "Conscience...acts *directly*, not *mediately*, and therefore it is not liable to the same mistakes as the eye." On this basis, he concluded that "conscience is the last appeal" and that "the man is degraded who disobeys it."[7]

As the controversy over Transcendentalism heated up in the press, Parker's pastoral and social activities were initially unaffected by it. He remained frustrated by the lack of religious fervor in his small congregation, but his sermon writing, work on De Wette, and parish responsibilities kept him very busy. But the conflict caught up with him at hitherto routine events where ministers on different sides met publicly. At the ordination of a young minister at Channing's Federal Street Church, for example, he witnessed two serious breaches of collegiality. Young Henry Bellows, who gave a mildly transcendental ordination sermon, was upbraided by Dr. Francis Parkman of the New North Church who said he was "exceedingly pained and grieved" to hear "dangerous doctrine" preached on the solemn occasion of ordination. Others complained that the Rev. Karl Follen, a German émigré with strongly romantic theological views had been asked to give the pastoral charge at the service. Parker was shocked to hear a normally genial colleague ask "why they got that 'Foreigner' to give the charge." In a religious culture that had long prided itself on liberality and cos-

mopolitanism, these altercations were unusual and indicated a deepening crisis
of identity.[8]

More serious to Parker's situation was the growing consensus among conservative Unitarians that some kind of creed, or test of faith, might be necessary
to prevent the spread of radical views. "Some of the ministers think we need to
have certain fundamentals fixed for all to swear by," he told his friend George
Ellis, "lest the new school among the Unitarians should carry the whole body up
to the height of transcendentalism." The Unitarian clergy preferred to think of
themselves as their society's natural religious leaders, but they were in fact denominational figures. Their ability to compete with the orthodox churches
hinged upon some level of theological unity. Emerson was no longer a Unitarian
minister, but his association with the movement was well known, and his het-
erodox theology raised serious questions about its character. It seemed essential
to declare his views out of bounds.[9]

The result was a decidedly illiberal display of intolerance. At the January
1839 meeting of the Boston Association of Congregational Ministers, for example, Parker heard older colleagues declare that Emerson was not a Christian because he denied Christ's divinity. One went as far as to call him "a downright
Atheist". The Association had no direct power over Emerson, but the meeting's
condemnation of the Concord philosopher had implications for young ministers
who subscribed to the "new views" but who also sought to remain in good
standing with their older, more conservative colleagues. A change of policy and
a new list of theological "fundamentals" would most certainly exclude Parker
unless he was willing to trim his sails.[10]

For the first time he wondered if a permanent division had emerged among
the liberal clergy. "It is quite evident there are now two parties among the Unitarians," he wrote after the meeting. "One is for progress with Dr. Channing at
its head; the other says 'Our strength is to stand still.'" Parker continued to hope
that Channing, and his allies among the younger clergy, would move the denomination toward a fully pluralistic position where consensus could be
achieved through open dialogue rather than creedal conformity. But concerns
about his own position were starting to mount. "You will have all the clergy
about your ears," an older minister warned him after hearing his views on theology. "You will not stay in your pulpit seven years."[11]

Channing and Strauss

Parker placed great hope in William Ellery Channing. Nearing sixty at the time
of the Transcendentalist controversy, Channing was a magnet for young intellectuals who were dissatisfied with the state of New England religious and cultural
life. As Parker's frank disagreements with him over the idea of conscience
show, Channing invited open discussion on pivotal theological issues. Transcendentalist Elizabeth Peabody, who spent time as Channing's personal secretary, said that "there never was a person more desirous of breaking down all

barriers of reserve and formality that would interrupt free and open communication between mind and mind."[12]

Yet for all his affinities with younger ministers, Channing encouraged them to moderate the tone and pace of their reformism. He was unwilling to take "the leap" beyond historical Christianity, with its emphasis on the special revelations of Christ, which so offended the radical idealism of Emerson and his circle. These differences became apparent to Parker in the spring of 1839 during another of his conversations at Channing's house. The subject of their talk was Parker's interest in producing an English translation of David Strauss's *Life of Jesus*, a work which took the revolutionary step of applying the Higher Criticism of the Bible to the Gospels. Parker was one of the first Americans to read the book and he quickly became an admirer of its attempt to separate the historical and mythical elements of the Synoptic texts.

Strauss's effect on Parker's thought was quite dramatic. A month or so before his talk with Channing, he had quite casually asked Convers Francis to consider the possibility that "all the miracles belong to the mythical part" of the Gospel narratives. "Is not Strauss right, in the main," he went on, "when he says the N[ew]. T[estament]. is a collection of mythi?" Perhaps Strauss's iconoclastic method went "too far", but "pray tell me," he asked, "where *is* far enough?" After all, if Christianity was rooted in human nature, it was "older than Abraham" and "would stand forever" without the support of any text. What was the point of inventing elaborate systems of interpretation to "save [the] credit" of Gospel miracles when the essence of the faith was "older than creation" itself. And finally, in what amounts to the most radical statement of his thought to date, he confessed that "I have sometimes thought that [Christianity] would stand better without the N[ew] T[estament] than with it. Certainly I should not send a skeptic to the Bible to convert him."[13]

Once again, Parker's elders told him not to take such ideas into the public square. When he told Channing that he was considering a published translation of Strauss's work, the older man proclaimed "very archly" that he "would not advise me to do it." Channing had heard rumors that the followers of Boston's best known freethinker, Abner Kneeland, were planning to put out a translation, and he was "very sorry" to hear it. Kneeland had been imprisoned for blasphemy earlier in the decade and he had emerged as a leading anticlerical voice in Boston. Channing likely assumed that Kneeland's followers would use Strauss to discredit the city's ministers. A scholarly translation like the one Parker proposed would lend credence to such attacks and would weaken the ability of the church to guide the public mind. Channing remained enough of an establishment figure to worry about the dangerous social consequences of placing the ideas of a thinker like Strauss in the hands of the multitude.[14]

Neither Channing's moderation, nor his social conservatism suited Parker's emerging worldview. He was convinced that false ideas of the Bible and of Jesus were at the root of the spiritual indifference he encountered in his own congregation. Strauss's book had the potential to sweep away the outmoded baggage of historic Christianity and generate a robust public discussion of the Bible.

A new image of Jesus as "the highest form of man," as one who overcame his "little faults and weaknesses" to become "a perfect incarnation of the word," might replace the mythical Christ of the Gospels. Such an image would encourage the faithful to see the potential of their own perfectibility. The book also offered a reaffirmation of the Transcendentalists' position that miracles were too shaky a foundation upon which to build a vital religion. But instead of a translation of Strauss, Parker decided to compose a lengthy review of the work for the April 1840 issue of the *Christian Examiner*, Unitarian's premier theological journal.[15]

If the subject of Parker's review was potentially explosive, its tone was still careful and measured. He was frustrated that he "could not say all I would say" and still have the review accepted by the cautious editors of the *Examiner*. In sixty, densely-packed pages, he laid out Strauss's "mythic" hypothesis in scholarly, rather than polemical terms. Nor was he uncritical of his subject. For example, he rejected as "absurd" Strauss's notion that the mythic stories of the New Testament have no basis at all in fact. Parker believed that Christ was a real person, not simply an idea as Strauss had suggested. But elsewhere Parker clearly admitted his admiration for the radical German critic, especially his courageous application of historical method to the New Testament. He praised Strauss for engaging in a process of creative destruction that would ultimately unlock the floodgates of religious progress. "Someone must plunge in," he argued, "before mankind could pass over the great chasm between the frozen realm of stiff supernaturalism ...and the fair domain of free religious thought." Strauss's virtue was his readiness to perform the intellectual violence necessary for a new era of religious liberty to emerge. Parker painted an image of Strauss that mirrored his own emerging self-conception quite closely.[16]

Parker's decision to ignore Channing's advice and link his name with Strauss demonstrates his increasingly direct role in the public debate over Transcendentalism by fall of 1839. Now he was reading drafts of George Ripley's rebuttals to Norton, and applauding his friend's defense of Christian liberty as "excellent, both in design and execution." He was especially pleased that Ripley's restrained style cast Norton in the role of aggressor. At the same time, however, he struggled to contain his own feelings of aggression against a man who seemed bent on crushing innovation. "The Professor may well thank Heaven that he has fallen into the hands of a Christian man" like Ripley, Parker told William Silsbee. "Some men would have treated him as the Giant charitably designed to treat Jack—would have broken every bone in his body."[17]

The Thursday Lecture and Levi Blodgett

In October, Parker took a break from his domestic and pastoral routine to go on a walking tour in the Berkshire Hills of Western Massachusetts with a group that included George Ripley. He relished the chance to get away from the ongoing tensions with Lydia and Aunt Lucy. He had tried to compensate for his isolated home life by spending time with his neighbors, the Shaws. But that provided little relief as it generated local gossip about his relationship with Anna Blake Shaw, Frank's attractive and well-educated younger sister. His journal contains several references to Anna Shaw, including some romantic-sounding poetic tributes. But there is no evidence of anything beyond a flirtation. The Berkshire trip provided a temporary respite from all of this. Sunny days were spent "roaming among the hills of Berkshire county" while rainy ones provided a relaxed opportunity for light reading, discussion and observation of life in local taverns. The "scent of the barroom," the "jingling of crockery, the neighing of horses, and cackling and crowing of little hens and cocks" at least temporarily took his mind off his domestic and professional problems.[18]

By the time he returned, however, he was ready to "plunge in" to the Transcendentalist controversy. His first opportunity came on January 2, 1840, at the Thursday Lecture, a monthly gathering of eastern Massachusetts clergy at the First Church in Boston. These lectures were typically theological in nature and were given by members of the Boston Association of Ministers on a revolving basis. The caution that was evident in his review of Strauss was certainly not on display that winter afternoon. Choosing to preach on the "Doctrine of Inspiration," a subject he had been working on privately for several months, he insisted that inspiration was universal in all men, not miraculous and particular to one special man. Christ was certainly a religious genius, unsurpassed in his own and subsequent generations, but his inspiration was distinctive only in its completeness, not in its miraculous character. It was possible, he told a shocked audience, that human religious development might produce a future genius whose contributions to man's religious progress would surpass even those of Christ. "It is folly, even impiety," he believed, "to say that God cannot create a greater soul than that of Jesus of Nazareth."[19]

Future Christs? To many in the audience, such a concept was bewildering at best, revolting at worst. The lecture was particularly infuriating to the more conservative clergy, who correctly understood his blunt condemnations of "folly" and "impiety" as an attack on them. They resented such breaches of deference and told him so. As Parker chatted amiably with Convers Francis after the lecture, he found himself caught in an embarrassing scene with an infuriated Dr. Francis Parkman. Parkman had earlier upbraided young Henry Bellows for a much milder transcendental sermon. Now he was so angered by Parker's lecture that he called it "impious" and declared that the idea of future Christs was unbearable. Despite his confident exterior, Parker was unprepared for the harshness of this harangue, and he rushed out of the church to avoid further mortification. "I was so grieved that I left him not in anger, but in sorrow," he wrote later that day, "and I went weeping through the street." [20]

Parker's emotional distress was real enough, but it only reinforced his commitment to telling the truth as he saw it to as many people who would listen. If ministers like Parkman were unwilling to hear the truth spoken plainly, perhaps the debate over Transcendentalism could be taken to a new audience. Determined to re-engage the most fundamental issues separating the Transcendentalists from their critics and to engage a broader readership, Parker quickly authored a pamphlet entitled *The Previous Question Between Mr. Andrews Norton and His Alumni*. Appearing in the Boston bookshops at the end of April 1840, the pamphlet bore the psuedonym "Levi Blodgett" who described himself as a Yankee "plain man" concerned about religious matters "affecting the whole community." Apologizing for his "humble style" and "uncouth phraseology," Blodgett announced that he wished to "offer only a few thoughts in my own homely way."[21]

The Blodgett character was not a fully developed literary device, nor was the pamphlet entirely successful in engaging a broader audience. Parker spent most of it discussing theological issues in language that was hardly in keeping with a man whose "life has been spent at the plough." But the pseudonym was intended to refute Andrews Norton's charges that Transcendentalism would destroy public morals and undermine social order. Parker insisted that plain men of common sense could easily understand that the miracles of Christ were too weak a foundation upon which to rest the case for Christianity. Turning Norton's argument on its head, Parker again insisted that it was traditional theology, with its demands for miraculous proof, which undermined public confidence in religion. "To leave religion in this state," said "Blodgett", "is to place it on a foundation that every scoffer may shake." Reliance on second-hand accounts of miraculous events was evidence "too weak to be trusted in a trifling case that comes before a common court of justice." Whatever its merits as a statement of principle, the Levi Blodgett pamphlet represented something new in the public discourse over Transcendentalism. Common people, it implied, could be, and should be arbiters in a public discourse about religion in which *everything* was on the table.[22]

By the time the Blodgett pamphlet reached the bookshops, Parker's radicalism was becoming widely known among the Boston clergy and his relations with them were increasingly strained. He had made his choice, and the consequences were apparent. He had frequently exchanged pulpits with more conservative ministers during his first two years in West Roxbury, but many of them no longer answered his solicitations for the courtesy. One embarrassed minister, who encountered Parker by chance in a Boston bookshop, obviously feigned illness in order to be excused from a previous commitment to preach in West Roxbury. "His color came & went, his voice faltered & his hand trembled," Parker remembered. "His eye did not meet mine as a man's." Refusal to exchange was tantamount to a personal insult in the genteel world of Boston Unitarianism. It suggested that Parker could no longer be trusted to deliver theologically or morally acceptable sermons. "By withholding from our neighbor the opportunity of use our pulpit for the propagation of what we regard as error," wrote conservative Ezra Stiles Gannett, "we say that we consider it error, and do not wish to help its diffusion."[23]

Though he was wounded by these rebuffs, Parker responded with feelings of defiance and even vengeance. "I should laugh outright to catch myself weeping because the Boston clergy would not exchange with me," he wrote in November 1840. "Their answer decides my course for the future. Let us see!" Though he repeatedly disavowed any intention of becoming a martyr, Parker prepared for a confrontation with his clerical detractors that would ultimately decide the fate of his professional life.[24]

V
THE MAKING OF A PUBLIC RADICAL
1841–1842

The intense controversy that engulfed the final two decades of Theodore Parker's life was at least partly due to his driving need for personal distinction. In language that expresses the sometimes self-destructive elements of his inner world, he confessed to his journal in 1840 that "I must do or die." For all his love of scholarship, Parker's staggering work schedule and his relentless productivity were also forced upon him by the demands of his own ambition. At times he felt "consumed by self-reproach for the [naught] I have accomplished, for the nothings I have undertaken." As his expectations for himself grew, so too did his dissatisfaction with the life of a country pastor. His parishioners liked him but they lacked the sophistication to fully appreciate what he offered them. He dreamed of "a larger sphere, a greater number of hearers, and those more intelligent and cultivated than the majority at Spring Street." Unlike some of his colleagues in the liberal ministry, Parker was not an aristocrat. He appreciated and admired the plain folk of his parish and he interacted with them without condescension. But at the same time, he possessed an intellectual intensity that sought out equals on the field of battle. Sunday sermons to the faithful at West Roxbury provided little to satisfy a mind like his and he began to wonder if he could "accomplish more through the Press than the Pulpit."[1]

Parker's immersion in Christian ministerial culture prevented him from fully acknowledging his ambition either to himself or to others. Open ambition might be acceptable in American politics or the marketplace, but clergymen were expected to display their talent and learning only in service to others. The notion of conscience, therefore, played a critical role in mediating between his deep need for distinction and his more overt personal and vocational identity. To those who accused him of using his prodigious preaching talents and radical theology to gain the attention of the credulous multitude, he retorted that simple duty called him to risk "a bad reputation" in order to "make men better." He refused to accept the criticism of those who were shocked by the bluntness and sarcasm of his preaching. In his own defense he fell back on the demands of a conscience that required that the truth be told without polite obfuscation. "I shall always take the liberty to call things by their right names, so far as I am able," he told one clerical detractor.[2]

Parker's ambition was real, and it was an ambition to do good. But the seriousness of his challenge to traditional thought and institutions required great inner confidence. The idea of conscience, especially the strong version of that idea espoused by the Transcendentalists, supplied those resources and allowed Parker to preserve his self-esteem in the face of relentless criticism. After all, there was no shame in persecution for conscience's sake. "No doubt my life is to be outwardly a life of gloom and separation from old associates," he told a colleague almost proudly in 1843. "I know men will view me with suspicion, and ministers with hatred."[3]

The South Boston Sermon

Theodore Parker's role as a lightning rod for theological conflict began on May 19, 1841 in the Hawes Place Church in South Boston. He had been given the honor of preaching the ordination sermon for Charles Shackford, a recent graduate of Harvard Divinity School. Among the other clergy taking part in the service were Samuel K. Lothrop, a Unitarian minister and editor of the liberal weekly *Christian Register*, and three orthodox Protestant ministers John H. Fairchild, Thomas Driver and Z.B.C. Dunham. At what was usually a solemn ceremony charging a new minister with the responsibilities of his office, Parker preached a sermon that led one young Divinity School student to wonder what was left of his own liberal faith after the preacher had wielded his dissecting knife. "Where are all our hopes of repentance, regeneration, our assurances of immortality?"[4]

Parker's motives for delivering the controversial sermon at Shackford's ordination are unclear. He claimed later that he was surprised by the firestorm it created, saying that the ideas had been staples of his recent preaching in West Roxbury. "I had preached them so often without rebuke, that I was not aware of saying anything that was severe," he told Caroline Healey. But this seems difficult to believe. Parker could hardly have been oblivious to the impact his words would have at an official ceremony attended by both liberal and orthodox clergy as well as representatives of the local elite. It is far more likely that he hoped to force his more timid colleagues to state their views on the Bible and historical Christianity openly. Initiating a public debate over the central premises of historical Christianity would certainly open up a "larger sphere" to one who was willing to risk his reputation in doing so. Contrary to his remarks to Caroline Healey, but probably closer to the truth, he told his orthodox brother-in-law, Charles Miller, that "I never in my life wrote a sermon with a deeper conviction of its truth or of the good it would do in the world."[5]

Parker's goal for the sermon, which he called "The Transient and Permanent in Christianity," was to separate the permanent truths of Christianity from the transitory theological opinions that had, from time to time, demanded the assent of believers. Christians, he argued, paid too much attention to the outward forms of religious expression which are subject to great change from one age to the next. In so doing, they slighted the innate ideas of God and human dependence that were the inward sources for those expressions. Religious institutions, doctrines, and texts, in other words, should not be confused with religion itself. "More attention is commonly paid to the particular phenomena," he complained, "than to the general law." Doctrines and creeds are merely "the language in which religion speaks...the robe not the angel...the accident of Christianity, not its substance." They should be understood only as approximations of truth, not truth itself. Perhaps paradoxical in a man who spent so much of his life formulating and analyzing theology, Parker pushed his audience to see theology not as an end in itself, but rather as an imperfect, finite vehicle for the expression of infinite truths revealed internally by "Reason, Conscience, and Faith."[6]

Had Parker remained on the level of these generalities, the sermon would have provoked little reaction at least from the liberal clergy. Many in the audience had no difficulty consigning Catholic or orthodox Protestant dogmas to the realm of the "transient." Most Unitarians believed in some form of religious progress with which they identified their own denomination. In the abstract, they could agree with Parker's argument that "what is falsehood in one province often passes for truth in another," and that progress depends upon fidelity to the "great truths of morality and religion." Nevertheless, many listeners, especially the conservative clergy present, objected to Parker's assertion that those truths had not been miraculously revealed to human beings by a divine messiah, but rather were "perceived intuitively, and by instinct." Christ's authority, which an imperfect, transient theology had rooted in a virgin birth and miracles, derived instead from "the voice of God in your heart."[7]

Echoing ideas from the Levi Blodgett pamphlet of the previous year, Parker told his audience that to defend the truth of Christianity upon the personal, infallible authority of Jesus was a terrible mistake. Any village scoffer who showed that Christ had been wrong about even the smallest matter could logically conclude that his authority as an infallible revelator was misplaced. No, the words of Jesus were not miraculously revealed truth, but rather "the music of heaven, sung in an earthly voice," and made "clear and beautiful in his life." And if "our elder brother" Jesus lived such a life, in which reason, conscience, and faith reached their fullest potential, so could every human being. "Christianity," he argued,

is a simple thing, very simple, it is absolute pure morality, absolute pure religion; the love of man; the love of God acting without let or hindrance. The only creed it lays down is the great truth which springs up spontaneously in the holy heart—there is a God. Its watchword is, Be perfect as your father in heaven."[8]

In addition to his radical Christology, Parker also used very strong language in reference to theological views which others regarded as essential. He described Christ's divinity and the infallibility of the Bible as idolatrous concepts, the residual influence of Christianity's contact with Judaism and "heathenism." The worship of a book or of a man, in other words, had corrupted and replaced Christ's simple call to worship God and love others. "Many tenets that pass current in our theology," he argued rather scornfully, "seem to be the refuse of idol temples," or holdovers from earlier, more ignorant cultural periods. The greatest threat to Christianity came not from heretics or "infidels" who questioned the authenticity of biblical miracles, but from those who demanded belief in an outmoded, transient theology as a test of faith. "Matters have come to such a pass that even now, he is deemed an infidel...whose reverence for the Most High forbids him to believe that God commanded Abraham to sacrifice his son, a thought at which the flesh creeps with horror." Again, the conscience was the judge of the Bible, not the Bible of the conscience.[9]

If the sermon did not already contain enough incendiary material, Parker included a final flourish that would alienate many potential allies in the liberal ministry during the ensuing months of controversy. In matters of religion and morals, he argued, truth-telling and fidelity to conscience were essential. Christian congregations needed ministers who would not "prophecy smooth things, and say, It is peace, when there is no peace." If transient doctrines and low ideals of life were ever to give way to truth and progress, courage was needed in the pulpit. And so for those ministers who held views like his own but who spinelessly or hypocritically refused to publicly endorse them, Parker had little respect. "Alas for that man who consents to think one thing in this closet, and preach another in his pulpit!" he charged. God would undoubtedly deal with such men in "his mercy" rather than "in his wrath," but Parker could not respect them. "Over his study and over his pulpit might be writ—EMPTINESS: on his canonical robes, on his forehead and his right hand—DECEIT, DECEIT." This rather puritanical statement, rhetorical as it was, could not help but sting many of his closest colleagues. After all, it was Convers Francis, Parker's mentor and longtime friend, who had once advised him to go slowly in mixing "the Bible for our study & the Bible for our public assembly."[10]

Parker hoped that his sermon would generate a debate over the Bible and traditional theology, but its most immediate effect was to reignite sectarian conflict in Massachusetts. Though they fully realized that Parker represented the Transcendentalist wing of the Unitarian clergy, the orthodox, Trinitarian ministers at Shackford's ordination seized the opportunity to tar all liberals with Parker's heresy. Working from "copious notes" taken at the service, they printed a brief abstract of the sermon in the *New England Puritan*, accompanied by a letter asking pointedly, "if the sermon then preached was to be regarded as a true exhibition of the sentiments of the Unitarian clergy"? The rest of the orthodox religious press jumped quickly on board. The *New York Evangelist* reprinted the article from the *Puritan* with its own commentary denouncing the "downright Pantheism" into which Unitarianism had sunk. The *New York Observer* remarked rather smugly that Unitarians had become victims of their own opposition to creedal tests. To denounce Parker would be "eating the most efficient words they ever uttered against the 'orthodox'." Closer to home, the *Trumpet and Universalist Magazine* of Boston compared Parker to the convicted atheist Abner Kneeland, and argued that much of the preaching "which goes under the name of Unitarianism, of fearful tendency."[11]

The Unitarian establishment recognized the need to respond quickly to these charges, but they did so in full retreat from Parker's views. Samuel Kirkland Lothrop, who had been present at the sermon, fired off a letter to the *Boston Courier* blasting Fairchild, Driver and Dunham, for creating the "false impression" that other Unitarian ministers approved of Parker's theology. Given that liberals imposed no creedal tests on their clergy, he said, "neither the members of the [Ordination] council nor Unitarians generally can thus be considered responsible for Mr. Parker's individual peculiarities of opinion." Proclaimed at a public ceremony, these "peculiarities" were now a serious liability for elite liberals who had worked hard to maintain their position in Massachusetts' religious order against Trinitarians who accused them of urbane heresy. Under these conditions, Lothrop had no intention of defending the West Roxbury minister. He said that readers would have to judge Parker's sermon for themselves once it was published, but he was ready to make it plain where he stood. Not only was the sermon "subversive of Christianity as a divine revelation," but he was ready to say that "if I entertained some of the opinions which I understood Mr. Parker to present . . .I should think that I ought to leave the Christian pulpit."[12]

As battles raged in the press during the summer of 1841, Parker and his views became the subject of widespread debate in the parlors and drawing rooms of respectable Boston. Twenty-year-old Caroline Wells Healey, the daughter of a prominent Boston family, found her own social circle in a "great state of excitement" over the controversy. Healey had heard Parker preach at the Purchase Street Church a month before the South Boston sermon, and she had come away with mixed feelings of "admiration and dread." Recognizing his extraordinary ability and confessing that "his talents...might do what they pleased with me," she worried that "upon a common mind, his views would have the worst effect." Would Parker's scorn for traditional Christianity undermine popular faith in religion and morals? Was his theological draught too heady for common minds? Despite these nagging questions, Healey, who would go on to a career of her own as a writer and reformer, was fascinated by Parker. She could not help but defend him to her friends even if it meant that she was considered "an infidel for my pains." She came to regard the "alarm" over Parker's sermon as "nonsensical" and defended his blunt language as simply the full expression of his conscience. Parker often "says more than he means," Healey argued, because he is "so afraid that he shall not be independent enough." Determined to show the world his principles, she wrote of Parker, "abstract truths as other people state them...are taking the likeness of the rankest infidelity in his pages."[13]

Another young Transcendentalist, Elizabeth Peabody, had similar views of the situation. Peabody had met Parker at the Transcendental Club and the two became close friends, despite the young woman's disapproval of Parker's tendency to use "sarcasm" in public controversies. Peabody had gone to hear Parker preach whenever should could and often returned enthralled. "The deep music of his voice moved me as I am seldom moved," she confessed to their mutual friend John Sullivan Dwight. "He has got on fire with the velocity of his spirit's speed—& the elements melt in the fervent heat of his word." As for the South Boston sermon, Peabody called it a "consuming fire" and condemned "Lathrop [sic] and the other philistines that blasphemed it."[14]

Peabody's support was echoed in other quarters, though most expressed their approval privately. Caleb Stetson, a Unitarian minister in Medford, Massachusetts and sometime member of the Transcendental Club, said that he had read the sermon with the intent to criticize it, but ended up writing only notes of admiration in the margins. Stronger sentiments came from James Freeman Clarke, the minister of the reform-minded Church of the Disciples in Boston. Clarke sent Peabody a note calling the sermon "the best defense of true Christianity I have seen." John Pierpont, the longtime minister of Boston's Hollis Street Church, said that he could endorse Parker's discourse save just one or two sentences.[15]

Yet for all their private admiration of his talent and courage, Parker's supporters faced serious problems when they made their views public. James Freeman Clarke, for example, had invited Parker to fill his pulpit at the Church of Disciples before the controversy over the South Boston sermon erupted, and he courageously refused to rescind the invitation even when opposition to the exchange emerged in his parish. Parker preached at Clarke's church unaware of the controversy, and he "charmed the people" with a beautiful and uncontroversial sermon on human sympathy. But he became irritated when he learned that some had opposed his presence and wrote an angry letter to Clarke, saying he would not have preached had he known of feeling against him. Clarke felt that he had risked a great deal to support his controversial friend, and was offended by the tone of the note. Peabody worked hard to soothe the feelings of the two young, radical ministers who were both working under intense pressure. She chided Parker about writing hasty letters with too much "innuendo or sarcasm" and she urged Clarke to see Parker's reaction in light of the controversy swirling around him. Thanks in part to Peabody's good offices, the two men remained friends, but pulpit exchanges were becoming a grave problem for Parker.[16]

In the midst of these trials, both public and private, Parker worked to produce a more polished copy of the South Boston sermon for the press. But when it appeared, there were complaints that its original language had been softened to remove its sting. The *Boston Recorder* accused Parker of being "frightened at the shadows of his own creating" but confessed that even with the alterations the sermon was "bad enough." The *Christian Register* objected that the sermon should have been "printed just as it was preached," bad grammar and all, so that the public could make up its mind about the fairness of the orthodox ministers' original accusations.[17]

Yet with the sermon in print, Parker now demanded substantive responses from the Unitarian leadership about their objections to his views. On June 21st, he penned a brief note to the *Christian Register* asking for an explanation for that journal's earlier description of his views as the "peculiarities of an eccentric individual." Saying that he had no objection to being "stigmatized" in that way, he demanded specific references to "the passages that grossly outraged your feelings?" He got what he asked for. Editor Lothrop answered him point by point but focused mainly on what he regarded as the flippancy of the sermon. Regretting that Parker's "researches have led him to results which seem to us fatally injurious to the Gospel of Christ," the *Register* objected much more strongly to the "sneer and ridicule" that pervaded the language of the sermon. For many reasons, Lothrop was infuriated by Parker's insinuation that liberal ministers think "one thing in the closet and preach another in the pulpit," not the least of which was the sectarian hay his orthodox attackers had made out of that charge.[18]

Conservative Unitarians had been so preoccupied by the renewed debate with orthodox Protestants that they had taken little time to respond to the more substantive theological issues Parker's sermon had raised. Given the denomination's reputation for scholarly discourse, the shrill tone of the controversy so far had been something of an embarrassment. To make matters worse, it was well known that Orestes Brownson, another heretical thorn in the side of conservatives, was praising the sermon in his own journal, the *Boston Quarterly Review.*

Efforts to remedy this situation came in September 1841 when Andrew Peabody, a Portsmouth, New Hampshire Unitarian minister and future editor of the conservative *North American Review*, reviewed the sermon for the learned readers of the *Christian Examiner.* Like Lothrop, Peabody saw Parker's views as a threat to Christianity, and placed him in the tradition of Enlightenment skeptics David Hume, Edward Gibbon, and Thomas Paine. But Peabody also accused Parker of "writing illogically" and of substituting "sweeping general statements" for careful scholarship. Parker was presumptuous, even arrogant, to claim that Christ had not believed himself the fulfillment of Old Testament prophecy. To dismiss such views so blithely was to write off generations of careful scholarship. How dare Parker treat beliefs which the "choicest minds of our race" regarded as essential to faith as if they were "the mere daydreams of irresponsible fanatics"? But perhaps most insightfully, Peabody argued that Parker's simple definition of Christianity as "absolute pure morality; absolute pure religion" failed to account for human sin and for Christ's role in human redemption. Parker's "religion of the perfect—of the unfallen" had been taught by Socrates and Plato before Christ's more specific, and more important, revelation of divine forgiveness through faith. Peabody concluded that the sermon failed to deal with the problem of evil, robbed believers of an essential faith in the value of supernatural revelation, and offered only a vague naturalism in its place.[19]

By the fall of 1841, Parker's life was taking on a strange character. No longer the obscure parish preacher he had so often feared becoming, he now faced a special, New England style of ostracism reserved for those who had broken ranks with their colleagues. Fellow ministers, once friendly and encouraging, now avoided him and found excuses to back out of pulpit exchanges. "Most of my clerical friends fell off, some would not even speak to me in the street, and refused to take me by the hand," Parker remembered later with bitterness. Convinced that he would be denied access to any pulpit but his own, he contemplated a long, lonely career spent writing "120 sermons a year, for 720 people— half children." The public square would be closed to him, and his ideas would wither on the vine.[20]

The Ferment of Reform

Important as they were to the controversy over Parker's sermon, theological issues explain only part of the reaction. To many conservatives, the South Boston sermon was yet another assault on tradition and authority at a time of unsettling change. Boston itself seemed almost wild with enthusiasm for new ways of doing things. Just six months before Parker preached in South Boston, for example, he had attended a three day meeting of reformers at the city's Chardon Street Chapel. There, "the institutions of the Sabbath, the Church and the ministry" all came under intense scrutiny and criticism. Ralph Waldo Emerson's oft-cited account of the gathering emphasized the fulsome eccentricity of the participants whose views ranged from the "straightest orthodoxy to the wildest heresy." Although many "cultivated persons" attended the meeting, including the venerable William Ellery Channing, the convention's spirit of "plebeian religious radicalism" meant that almost anyone could take the floor and have their say. Among those who did were abolitionist leader William Lloyd Garrison, women's rights activist Abby Folsom, and Jones Very, the mad and mystical transcendental poet.[21]

To the reformers, Chardon Street signaled the arrival of a new spirit of democratic social criticism in which new voices and more unrestrained modes of dissent could be heard. Emerson said that the best speech was made by Nathaniel Whiting of South Marshfield, Massachusetts. Whiting was "a plain, unlettered man" whose "eminent gifts" of thought and oratory had been cultivated not in libraries or universities but in the "Anti-slavery, Temperance and Non-Resistance Clubs." He lamented that the authority of the Church rested on the flawed authority of a miraculous Bible, and he called his listeners heed "the God within their bosoms, and decide all questions according to their own understanding and consciences." Here was the Levi Blodgett of Parker's imagination made flesh. Though it adopted no resolutions, the Chardon Street Convention demonstrates the roiling ferment of thought in antebellum Boston that worried conservatives and that would soon provide a large urban audience for Theodore Parker.[22]

Parker did not comment directly on the events at Chardon Street, but his presence there reflects a growing engagement with the wider reform culture. In September 1840, for example, he had begun reading Albert Brisbane's work on the French Socialist Charles Fourier with its biting criticism of market economics. Parker's friend and colleague George Ripley, who was in the process of leaving the Unitarian ministry to create the Brook Farm community, would later use Fourier's ideas to organize his new society. Parker's thoughts on social questions centered on a deep conviction, rooted in his agricultural background, that manual labor was both a necessary and natural part of human life. In the April 1841 issue of the Transcendentalist magazine *The Dial*, for example, he argued that the "terrible excess" of toil that fell on laboring people in New England was a perversion of the natural social order in which productive work would be performed equally, and enjoyed equally, by all. The problem of inequality, he believed, stemmed from the biblically-sanctioned belief that labor was a curse rather than a blessing. This fatal error led the rich to seek out idleness, and to shift their own responsibility for productive labor onto an increasingly overburdened, cultureless poor. In stinging language that would become the hallmark of his social criticism and antislavery rhetoric, he declared that "a small body of men" should not be "pampered in indolence, to grow up into gouty worthlessness," while the "large part of men" were "worn down by excessive toil ...before half their life is spent."[23]

Parker's research into new forms of social and religious life had also been inspired by the extraordinary meetings he had attended in the summer of 1840 at the Christian Union Convention in Groton. Along with Ripley, Emerson, Alcott, and Christopher Pearse Cranch, Parker had listened to speeches by radical Cape Cod "come-outers." These were men and women who had left their churches to create purer, less coercive religious societies ruled by egalitarian principles. They rejected most traditional religious practices including Sabbath observance, the use of formal church buildings, formal preaching and prayer, a paid ministry, and doctrinal exclusivity. Parker was fascinated with them generally, but he was especially intrigued by Joseph Palmer, a self-educated butcher from Leominster whose principled, if eccentric, refusal to shave his beard had once led to a confrontation with local citizens and a year's jail sentence. Palmer was the embodiment of an emancipated conscience. "He is an abolitionist; a no property man; a non-resistant, and a no government man," Parker wrote in his journal. Perhaps most importantly to Parker, "he takes the Bible for what it is: "[Christ] for our brother, not our master."[24]

These plain farmers and mechanics lacked polish and learning, but they confirmed Parker's belief that the essence of religion could be separated from its transient forms and in the process strengthen the lives of real people. In freeing themselves from "the shams of the [Christian] Church," he said, the come-outers had "made actual my own highest idea of church." Inspired by the commitment of the people he met there, Parker gave a speech to the group that certainly met their standards of radicalism. "Where the Spirit of the Lord is, there is liberty," he told them. "But where the spirit of the church is, there is slavery!"[25]

The Discourse of Religion

The hothouse environment of religious and social reform provided a ready audience for the views of an iconoclastic preacher like Parker. As the press battles
over the South Boston sermon heated up, in fact, he received a note from a
group calling itself the "Friends of Liberal Religious Thought," inviting him to
deliver a series of lectures at Boston's old Masonic Temple, a neutral venue
where Ralph Waldo Emerson had once spoken. The group's readiness to offer
Parker a platform highlights the intense interest of young, educated Bostonians
in ideas that challenged the status quo. A good example of this was twenty-three
year old Charles Mayo Ellis who signed the letter inviting Parker to speak at the
Masonic Temple. A native of West Roxbury, Ellis had recently graduated from
Harvard Law School and was about to begin a career as an attorney in Boston.
Full of romantic idealism, he admired all things transcendental, supported aboli-
tionism and believed that "truth, goodness and beauty are the only existences."
Men like Ellis wanted to hear Parker, and Boston was full of lecture halls.
Though Parker initially turned down the offer to speak in the city he changed his
mind later as opportunities for pulpit exchanges became scarce.[26]

According to those who admired and sympathized with him, the five lectures he delivered in the fall of 1841 were a great success. The hall was full, and
the speaker's deep, rich tones moved many in the audience to re-examine their
assumptions about religious life. But young Caroline Healey experienced what
must have been a common feeling, even among those who had grown up in the
most liberal churches of eastern Massachusetts. Healey could sympathize "in
every word he said" about the defects of the Old Testament, but she "rather
shrank" from the implications of his views for the life and miracles of Jesus.
Surrounded by friends who whispered their own views in her ear as Parker
spoke, she struggled to discriminate "fairly between the transient and the permanent" in her own spiritual values. She worried that embracing Parker's "new
faith must separate me forever" from the community at the West Street Church
where she went with her family on Sundays. Could religious, moral and social
life survive without the traditions of scripture, miracle and church?[27]

Yet even as she wrestled with the potential costs of accepting Parker's
views, Healey could not help but admire his willingness to follow his conscience. Hearing him tell the audience that he spoke "well knowing what it
meant," she "loved him for his independence" and "wondered if I too—could do
this." Seated close to the podium, she could see "the perspiration starting to his
forehead" and "his lips trembling" as he predicted his own ostracism. It is clear
from Healey's response that Parker's increasingly dramatic self-conception as a
man of conscience, willing to risk the loss of "his brother's heart" and having
"every man's hand against him" was becoming an indispensable and deeply
effective part of his public persona.[28]

During the winter of 1841–42, Parker worked ten to fifteen hours a day to
enlarge the Masonic Temple lectures into a book-length, theological treatise
which appeared in May as *A Discourse of Matters Pertaining to Religion*. Like

his two earlier contributions to the Transcendentalist controversy, the *Discourse* distinguished between the eternal and the ephemeral in religious life. It insisted that religion was innate in man. Just as legal institutions were outgrowths of man's "moral nature," religious doctrines and institutions were outgrowths of a "religious element" rooted "deep and permanent in the constitution of man." Parker believed that the existence of the religious element was grounded in human consciousness, where a "sense of dependence" sprung up spontaneously in the mind. To readers who were wedded to empirical modes of thought, he pointed out that the universality of religious phenomena in human societies was inexplicable in the absence of an innate human impulse. "[I]f there is no religious principle in man," he remarked, "then there are permanent and universal phenomena without a corresponding cause." Derived from his reading of the German philosopher Friedrich Schleiermacher, the concept of a "religious element" in man was the foundation upon which so much of Parker's religious and social thought rested. Religion was located securely and permanently within the fortress of human nature. Its outward manifestations could therefore be reformed, even in the most radical ways, without weakening its hold on human culture.[29]

It was the reform of religion, of course, that occupied most of Parker's time in the *Discourse*. Giving fuller development to concepts implicit in the South Boston sermon, he made a key distinction between what he called the *idea* and the *conception* of God. The pure idea was innate, but more specific conceptions of it took on the transient elements of the cultural contexts in which they were expressed. "Since men exist under the most various conditions, and in widely different degrees of civilization," he argued, "it is plain that the religious consciousness must appear under various forms." The more primitive the culture, he argued, the more primitive and anthropomorphic the conception of God. Angry, vindictive, warlike conceptions of God reflected earlier stages of human development in which violence and tyrannical political systems dominated human life.[30]

Parker's evolutionary model of religion and culture borrowed quite heavily from the French positivist philosopher August Comte. Comte had placed spiritual change on a progressive continuum, beginning with fetishism, moving into polytheism, and culminating in the monotheistic systems. When the forms, rituals and theology of one system failed to keep pace with the progress of human thought and culture, they were replaced with newer and purer ones. Christ's conception of God as a loving father, for example, represented a major leap forward just as it generated opposition from those who clung to old forms out of ignorance or fear. To Parker, Jesus was not a God, but a man with a "genius for religion" whose followers were so stunned by the truth of his preaching that they worshipped *him* rather than the God he described. Christianity was a higher form of religious culture not because it rested upon the special authority of Christ, but because Jesus' conception of God was closest to the pure idea revealed universally in human consciousness.[31]

But Parker's use of Comte was neither slavish nor uncritical. He firmly rejected the philosopher's view that scientific progress would ultimately replace faith. Instead, scientific thought and critical inquiry would do their purifying work on Christianity, purging its worn out dogmas and its vestiges of fetishism and polytheism. In so doing, it would usher in a new era of "Absolute Religion" in which innate spiritual intuitions were expressed in perfect love to God and man. Yet in defining Absolute Religion as the ultimate destination of religious progress, Parker posed a question that drove to the very heart of the theological challenge he posed to his contemporaries. Was Christianity the same as absolute religion or was it only another stage in the ongoing religious development of humanity?

His answer took up nearly half of the *Discourse* and it focused on the theological, scriptural and institutional expressions of the Christian faith. If Christianity meant a belief in miracles, the special, personal authority of Christ, the worship of an inerrant Bible, and authority of the institutional church over individual conscience, then it fell short of Absolute Religion. So critical was Parker of these historic traditions that one commentator has described the second half of the *Discourse* as taking on "the atmosphere of a shooting gallery." But if Christianity meant Jesus' simple embrace of perfection, his admonition to serve God through "the normal use, discipline, development, and delight of every limb of the body, every faculty of the spirit, and so of all the powers we possess," then the answer was yes. Parker did not seek to substitute Absolute Religion for Christianity. He vehemently denied that he was attempting to found a new religion. Instead, he called for the reformation of Christianity, so as to make it synonymous with the Absolute Religion found within the self.[32]

Parker always resented the accusation that he was merely a destructive critic, but the reformation envisioned in the *Discourse* was radical. If implemented, it left very little that was recognizable in the religious life of most ordinary American churches. As historian Gary Dorrien has observed, Parker was totally uninterested, except in a critical way, in form, ritual, symbol, and liturgy. Yet these remained central to the religious experiences of most individuals and communities in the United States. The *Discourse* did include passages of great stylistic beauty and Parker believed to his core that true piety would place human beings in right relation to one another, to God, and to nature. He spoke of Jesus' highest teachings as "a beam of light shot into chaos" and he was certain that Absolute Religion would lead man "to the light, to the tree of God, and tree of life." But on balance, the work displayed more of Parker's skeptical and rationalist side than it did his spiritual one.[33]

These stylistic problems, along with the uncompromisingly radical message of the book, clearly affected its reception. William Ellery Channing, for example, confessed to finding the *Discourse* rather dispiriting. "I have read a part of Parker's book with much pain," he wrote only a few months before his death. "I do not esteem him the less for his errors—but I am grieved that he would rob himself and others of a faith which I would not resign for the world." Parker certainly possessed the intellectual power to initiate a liberal Christian reformation in America, but he lacked the patience to express it in less blunt and shocking terms. Convers Francis, who still claimed to "love and admire" Parker on a personal level, found the *Discourse* repellent. He described its spirit as "bad, sarcastic, arrogant,—contemptuous of what the wise and good hold sacred." The final phrase in Francis's description says much about the differences that were emerging between the two men.[34]

By the time his book appeared in 1842, Parker was becoming a pariah among the liberal clergy of Massachusetts. His theology had been formally repudiated by all the major Unitarian periodicals in Boston, and there were few among his colleagues willing to exchange pulpits with him. He continued to attend meetings of the liberal clergy, but his letters began referring to "the Unitarians" in a sense that clearly distinguished him from the group. Parker occasionally thought of leaving the ministry as Emerson, Ripley, and Brownson had done, but he still retained the support of his small congregation in West Roxbury and he was naturally more inclined to confront his opponents than to run from them. "What I have seen to be false I will proclaim a lie on the housetop," he insisted to Convers Francis. "Just as God reveals truth I will declare his word come what may come."[35]

VI
A Reckoning with Ministers
1842–1843

It is possible that had Parker confined himself to challenging the theology of the Unitarians, he might have been able to forge an uneasy peace with them. In an otherwise scathing review of the *Discourse* in the *Christian Examiner*, for example, New Bedford Unitarian minister John H. Morison repeatedly refrained from accusing Parker of deliberate maliciousness. Instead, he preferred to believe that Parker simply did not understand "the force and bearing of his words." But in the wake of the *Discourse*, the theological and social elements of Parker's conflict with Boston's clerical establishment began to converge. His critics soon came to believe that their wayward colleague was deliberately undermining the authority of the church and impugning the reputation of its ministers.[1]

Unfortunately, they had more than enough evidence to sustain such views. Even as the controversy over the South Boston sermon was erupting, Parker persuaded Ralph Waldo Emerson to publish an article he had written called "The Pharisees" in the July 1841 issue of the *Dial*. The article was Parker at his most blunt and sarcastic. Pharisees, he wrote, were those who opposed truth and moral progress out of concern for their own power and prestige. They had existed in the time of Christ, but the "last of the Pharisees has not yet been seen." Now they could be found in every walk of life including politics, business, and journalism, and their aim was to "*seem* good and excellent, not to *be* good and excellent." But of all varieties of Pharisees, the "Pharisee of the Pulpit" was the worst.

> He keeps up the Form, come what will of the Substance...He wonders at the 'perverseness of the age,' that will no longer be fed with chaff and husks...His thought might not agree with the form, [but] since he loves the dream of his fathers better than God's truth he forbids all progress in the form...These men

speak in public of the inspiration of the Bible, but at home the Testament is a collection of legendary tales.[2]

As the language of the article suggests, Parker had no intention of limiting his reformism to theology alone. Indeed, he quickly emerged as one of the most outspoken critics of the institutional church in New England. Part of the vehemence of his assault stemmed from his belief that his colleagues were trying to have him "put down" like a "bull whose roaring cannot be stopped." But it also emerged out of the critique of institutional Christianity he shared with the Transcendentalists and other radical reformers. Transcendentalists had from the beginning been trenchant critics of the Unitarian clergy for what they viewed as coldness in the pulpit and a lack of moral leadership in society. In his famous "Divinity School Address," for example, Emerson had complained that "historical Christianity destroys the power of preaching," and that as a result, "the village blasphemer sees fear in the face, form, and gait of the minister."[3]

Emerson's address had the broadest impact, but nearly all of the major Transcendentalists had leveled attacks on the clergy in the late 1830s. In his 1837 book *Conversations with Children Concerning the Gospels*, the radical school reformer A. Bronson Alcott had outraged the Boston clergy by allowing his students to poke fun at overly sober ministers. At one point Alcott asked a boy of seven, "Do you think that ministers put on a sober look?," and was told "Yes...they don't look as they feel." In his letter of resignation from the Purchase Street Church, George Ripley criticized the Unitarian leadership for retaining an outmoded view of the ministry that separated "the pastor of a church from the sympathies of his people, [confining] him to a sphere of thought remote from their usual interests." Ripley's vision of a more democratic church, bereft of the unnatural authority of a minister, was ultimately realized at Brook Farm. "The true followers of Jesus are a band of brothers," he told his congregation in his 1840 resignation letter. They "compose one family...feeling they are one in the pursuit of truth." Orestes Brownson argued that the church's failure to keep up with human intellectual and social growth had destroyed its influence. "What remains of it is only the body after the spirit has left it...it is a by-word and a mockery."[4]

Conscience and Institutions

At the core of the Transcendentalists' critique of the clergy was a belief that churches confined the human conscience within traditional forms of worship and that theological creeds were obstacles to religious and social progress. Parker was certain that "those pious souls who accept the church's Christianity are, in the main, crushed and degraded by their faith...Conscience cannot speak its mother tongue to them." A society in which divine intuitions were stifled by overbearing political and religious institutions was a society without a moral anchor, a society in which no collective witness could emerge from its people. In its suspicion of traditional institutions, the direction of Transcendentalist thought ran parallel with several groups of evangelical reformers whose belief in radical individualism led them to reject ministerial authority and to withdraw from traditional churches. Parker had already met the Cape Cod "Come Outers" who had renounced their allegiance to ministerial authority and by the early 1840s radical abolitionists in Boston had adopted similar concepts of romantic perfectibility drawn from neo-orthodox Protestantism. William Lloyd Garrison's New England Non-Resistance Society, a group of radical antislavery and peace activists, renounced all forms of human authority, including that of ministers, as sinful usurpations of Divine sovereignty.[5]

If Transcendentalists and abolitionists had not yet made common cause, both were targets of elite condemnation. The conservative press rather tellingly paired "Parkerism" and "Garrisonism" when listing threats to social stability in the early 1840s. The anti-institutionalism of both groups disturbed the tight-knit alliance of ministers, merchants, and politicians that ran eastern Massachusetts. Increased immigration, democratic politics, and rising class conflict had convinced elite Bostonians that the organic social order of the eighteenth-century city was in danger of slipping into history. The moral and intellectual authority of the churches, therefore, represented a critical source of tradition and deference in a city that seemed increasingly ungovernable. But in men like Parker, they perceived one who, as Rev. Ezra Stiles Gannett put it, "considers it his duty to undermine the foundation on which the faith of the multitude rests." To Gannett, and those who thought like him, this was no time to trifle with the "multitude" and no time to question the integrity of the churches or their leaders.[6]

By the summer of 1842, a critique of wealth and its deadening impact on the church was emerging in Parker's writing. In a letter to Convers Francis he fumed that "no body of men was ever more sold to the sense of expediency," than Unitarian ministers. "Stuff them with good dinners & Freedom, Theology—Religion may go to the devil for all time." Perhaps "the abolitionists and temperance men are half right when they say '*the Church is a* Humbug." The other half of the story, he now believed was that "*the ministers are ditto.*" Francis's response to this letter is not preserved, but his friendship with Parker placed him in an extremely difficult position. He had recently accepted an offer to become Parkman Professor of Pulpit Eloquence at Harvard Divinity School, an appointment that would take him to the heart of the establishment that Parker now had in his sights. In order to secure the position, he had earlier ceased exchanging pulpits with Parker. It was a turning point in what had been an extraordinarily fruitful friendship, but it also represented a change in the direction of Parker's thought. In identifying his theological opponents with particular social and economic interests, Parker implied that Unitarian ministers were the willing captives of the conservative elite. These accusations were at least as disturbing to his colleagues in the Boston Association of Ministers as his ideas about the Bible or the divinity of Christ.[7]

These new views were on public display as Parker intervened in a controversy between Rev. John Pierpont of Boston's Hollis Street Church, and his wealthy congregation. Pierpont, who had served as pastor of the Hollis Street

Church for more than two decades, was a deeply committed temperance activist. He had helped draft the 1838 Massachusetts law forbidding the sale of "Spiritous Liquors" in less than twenty-eight gallon containers. Unfortunately for Pierpont, some of his wealthiest parishioners made their money in the liquor business. Four rum distillers and eight wine or molasses merchants sat in the front pews each Sunday morning. To these men, Pierpont's sermons on the evils of alcohol, and his condemnations of those who profited from the misery of others, were intolerable and they exerted their power as pew owners to force him out of the pulpit. Echoing language that was sometimes used to describe Theodore Parker, Pierpont's critics said that sermons against "lawful dealings and business" of some of "his most respectable parishioners," lacked "prudence, moderation, [and] sound judgment." In other words, Pierpont had refused to check his conscience or his tongue where the interests of the wealthy and powerful were concerned.[8]

After a lengthy and embarrassing battle in the press, the Boston Association of Ministers convened an ecclesiastical council, led by the Unitarian ministers, to arbitrate the dispute. While the "Hollis Street Council" as it was called, exonerated Pierpont from many of the charges, it did censure him for excessive attention to the divisive issue of alcohol production and recommended that his relationship with the Church be dissolved. Many members of the group agreed with Pierpont's principles, but they were critical of the "harshness, levity, personality, ridicule and sarcasm" that crept into his speech and writing. The gentility and balanced character expected of Boston's clerical elite was clearly lacking in Pierpont, just as it was in Parker.[9]

Parker knew and admired Pierpont and he was outraged by the Council's failure to see that the controversy at Hollis Street was at root a conflict between conscience and expediency, prophecy and power. Although Parker agreed with Pierpont's temperance principles, it was the issue of conscience that generated the heat of his defense of the older minister. The Council had shirked its responsibility to support a courageous Christian minister who had spoken with a prophetic voice, courageously condemning the sins of the people. Reviewing the whole matter for the *Dial*, he compared Pierpont to the Prophet Jeremiah and, implicitly at least, suggested that his critics had sacrificed principle to the pagan idols of wealth and power. He heaped scorn on the Council's view that Pierpont had not taken into account "the peculiar circumstances" of his congregation when speaking on temperance matters. "The peculiar circumstances of his parish," Parker insisted, were "Rum Selling, Rum Making, and Rum Drinking." Nor did he have any time for genteel disapprovals of the minister's manner of speech. Hadn't Jeremiah spoken harshly against sin? Hadn't the apostle Paul once called his enemies "whited walls"? Under the guise of reprimanding Pierpont for immoderate speech, Parker charged, the Council was in fact punishing him for speaking "against the sins of his own parish." Pierpont was a man of conscience above all. If he got a bit overheated in the midst of battle, so what? "Are we speaking of Angels?" Parker asked with more than a hint of sarcasm.[10]

The Association Conference

In January, 1843, Parker's relationship with his colleagues in the Unitarian ministry reached a crisis point. Offended by his insinuations in the *Dial* and determined to disassociate themselves from the stain of his heresy, leading members of the Boston Association of Congregational Ministers sought to end his relationship with their group. His chief detractors were older, conservative Unitarian divines, including Ezra Stiles Gannett, Nathaniel Frothingham, and Francis Parkman. All three were on record as fervent opponents of Transcendentalism, and two of them had been directly involved in the Hollis Street Council affair. At meetings of the Association in late 1842, Parker became a topic of heated conversation among these men and they searched for ways to deal with the threat he posed to their public influence. Yet in considering their course of action, they faced a difficult problem. The traditional liberal hostility to creeds meant that Parker had made no confession of faith before joining the Association. There was no way to expel him on the basis of theological apostasy alone. But perhaps they could *persuade* him to resign. With this end in view, they invited him to attend a special meeting of the Boston Association on January 23, 1843, at Rev. Robert C. Waterston's home on Temple Street in Boston. For Parker, who recorded the events of the meeting in excruciating detail in his journal, the clash of personalities and ideas was both traumatic and exhilarating.[11]

Assembling in the afternoon of a cold, mid-winter day, the assembly of twenty-one ministers began in typical elite Boston fashion, with tea. Given the bruised egos in the room and the delicate purpose of the gathering, however, it is unlikely that there was much conviviality. With "a considerable degree of embarrassment," Rev. Parkman formally opened the proceedings and called on Nathaniel Frothingham to state the Association's litany of grievances against Parker. Frothingham explained that while many in the Association were happy to continue "friendly and social intercourse" with Parker, most were unwilling to endanger the spiritual welfare of their congregations by exchanging pulpits with him. The *Discourse,* he stated, was "vehemently deistical," and "subversive of Christianity as a particular religion, for it aimed to dissolve Christianity in the ocean of absolute truth." Parkman chimed in at this point to add that theology was not the only issue. The Hollis Street Council article was also grounds for severing professional ties because it had offended important members of the Association. As far as Parkman was concerned, the deistical character of Parker's theology was not really up for debate. The only real question was how to sever the remaining ties between the Association and its wayward colleague.[12]

Parker waited for the charges to be fully stated before responding, but when he did so, his comments reflected a remarkable degree of self-assurance and a stunning lack of deference to his older, more established colleagues. Here was a man, just thirty-two years old, with less than six years' experience in the ministry, facing down almost twenty hostile stares hoping for his withdrawal. But instead of taking their broad hint to leave the group, Parker threatened to expose their hypocrisy instead. He reminded them that he remained in possession of letters from several members, letters that could be published, proving that their unwillingness to exchange pulpits with him had little to do with theology and much more to do with pressure from leading ministers. As for ministerial exchanges generally, Parker said that he would not complain much since he was now regularly speaking to large audiences in Boston and elsewhere. Indeed, he suggested that it was the harsh treatment he had received from "the Unitarians" that had generated so much public interest in his ideas. Professional ostracism made him more interesting to the public. But "on myself," he said curtly, "it had no effect."[13]

When Parkman and Frothingham failed to convince Parker to withdraw over theological differences, Gannett and others turned to the deeper and more volatile issue of legitimate public discourse. They drew the attention of the group to the polemical language of Parker's articles in the *Dial*. "One man said I slandered the brethren in the Sermon of Pharisees," Parker wrote, "another in the conclusion of the South Boston Sermon, and Gannett that I had held him up to scorn in the article of the Hollis Street Council." Refusing to be intimidated by the rising anger in the room, Parker said he found it revealing that although he had spoken of six classes of Pharisees in his article, only the ministers had complained! This provocative remark confirmed the suspicions of most members that the article had been aimed directly at them. Turning next to the article on the Hollis Street Council, members quoted directly from the text emphasizing Parker's use of the words "cowards, knaves and hypocrites" as evidence that he "dipped his pen in gall and his razor in oil." Parker repeated several times that he had "no individuals in mind," but nearly all present were certain that he did. In a moment of exasperation, Gannett exclaimed: "I will say that I freely and from my heart forgive him, as I hope Almighty God can forgive me, but I can never grasp him by the hand again cordially." At that point, Parker noted that his colleagues stopped referring to him as "Brother Parker" and began using the more formal and distant title of "Mr."[14]

Gannett's angry declaration brought the proceedings to a head. For Parker, it removed some of the need to couch his self-defense in decorous terms and he quickly revealed a key source of his animosity toward the men in the room. Much of what had been discussed at the meeting, he stated, was only "theological matter at best." The real difference lay in the lines "drawn immediately after the South Boston sermon" when ministers, who should have come to his defense in the face of orthodox attacks, had instead cut him off to serve institutional ends. Whatever its faults of style and argument, Parker insisted, the South Boston sermon had contained ideas familiar to nearly all Unitarian ministers. None of it should have surprised them and only hypocrisy could explain their stampede to disown views they entertained privately. Again he reminded them that he had "a collection of curious letters on that theme, which I might publish one day." In his own rendition of the moment, Parker presented himself to his colleagues as a truth-teller, a lone, courageous voice abandoned by those whose self-interest was stronger than their devotion to truth. Without mentioning his old friend Convers Francis by name, he confessed that he had been "grievously disappointed" in close friends whose views were very similar to his own, but who had deserted him, and deserted the truth.[15]

As Parker's raw emotions rose dangerously close to the surface, the Association coaxed him toward voluntary withdrawal. "Since Mr. Parker finds the feeling in respect to him so general," Rev. Chandler Robbins stated flatly, "I think it is his duty to withdraw from the association." Robbins, who preached at Boston's Second Church, had once been very close to Parker and still professed love and admiration for him. But his suggestion drew instant support from the others who complained that Parker's presence in the group compromised its authority and effectiveness. To the shock and chagrin of Frothingham, Gannett, and Robbins, however, Parker refused to agree. This was, after all, a matter of conscience. "I told them that if my personal feelings alone were concerned I would do so," he wrote in his journal, "but as the right of free inquiry was concerned, while the world standeth I will never do so." He reminded his colleagues of the toleration that had always marked relations among the liberal clergy and he asked them to remember that he had made no theological confession upon admission. No, to quit the Association was to abandon a post of duty and he would not count the costs of adhering to principle. As the clock approached nine in the evening, it was clear that after nearly three hours of deliberations, no clear result was forthcoming. Parker was exhausted and emotional. When several members of the group assured him of their personal esteem, the young minister burst into tears and left the room. Yet a few days later he told Robbins not to feel sorry for him. "Some of my relations, 200 or 300 years ago, lost their heads for their religion. I am called to no such trial, and can well bear my lighter cross."[16]

Until his congregation sent him to Europe for a year in September 1843, Parker endured seven months of constant preaching and nearly incessant intellectual labor. In the spring and early summer of 1843, he prepared the final version of De Wette's *Introduction to the Old Testament* for publication, and edited a collection of his own "Critical and Miscellaneous Writings." By September, however, he was ready to take Lydia on a pilgrimage to the European centers of learning that had done so much to influence his life and thought. Before departing, however, he delivered a sermon to his congregation reviewing his six years as their pastor and laying out his ideas for the future. In it, he said that all ministers faced two opposing threats to the effectiveness of their work. One threat was born of "excessive confidence," in which a learned man becomes "opinionated, and teaches mere whimsies and specters of his own brain instead of everlasting truths." Such men see no limit to their own powers and therefore "aspire to lead where [they] are only competent to follow."[17]

The second threat, which Parker developed at much greater length, was the temptation to "succumb to things as they are" and to become simply an echo chamber for the views of sect, of public opinion, or of the market place. Such ministers wasted their natural gifts, their learning became a flimsy ornament, and they were fit "only to dangle about the tables of rich men." Unlike his colleagues in the Boston Association who insisted upon the use of elite authority to police the boundaries of public discourse, Parker had come to believe that the legitimacy of institutions depended upon their ability to withstand open critical debate. Rules of decorum were simply crutches that propped up falsehood and stood in the way of progress. Having placed all his hopes upon the reliability of human conscience, he had little fear that his own ministry bore the faults of over-confidence. He was willing to teach true religion without the "authority of any church, any book, any man." Praising his congregation for continuing to trust a man who trusted himself, he vowed to preach the truth under the "open sky" if no other place could be found.[18]

VII
CHURCH AND SOCIETY
1843–1845

By 1843, Theodore Parker had emerged as a lightning rod of theological controversy in New England and he had become a trenchant critic of the region's clerical Standing Order. Yet for all his radicalism on theological and ecclesiastical questions, he had yet to fully apply his thought to the social issues that were preoccupying some of the greatest minds of his generation. Problems like slavery, intemperance, social inequality, and women's rights, had produced a rich array of movements and ideas that engaged the consciences of Americans as dramatically as did religious reform. Indeed, it seemed to Ralph Waldo Emerson that the fervor and zeal that once belonged exclusively to the church had left it only to re-emerge in "temperance and non-resistance societies, in movements of abolitionists and socialists." And if Parker had done little in this area, other members of the Transcendentalist circle were deeply engaged in the application of romantic thought to social problems. During the summer of 1840, for example, George and Sophia Ripley were in West Roxbury planning the Brook Farm community which they would soon create only a few miles from Parker's house on Spring Street. In the midst of their preparations, they took the time to remind the town's brilliant young minister that theological reform would mean very little without practical action to relieve the suffering so evident in American society. "Mrs. R. gave me a tacit rebuke for not shrieking at wrongs, and spoke of the danger of losing our humanity in abstractions," he wrote in his journal. It was a problem he recognized, but took several years to resolve.[1]

Sophia Ripley's "rebuke" of Parker in 1840 is indicative of a growing split within Transcendentalism. Having rejected the outmoded theologies and religious forms that stunted the intuitive powers of the individual, this restless group of loosely affiliated intellectuals struggled to find the best means of effecting their proposed "reformation" of American culture. For Ralph Waldo

Emerson, Margaret Fuller, and Henry David Thoreau, reform was primarily an act of "self-culture" in which the emancipated individual shed outward associations in pursuit of the truth within. At times, this radical individualism produced a suspicion of reformers who located the self within in a web of responsible social relations. "Do not tell me, as a good man did today, of my obligation to put all poor men in good circumstances," Emerson wrote in his essay "Self-Reliance". "Are they my poor?" he asked. Yet others within the orbit of transcendentalism saw the matter differently. Drawn from their experience with the urban poor, George Ripley and Orestes Brownson, saw the promise of the emancipated self-threatened by a ruthless, materialistic, and class-divided society. What chance did the industrial poor have for self-culture, deprived as they were of education, and decent living conditions? Did the obligations of conscience apply only to the self, or did they constitute the means through which a new understanding of ethical social relations could be created?[2]

Although theology had absorbed most of his attention during his early years in West Roxbury, Parker naturally gravitated toward the more socially-engaged aspects of Transcendentalism. He was almost instinctively critical of the genteel model of literary self-culture that emerged in the *Dial* under the editorships of Emerson and Fuller. As early as 1840 he had mocked the journal as weak, over-refined, and lacking in social relevance. If Brownson's reformist *Boston Quarterly Review* could be represented visually as "a body of stout men in blue frocks, with great arms and hard hands," he once wrote that the *Dial* could only appear as "a baby and a pap spoon and a cradle." For all his intellectual distinction and his socially advantageous marriage, Parker remained the son of a Lexington farmer whose intellectual development had suffered under the unremitting struggle against poverty.[3]

But Theodore Parker's social conscience developed over several years. It took shape in response to conditions he observed in Europe, to the work being done by his fellow Transcendentalists, and to his ongoing re-imagination of the relationship between the individual conscience and society. As he struggled to apply his religious ideas to social problems, he came to see the need for a new kind of church, one that could reach out to a broader social constituency and nurture the ability of its members to apply conscience to society in uncompromising ways. If Emerson believed that zeal for righteousness had left the church and generated reform societies, Parker sought to reconstruct the church so that could bring the resources of Absolute Religion to bear upon the problem of social evil. If this did not always mean radical change, it did mean that the perpetrators of social wrong could be exposed and criticized openly in the public square.

Europe, New England, and America

Parker left the United States for Liverpool, England in September, 1843 a troubled man. His health had become precarious, the Boston Association of Ministers had all but expelled him, and old friends like Convers Francis had become distant for their own professional good. But as he and Lydia travelled through England and Italy in the fall and winter of 1843, and then Germany and Austria in the spring and summer of 1844, Parker regained his health and his confidence. Freedom from writing two weekly sermons and a hiatus from the endless round of parish responsibilities allowed his mind to roam freely. He relished the opportunity to meet the English and German theologians who inspired his theology, and these encounters strengthened his convictions and restored his optimism. He delighted in his ability to tell nearly every German and English scholar he met that "I have read your books" and he seems to have made a good impression on his hosts. The great essayist Thomas Carlyle found Parker a "hardy, compact, clever little fellow" whose combination of "decisive utterance" and "good-humor" made him a delightful companion.[4]

Another meeting of strong minds came in July 1844, when Parker traveled down the Rhine River to the Swiss city of Basle to attend the lectures of Wilhelm De Wette. Spending several evenings with this "compact little man with a rather dry face," Parker presented his hero with the annotated translation of the *Introduction to the Old Testament* which had just been published in Boston. If Parker was somewhat disappointed with De Wette, who had lost some of the fire of his early years, his own self-esteem rose by comparison. Experiencing no feelings of inadequacy in the presence of the great scholar, Parker described De Wette as "a little irritable" and surprisingly detached from his earlier commitments to German romantic nationalism. As he left Basle on July 4, Parker wrote in his journal regarding De Wette, "I do not think my interviews have either raised or diminished the esteem I have for the man."[5]

But the most important effect of Parker's European travels was its role in the development of a social conscience. The highly detailed observations of European life which filled the pages of his journals and his letters home, reveal a man who was fascinated with Europe's art and learning, but horrified by its religious and social institutions. He gloried in the architecture of French Cathedrals like Notre Dame and St. Eustace, but his anti-Catholicism mirrored that of other New England travelers from this period. "I hate it[s doctrines its rites, & its general effects] all the more in Europe than I did at home," he said of the Church. He was also struck by the vast disparities of wealth he found in cities like Rome and Naples and the lack of spiritual and intellectual development among the masses of Europeans. "[T]he distinction between rich and poor is not only greater here than it is with us, but far more distinctly expressed in all places," he wrote to his parishioners in West Roxbury. The opulence of the Roman aristocracy disgusted him, and he praised by contrast the republican virtue of American elites who he felt were "very properly ashamed of much splendor."[6]

As for the education of most Europeans, Parker found that little had been done in contrast to the growing public education system in New England. "There are no free schools and few schools not free, and of course the people are ignorant." How could there be "so many scholars—ripe and good ones too—and yet so much ignorance"? Urban poverty in Italy also shocked him, and he was dismayed to find that what local support there was for the abandoned children

who "swarm the streets," was grafted by corrupt politicians. With an uncompromising pride in New England enterprise, he criticized the "inefficiency" with
which everything was done in Europe. "It is amusing for an American to see the
clumsy way in which the Italians go to work in all the common affairs of life,"
he told one of his parishioners. Reflecting the republican political culture of his
era, he could find no other explanation for this phenomenon save "the servile
respect which is paid in Europe to Rank." Aristocracy and other artificial social
distinctions were, for Parker, obstacles to intellectual and material progress, and
after a month in England and four months in Italy, he confessed that "I don't
find that my love of home, or of American institutions has abated, on the contrary it has grown." Yet in speaking of America, it was clearly New England's
institutions, its schools, its agriculture, its traditional opposition to displays of
wealth that Parker was thinking of. Like many Americans of his generation, his
nationalism was regional culture writ large.[7]

Yet even as his observations of European society reinforced a sense of
Yankee pride, Parker was aware that some of his fellow Transcendentalists had
exposed problems in the American industrial system that mirrored the evils of
the Old World. In the pages of his *Boston Quarterly Review*, for example, Orestes Brownson had denounced the wage labor system for reducing the working
class of the North to the slaves of parasitic capitalists. "We stand and look at
these hard working men and women hurrying in all directions, and ask ourselves, where go the proceeds of their labors?" In a scathing article on the "The
Laboring Classes" written in 1840, he had denounced the "city nabobs, reveling
in luxury" who forced workers to toil "like so many slaves." When George Ripley resigned from his prestigious position at the Purchase Street Church in 1840,
he told his congregation that he could not witness "the glaring inequalities of
condition" without concluding that "the spirit of Christ has well-nigh disappeared from the Churches." Since workers were "held to unrequited labor at the
will of another and destitute of the means of education," they and their families
were "doomed to penury, degradation and vice."[8]

During his travels in Europe, Parker kept up to date with the latest news on
these reform activities. He learned from Convers Francis that a society devoted
to Fourierist socialism had been created in Boston with George Ripley as its
president. Francis dismissed the efforts of men like Ripley as only a "fly on the
great ox of conservatism," but he conceded that they came "from the heart of
humanity." For his own part, Parker was delighted to hear about the activities of
his reform-minded friends. He rejoiced "in the Fourier movement," not because
he agreed with its particulars, but because he was coming to believe that "the
existing state of society is irrational and un[Christian]." Such irrationality had
been most evident to him in England, "the richest country in the world, but that
in which there is the most misery." He feared that America was "going in just
the same way as the English." Only a change in the whole system would prevent
his country from replicating the evils of political corruption and social inequality. "We shall come to just the same result, and have the Christian Feudalism of
Gold in Boston as in London." If Parker was not attracted to Fourierism, with its

precise, 1680-member phalanxes, and its rigid divisions of labor and leisure, he was still unwilling to stand by as the shared dignity of work became the crushing drudgery of the masses.[9]

Yet what did Parker propose to do? Were the social evils besetting Europe and America products of a bad social system or of bad ideas? And how had such evil come to exist in the first place given Parker's own faith in God as a benign creator? The answers to these questions would develop over the next several years, but his starting point was always rooted in the individual conscience. As in religion, true social reform must proceed from innate sentiments, proceed from there to clear ideas for change, and then culminate in action. He sensed that the socialists had the right sentiment, but felt that their ideas were confused and ill-suited to the American context. "If their Idea be wrong," he concluded, "so must their Action be." As a romantic reformer, Parker was certain that social change began with individuals, not groups or artificial social arrangements. It succeeded when the human conscience broke free from its restraints and realized itself in practical ways. A liberated conscience worked from the foundation of unshakable truth and gathered other liberated souls to its standard. "I see no cure for the evil but this," he told Francis. "Give each individual clear views of the Right—& then leave it to him to do what he thinks is best." When Parker spoke of a "complete revolution," he spoke not of a social revolution along the lines of a Fourierist phalanx, but of a revolution in thought powerful enough to replace the ethic of greed with the ethic of love.[10]

Old Enemies and New Audiences

Parker returned to West Roxbury in the late summer of 1844 full of restless energy and more confident than ever. After a quick and easy ocean voyage of just twelve days, he and Lydia arrived home and were received warmly by the Russell family, their loyal friends and neighbors. But if such friends had hoped that time away from the cut and thrust of theological controversy would produce a thaw in relations between Parker and his critics, they were sadly mistaken. Disappointed to see him back in their midst, Parker's adversaries were determined to exert institutional and financial pressure to isolate and silence him. The efforts of conservatives focused on Boston because it was there that the popular interest in Parker seemed greatest. But in what was becoming a pattern, Parker sensed the opportunity that these renewed attacks presented. In repelling them publicly, he saw the possibility of addressing new and larger audiences who were more receptive to religious and social reform. In seeking out such audiences, moreover, he moved toward democratic modes of speech and church organization to spread his message and satisfy his conscience.

This process began less than two months after his arrival home, when the Rev. John Turner Sargent, minister of Boston's Suffolk Street Chapel, was forced to resign from his position for exchanging pulpits with Parker. The Suffolk Street Chapel had been created several years earlier as part of Unitarianism's spiritual outreach to the Boston poor. In 1834, a group of nine churches in the city had created a Benevolent Fraternity with funds to support four "ministers at large." Sargent was one of the four, and he soon immersed himself in the business of visiting the "deserving poor" in his area and bringing them into the Suffolk Street congregation. Although dispensing relief was within the remit of the minister at large, the main purpose of the Fraternity was to "improve the moral state of the poor and irreligious" in Boston.[11]

The wealthy churches that ran the Fraternity kept a tight hold over its activities. Each of them sent delegates to an executive committee which had the final say over the appointment or removal of the ministers at large. When the committee demanded assurances from Sargent that he would never allow Parker into his pulpit again, he resigned in protest. The fact that Sargent was universally admired and utterly devoted to his work seemed compelling evidence that the conservative Boston churches regarded the enforcement of the ban on Theodore Parker as more important than the needs of the Boston poor. Parker immediately condemned the "shabby conduct" of the Fraternity, and praised Sargent's refusal, "for conscience' sake," to submit to pressure. In a public letter to the Boston Association of ministers, he wondered whether the Suffolk Street Chapel should be called a "vassal church" and the Fraternity its "feudal superiors." Parker's European trip was still very much on his mind.[12]

Because the Suffolk Street Chapel was a missionary institution and not an independent congregation, Sargent lacked the protection from elite interference that other ministers enjoyed within the congregational system. But even Parker's friends among the settled ministers faced serious consequences for exchanging with him. When James Freeman Clarke again invited Parker to preach from his pulpit at the Church of the Disciples, several prominent members of the church threatened to leave. Less than five years old, the Church of the Disciples was highly democratic in its structure and quite progressive theologically. It had abolished the practice of renting or selling pews to prominent members and relied solely on the voluntary financial contributions of members. Its statement of purpose remained explicitly Christian, but traditional Christian ordinances like Baptism and Communion were optional. No statement of faith was required for full membership. Yet even in a church like this, Parker's views were hardly uncontroversial, and two members of the society appeared in West Roxbury begging him to cancel the exchange. Refusing on the grounds that Clarke's invitation represented his commitment to ministerial fellowship, Parker preached to the Disciples in late January 1845. Clarke called the day "Black Sunday" with good reason, as fifteen prominent families left in protest. Ironically, the sermon Parker preached that day, "The Excellence of Goodness" was among his least controversial. At the end of the service, an elderly lady stood at the door to praise the visiting minister saying she sorely wished "Theodore Parker could have heard *that* sermon"![13]

Parker's decision to preach on moral rather than theological issues at the Church of the Disciples in no way signaled a retreat from the radical position he had taken before his trip to Europe. Indeed, he seemed to thrive on the opportunity to thrust his thumb into the eyes of his critics even as they tried to silence him. Even as the renewed conflict over exchanges engulfed Clarke and Sargent, Parker preached a highly confrontational sermon at the First Church in Boston as part of the rotating Thursday Lecture series. The minister there was Nathaniel Frothingham, a theological conservative who had denounced Parker's *Discourse* as "vehemently deistical" at the ministerial Conference two years earlier. According to the minister's son, a young divinity school student who served as the organist at the First Church, the Thursday Lectures were usually sparsely attended, often bringing out "venerable old ladies" who carried smelling salts to prevent drowsiness. Yet when Parker preached, the hall was so crowded that even the stairs and the choir loft were full of curious, if sometimes disapproving faces. The sermon they heard, "The Relation of Jesus to His Age and to the Ages" was long remembered for its statement that while Jesus was the greatest man in human history, "God has yet greater men in store."

Such views were anathema to conservative Unitarians and they immediately took steps to ensure that they would not appear in the Thursday Lecture again. Within weeks, the terms of the series were altered giving the minister of the First Church, in this case Frothingham, unilateral control over the choice of future preachers. Parker, and those who were suspected of harboring similar views, would henceforth be excluded. To Parker, the proscription of innovative theology at important denominational forums signaled the weakness of the Unitarian movement and vitiated its claims to spiritual leadership. In the same letter of protest that defended John Sargent, Parker denounced this "intricate confusion" and demanded that the Association either drop its ban or adopt "a standard of Unitarian orthodoxy."[14]

But in focusing on the theological issues in Parker's 1845 Thursday Lecture, his critics missed the equally important social message that wove through its pages. In his descriptions of Jesus' enemies, the Sadducees, Pharisees and Essenes, Parker made pointed allegorical references to American life and institutions. The Sadducees represented the conservative political and mercantile establishment. They "had wealth and believed in it too," they believed in the "state, in the laws, the constables, the prisons, and the axe." The Pharisees stood for New England's religious leaders whose business it was to preserve the status quo. They "adhered to the words of old books, the forms of old rites, the tradition of the elders." Yet in the Essenes, Parker seemed to find his model for the Fourierists and other reformers whose sentiments were right, but who lacked a clear understanding of the world. Essenes, he said, were "come outers" who had despaired of the "church and the state" and who built their institutions "free, as they hoped from all ancient tyrannies." But the Essenes were also separatist ascetics, "hostile to marriage...and had all things in common." They had "faith in man" but were "imprisoned by their own organization." Parker's Jesus steered a course between these extremes, rejecting the materialism and worldly power of the conservatives while refusing to renounce the world in favor of artificial associations. Instead he had chosen to work "for men, with men, by men, trusting in God." Rejected by the guardians of order and orthodox learning, Jesus was accepted by those considered "unlearned and ignorant men" by their "betters".

He had had no fear of "church or state, and trembled not, though Pilate and Herod were made friends only to crucify him." To anyone who cared to listen closely, Parker's sermon was much less a theological document than a social allegory that pointed to the direction his own ministry was taking.[15]

If the "unlearned and ignorant" had flocked to Jesus, so, it seemed, they were flocking to Theodore Parker. During this same winter of 1844–45, he spoke more than twenty times to audiences on the lyceum circuit, an increasingly popular lecture system supported by small admissions fees. Like Ralph Waldo Emerson before him, Parker found that the lecture format allowed a greater freedom of expression than was possible from the pulpit, and reached a more diverse audience. Sometimes held in churches, lyceum lectures otherwise bore no formal relation to religious institutions or denominations and Parker felt free to choose topics and take positions that he might have modified if delivered in his West Roxbury church. As a democratic intellectual medium, the lyceum circuit served as an end run around the ecclesiastical structures that seemed more and more closed to his influence. It was liberating. "I found I could say what I pleased in the lecture room," he reflected later in life. Perhaps it was the people, not their betters, who were ready and able to hear what he had to say. "I spared no labor in preparation or delivery, but took it for granted [that] the humblest audience, in the least intelligent town or city, was quite worthy of my best effort, and could understand my facts and metaphysic reasonings."[16]

Parker's success on the lyceum circuit indicates an emerging ability to move beyond abstruse philosophical argument or intricate questions of biblical criticism toward more democratic approaches to public speech and performance. Unlike church goers, lyceum audiences paid a fee to attend and they expected to be entertained as well as educated. Those who came to Parker's lectures found an indefinable charisma in his performances and came away feeling that they had gotten their money's worth. A Connecticut woman who attended one of his lectures said he possessed "acute analysis, keen satire, and learned illustration." But she was more intrigued by his style of address, noting that "his concise and nervous language requires a verbatim report" because "condensed newspaper sketches do him injustice." Another report also struggled to describe a "certain something in his speech which steals upon the sympathies." The same observer confessed that while he did not concur with Parker's "ultra-theological views," he was certain that the speaker was "a man of genius and originality."[17]

Parker's success as a lyceum lecturer stemmed at least in part from his adoption of a democratic persona. Nearly all reviewers noted that he had jettisoned the traditional high-style of public address with its extended classical allusions and highly structured format in favor of a more informal, yet deeply learned presentation. He spoke "without any flourish of trumpet" said one, while another emphasized the lack of "disguise or verbiage" in his address. Used to lectures in which profound learning came in stylized, genteel packages, Parker's audiences were intrigued by the contrast between his unpretentious demeanor and the vast knowledge displayed in the content. "His manner is modest...his stature is of the medium make with a trim and well-packed body and limbs," wrote the *Waterbury American*. But he spoke for two hours, "without notes" and delivered a lecture of surpassing "strength, originality and point." By the 1850s, Parker's reputation as a star of the lecture circuit rivaled Emerson and Henry Ward Beecher.[18]

The notes that Parker compiled for these lectures indicate that he argued forcefully for the application of Absolute Religion to social life. In a lecture on slavery, for example, he looked closely at the position of labor in New England, and came quite close to the ground that Orestes Brownson had taken in 1840. The "idle and oppressive classes" of Northern society had created a permanent class of laborers who saved them from performing what they considered "degrading" manual labor. "We shut up our slaves in damp cellars—or banish them to hot garrets," he argued. "I look for little good from the rich;...the money lords are as bad as the sword lords of other days." Parker was unsure as to whether the situation was improving or deteriorating, but he clearly felt that "the rights of labor are not respected." Parker's definition of slavery encompassed a wide variety of unequal social relationships in which individuals or classes controlled the physical and moral destiny of others. "When one claims it right to have others do for him what degrades them in his eyes, their eyes or those of society," he argued, "there is the spirit of slavery." Only when this spirit was eradicated and absolute human self-ownership took its place could society right itself.[19]

But the strident tone of these assertions masked some indecision about the direction his social conscience was taking. He was clearly appalled by inequality, which he traced to false ideas about the indignity of labor, and he decried materialism, ignorance, intemperance, and greed as destructive of moral, intellectual and spiritual growth. But his solutions remained vague, and his emphasis upon the individual conscience placed limits on the nature of his calls for change. As he saw it, the duty of man was to "make himself", to govern himself in ways that reflected the law of his being, to discard low, or destructive ideas that prevented the full use of reason, religion and conscience. This concept of individual self-ownership was the only basis through which collective action could be taken and encouraging it was one of the main purposes of government.[20]

But *how* could society be remade by the innate capacities of man? How could conscience be connected to social change? In December, 1844, he went back to the ideas of Charles Fourier and found a compelling indictment of the social contradictions inherent in the new market economy. "The rich man with all the money in the world does nothing for society," he wrote in his journal. "On the other hand a poor blacksmith who toils 14 hours a day finds it difficult to support his wife and children." Yet he could not accept Fourier's system of association, nor could he agree that private property was the root of the evil. The ownership or transmission of property reflected a natural impulse toward self-preservation and generally acted as a positive force in society. The problem was the immoral desire to escape from the physical labor of creating wealth, and the cynical attempt to cast its burden upon others. In "the love of low things and the idea that work degrades," Parker found his culprit. Society could be reformed when its individual members recognized that "labor elevates man" and that there were "better things than gold can buy."[21]

Parker did not even need to leave the shady groves of West Roxbury to see such ideas in practice. George Ripley's Brook Farm community was but a few minutes' walk from Spring Street, and some of his parishioners were members of the group. The community had recently been reorganized as a Fourierist Phalanx after three years under a looser system of principles. The basic goal of the experiment was to provide an alternative to the wage labor system which reformers believed was at the root of class divisions and social misery in the urban North. Labor was shared and rotated at Brook Farm and all members had access to leisure, education and other means of self-improvement. Brook Farmers were determined to fight the destructive separation of human society into artificial classes of workers and thinkers. As George Ripley put it, the community would create "a more simple and wholesome life, than can be led amidst the pressure of our competitive institutions."[22]

On a beautiful spring day in April 1845, Parker attended Brook Farm's celebration of Charles Fourier's birthday. Several members of the Spring Street church participated in the festivities and they were treated to coffee, milk, sandwiches and fruit. In his private account of the visit, Parker called Brook Farm a "noble enterprise" but it is not clear that he took it very seriously as a solution to the social problems now occupying his attention. He seemed non-plussed by it, focusing mainly on the "entertainment" provided for the guests rather than the social principles that guided the community. Perhaps he was on to something real. As one historian has described it, "[a]t Brook Farm there was an almost insatiable desire for pleasure: music, dancing, card playing, charades, tableaux vivants, dramatic readings, plays, costume parties, picnics, sledding and skating." Whether such amusements were on display when Parker visited is unclear, but he came away from his "pleasant" visit to the community ready to attend to more important business. In Parker's mind, at least, Brook farm was a bit like the *Dial*. It was agreeable enough in its way, but it left him with a taste for something stronger.[23]

The Twenty-Eighth Congregational Society

As it had been for most of his adult life, Boston remained the focus of Parker's imagination. For all his love of nature, his dynamic and tumultuous inner world found better analogues in the busy streets and crowded lecture halls of the American Athens than in the verdant calm of West Roxbury. He basked in the roiling reform culture that pulsed around the edges of this growing, commercial city. A month after his visit to bucolic Brook Farm, for example, he attended the Anniversary Week reform conventions in Boston where he mixed with activists from a variety of backgrounds and ideological commitments. At a meeting of the Clerical Anti-Slavery Society, he cheered as anti-slavery laymen refused to allow the conservative clergy to dominate the proceedings. On subsequent days, he attended a Fourierist meeting, a conference on the anti-slavery Liberty Party,

and an anti-capital punishment convention. The last of these was particularly
heartening to Parker, who had become convinced that "'justice' catches only the
petty rogues, never forgiving their offenses—gradually makes them worse and
at last hangs them." It was a positive "sign of the times" that "soon this sin of
judicial murder will be over."[24]

The most positive sign of the times for Parker in 1845 was the movement to
establish a permanent preaching venue for him in Boston. Just after returning to
West Roxbury from Europe, he had received an invitation from a group of supporters in Boston to preach once a week to a recently-organized congregation at
the Melodeon Theatre on Washington Street. The Melodeon was the home of
the city's Handel and Haydn Society, but it also served as a lecture and convention venue with a seating capacity of fifteen-hundred. Given the size of the audiences who came out to hear his theological lectures in the winter of 1841–42,
and his success as a lyceum speaker, it did not seem outrageous to imagine that
Parker could make good use of the Melodeon's "commodious" interior. The
founders of the church, who incorporated themselves as the Twenty-Eighth
Congregational Society of Boston in November, 1845, had been horrified by the
heavy-handed tactics of Boston's conservative establishment. As Dean Grodzins
has shown, many leading lights of the Society had been members of John Sargent's Suffolk Street Chapel or John Pierpont's Hollis Street Church before the
two embattled ministers had been forced to resign. In bringing Parker to Boston,
men like John Flint, Francis Jackson, and Samuel May Sr. sought a measure of
revenge while at the same time supporting the cause of religious freedom.[25]

The feelings of betrayal that conservatives had engendered in Boston's liberal, reform-minded circles cannot be overstated and it is clear that those who
began attending Parker's services at the Melodeon in 1845 used their presence
there to express their anger at the self-styled custodians of culture. Caroline
Healey, who had recently married the Unitarian minister Charles Dall, said that
"I never knew what it was to lose friends—to feel the coldness and neglect of
those who had been kind—until the Boston clergy taught me." Her father, the
Boston merchant Mark Healey, was a key figure in the organization of the
Twenty-Eighth, and Caroline was disgusted by the cold treatment he received
from the Boston clergy as a result. Perhaps Caroline felt guilty since it was she
who had introduced her father to Parker's preaching in 1842 and thereby set
forces in motion that would lead him to a costly public association with the controversial minister. For her husband Charles, who was just then seeking a permanent position in the Unitarian ministry, the creation of the new church, and
his family's public connections with it, created equally difficult problems.
Charles Dall was not a Transcendentalist, but he was sickened by the personal
attacks his fellow ministers leveled at Parker. "They are grievously unjust towards him," he told Caroline one evening in February, 1846. He had spent most
of the day arguing "against six of them...who said [Parker] was a *dishonest*
man."[26]

The creation of the Twenty-Eighth Congregational Society represented
Parker's strongest effort to resolve the tensions between his moral individualism

and his recognition that collective action was essential to reform society. The "true" Church, he said in his installation sermon, should exist to perfect its members in their infinite variety, but then send them into the world to work for the common purpose of human improvement. Individuality was never to be sacrificed. But just as organs "must have pipes of various sound" that could be tuned to harmony by a "skilful artist," Parker believed that a Church committed to truth as the only authority could accomplish great ends without sacrificing "the man to the mass." The Twenty-Eighth, therefore, would model the critical public culture that Parker believed was essential to the reform of society at large. It seemed less important to him to arrive at specific solutions to social problems than to create an open discourse in which such solutions could eventually take shape in the moral imagination of its participants. As Boston's wealthy Unitarian churches closed off opportunities for open declarations of conscience, Parker's church would become a vital oasis of dissent and social criticism.[27]

As it encouraged the full flowering of individual conscience, Parker's "true church" would pool the moral capital of its members to accomplish real social change. Looking out upon his new flock, he counted many who were already active as social reformers. Charles M. Ellis, Walter F. Channing, and John Augustus were engaged in medical reform, public education, prison reform, abolitionism and temperance work. Unlike the well-intentioned experimenters at Brook Farm, such men were in and of the world, working to improve the lives of society's most vulnerable people. Under the institutional umbrella of the Twenty-Eighth and the theological banner of Absolute Religion, such reformers could "apply Christianity to life, and make the world a better place." Implicit in his installation sermon, and explicit in his journals and later writings, was a conviction that unless the churches reformed themselves, the positive religious energy of nineteenth-century America would leave them. To remain faithful and relevant, the churches must lead the people boldly and fearlessly in the great causes of human improvement. Rather than driving out reformers like John Pierpont and John Sargent who welcomed innovation and challenged social evil, the "church of the nineteenth century must honor such men." Otherwise, "it is a dead church, with no claim on us, except that we bury it."[28]

To ensure that his own congregation did not devolve into a bastion of conservatism and privilege, Parker had come to an agreement with lay leaders that the society's finances would be based on voluntary contribution rather than the traditional method of selling pews. All would be welcome to attend, and the seating arrangements would be open rather than assigned according to class, gender or race, as in most American churches. Like his theological work, Parker understood ecclesiastical reform as an attempt to save the church from becoming a relic, "mewling and whining, its faced turned down, its eyes turned back." The Twenty-Eighth Congregational Society at least would model the heroism of Jesus and look up and outward toward a world that needed better ideas and better solutions to social problems.[29]

VIII
CLASSES, FAMILIES AND REFORM
1845–1848

As the new church and its minister looked up and outward, however, they found a city with problems that no church could solve on its own. Parker's parish was no longer a small town whose families could receive direct pastoral care, but a rapidly industrializing city that reminded him of what he had seen in Rome, Paris, and Liverpool. Boston society had changed rapidly since he had arrived there as a young school teacher fifteen years earlier. Not only had the population nearly doubled during those years, but its composition had altered radically. In 1830, native-born Americans comprised some ninety-five percent of the population, while in 1845 nearly one out of four city dwellers was of German, Irish, or English origin. The steady influx of mostly unskilled, Irish-Catholic immigrants might have provided a cheap source of labor for urban industrial development, but most manufacturers in antebellum Massachusetts chose to locate outside of Boston where land was cheaper. As a result, the years before the Civil War saw unprecedented residential mobility among the population of Boston with turnover rates averaging thirty percent.[1]

For those immigrants who remained in the city's core, poverty and squalid living conditions were endemic. Areas "full of sheds and shanties" became a permanent part of the urban landscape and the system of poor relief was stretched to its limit. Without adequate city services, public health remained a constant problem. Cholera epidemics carried off hundreds of victims, disproportionately Irish, each year during the late 1840s. To prosperous Bostonians, whose neighborhoods were less affected by such diseases, the prevalence of sickness in poor immigrant wards proved that their inhabitants followed "dissolute" ways. Anti-Catholic sentiment at all levels of native-born Protestant society simply exacerbated the social polarization evident each day on the streets of Boston.[2]

The house that Theodore and Lydia Parker chose to live in was located several blocks from the most poverty-stricken areas of the city. For all of his concern with the moral and physical condition of Boston poor, Parker had no intention of living among them. Exeter Place was in a prosperous area not far from Boston Common and his neighbors were men like Wendell Phillips, the son of an old, elite family who had broken with his class to join the ranks of the abolitionist movement in the 1830s. Visitors to the Parker's house found it quite elegant with handsome engravings, chosen by Lydia, decorating the walls of the second floor parlor. Living together as a married couple for the first time without Lydia's Aunt Lucy, who remained at the old house in West Roxbury, the Parkers were now free to create a home on their own terms. At the core of it was the minister's study, where Parker's ever enlarging collection of books filled every available space. By the time the black abolitionist and educator Charlotte Forten Grimke visited it in the late 1850s, the study could no longer contain the collection and she noted that the overflow of books had spilled into every room in the house.[3]

Yet even amidst this growing monument to Parker's erudition, there were token symbols of the personal losses and blighted expectations he been forced to confront in his life. In a small corner of the study was the "little chest of drawers in which his mother kept his clothes when he was a child." Another compartment was filled with toys he had purchased to amuse the children of his guests. Even as his influence and celebrity grew, the childlessness of his marriage and the early loss of so many of his natal family members remained powerful reminders that for all its divine potential, human life remained fragile and subject to disappointment.[4]

Dangerous and Perishing Classes

If the house on Exeter Place was in many was a typical Victorian "domestic refuge," Parker refused to avert his eyes from the grinding poverty that lay just around the corner. Ragged, destitute children, who roamed the streets of Boston in greater numbers during this period, were a constant reminder of the city's moral failure, and they exemplified the consequences of inequality for the most vulnerable members of society. "Last night I saw two boys with faces so low and animal and even demonical that it astonished me," he wrote a few months after moving to the city. He tried to speak to them and offer assistance, but found that "they would not bear me" and ran off into the night. "Their language was bad—their manners obscene and savage—they are the savages of our civilization."[5]

Yet unlike those who blamed the poor for their own plight, Parker refused to pass judgment on such children or their families. He preferred instead to indict those who failed to offer a helping hand and insisted that "every beggar, every pauper, born and bred amongst us, is a reproach to our civilization." He asked his congregation how it was that "in a land of abundance" there are people, "for no fault of their own born into want, living in want, and dying of want?" The contrasts between abundance and poverty, civilization and savagery, education and ignorance, health and sickness were unbearable to Parker because he believed that they were so unnecessary. Using his new pulpit in Boston, he intended to reform the public conscience of Boston and force its leaders to re-examine their responsibilities to the poor.[6]

This notion of elevating the poor, of securing to them the benefits of modern intellectual, spiritual, moral, and material progress was at the core of Parker's reformism. It rested upon a secular concept of social development that mirrored the religious evolution he had outlined in the *Discourse of Religion*. Always preferring evolutionary models to the "artificial" arrangements he had encountered in Fourier, Parker once again drew on the writings of August Comte. In his 1847 "Sermon of the Dangerous Classes," for example, a discourse on the origins of crime which he delivered not long after moving to Boston, he divided human history into overlapping stages. From its origins in an "animal period," in which food, sleep and reproduction dominated life, human beings had moved into a savage and barbarous stage characterized by violence and self-interest. Finally, human society would reach a civilized state in which enlightenment, religion and conscience replaced ignorance, selfishness and vice. Mankind, he believed, had reached the last stage and was in the process of perfecting the intellectual and religious powers. But each child, in the process of growth, must recapitulate this progression in the development of his or her own individual nature. "Each new child is born at the foot of the ladder," he maintained "To attain to the present civilization he must pass over every point which the race has passed over."[7]

Here, of course, was where the roots of crime and social disorder lay. The effect of the urban environment, its entrenched poverty, inadequate education, rampant disease, and overwork, stalled or blocked the natural process of growth in the children of the poor. Those who lacked the atmosphere of improvement, through no fault of their own, were doomed to remain at the bottom of a developmental ladder that others, more fortunate, were climbing. The price that society as a whole would pay for injustice done to these "dangerous classes" was the violence and crime that impeded the larger progress of human values. One great task of the reformer, then, was to prick the conscience of those higher on the ladder to improve the urban environment, creating the conditions in which the natural laws of individual and social advancement could unfold. At the very least it was the job of those whose conscience had developed normally to express themselves in the public debate on behalf of the poor and give voice to the voiceless.[8]

Parker's use of an evolutionary model to explain social differences was fraught with perils. One was the tendency to view the poor as objects of paternalistic condescension. Another was the seemingly irresistible temptation to apply the concept of evolutionary stages to explain racial differences. Both were present in his sermon on the "Dangerous Classes." He spoke of the "dangerous classes" as those who "loiter behind our civilization" and as "the backward children of society." In a section in which he asked what could be done for "thieves, pirates, housebreakers, murderers," moreover, he slipped easily into a similar question about "the humbler nations—Irish, Mexicans, Malays, Indians, negroes." In the long run, he implied that those who had learned how to use their consciences should work to uplift those who had not.[9]

But in the meantime, he thundered against the impulse to punish rather than reform criminals. "Our whole criminal legislation is based on a false principle—force not love," he wrote. Long term imprisonment, social stigma, and especially capital punishment were themselves relics of a more barbarous age, and indications of society's refusal to embrace its responsibility to reform the lawbreaker. Jails would never be able to do the work that good homes, a decent education, and benevolent churches were meant to accomplish. He praised the "special work" of his parishioner, Boston boot maker John Augustus, who had established an informal probation system for those convicted of minor offenses. Augustus provided bail for petty criminals who remained in his custody for a month and, if they showed repentance and "some improvement in character and prospects," were discharged by the municipal court with a one-cent fine. By the time Parker moved to Boston, Augustus was overseeing more than a hundred cases each year.[10]

Despite those elements of his reformism that reflect paternalism and a desire to "civilize" the urban masses, Parker was quite clear that pernicious social inequality, not individual moral failure, created pauperism and vice. In seeing the "dangerous classes" and "perishing classes" of Boston as the victims of social forces beyond their control, Parker dissented from the dominant views of evangelical reformers who regarded the poor as victims of their own improvidence and depraved appetites. As historian Bruce Dorsey has shown, poverty in the antebellum city had been defined by most reformers as a problem that could only be solved by changing the *spiritual* condition of the poor, not by altering their material circumstances. The Presbyterian minister Ezra Stiles Ely of Philadelphia, for example, was certain that the inmates of that city's almshouses were there because of their "drunkenness, idleness, extravagance, improvidence, laziness, lust, and the righteous curse of unchastity." He even advised the overseers of the poor to withhold firewood during the winter in order to encourage the "improvident" to plan better for the future.[11]

Parker believed that such views betrayed a total ignorance of the poor and of the stultifying consequences of poverty. The poor were not improvident, they were robbed by unscrupulous landlords, charged higher prices for flour because they purchased in smaller quantities, and denied decent wages because the "capitalist can control the market for labor." If poor men sometimes drank away their earnings or spent them on luxuries they could not afford, this was the consequence of deprivation. "The recklessness of the poor comes unavoidably from their circumstances," he argued, "from the despair of ever being comfortable, except for a moment at a time." In his sermon on the "perishing classes," he vividly described the fate of the abandoned children of the city who grew up in abject poverty amidst the scenes of wealth. "Amid all the science and refined culture of the nineteenth century, these children have little," he argued. "In the intense life around them they unavoidably become vicious, obscene, deceitful, violent, they will lie, steal, be drunk; ...how can it be otherwise?"[12]

Parker's rejection of the dominant spiritual explanation for crime and poverty, and his embrace of environmental explanations, led him to the innovative use of statistical information to study urban problems. Here, he believed, was a way to speak on behalf of the poor that could withstand charges of partisanship or special pleading. Like other antebellum reformers, he realized that audiences would give his statistical claims a "superior credibility" and would reinforce his larger moral argument. Using data derived from an 1838 study of Boston, for example, he painted a frightful picture of child mortality, crime, grinding poverty, intemperance, and prostitution which he blamed on the inequalities of modern economic relations. He demonstrated that sixty-one percent of Catholics who died in Boston from 1833–38 were less than five years of age. His statistics on crime showed that offenders came disproportionately from the ranks of urban poor who were jailed for "crimes over which they had no control." Unless something was done to improve the urban environment, Parker's statistical evidence showed, criminals, including prostitutes, were quite likely to repeat their crimes and be jailed again. "Here are the poor, daughters and sons, excluded from the refining influences of modern life," he sadly concluded, "shut out of the churches by that bar of gold—ignorant, squalid, hungry and hopeless, wallowing in their death."[13]

Intemperance was a vice that many reformers used to condemn the moral character of the poor, but Parker saw poverty and hopelessness as the root cause of drunkenness. The issue was a personal as well as an intellectual problem. Parker's older brother Hiram, one of his two remaining siblings in the 1840s, was a factory hand in the Lowell mills, and had repeated problems with alcohol. Theodore was often obliged to send money to Hiram's family, and on occasion he traveled to Lowell to offer encouragement. Just before his trip to Europe, Parker had visited Hiram, and told his brother Isaac that "H. promised to do better, [he] signed the temperance pledge again and seemed likely to do well." Despite this optimism, he begged Isaac to contact Hiram and "say a word or two of encouragement." He acknowledged that individual weakness was a source of intemperance, but Parker condemned the unrestrained quest for profits among the rum merchants with much greater ferocity.[14]

With the expulsion of John Pierpont from the Boston Association of Ministers still fresh in his mind, Parker argued that the liquor industry in the city was supporting the destruction of individual workingmen and their families by the unchecked importation and retailing of alcohol. He calculated that over two million dollars per year was spent in "dram shops," and shocked his congregation by showing that "this sum is considerably more than double the amount paid for the whole public education of the people in Massachusetts." He praised the Washingtonian Temperance Society, organized mainly by working class men, and he lamented that "respectable men" had failed to support it. Parker saw drunkenness, like poverty and crime, as signs of moral failure not on the part of the poor who were its victims, but upon the rest of society, which allowed the strong to exploit the weak for profit and gain. Those whose consciences were not blunted by ignorance, poverty, and unremitting toil had no excuse for their failure to act upon them.[15]

Many of Parker's early sermons at the Melodeon were blistering critiques of the wealthy and powerful elements in New England society who were failing to address the conditions of the Boston poor. Unlike many contemporary reformers, Parker regarded wealth as a decidedly mixed blessing. The moral temptations many middle class reformers associated with the poor, he instead linked with the rich. Their "inordinate desire of wealth," their "temptations to fraud," their tendency to use "position to the disadvantage of the weak" and the danger of using "political power to the disadvantage of the nation" were chief among them. Wealth and conscience, it seemed to Parker, did not coexist easily.[16]

In his "Sermon of Merchants," preached and published in November of 1846, he returned to the concerns about "money lords" that had emerged during his trip to Europe. Again employing his developmental model, Parker acknowledged that European and American merchants were a great improvement over the warrior nobles of feudal times and the idle, hereditary aristocracy of later periods. Unlike their predecessors, merchants were at least men whose wealth and power flowed from "practical skill, administrative talent" and the ability to "make use of the labor of other men." Yet judged by "the standard of justice, of absolute religion," the mercantile elite were sadly wanting. Despite their enormous power to promoted social improvement, Parker found that most were pro-slavery, sold rum to the working class, supported capital punishment and imprisonment for debt, and manipulated politics for their own narrow class interests rather than for social good. If the "wicked baron, bad of heart, and bloody of hand" had passed into history, Parker was certain that the "bad merchant still lives."[17]

Such condemnations of the merchant class formed the very core of the dissenting discourse that Parker and his congregation were injecting into the public culture of Boston. In their own defense, wealthy Bostonians pointed to their massive financial support for the Massachusetts General Hospital, the Boston Athenaeum, the Boston Public Library, the McLean Asylum for the mentally ill, and Harvard Divinity School. Conservative minister Ezra Stiles Gannett was appalled at Parker's attack on the elite, accusing him of "bad taste" and irresponsible accusation. "Some persons, perhaps, may be pleased," Gannett wrote rather archly, but others "whose esteem you would be glad to retain," would be offended. Gannett reported that many among his former colleagues were becoming convinced that Parker's sermons proved that he was now overcome by "sourness," "disappointed ambition" or even a "mutated mind."[18]

But Parker was unrepentant. In an emotional response to Gannett, he denied any intention to offend, but only to tell the truth. "The things which sound so hard when I say them...are said wholly in sorrow, I weep when I write them," he claimed. "I wrestle with myself afterwards, say I can't say them. I won't." But then, he told Gannett, "the awful voice of conscience says *who art thou, that darest to disobey thy duty!* So I say them—tho' it rends my heart." As it did in his theological battles, conscience supplied both the method of social reform and driving personal force behind it.[19]

Family and Gender

Parker's conservative critics accused him of attacking the very roots of social order, substituting the individual conscience for all traditional sources of authority. Yet for all his critique of institutions, the family remained a critical anchor for his developing social ideology. Here is where the "ethic of love" could be nurtured and preserved even in the midst of rapid social change. Like many in his generation, he disdained movements such as Shakerism and Mormonism that experimented with family structure. Along with private property, he believed, family bonds were rooted in human nature and served a critical function in social life. "It seems to me the best qualities of human nature are developed by [the family] connection," he once told the Shaker leader Robert White. Families were "united by the most sacred and most beautiful and most endearing ties, each [member] is a complement to the other." In the morally vitiated environment of the city, where families were sometimes destroyed by poverty and drunkenness, abandoned children were left to absorb the worst aspects of their environment. "What have these abandoned children to help them?" he asked. "There is nothing about them to foster self-respect; nothing to call forth their conscience, to awaken and cultivate their sense of religion." Parker was always careful to note that families did not *create* conscience, but he acknowledged that without them conscience would remain unused.[20]

Parker saw the family as the only social institution where the "spirit of Christianity" was consistently practiced. He also insisted that women, in their domestic roles as wives and mothers, played a disproportionate role in the maintenance of affectionate family bonds. Drawing on a hazy, rather idealized memory of his mother that blended easily with Victorian family norms, he argued that women constituted the moral center of family life. Their "unique" qualities could shape the institution as a Christian enclave in society where conscience had been drowned out by materialism and self-interest. "Sometimes you see a woman of lofty aims applying her ideal to life, not with much talk at the corners of the street, but with humble perseverance in the intellectual, moral, and religious education of her family," he preached in 1845. "By and by, her child has become a man, and men wonder whence has he this wisdom, this moral power, this soul of faith?" Just as his own mother had taken "great pains with the moral culture of her children," Parker suspected that each moral man owed a tremendous debt to "the soul of that mother, over whose grave the bee gathers honey in June."[21]

Parker's general views of women mirrored commonly accepted notions of female domesticity that dominated middle-class American thought in the nineteenth century. Supported by popular, prescriptive literature, the domestic ideal held that women served the interests of their family, society, and nation by remaining at home where their "natural" qualities could best be employed in the

moral cultivation of the young. For a man who felt little compunction about
challenging other aspects of popular thought, Parker sounded remarkably conventional about gender. He was certain, for example, that "man will always lead
in affairs of the intellect—of reason, imagination, understanding—he has the
bigger brain." But women possessed "pure and lofty emotion...moral feeling,
affectional feeling, and religious feeling" that was "well in advance of man."
Associating "manliness" with the rational intellect, force of personal character,
and even physical courage, he associated womanliness with "eminence of conscience" and a "mighty heart." Parker never described women as inferior to
men, but he never doubted that the sexes possessed distinct qualities that prescribed divergent social roles. Since "male" qualities tended to replace conscience with force, it was crucial that women remain the domestic guardians of
society's "higher" values.[22]

Having assigned such qualities and roles to women, Parker was remarkably
intolerant of those women who did not live up to them. He judged fellow Transcendentalist Margaret Fuller very harshly for what he called her "violence and
unregenerate passion." Fuller possessed the "power of mind" and character that
Parker associated with men, and he found her unnerving as a result. Evaluating
her in explicitly gendered terms, he regretted to "see a woman give way to petty
jealousies" and "contemptible lust of power." Fuller and Parker were never on
close personal terms, but even Parker's staunchest women supporters sometimes
bristled at his attitudes. After attending a Sunday evening conversation at his
house in Boston, for example, Caroline Dall came home fuming about comments he had made about the French novelist Amandine Dupin, better known as
George Sand. Sand had become a controversial figure in Europe, wearing men's
clothes, smoking tobacco in public and carrying on extramarital relationships.
Parker disapproved of such departures from domesticity and, to Dall's intense
irritation, he condemned Sand as living a "licentious life." This was clearly not
the first time that she had been exasperated by Parker's conventionality. She
confessed that his "mannish views of women" regularly "provoked" her and she
wondered why men so often "took the lowest view" of unorthodox women.[23]

Although it was largely in keeping with convention, Parker's acceptance of
gender essentialism did not preclude an expanded public role for women. He
was certain that women, especially those who engaged in local benevolent work,
constituted an indispensable part of the nation's public conscience, not just of its
domestic hearths. The aggressive, competitive, and harsh attributes of men required a countervailing force if society was to eliminate its most brutal, inhu-
mane practices. "Woman is to correct man's taste, mend his morals, excite his
affections, inspire his religious faculties," he wrote in 1853. "[I]t seems to me
God has treasured up a reserved power in the nature of woman to correct many
of those evils which are Christendom's disgrace today." In his congregation
were many women who fit this description. Matilda and Lucy Goddard, for example, were the daughters of a wealthy Boston family who spent a lifetime in
charitable work with "destitute infants" and indigent widows. Although Matilda
Goddard never married, she became a kind of "public mother" to what Parker

had called the "perishing classes" in the city. He referred to her as "Saint Matilda" for her dedication to the less fortunate. Although their work was predicated on the notion of distinct and essential female qualities, women at the Twenty-Eighth Congregational Society were encouraged to participate in a wide variety of social reform endeavors that took them well beyond the domestic sphere.[24]

While recognizing the conventional elements of Parker's gender ideology, it would be a mistake to dismiss him as just another proponent of domesticity. Perhaps most important to the emerging women's rights movement was his assault on the theological sources of traditional patriarchy. He understood that the expanded role he envisioned for women could never be achieved until false, degrading ideas of female inferiority were overthrown. At the root of the problem, he believed, was the Bible which, if read literally, suggested that women were "created as an afterthought" as man's "instrument of comfort" or his "medium of posterity." Such false ideas were rife in a Christian history dominated by men who were taught to regard women as "pollution." He was convinced that the exclusion of women from theological writing had led to partial, and in some cases false ideas of God. Leaving "nothing feminine in the character of God," he argued, popular conceptions of religion dwelt too exclusively on God's power and stern judgment. Parker doubted that any woman would have preached the doctrines of infant damnation or innate depravity since they conflicted with women's natural inclinations toward motherhood and forgiveness. Despite accepting inherent differences between the sexes, he argued that the male and female aspects of human nature closely mirrored the all-encompassing character of God. To the great delight of woman's rights activists in Boston, he often referred to God in his public prayers as "thou who art our Father and Mother."[25]

The value that Parker placed on the moral and religious qualities of women led him to support many of the specific goals of the woman's rights movement. He agreed with activists like Margaret Fuller that domestic drudgery robbed women and their society of precious gifts. "I don't believe a woman will arrive at the 'science of universals' in frying fish all her life," he told Caroline Dall in 1846. After all, he said, if ten women were left to "fry fish all their lives," it was likely that "nine of them will know nothing but how to fry, stew, boil and bake." He understood that without property rights and political equality "woman is treated as a doll or a drudge, not a free individuality but a dependent parasite or a commanded servant." Parker expressed unqualified support for the education of women, and he advocated equality in property rights, legal custody of children, and access to the professions.[26]

Since open access to the public square was a critical dimension of Parker's vision of social change, his church became a place where radical women could raise their voices. Abby Folsom, the eccentric women's rights activist, took that invitation quite literally, periodically interrupting Parker's Sunday sermons to provide her own commentary. When he asked her "very gently" to wait until the end of the service, she sometimes preached a whole sermon as the organist played the recessional. But other women's rights leaders, including Elizabeth

Oakes Smith and Antoinette Brown, gave more traditional addresses from the pulpit of the Twenty-Eighth. Smith claimed that Parker actively encouraged her writing and public speaking, telling her that there was "no reason why a woman should not speak if she had something to say." Brown was the first woman licensed to preach by Oberlin College, and she had fought a protracted battle against the school's refusal to train women in rhetoric and public oratory. It is clear that Parker supported Brown's professional aspirations, but the strangeness of addressing her by the formal ministerial title amused him. "I was present one Sunday when he announced to his congregation that the Rev. Antoinette Brown would address them on the Sunday following," remembered Julia Ward Howe years later. "As he pronounced the word 'Reverend,' I detected an unmistakable and probably unconscious curl of his lip."[27]

Unconscious or not, Parker's amusement at Brown's title betrays an underlying ambivalence about women's rights that prevented him from playing a prominent role in the movement. His attacks on the biblical and theological foundations of traditional patriarchy were useful to women's rights activists, but he was unable to shed his "mannish" views of women. His best known work on gender, the 1853 "Sermon of the Public Function of Woman" insisted that the public activities of women began only when the more important domestic functions had been completed. "Woman's function, like charity, begins at home," he argued, "then like charity goes everywhere." He admitted that there were some women who "had no taste and no talent for the domestic function," but his stated ideal was that of the "domestic woman" whose hard work and efficiency left her time for other work. This amounted to a kind of superwoman who was able to merge "the useful of the drudge and the beautiful of the doll into one womanhood, and have a great deal left besides." The sermon advocated equal political rights and equal access to education and the professions, but Parker never took these goals as seriously as he might have. He doubted, for instance, "that women will ever take the same interest as men in political affairs, or find therein an abiding satisfaction." He went on to say that every "woman is a nurse and half-a-doctor by nature, and yet I believe no woman acts as a lawyer." Politics and law would remain the province of strong-minded, rational men. But women might extend their role as domestic guardians into the public sphere as nurses, teachers and ministers.[28]

Like his larger reform vision, Parker's ideas about family, gender, and women's rights were a mix of the conventional and the unorthodox that reflected the views of a reform-minded, but largely middle-class Boston congregation. He recognized that domesticity hindered women's ability to bring conscience to bear upon the public sphere, but his commitment to the Victorian family as the cradle of conscience prevented him from developing a full critique of its gender conventions. As he would do later with the contradictions inherent in using violence in a righteous cause, however, Parker subsumed the ambiguity in his views of women in the larger context of human progress. "All these are transient things, and will soon be gone," he once said of oppressive views of women. One day they would be regarded as just "the noise and dust of the wagon that brings the harvest home." Ultimately, he preferred causes where conscience and injustice could be more easily pitted against one another in dramatic and confrontational ways. The slavery issue would soon provide more than enough to satisfy his appetite.[29]

IX
SLAVERY, POLITICS AND THE REVOLUTION
1841–1847

At the end of January, 1841, several months before preaching his explosive ordination sermon in South Boston, Theodore Parker had addressed his congregation in West Roxbury on the subjects of slavery and abolition. He began with a
firm condemnation of human bondage and those who perpetuated it. Slavery
was wrong and stemmed from consciences blunted by greed. "Men who wish
for wealth and luxury, but hate the toil and sweat which are their natural price,
brought the African to America," he argued. "If these men spoke as plainly as
they needs must feel, they would say 'Our Sin captured these men on the African sands, our Sin fettered him in slavery, and please God our Sin shall keep
them in slavery till the world ends." In the same sermon he defended abolitionists like William Lloyd Garrison from the nearly universal charges of fanaticism
and demagoguery. He admitted that abolitionists were sometimes extravagant in
their speech, but that was understandable given the apathy and indifference
shown by so many. After all, "honest souls engaged in a good work…sometimes
forget the settled decorum commonly observed in forum and pulpit, and call sin
sin," he argued. John the Baptist and Jesus of Nazareth had done the same, and
paid for their bravery with their lives. Although Parker was defending the abolitionists, he could easily have used the same words to defend himself.[1]

Yet less than two years later, after Boston abolitionists had called a mass
meeting at Faneuil Hall to prevent the return of George Latimer, a fugitive slave
from Norfolk, Virginia, Parker declined an easy opportunity to ally himself publicly with the antislavery movement. After securing Latimer's release, the abolitionists had organized a massive petition drive calling for the passage of a
"Latimer Law" preventing state authorities from assisting slave catchers or using
public property to incarcerate accused fugitives. One of Parker's own parishioners, Frederick Cabot, had helped to found the *Latimer Journal*, a publication

designed to raise awareness of the case and to promote non-violent assistance to fugitives. As the petition drive picked up steam in November 1842, Cabot asked Parker to promote the petition at the end of a lecture he was giving at the Marlboro Chapel. But with the large crowd filing out of the building, Parker lost his nerve and, to the horror of the abolitionists, said nothing about the petition. Abolitionist Maria Weston Chapman, who had publicly supported Parker during the conflict over the South Boston sermon, was furious. She told a friend that Theodore Parker had "just enough moral courage for himself and not enough for the [antislavery] cause." George Adams, a Boston printer and Garrison protégé, sent Parker a letter directly reproving him for backwardness in the cause of justice. In a rather unconvincing reply, Parker claimed that he had no fear of associating himself with abolitionism, only that he had become convinced, after due deliberation, that he would not "do the Slaves a service for presenting the petition at this time." He said he realized that his actions would make him unpopular with the abolitionists, but "fear of man never stopped me when conscience said 'Go'. Perhaps it will in time to come." Parker told Adams that his zeal on behalf of the slaves was strong, but admitted that he didn't "come up to my ideal" on the issue.[2]

Parker's ambivalence about abolitionism in 1842 stands in marked contrast to his personal involvement in the movement after 1845, his violent opposition to the Fugitive Slave Act of 1850, and his involvement in the Secret Six conspiracy which funded John Brown's raid on Harper's Ferry in 1859. He had to overcome serious doubts about the propriety and efficacy of anti-slavery agitation before he could embrace it. His colleagues among the liberal Unitarian clergy and members of the Transcendentalist circle opposed slavery, but some feared the social consequences of immediate emancipation. Others recoiled from the invective and hyperbole that abolitionists employed. The story of Parker's eventual alliance with abolitionism, then, is at least in part the story of his detachment from these groups. It is not surprising that as his radical theology and zealous pursuit of social justice resulted in ostracism from genteel Boston, he became less critical of those whose passionate condemnations of slavery earned them a similar pariah status.

Transcendental Ambivalence

Parker's refusal to sign the Latimer petition and his defensive explanation are indicative of an early ambivalence about the abolitionist movement that he shared with other New England intellectuals. Since its inception in 1833, the movement for the immediate abolition of slavery in the United States had suffered a reputation for radicalism, ideological rigidity, and a bitterness of style that alienated many whose sympathies ran in a similar direction. Among the conservative elite of Boston, who feared that immediate emancipation would bring about social disorder and disunion, abolitionism was condemned as irresponsible fanaticism. Young Unitarian ministers stood to lose much by any association with the movement. Parker's friend and colleague Samuel Joseph May, for example, had been forced to resign his Unitarian pulpit in South Scituate, Massachusetts because of his abolitionism. In 1840, respectable Unitarian churches of Boston had even refused to perform the funeral of German émigré and abolitionist Charles Follen. The American Unitarian Association, which was attempting to establish congregations in southern cities, refused even to discuss the moral issue of slavery until 1850.[3]

Among those Unitarians and Transcendentalists who were concerned about slavery, most preferred to keep a safe distance from organized abolitionism. The most articulate spokesman for this group was William Ellery Channing, whose widely read work *Slavery* supported a gradual approach to emancipation and a more elevated tone in antislavery discourse. Channing was roundly critical of the abolitionists' intemperate and indecorous manner. Their writings, he argued, "have been blemished by a spirit of intolerance, sweeping censure, and rash, injurious judgment." Revealing his Federalist origins, Channing wished that there were more "men of strong moral principle, judiciousness, and sobriety" in their ranks to give abolitionism a gentler, more respectable air.[4]

More galling to the abolitionists was Channing's argument that organized action in reform societies vitiated the ability of the individual to rely fully upon conscience. He feared that the "age of individual action is gone," and lamented that the truth "can hardly be heard unless shouted by a crowd." He saw abolition societies, like political parties and religious sects, as divisive forces demanding narrow loyalties that sapped the independent conscience of the individual. "This moral independence" he argued, "is mightier, as well as holier, than the practice of getting warm in crowds, and of waiting for an impulse from multitudes." Part of Channing's hostility to abolitionism was rooted in his unease with the democratic impulse, but it also came out of a religious tradition that stressed self-culture as a means to achieving salvation.[5]

Leading Transcendentalists shared Channing's concern about the violence of abolitionist rhetoric and sought ways to distinguish their own opposition to slavery from that of the agitators. Both Emerson and George Ripley adopted Channing's preference for individual antislavery work over organized societies. They justified their cool attitude toward abolitionism on the grounds that reform societies necessitated an adherence to a kind of creed. "I would not be responsible for the measures of a society," Ripley told his Boston congregation in 1841. "I would have no society responsible for me." Along the same lines, Margaret Fuller told the Garrisonian abolitionist Maria Weston Chapman that "the abolition cause commands my respect as do all efforts to relieve and raise suffering human nature." But like Channing, she believed that "the faults of the [abolitionists] are such as, it seems to me, must always be incident to the partisan spirit." To Fuller, partisanship in any form was an insincere and sectarian form of public discourse that undermined individual autonomy and self-culture. Like others who were uncomfortable with the tumultuous nature of abolitionism in Boston, Fuller confessed to Chapman that she felt "sympathy with your aims if not your measures."[6]

In the early 1840s, Parker shared elements of this critique of abolitionist style. He remained independent of formal abolitionist organizations even while supporting them with his money and talent. But his own confrontations with conservative Unitarianism over theology and social reform made him more sympathetic to the crusading spirit of abolitionism than either Channing or the Transcendentalists. One key to this difference lies in the battle over antebellum public speech that placed Parker and the abolitionists on one side, and many of his fellow Transcendentalists on the other. It is important to remember that the censure Parker received for using "sneers" or "sarcasm" in public controversy often came from friends as well as enemies. Transcendentalist Elizabeth Peabody, who generally liked and admired Parker, often rebuked him for being too "sudden and quick in quarrel" and for using "innuendo" against his foes. Similar sentiments came from Caroline Healey Dall who repeatedly chided him for the use of "shock tactics" in public discourse.[7]

But Parker's conflict with his critics made him something of a partisan in the religious culture of his era and he adopted that spirit quite naturally. Indeed, he seemed always to be moving toward more confrontational modes of speech. A correspondent from the *New York Herald*, who attended Parker's Fast Day sermon in April 1846 repeatedly used words like "bluntness," "severe," "sarcastic," and "withering," to describe the talk. Yet Parker brushed all of this aside. Like the abolitionists, he had come to recognize the ways in which polite speech, conventional decorum and rhetorical obfuscation could mute the full force of conscience. "If I lose all my friends, I can't help it—I must be true to my truth not to theirs," he told Dall. For their part, the abolitionists sensed that Parker's confrontational style of address was similar to their own. As early as 1841, Garrisonian abolitionist Edmund Quincy predicted that Parker would ultimately embrace the cause without "any Emersonian or Channingian qualifications" and that "we shall get some good work out of him in some way."[8]

The criticisms that Parker received from fellow Transcendentalists indicates a growing detachment from that small circle of intellectuals. Although he had published many articles in the movement's periodical, the *Dial*, he had never been happy with what he regarded as its effete literary and philosophical tone. There was too much "Dialese" in it, by which he meant vague, insubstantial language that could only issue forth from "the 'authentic circles' of 'transcendental' men and maidens." "I suppose it is the smoke of the torches of young genius," he told Emerson rather sarcastically. "But I have sometimes found it where there was no *flame*." He found Bronson Alcott's articles particularly annoying, believing them devoid of logic and full of ill-considered, mystical "nonsense."[9]

For their own part, the *Dial's* editors sometimes recoiled at Parker's polemical style. Emerson called Parker's article on the Hollis Street Council "unpoetic, unspiritual and Un-Dialled," and he agreed to print it only "out of honor to the contributor." Parker had been much happier with the hard-hitting social criticism of Oresetes Brownson's *Boston Quarterly Review*. But Brownson's encounter with the writings of French Catholic socialist Pierre Leroux, had led him to Catholicism in 1844 and he was now using his journal and his prodigious intellect to attack the Transcendentalists generally, and Parker in particular. Finally, the fact that the Brook Farm experiment had failed to fire Parker's social imagination meant that there were fewer opportunities to work directly with those in the Transcendental orbit.[10]

As his relationships with leading Transcendentalists became more attenuated, Parker's connections with the abolitionists became stronger. During his early years at the Melodeon, he found that William Lloyd Garrison's crusading abolitionist weekly *Liberator* could be relied upon to defend him vigorously against his critics. It also promoted the Twenty-Eighth Congregational Society, where numerous abolitionists were on the membership list. Garrisonians, after all, were at least as severe in their criticisms of the churches and of social wrong as Parker was, and they recognized that his large, reform-minded congregation was a major asset in a city where opposition to abolitionism was widespread. The paper carried glowing articles on his installation service at the Melodeon including a summary of the sermon. The articles went out of their way to suggest how well attended the service was, noting that "all the seats of house, gallery, and orchestra" were filled and that the "aisles were filled with people sitting on stools."[11]

Garrison's paper also defended Parker's views in print at a time when both the liberal and orthodox religious press were attacking him and denying him the opportunity to respond. In 1845, for example, the Rev. Sylvanus Cobb of the Universalist *Christian Freeman* declared that Parker's denial of New Testament miracles made him little more than an atheist. His preaching, the editor snarled, made "Christ an imposter" and the Gospel writers "fabulists." When Cobb refused to print a letter defending Parker's right to call himself a Christian, Garrison not only published the letter in the *Liberator*, but also condemned Cobb for "unjust and unmanly conduct" as an editor. Garrison and Parker did not agree on everything, but both were passionately committed to an open and democratic public discourse.[12]

After establishing his new congregation in Boston, Parker began appearing more regularly at abolitionist events. On August 1, 1845, for example, he traveled to Dedham to speak at the West India emancipation celebration. Although disappointed by the paltry turnout for the opening procession, the event turned out to be a significant one in his public association with the antislavery movement. On the podium that day were some of the leading lights of Massachusetts abolitionism, including Edmund Quincy, Maria Weston Chapman, and Garrison himself. One of the organizers of the event was Frederick Cabot, the young West Roxbury abolitionist who had been so disappointed by Parker's refusal to read the Latimer Petition three years earlier. When called on to introduce Parker, Garrison made reference to an earlier speaker who had criticized the churches for calling abolitionists "infidels." Keenly aware that Parker had been called by the same name many times since the South Boston sermon, Garrison lightheartedly asked if he would "confirm his title to that name by antislavery action with us today?" In a symbolic gesture, and Garrison was good at those, the crusading editor affirmed the public link between Parker's new status as an activist out-

sider and his own. Parker responded in kind. Saying he knew that Garrison was
not above name calling, he was delighted to be called a name he could easily
answer to![13]

Although the turnout at Dedham was small, Parker's presence there was a
success. Elite Boston abolitionist Maria Weston Chapman, who had been so
disappointed in Parker in 1842, found his Anniversary Day speech "exceedingly
interesting and eloquent." He had pointed to an antislavery circular letter recently signed by sixty Unitarian ministers and told his fellow activists that there
were important signs of a change in public sentiment. The Dedham anniversary
event was not exactly a coming-out for Parker as an abolitionist, but his confident performance there represented a significant departure from the nervous,
hesitant minister who had disappointed the friends of Latimer in 1842.[14]

The Slave Power and the Revolution

By the time he delivered his remarks at Dedham, Parker's attitude toward the
antislavery movement in America was being transformed by events far beyond
Massachusetts. Less than six months earlier, on February 18, 1845, the Democrats in the United States Congress had forced through a joint resolution making
Texas, formerly a self-declared independent, slaveholding republic, a part of the
United States. Parker had cast his ballot for Whig candidate Henry Clay in the
1844 presidential election, hoping that the Whigs would block attempts to acquire Texas. Though he had never shown a great interest in politics, his recent
trip to Europe had heightened concern about the direction of American society
and deepened his awareness of national policy. "The most important element in
the education of a people is always the political action of the people—or the
nation," he wrote in his journal. But if political life acted as the nation's school-
master, the victory of Tennessee Democrat James K. Polk in 1844 ensured that
the lessons were going to be taught by southern slaveholders. "Education they
suspect, slavery they allow," he said of the Democrats. "I dislike their morals
and their men."[15]

In the annexation of Texas, Parker perceived the beginning of a new and
more critical era in the history of American politics dominated by the polarity
between slavery and freedom. Like Massachusetts Congressman and former
President John Quincy Adams, Parker viewed the mania for Texas annexation as
a clever bid by southern politicians to upset the sectional balance in Congress
and to open a huge western market to the domestic slave trade. As the Texas
issue linked slavery with America's political destiny, Parker's rhetoric became
stronger than before. "It is the infamy of the whole nation; it is the curse of the
very South which clamors for it with such foolish speech," he wrote not long
after annexation. "It is the drug of an evil prophet thrust into the mouth of that
fair statue our fathers set up to the Genius of Freedom."[16]

Frustrated by the weakness of the opposition, he vented his anger on George
Bancroft, the most prominent Democratic politician he knew. Bancroft had recently been defeated as the Democratic candidate for governor of Massachusetts

and he was now serving as Secretary of the Navy. In a strongly-worded letter, Parker demanded that the historian-politician either resign his post or bear the guilt of betraying American principles. "I would rather posterity said of me that, holding a place in government of the United States, I opposed that Government in its scheme of annexing a slave territory as big as the Kingdom of France," he told Bancroft. "If you do not, you falsify your own bravest words." He could only conclude that Bancroft's conscience had succumbed to lure of preferment.[17]

The growth of slavery, the blunt rejections of his theology, and his emergence as the minister of a dissident urban congregation not only prompted Parker to re-evaluate his earlier ambivalence toward abolitionism, but also to reach back into the past to reconnect with the earliest sources of his identity. On the 30th of July, 1845, just a day before his abolitionist speech at Dedham, he had gone back to his childhood home in Lexington. While there, he made a point to seek out Jonathan Harrington, the last surviving participant in the Battle of Lexington. Harrington vividly described the battle and Captain John Parker's firm command of the frightened militiamen. Accurate memories of the battle and of his famous grandfather's role in it were important to Parker that day, and he carefully took down the old man's words. "He said that Captain Parker looked as if he could face anything, and so he could," Parker wrote later. When "some offered to run," Harrington remembered, "Captain P. drew his sword and said he would run through any man who offered to run away."[18]

Listening to Harrington's narrative, Parker was struck by the parallels between Captain John Parker's part in the struggle for American independence and his own growing opposition to the designs of the Slave Power. It was as if the present had suddenly become an extension of "revolutionary time," a recapitulation and extension of the heroic world of the revolutionary past. Seen through this lens, the sectional conflict appeared to be moving toward a second confrontation between tyranny and freedom. Would Parker play a part equal to his grandfather's heroism? Were there ways of bringing American Revolutionary values and memories to bear upon the present generation's public culture? With this grandiose self-conception taking shape in his mind, the Dedham Anniversary celebration, with its small crowd, could not but disappoint him. "It was a failure," he complained that evening. "It was only a display of our nakedness."[19]

Fortunately, speaking against slavery on rural platforms with Garrisonians was not the only option. Political action, which Garrison dismissed as moral compromise appealed to a new generation of Bay State activists. Many were followers of the "Old Man Eloquent," former President John Quincy Adams who represented the Plymouth district in the House of Representatives. Adams was a hero to political antislavery activists because of his vehement protests against the Congressional "gag rule" on antislavery petitions. Carrying the mantle of the American Revolution and the prestige of an ex-President, Adams had forged a new political rhetoric that cast opposition to slavery and southern power as fidelity to America's deepest traditions. As Parker revisited the imagined terrain of revolutionary Lexington, Adams wielded the rhetorical power of the nation's past against the present ambitions of the South. During the debates over the annexation of Texas, for example, he had charged that revolutionary principles were being sacrificed to the expansion of slavery and southern power. The Founders, Adams insisted, had "pledged us, their children, to labor with united and concerted labor from the cradle to the grave, to purge the earth of all slavery."[20]

In the wake of Texas annexation, Adams led an insurgent group of Massachusetts anti-slavery or "conscience" Whigs against party regulars because of the conservatives' unwillingness to oppose the territorial designs of the South. Among his supporters was Charles Sumner, a graduate of Harvard Law School and scion of a prominent Boston family. Sumner had defied his class over the slavery issue, and now sought to build a broad-based political movement in opposition to its expansion. He condemned slavery on moral grounds, but also denigrated it as an inefficient labor system and as a violation of America's political ideals. The anti-slavery movement, he believed, "should unite the freemen of the North by all considerations of self-interest and by those considerations founded on the rights of man." Parker, whose emerging antislavery vision was comprised of similar elements, found him intriguing.[21]

In July 1845, Sumner delivered the annual Boston Fourth of July Oration on the subject of "The True Grandeur of Nations," where he first came to the attention of Theodore Parker. He had argued that "the surest token of the grandeur of nations is that Christian Beneficence which diffuses the greatest happiness among all, and that passionless, godlike justice which controls the relations of their nation to other nations." Like Adams, Sumner saw annexation as an unprincipled exploitation of weak Mexico and as a naked attempt to extend slavery. Parker was impressed by Sumner's prodigious learning and by the courage he had shown in raising the subject of slavery in public. "I wish to express to you my sense of the great value of that work and my gratitude for delivering it on such an occasion," he wrote Sumner after reading the address for the second time. "I know the reproaches you have already received from your friends—who will now perhaps become your foes."[22]

Parker keenly sympathized with Sumner's personal sacrifices and soon immersed himself in Conscience Whig writings about the slavery controversy. In the pages of their recently acquired newspaper, the *Boston Daily Whig*, Sumner, Charles Francis Adams and former Divinity School professor John Gorham Palfrey, interpreted recent political events in highly conspiratorial terms. Palfrey, whose work on biblical criticism Parker had once ridiculed, wrote at length about the existence of a "slave power" conspiracy which he defined as a corrupt alliance of southern slaveholders and short-sighted, northern merchants. This unholy brotherhood, he charged, controlled the Democratic Party and was conspiring to extend and perpetuate an institution which was totally hostile to republican values and northern interests. Palfrey also attacked Whig Party conservatives for "thinking more of sheep and cotton than of men" and for "truckling to expediency in everything, for the sake of slaveholding gold." Parker now looked with new eyes on his old theological opponent, whose "manly position with regard to slavery" he contemplated with both "admiration and delight."[23]

In the slave power conspiracy, Parker found an idea that resonated with his background, his political instincts, and his emerging critique of the merchant classes of Boston. By 1846 his sermons at the Melodeon offered his congregation much the same view of history as that being put forth by his dissident Whig friends. "It was not enough to have Louisiana a Slave Territory" he told his congregation at the Melodeon. "We must have yet more slave soil...to bind the Southern yoke yet more securely to the Northern neck." Drawing on Adams and Sumner, Parker told his flock that the annexation of Texas was a "movement hostile to the American idea—a movement to extend slavery" and blamed it on the "politicians who pulled the strings." The South was the primary target of his jeremiad, but he pointed out that northern opposition to the political demands of the Slave Power was paltry. The selfish monetary interests of the northern merchants, he suspected, were again blunting the conscience of New England and threatening to bury the revolutionary tradition. "The eyes of the North are full of cotton," he told his congregation at the Melodeon. "They see nothing else, for a web is before them; their ears are full of cotton and they hear nothing but the buzz of their mills."[24]

As in his sermons on the "perishing" and "dangerous" classes of Boston, Parker refused to question his faith in conscience as the engine of progress, but instead castigated those who had little excuse but their selfishness in not acting upon its dictates. Yet in all of this, there was a personal dimension. In preserving the "American idea" and defending the legacy of the Revolution, Parker believed that he might now stand in his Grandfather's place.

The Mexican-American War

As the United States moved closer to war with Mexico in the spring of 1846, Parker began experiencing signs of physical breakdown. For nearly a year before his permanent move to Boston, he preached in both West Roxbury and Boston each week while giving a full complement of lyceum lectures. In Boston, his days were filled with parish visits, sermon and lecture writing, requests for financial assistance, meetings with committees and, of course, intense reading. Some of the burden was eased by the services of Hannah Stevenson, an unmarried, thirty-nine year old parishioner who began living at the Parkers' Exeter Place home. Reform-minded and supportive of abolitionism, Stevenson acted as Parker's personal secretary and sounding board. Perhaps her most important task was to fend off throngs of visitors who might overtax the minister's health.[25]

But Stevenson could do little to break the habits of overwork that Parker imposed on himself. He began experiencing problems with balance, blinding headaches, and the onset of a serious respiratory infection which he feared might be tuberculosis, the disease which had carried off most of his family. Later he would complain that when he awoke in the morning, the left side of his body, and both hands, were numb. In July 1846, he left Boston for a month vacation in upstate New York and lower Ontario, but returned without fully recovering of his health. He couldn't ride a horse very long without becoming exhausted and he sometimes found that writing sermons was beyond his endurance. Still, he agreed to give more than twenty lyceum lectures all over eastern Massachusetts and New Hampshire in the fall.[26]

Fighting through his physical problems, Parker read daily newspaper accounts of American forces advancing toward the Rio Grande River. Though the Polk administration claimed it was seeking a diplomatic solution to the border dispute with Mexico, antislavery critics suspected that Polk's demands for new slave territory would not stop at the Rio Grande. They asked how a diplomatic solution could be reached while American troops moved against Mexican positions. When war was declared, Whig Governor George Briggs of Massachusetts called for volunteers to represent the Bay State in the United States Army. Parker was indignant and he volunteered to speak against the war at the New England Antislavery Convention at Faneuil Hall on June 4th. The hall was filled, and the atmosphere was decidedly rowdy as a crowd of "noisy and reckless youths" continually interrupted the speakers with boos and catcalls.[27]

This was a new environment for Parker, nothing in his experience as a preacher or lyceum lecturer could have prepared him for it. Yet despite his illness, he was thrilled by the experience, interacting easily with the crowd and talking back to the young toughs who challenged him. Resting on his oratorical and performance skills, rather than on his authority as a minister, he waded into the roiling debate with supreme confidence. At one point he asked: "would any Democrat march to Mexico to extend the area of slavery?" When hecklers shouted "Yes!", Parker immediately shot back "Then Go!" and received the applause and laughter of supporters. This was not exactly the Lexington town green in 1775, but here was the grandson of the famous Captain braving the displeasure of a potentially violent crowd with great coolness and determination. According to observers, the overall effect of his speech was "electric."[28]

The content of the remarks he offered that night foreshadowed the explosive mixture of moral individualism and American Revolutionary memory that would supercharge his activism in the following decade. He argued that the Slave Power had "trodden the Constitution under foot" by annexing Texas, and charged that Massachusetts was showing itself an apostate to its revolutionary heritage by obeying Gov. Briggs's request for volunteers. Once again his diagnosis was that the lust for profits was blunting the force of conscience. "The former creed was 'I believe in God Almighty,'" he told a crowd that cheered and hissed him at the same time. "Now it is 'I believe in the Gold Eagle Almighty, I believe in the Silver Dollar almighty, I believe in the copper cent almighty.'" According to the Boston Bee, Parker recommended "no cooperation" with Briggs's request, and compared the refusal to fight against Mexico with "refusing to obey Hutchinson and Gage." Later that evening, he put his name to a series of resolutions that denounced the Polk administration as a "pack of lawless murderers" and calling for "primary assemblies of the people" to establish "a new bond of a Union." As for individual citizens, the convention resolved that "no citizen is under any obligation of patriotism or of honor to aid this unparalleled outrage against a sister republic."[29]

Parker denounced the war a second time less than a week later at the Melodeon. This time, however, he did so in terms that reflected the northern sectional values of his friends among the Conscience Whigs. His "Sermon of War" condemned military aggression as "a sin—a national infidelity," but his central theme was the incompatibility of military conflict with northern economic prosperity. "In war the capitalist is uncertain and slow to venture," he explained. "So the laborer's hand will be still and his child hungry." Using a massive collection of statistics drawn from government sources, he showed that military spending diverted precious capital resources away from productive industry that would otherwise benefit the nation as a whole. "Your fleets, forts, dockyards, arsenals. . . and the like are provided at great cost and yet are unprofitable," he argued. "They weave no cloth, they break no bread."[30]

But if the war posed an economic threat to the North, Parker was just as convinced that it eroded the moral discipline essential to republican government. "The Soldier's life generally unfits a man for the citizen's," he asserted. "Every camp is a school of profanity, violence, licentiousness, and crimes too foul to name." The passions which war excited, and the negative ideals of violence and destruction that it taught young men were proof, just as Sumner had argued, that it belonged to a barbarous age. In a revision of older republican thought, he told his parishioners that the immorality which surrounded a soldier undermined his subsequent ability to live as a sober, vigilant, and independent citizen in a republican society. The American Revolution had been a struggle for "the unalienable rights of man," but Parker noted that many of its veterans had been "ruined for life—debauched, intemperate, vicious and vile."[31]

Yet Parker saw a marked contrast between the Mexican-American War and the Revolution. The latter was a war "for the idea that all men are born free and equal," while the former was "a movement for the extension of slavery." Since the Slave Power had provoked the conflict to extend its economic and political power, Parker advised his congregation not to support it in any way. "Men will call us traitors," he warned, "but that hurt nobody in '76." Slavery was a retrograde force in American history that threatened to undo the work of the revolutionary generation, so a new kind of republican vigilance was necessary to preserve the ongoing work of liberty. He confessed that he thought very "lightly of what is called treason against a government," and warned his parishioners that treason might, under certain circumstances, become a duty. "Certainly it was our father's duty not long ago," he reminded them. Once again, the revolution was becoming a present reality.[32]

The "Sermon of War" was very popular with the abolitionists. The Liberator called it "fearless and timely," and Garrison estimated that "ten thousand dollars could not be better expended than in giving it a gratuitous circulation throughout the country." Several editions of the sermon did appear in 1846, with at least one of them reaching the army itself. Major Ethan Allen Hitchcock, a Vermont Unitarian on his way to Mexico aboard the U.S.S. Massachusetts, sent Parker a letter stating his agreement "with your view of this abominable war." Hitchcock was a career army officer and had just been appointed to General

Winfield Scott's personal staff as the coordinator of military intelligence. He had read everything of Parker's he could find, including the *Discourse of Religion* and the translation of De Wette. Sensing a deep conflict between his duty as a military officer and his disgust at what he believed was an "unjust" and "needless" war, Hitchcock resigned himself to "obey the orders of the constituted authorities of the government until the people shall see fit to change the government." But in the meantime, he hoped his letter to Parker would ensure that he would "not fall victim to this war without uttering my protest."[33]

The annexation of Texas and the Mexican-American War had radicalized Parker's views on the slavery issue. But there is no better gauge of the distance he had travelled than his response to the fugitive slave crisis of September 1846, the biggest case of its kind since the Latimer affair four years earlier. A slave known only as "George" had hidden himself aboard the brig *Ottoman*, which had sailed to Boston from New Orleans. The crew discovered the stowaway before the ship reached Boston harbor, but he escaped and reached the South Boston shore before being recaptured by the *Ottoman*'s captain James Hannum. He was then chained and taken aboard the *Niagra*, a commercial bark scheduled to return to New Orleans in short order. In a desperate attempt to prevent the man's return, the abolitionists secured a writ of habeas corpus from Judge Samuel Hubbard of the Supreme Judicial Court of Massachusetts. Unfortunately, the Deputy Sheriff's delay in serving the writ allowed the *Niagra* to leave Boston with the chained fugitive still on board.[34]

Boston's antislavery community called a mass meeting at Faneuil Hall to register disgust at the city's shameful conduct in the affair. Chairing the meeting was John Quincy Adams and other speakers included abolitionist Wendell Phillips, reformer Samuel Gridley Howe, and antislavery Whig Charles Sumner. Theodore Parker was also there, and he was on fire. Later, when he was accused of giving a "rowdy speech," he could only say that he had had "the soul of a rowdy that night" and that an "honest blood spoke in me, through me." He called for bold action against laws that justified war and that permitted the enslavement of human beings to take place on the sacred soil of Boston. Once, he said, a small group of stout men had met in Faneuil Hall and passed resolutions that "went abroad" and shook the world. Now political parties passed resolutions that "cannot be heard from the North End to the Neck." What was needed was braver men whose "lives show they can be trusted in the times that try men's souls." God's law was imprinted upon the hearts and minds of all human beings and none could claim ignorance of its demands. It "transcends and over-rides all the statutes of men." Parker's revolutionary conscience was beginning to take shape.[35]

X
MAKING ANTISLAVERY CULTURE
1847–1850

In the late 1840s, Parker carved out a distinctive place for himself on the ideo-logically charged landscape of the New England antislavery movement. On the one hand, he had fully identified himself with the abolitionists, speaking from their platforms, joining their protests, and writing for their periodicals. In his withering, often sarcastic criticisms of the church and state, he could sound like a Garrisonian and suffered the censure of friends who thought he went too far. At the same time, however, he refused to forsake political approaches to aboli-tionism and built productive relationships with non-Garrisonian forces among the Massachusetts abolitionists. And he worked exceptionally well with Con-science Whigs like Charles Sumner who were sympathetic to abolitionism but who refused to endorse immediate emancipation as the antislavery societies did.

The pluralistic public culture that Parker had endorsed in his conflict with Unitarian and orthodox religious leaders now spilled over into his role as an abolitionist. He believed that in reform movements, as much as in theology, progress depended upon free and dialogic expressions of conscience, especially when real differences existed between sincere people. He attempted to forge an irenic antislavery culture embracing abolitionists from across the movement's complex ideological spectrum. His success in this endeavor hinged upon a re-markable ability to rework the symbols of American Revolutionary memory and the themes of New England's regional culture, in ways that appealed to a broad array of activists. The vehicle he chose to develop this point of view was the *Massachusetts Quarterly Review*, a journal which he edited for three years. Like the Twenty-Eighth Congregational Society, where the various manifestations of conscience were harmonized by its minister's larger commitment to progress, the *Massachusetts Quarterly Review* used history and memory to unite the dis-parate voices of Massachusetts' dissenting culture.

'The Field is Broad Enough for Us All'

The fact that Parker's abolitionism transcended the ideological boundaries which divided the opponents of slavery in America was at least in part a function of timing. A relative latecomer to the movement, he had not been a party to the bruising battles of the late 1830s when conflict over strategy and tactics had fractured the American Anti-Slavery Society. Such battles had little meaning for him, and he repeatedly used his position to call for unity in the movement. New York antislavery Whig William Seward was one of the few who understood Parker's potential as a consensus builder. "You seem to have apprehended things which the Anti-Slavery men are too slow in learning, that the field is broad enough for us all, of all parties, and of all positions."[1]

Yet even as he sought to transcend abolitionism's internal divisions, those conflicts were nevertheless quite real and persistent. Early abolitionists had agreed that slaveholding was "a heinous crime in the sight of God" and that "the duty, safety, and best interests of all concerned require its immediate abandonment." But by the late 1830s disagreements over the character of the movement became acute. On the "radical" side were the followers of William Lloyd Garrison who had issued blistering denunciations of northern churches for failing to endorse immediate abolition. Some Garrisonians had also adopted non-resistance, a form of Christian anarchism that rejected violence of any kind and condemned coercive human institutions, including governments, churches, and traditional marriage, as equivalent to slavery. Convinced that the Constitution and the Federal Union were fundamentally proslavery, Garrisonians condemned political parties for implicitly reaffirming the legitimacy of an evil system of government. They instead called for the dissolution of the Union and its reorganization upon the principle of universal liberty.[2]

For other abolitionists, whose hatred of slavery was as deep and sincere as that of the Garrisonians, such positions went too far. Evangelical reformers, like New York City's Arthur and Lewis Tappan, believed that radical attacks on the churches and on traditional gender roles were both offensive and counterproductive. More conservative in their theology and devoted to church-oriented reform, the Tappanites resisted Garrison's attempt to convert abolitionism into a universal reform movement. From their perspective, perfectionism, non-resistance, and especially women's rights activism, subsumed the already unpopular cause of the slave in a host of irrelevant and highly controversial issues. "They are the prolific fountain of all the evils which retard and injure the cause of abolition," wrote one such evangelical. More politically-minded activists like Gerrit Smith, James Birney, and Elizur Wright, joined the evangelicals in their revolt against Garrisonian leadership.[3]

Society when evangelical abolitionists seceded from the organization to create the American and Foreign Anti-Slavery Society. That same year, in upstate New York, political abolitionists formed the Liberty Party, an abolitionist third party dedicated to the election of immediate abolitionists to office. Expressing the hope of this new party, Elizur Wright looked forward to seeing "the executive power of this government wielded...to the utter overthrow of slavery, and the liberation of millions."[4]

When Parker entered the movement in 1845, these factions were more polarized than ever. The Garrisonians saw the annexation of Texas and the war with Mexico as confirmation of their position on the Constitution and the Union. They were disgusted that Liberty Party leaders, who had fared poorly in the 1840 and 1844 elections, were now reaching out to more moderate anti-slavery forces, including the Conscience Whigs, who merely demanded limits on the spread of slavery. Such alliances, the Garrisonians believed, would dilute the antislavery gospel with political compromises and half-measures. In its annual report for 1846, for example, the Massachusetts Anti-Slavery Society renewed its warnings against political abolitionism and instead called for the moral reconstruction of American society and politics. The M.A.S.S. secretary Francis Jackson was one of Parker's parishioners. "There is no remedy but REVOLUTION!" he wrote in the report. "A Revolution in the hearts and minds of men, but manifested in the disruption of our present delusive Union and in the overthrow of our present deceptive Constitution."[5]

Political abolitionists, by contrast, believed that the anti-southern passions awakened by the Mexican-American War created possibilities for a broader political challenge to slavery. They were elated that the Wilmot Proviso, a proposed ban on slavery in territory acquired from Mexico, had received substantial northern support in the House of Representatives. The fact that the proviso was introduced by a northern Democrat suggested that growing opposition to the designs of the Slave Power had the potential to transform the party system and force the slavery issue to the very center of American politics. Although dedicated to immediate abolition, Liberty Party leaders like James Birney and Gamaliel Bailey were open to political alliances with Conscience Whigs and antislavery Democrats who opposed only the extension of slavery. To these men, Garrisonian opposition to political action was either foolhardy or deluded.[6]

Parker was a natural mediator in this environment. In ideological terms, he was not a Garrisonian. He was critical of war and violence, but he never accepted the radical pacifism of the Non-Resistance Society. He could not help but praise the Revolutionary fathers who "fought with bloody hand," and he did not accept Garrisonian views of the Constitution. In his protests against the annexation of Texas, for example, he had argued that the Constitution's *spirit* had been violated, not that the document was itself fundamentally proslavery. Like the Bible, he argued, the Constitution's accommodation of slavery rendered it imperfect, not useless. Conscience could be a tool for reinterpreting the Constitution, just as it was for the Scriptures. The point was for the current generation to separate the document's transient proslavery errors from the permanent libertarian truths rooted in America's fundamental identity. The founders of the nation, like the authors of the biblical texts, had mixed deep insight with serious errors, but ongoing progress would build on the former and discard the latter.[7]

Yet for all of Parker's differences with them, the Garrisonians had to acknowledge his credentials as a religious radical, social critic, and bête noire of the Boston establishment. The ideologically eclectic nature of the Twenty-Eighth Congregational Society helped as well. His congregation included Garrisonians like Francis Jackson and political activists like Samuel Gridley Howe. He preached sermons against the injustice of slavery and he sought a moral revolution to eradicate it. But his mind naturally gravitated toward political solutions even as he warned against the potential compromises and temptations of political action. Underlying his preaching and activism, however, was an instinctive attachment to the memories and traditions of the American Revolution which all New England activists, black and white, shared with varying degrees of intensity.[8]

Parker took his role as a non-aligned figure seriously. When speaking from Garrisonian platforms, like the New England Antislavery Convention, he demanded unity and tolerance among the opponents of slavery. At the 1848 meeting, for instance, he argued that moral and political activism complemented each other. "We need not waste time by denunciation," he insisted. "I make no doubt it inspires the slaveholder's heart to see division among his foes." Preaching tolerance to the Garrisonians, Parker reminded them of the importance of political institutions in shaping the nation's future. "Some men will try political action," he told the New England abolitionists, "the action of the people, of the nation, it must be political." Without passing judgment upon the non-voting convictions of his Garrisonian friends, Parker exhorted them to support antislavery candidates at the polls. "I would appeal to you who are men, and have votes to cast, and see fit to cast them, to cast them on the side of right," he told a group of Worcester abolitionists in 1849. "Let us oppose slavery by sentiments, by ideas, and by actions in every form and in every place." Parker was convinced that the moral and political regeneration of America could be achieved simultaneously.[9]

The Massachusetts Quarterly Review

Parker's hopes for the regeneration of America began with his own native region. Like many antebellum New Englanders, his understanding of American national identity was rooted deeply in regional history and culture. The retrograde forces unleashed by the slaveholding South could only be resisted, Parker believed, if New England took the lead in awakening the nation to its more fundamental tradition of human rights. In late 1847, for example, he published a one-hundred page "Letter on Slavery" demonstrating his faith that New England's historic traditions could still redeem the nation as long as they were not forgotten by a generation besotted by luxury and self-interest. The march of freedom, he said, had begun with the Pilgrims who had "knelt in the sands of the wilderness" and laid the foundations of America's free institutions. Their faith had been vindicated by the sacrifices at Lexington, Concord and Bunker Hill, moments which Parker called the "Thermopylae of universal right." Would the great procession end with "the Negro Slave, bought, branded, beat?" Such could only be possible if the people of New England, in whose veins the blood of the

Pilgrims and the revolutionary heroes still flowed, forget who they were.[10]

Parker eagerly embraced the cultural work of reawakening New England, of forging a link between sectional memory and the antislavery movement, in the pages of the *Massachusetts Quarterly Review*, a journal which he co-founded in 1847 and which was devoted to "literature, politics, religion and humanity." Initially sharing editorial duties with Ralph Waldo Emerson and James E. Cabot, Parker took sole custody of the journal within a year and emerged as the dominant architect of its message. During his three years as editor, he used the *Review* to reinvent the politics and culture of New England as the larger nation struggled with the issues of war, expansion, and slavery. He was also the journal's most important contributor. His articles forged a bridge between New England's role in America's republican past, and its crucial role in transforming the nation's present. Reworking the old symbols of Puritanism and the Revolution, he derived new sectional meaning from materials as diverse as abolitionism, Free Soil politics, and the life of John Quincy Adams. Ultimately, Parker hoped to establish a New England antislavery culture that would transcend the antislavery movement's ideological divisions in ways that mirrored his personal role.[11]

This was no simple task. The new journal shared an already crowded periodical market with better established alternatives like the *North American Review*. The editors of that Brahmin publication, men like Jared Sparks and Edward Everett, were highly conservative in their understanding of New England's identity. As conservative nationalists, they equated respect for New England's past with loyalty to the Constitution and the Union, and deference to the region's genteel leadership class. For them, history was a means by which to bind Americans, especially New Englanders, to existing political arrangements and social institutions. They condemned the "vandal spirit" of abolitionism as the most serious threat to order and institutional authority. "We regret to see the abolitionists of the day seizing upon the cruelties and abuses of power by a few slaveholders," wrote Emory Washburn in the *North American Review*. "If…the Union be dissolved…our country will be plunged into the gulf."[12]

But the war and the renewed conflict over slavery raised serious questions about the proper response of New England's leaders to the growth of Southern power. When the first number of the *Massachusetts Quarterly Review* appeared in December 1847, for example, Parker used it to indict the region's prominent men for their ineffective opposition to the Mexican-American war. The problem, he argued, was the corruption of authentic sectional identity by the same merchant interests whose selfishness and greed left the "perishing" and "dangerous classes" to their fate in the streets of Boston. This time, it was the slaves who were being sacrificed on the altar of money. "New England could have prevented [the war]," he maintained, "but a false idea had gone abroad in New England—that southern slavery is profitable to the North." Convinced that New England possessed the latent moral and political energy to rescue the nation from its "delirium," he feared that the commercial ties between conservative New England textile interests and the slaveholding South had vitiated the section's ability to speak in its truest voice. "The 'chivalry' [of the South] and the 'morality' [of New England] have one common affection," he argued, "the love of gain." This unholy alliance had not only prevented New England's effective opposition to the war, but had also produced an attitude of base servility toward the South that betrayed the spirit of the revolutionary generation. Quoting Shakespeare, Parker suggested that New England had long ago learned "to crook the pregnant hinges of the knee/Where thrift may follow fawning."[13]

In choosing to fawn for commercial or political gain rather than to follow New England's historic principles, Massachusetts' conservative politicians became the central targets of Parker's editorial invective. Sensitive to the Puritan as well as revolutionary sources of New England's identity, he took great pleasure in castigating Boston's conservative Whig representative Robert C. Winthrop as the only member of his state's delegation to cast a vote in favor of the Mexican-American war. Winthrop bore one of the most famous names from Massachusetts' colonial past, and his Whig politics had made him a symbol of New England values around the North. But his vote on the war personified Parker's fears about the death of a vital sectional tradition and signified a fraying of the links between New England's present politics and its founding mythology. Invoking the same historical themes that men like Winthrop and Webster had long used to uphold national institutions, Parker now used the heart of New England's Puritan identity to shame them. "In that puritanic blood of theirs was there no tinge from the heart of the Pilgrim?" he wondered.[14]

If Parker used the *Massachusetts Quarterly Review* to accuse the conservatives of treachery to New England's historic identity, his editorial mission also reflected a forward-looking program for sectional rebirth. Intimately connected to his vision of a revitalized, antislavery New England culture was a desire to strengthen the position of Conscience Whigs whose vocal support for the Wilmot Proviso had put them at odds with Webster and Winthrop and threatened their place in Boston society. Having experienced the cold stares and stony silences of Massachusetts' polite society, Parker knew all too well the emotional and intellectual stamina required from those who engaged in robust dissent. Writing of the Conscience Whigs in an 1848 article in the *Review*, Parker remarked that "the members of the family of Truth are unpopular...while the members of the family of Interest are all respectable, and are the best company in the world; their livery is attractive." Parker saw the "Young Whigs" as a new breed of principled New England statesmen whose opposition to slavery needed intellectual support and personal encouragement. In accusing conservatives like Webster and Winthrop of betraying the memory of Pilgrim "outcasts," he hoped to shift the mantle of sectional authenticity to a new generation of antislavery leaders who could carry the banner of sectional culture into state and national government. [15]

Sending the first number of the *Review* to John Gorham Palfrey as a gift in December 1847, he praised the "manly position" Palfrey had taken since being elected to Congress in 1846 and encouraged him to defy the censure of those who lacked the moral courage to stand up for their region's principles. Parker consoled his former professor that censure always fell upon those whose moral sentiments were far in advance of their times. "It is not in the power of New Englanders often to do such deeds as you have done," he told Palfrey, and he promised to do whatever he could to "pluck a thorn out of your path." Intellectual support from the *Massachusetts Quarterly Review* was at least a partial attempt to fulfill that promise. Charles Sumner was impressed enough to send Palfrey a second copy of Parker's article on the Mexican-American War, urging him to read its "stinging conclusion against the course of leading politicians."[16]

As Parker's political friends attempted to regenerate the Massachusetts Whig Party on the basis of antislavery principles, he sought to provide them with models of political conduct that conformed to New England's "authentic" past. John Quincy Adams's death in February 1848 offered a unique opportunity to illustrate the qualities of a statesman whose name was almost synonymous with New England and whose political career abounded with antislavery and anti-southern principles. Appearing in the July 1848 number of the *Review*, Parker's "Discourse on the Death of John Quincy Adams" was the product of extensive correspondence with these same antislavery Whigs who had known Adams personally during his congressional career. Even though his discourse was presented as an "impartial" assessment of the former president's life, Parker's carefully crafted image of Adams actually reflects the same selective revision of sectional memory that marks so many of his contributions to the *Review*. Detailing aspects of Adams's life that supported an antislavery conception of New England's identity, Parker used the "old man eloquent" as an emblem of the region's potential and as standard by which to judge its current generation of politicians. As a form of "symbolic biography," his eulogy transmitted an understanding of Adams's life that would help commit New England to antislavery politics.[17]

As he constructed his work on Adams, Parker was acutely aware of the ongoing, high-stakes politics surrounding the memory of the former president's life. The conservative and antislavery wings of the Massachusetts Whig Party struggled mightily to harness the meaning of Adams's political career to their own values. In Congress, Robert Winthrop had already eulogized Adams without once mentioning the antislavery struggles that had so marked his post-presidential career. As speaker of the House of Representatives, he refused to recognize any member likely to mention such divisive issues. In Boston, Edward Everett's bland eulogy of Adams in the Massachusetts State House on April 15, 1848, was similarly devoid of controversial subjects. Conservatives like Winthrop and Everett were preparing to unite their party behind Louisiana slaveholder Zachary Taylor. To them it was crucial that Adams's commitment to the Union be emphasized above his antislavery principles. Antislavery Whigs like Charles Sumner were furious about these developments. Sumner complained bitterly that even Adams's physical remains were being attended by a Congressional Committee "on which was placed the most prominent Southern and South Western slaveholding partizans of General Taylor." He was convinced that this attempt to downplay Adams's antislavery views was part of a political conspiracy to rally Massachusetts behind unacceptable moral and political compromises over slavery in the territories.[18]

Responding to the conflict over Adams's legacy in the June 1848 number of the *Review*, Parker carefully constructed an image of the former president that emphasized both the antislavery aspects of his public career and his overall fidelity to New England's "authentic mission." Adams was a "New England man," whose childhood amidst "the roar of cannon at Lexington and Bunker Hill" gave him a direct connection to the Revolution. Unlike Daniel Webster or Robert Winthrop, Parker's Adams had never allowed New England's commercial identity to "violate the ideas of the Revolution" and had repeatedly refused to "put on the collar, lie lies...and consent to slavery." He had understood New England's identity and its interests in an expansive sense that linked democracy, morality, and economic progress to an unswerving commitment to individual liberty. Adams's public life, Parker asserted, transcended Daniel Webster's narrow commitment to commercial interests and instead embraced the unified brand of progress that only New England could offer the nation. "Mr. Adams loved his dollar as well as most New England men," Parker acknowledged, "but he loved justice more, honor more, freedom more." Clothed in Parker's rhetoric, Adams became a symbol of the bustling democracy, productive energy, and moral order of New England's towns and cities. The great challenge for the next generation of New Englanders was to prove that they were worthy of the legacy left by this regional hero.[19]

In his description of Adams's highly visible role in the protests against the return of the *Ottoman* fugitive slave, moreover, Parker used the former president's physical presence at Faneuil Hall to weave a symbolic link between New England's revolutionary leadership and the antislavery imperatives of the present. "That old man sat in the chair at Faneuil Hall; above him was the image of his father; around him were Hancock and the other Adams," he remembered. "Before him were the men and women of Boston, met to consider the wrongs done to a miserable Negro slave; the roof of the Cradle of Liberty spanned them all." While the omnipresent monuments and images of New England's revolutionary past were intended to consecrate the institutions of the founding generation, Parker now used his periodical to equate New England's identity and traditions with a higher law. The merchant interests of Boston were ready to cringe in obedience to the slaveholders, but Adams's "New England knee bent only before his God."[20]

The eulogy of Adams was well received by political antislavery forces in New England and beyond. "My article on [Adams] has met with more favor than anything else I ever wrote," he told a New York correspondent. "It has been circulated very widely and I hope it will do some good work." Veteran Liberty Party candidate James Birney was so pleased with it that he sent Parker a five dollar note for a year's subscription to the *Review* and proposed to write an article of his own on slavery for a subsequent issue. Birney understood that Parker's positive assessment of Adams's life reflected a profound dissatisfaction with New England's present class of leaders. "Compared with other public men now on the theater of action...I esteem him as highly as you do," he wrote. But he also commended Parker for refusing to write a traditional commemorative eulogy of Adams. Birney expressed disgust with eloquent eulogies that had suffocated the legacy of the dead in monotonous factual detail or rhetorical excess. "After reading through the dull sophomorical effusions which Mr. Adams' death gave rise to in Congress," Birney told Parker, "[your remarks] especially commend themselves to me as the first honest attempt to benefit the living by a public, impartial account of the dead." In combining symbolic biography with postmortem criticism, Parker's approach to the memory of John Quincy Adams verged on Birney's ideal.[21]

Parker's contributions to the *Review* continued the dissenting style of public speech that had angered his Brahmin critics and pleased his lyceum audiences. Unlike Webster and Everett, whose renderings of sectional history were often nostalgic or overtly celebratory, Parker's more critical approach to the past grated on the ears of conservatives and verged on the abolitionist style that so deeply offended them. In a review of Richard Hildreth's *History of the United States*, for example, he reminded his readers that Massachusetts had once passed laws punishing heretics with "whipping, banishment, or with death." He said he knew of some people who would be "glad to revive these pleasant statutes in the present day" and then use them against certain dissenting clergymen. These sorts of comments irritated the conservative guardians of culture. His pen "flourishes along too flippant a course to inspire much confidence in he who wields it," complained Boston's weekly *Christian Register*. The Unitarian *Christian Examiner* warned its readers that Parker's articles were likely to "disturb some sensibilities and offend some convictions." Unable to denounce the *Review* simply as an organ of radical abolitionism, Massachusetts conservatives were nevertheless aware that the new journal had emerged as a platform for alternative understandings of both past and present.[22]

Yet for all his success in creating a usable sectional memory, Parker's rhetoric sometimes created interpretive difficulties, especially when it confronted the rapidly shifting antebellum political scene. In 1848, for example, the dramatic revolt of Bay State Conscience Whigs and the formation of the Massachusetts Free Soil Party initially convinced him that Puritan self-reliance and the revolutionary spirit were replacing the false patriotism of conservative leaders. "Massachusetts has shown herself worthy of her best days," he wrote of the Free Soil vote in 1848. "Mr. Webster's thunder [fell] harmless and without lightning, from his hands." But New England's electoral weakness, its internal divisions, and the realities of political compromise made such an interpretation difficult to sustain. When the Free Soil convention chose former Democratic President Martin Van Buren, rather than New Hampshire's John P. Hale, as its presidential candidate, Parker was disappointed. That this noble New England conscience could be overlooked by the new party in favor of a calculating New Yorker like Van Buren was exasperating. It also undermined Parker's attempt to connect the free soil movement with his revised sectional memory. Grieved at the news of the party's choice, Parker sarcastically linked the New York "fox" to the mem-

ory of an earlier tempter of New England virtue. "Naughty men say Van is the
son of Aaron Burr," Parker told abolitionist Samuel May. "There is a certain
spiritual similarity between the two."[23]

The persistent ideological conflict within the New England antislavery
movement provided equally serious rhetorical problems. Believing that the Free
Soil movement represented an egregious dilution of moral principle, for example, Garrisonian abolitionists denounced it. While Sumner and other Free Soilers
had laid claim to New England's revolutionary memory in building their movement, radical abolitionists explicitly denied the legitimacy of such a connection.
"The Free Soil Party...is not in its nature and avowed purposes a Revolutionary
Party," argued the Massachusetts Anti-Slavery Society. "As long as it intends to
be true to the political compromises of the Constitution, it is a Pro-Slavery
party." Parker's editorial emphasis on sectional memory had been intended in
part as a bridge between New England's divided antislavery forces, but he discovered that New England's past was still very much contested ground.[24]

Unwilling simply to concede the field to Garrisonian criticisms, Parker returned to the *Massachusetts Quarterly Review*. His 1848 article on the "Free
Soil Movement" defended the new party's "revolutionary" significance against
doubtful radical critics, while building a case for its fidelity to New England's
sectional traditions. Not surprisingly, the result was a rather strained combination of generalities and contradictions. On the one hand, he declared that Free
Soilism represented an unstoppable "revolution in ideas" that linked the principles of 1776 to an inevitable future "revolution in deeds." In their opposition to
the "Dynasty of slaveholders" who were manipulating the federal government
into extending slavery, New England Free Soil politicians like Hale, Palfrey, and
Sumner were true heirs of the revolutionary generation's "determination to govern themselves." At the same time, however, he had to concede that the party
was not hostile to "the American state, and therefore makes no revolution there."
In accepting that Free Soilism was basically consistent with the Constitution,
Parker seemed to yield to the radicals' most basic point.[25]

But Parker's self-conscious role as a neutral broker between Garrisonians
and the political antislavery movement necessitated a strong effort to construct a
shared history and destiny. In a striking, commemorative review of New England's antislavery history since 1831, Parker depicted the abolitionists and Free
Soilers as interdependent forces for sectional progress. The Free Soil movement,
he contended, had benefited from seventeen years of heroic and successful New
England antislavery activism. He reminded his readers that Garrison and the
radical abolitionists had long endured "the scorn, the loathing, the contempt of
mankind" for the sake of "the most abused and despised class of men." Like the
Plymouth Pilgrims whose "small beginnings" had been "mocked" by their own
contemporaries, these latter day seekers had also "forgotten self interest in
search of a great truth."[26]

Just as the revolutionaries of 1776 had vindicated the sacrifice of their Pilgrim Fathers, so New England's support for the Free Soil Party in the 1848 election represented a partial vindication of the abolitionists' early sacrifices. "When

intelligent men mock at small beginnings, it is surprising that they cannot remember that the greatest institutions have had their times which tried men's
souls," he mused. Laboring mightily to elevate memory above ideology in uniting the progressive forces of his region, Parker described antislavery radicals as
New England's conscience and as part of the vital, living bridge between his
section's historic struggles and its present "revolution in ideas." Sometimes inconsistent, and always selective, Parker's periodical rhetoric recast New England's puritan and revolutionary experiences as wellsprings for transforming the
present. The result was an antislavery vision in which the past and present
merged in a progressive alliance that promised the inevitable "triumph of the
genius of freedom." [27]

In October 1850, Parker informed a correspondent in New York that there
would be no further numbers of the *Massachusetts Quarterly Review*. "[It] came
to an end directly through the failure of the publishers," he wrote, "though they
always found the *Review* profitable to them." After three extremely laborious
years as the journal's editor, leading contributor, and financial supporter, Parker
was frustrated at the failure of the project while at the same time relieved to be
free of its incessant demands on his time. Escalating conflict in Boston over the
Fugitive Slave Act of 1850 and Parker's role as one of the city's most militant
opponents of the law had already come to dominate his attention. A central figure in the organization of Boston's Vigilance Committee, he would soon emerge
as a valuable link between the city's black community, its abolitionists, and its
political antislavery forces. Moving comfortably between activists of widely
differing ideological persuasions, he consciously sought to build a resistance
movement upon the provocative sectional images that had emerged in his increasingly militant speeches and in the pages of his periodical. "Plymouth, the
altar stone of New England," and "Bunker Hill, the spot so early reddened with
the blood of our fathers," had now become monuments to the future as much as
to the past. It was on that imagined landscape that the grandson of Captain John
Parker would demand fidelity to a revolutionary conscience that that been nearly
two decades in the making.[28]

XI
CONSCIENCE AND THE FUGITIVE SLAVE ACT
1850

In November 1850, Theodore Parker wrote an emotional letter to his friend James Martineau in Liverpool, England about recent events in America. "The Fugitive Slave Act was passed last September," he began. "It is one of the most atrocious acts passed since the first persecutions of the Christians by Nero." In bitter language he described the basic provisions of the law. Federal court-appointed Fugitive Slave Commissioners were now empowered to hear evidence from southern slave hunters and to issue warrants for the arrest of alleged fugitives. "The slave hunter takes [the warrant] to the Marshal, the Marshal makes the arrest and the poor victim is hurried off to slavery as hopeless as the grave," he wrote. "[A]ll this may be done without allowing the fugitive to defend himself with no inquest by a jury." In addition to these offensive provisions, Fugitive Slave Commissioners would receive higher fees for handing down convictions rather than acquittals. Anyone caught assisting fugitive slaves or obstructing the law faced fines and imprisonment.[1]

Martineau was an English Unitarian with deeply held antislavery views and a belief in the sanctity of conscience that rivaled Parker's own. But the impact of the letter must have been especially powerful, as it was delivered in person by William and Ellen Craft, escaped slaves who had only narrowly avoided arrest and rendition at the hands of Boston authorities. The couple's flight from America embodied the terrible human costs of the new law. As their minister, Parker had helped send the Crafts to England in order to avoid further assaults on their freedom. Not surprisingly, he could not resist the grim irony of two fugitives from tyranny and oppression seeking their freedom in the land of the redcoats. "I thank God that Old England, with all her sins and shames, allows no Slave Hunter to set foot on her soil," he concluded.[2]

The Fugitive Slave Act created a harsh, new reality for African Americans in Boston and presented both serious challenges and new opportunities to the antislavery community. In eliminating jury trials and other basic due process guarantees, the new law made free black residents of the city even more vulnerable to kidnapping and enslavement. Slaveholders needed only a bill of sale and a single witness willing to swear to the identity of the accused fugitive. Defendants were prohibited from challenging the evidence against them, making race the over-riding evidentiary factor. Such obvious corruption of the law enraged abolitionists and raised doubts about the efficacy of the movement's commitment to non-violent activism. Organized resistance to federal enforcement raised the possibility of direct confrontation with slave hunters, the police, government officials, or even the military. But at the same time, the law represented a unique opportunity to move the fight over slavery out of the realm of ideas and into the streets of northern communities. Scenes of slave hunters chasing fugitives across the historic landscape of Boston generated outrage beyond the abolitionist community and offered the possibility of building a broader antislavery alliance.

Theodore Parker's deep sensitivity to Boston's landscape of memory was, along with his belief in the power of conscience to transform human history, the key to his opposition to the law. During the debate over the passage of the law and in the dramatic crises over enforcement that followed, he reminded his contemporaries of the ideal Boston, forged in the crucible of the American Revolution and lying just beneath the surface the city's contemporary life. As a romantic intellectual, he believed that the world of the senses offered analogies to a deeper, ideal reality which, when fully understood, could be reflected back upon the physical world in the form of transformative action.[3]

The battle to ensure that this ideal, revolutionary Boston played its part in defeating the Fugitive Slave Act involved struggles over the reliability of conscience and over the meaning of the city's public spaces. Massachusetts conservatives had their own understanding of the region's past and present, and they marshaled it in favor of the law and the preservation of the Union. They claimed Faneuil Hall and the Boston courthouse as symbols of conservative nationalism, a responsible, moderate approach to sectional differences built upon law and ordered liberty. They derided the notion that individual moral judgment could outweigh the demands of law and they celebrated the ties that bound the existing Union together. Parker and the abolitionists, however, claimed those same symbols and public spaces as monuments to their expansive conception of liberty. It was in these places where Boston, and by extension America, could find the inspiration to heed the dictates of conscience and resist the Slave Power's war upon freedom.[4]

The Conservative Conscience

Conflict over the Fugitive Slave Act began even before the law was passed, and it generated a fascinating debate over the meanings of conscience, patriotism and citizenship. On March 7th, 1850, the prestigious Senator from Massachusetts, Daniel Webster, shocked many of his constituents by calling for the passage of the fugitive slave bill and the other measures which became the Compromise of 1850. Webster was desperately trying to hold the national Whig Party together in the midst of intense sectional discord and to safeguard his own presidential prospects. His speech castigated northern and southern radicals for threatening the Union, but it also explicitly condemned the northern personal liberty laws as an unwarranted, unconstitutional break with traditions of interstate comity and cooperation. On that issue, he argued that the "South is right, and the North is wrong."[5]

Webster's influence in New England created significant political problems for opponents of the law, but his speech offered a deeper message that Boston's antislavery community would have to confront. In short, Webster argued that men like Parker over-rated the power of conscience to discern moral duty. Such certainty, he maintained, had produced a "fanaticism" in both sections that threatened the survival of the Union. Abolitionists and secessionists shared an arrogant dogmatism that stood ready to sacrifice America's most precious political institutions on the altar of their own fallible principles. The cardinal error made by the abolitionists, he said, was a tendency to "deal with morals as with mathematics" and a mistaken view that "what is right may be distinguished from what is wrong with the precision of a mathematical equation." Here was the establishment answer to the conscience-driven dissenting culture that Parker had worked so hard to create.[6]

Although ironic coming from a man with a legendary ego, Webster called for humility in moral judgment and for recognition that the claims of conscience must be balanced against other, equally legitimate duties. After all, he argued, did the authority of private judgment entirely outweigh the historic bonds forged between the sections at the time of the Constitution and the allegiance that all Americans owed to institutions created by the Revolution? To Webster, that kind of uncompromising moral certainty was incompatible with democratic forms of government which required an acceptance of human fallibility. It produced angry people who were "apt to think that nothing is good but what is perfect" and who were unwilling to make "compromises or modifications...in consideration of differences of opinion."[7]

Webster's decision to attack the antislavery understanding of conscience generated support from religious conservatives who had their own grievances against transcendental moral philosophy. Perhaps the most important endorsement came from the Rev. Moses Stuart, a renowned biblical scholar at Andover Seminary in Massachusetts. Stuart was an important backer of the Compromise of 1850 and an admirer of its Bay State architect. As the debate over Webster's speech heated up, Stuart weighed into the controversy with a long, sometimes rambling pamphlet entitled *Conscience and the Constitution*. Recognizing that the idea of conscience and its relation to traditional sources of Christian authority was at the core of the bitter debate over fugitive slaves, Stuart insisted that biblical sanctions for slavery and the political duties of citizenship overruled private moral judgment.

Stuart believed, as did most contemporary moralists, that the conscience was a real, but rudimentary faculty of the mind. To function properly, it required instruction from external sources of authority including the Bible, the Church and the State. After all, he argued, there are "all sorts of consciences, very diverse and even opposite." The idea of conscience that Parker preached was "wholly subjective" and could be used to justify any action. What distinguished a "Christian conscience" from the subjective "passions and prejudices" of individuals was fidelity to biblical principles. Stuart was not comfortable with southern arguments that slavery was a "positive good", but he believed that the institution could only be ended safely by a gradual process of reform and voluntary emancipation. In the meantime, the Bible, the law and the Constitution required American citizens to cooperate in returning fugitive slaves to their owners.[8]

The biblical component of Stuart's argument required some careful exegesis because of a well-known passage from Deuteronomy 23 that commanded the Israelites not to return a fugitive slave, but rather to allow him to "live among you wherever he likes." For once, the abolitionists believed that a literal interpretation of the Scripture strengthened their position. But Stuart's considered opinion was that Moses had meant such a rule to apply only to slaves of "heathen" origins whose masters were barbarous and cruel, not to Israelite owners whose treatment of their slaves was regulated by divine law. He supported this view by a close exegesis of Paul's letter to Philemon in which the Apostle returned a Christian slave to a Christian master. "Paul's Christian conscience," Stuart insisted, "would not allow him to injure the vested rights of Philemon." This view was not unique to Stuart. Historian Laura Mitchell, who has surveyed the public preaching record of northern ministers, both liberal and orthodox, between 1850 and 1854, could find only a handful opposed to Stuart's position.[9]

In addition to its reaffirmation of Webster's attack on abolitionist moral thought, Stuart's pamphlet was almost fawning in its praise of the senator's disinterested statesmanship and devotion to the Union. His sentiments were echoed by members of Boston's Whig establishment who publicly defended their leader. On April 12, the *Boston Daily Advertiser* carried a letter of thanks to Webster signed by over 700 citizens who lauded the Senator for his efforts towards "the preservation and perpetuation of the Union." Among them were the Presidents and leading lights of both Harvard University and Andover seminary, leading Unitarian clergyman, prominent Boston lawyers such as Rufus Choate and Edward Loring, and merchants like William Appleton, whose textile businesses depended upon smooth economic relations with Southern planters. For this group, the Fugitive Slave Bill was important not only as a Union-saving measure, but also because its enforcement in Boston would remove the radical taint placed on the city by incendiaries like Garrison, Phillips, and Parker.[10]

Yet even with the backing of Boston's Brahmin elite and the intellectual support of clergymen like Stuart, Webster was taking a terrible gamble. In endorsing a law that legally required the participation of Massachusetts citizens in the capture and rendition of fugitive slaves, the Senator exposed himself to the accusations of truckling to an aggressive Slave Power. Robert Winthrop believed that the 7th of March Speech would have "killed any northern man except" Webster, and he acknowledged that conservatives would have "hard work" to sustain themselves against critics of the speech.[11]

He was right to be concerned. Even the usually moderate editors of the *Christian Register* were shocked by Webster's dismissal of the moral dimensions of the slavery issue. They feared that he had gone too far in advocating "a law which must come directly in conflict with the moral convictions of the great body of the people in the Free states." More vehement condemnation came from Conscience Whigs like Charles Sumner who compared Webster's conduct to that of Judas Iscariot. Ralph Waldo Emerson, who was usually reticent on political subjects, could not help but register his disgust at Webster's betrayal of New England's interest and values. He declared acidly that "the word liberty in the mouth of Mr. Webster sounds like the word love in the mouth of a courtesan." Yet if all of this was going to translate into effective opposition to the enforcement of the law, a broader statement of principles in opposition to Webster and Stuart was necessary.[12]

A Revolutionary Conscience

Parker constructed just such a statement, in three installments, between March and September of 1850. At Faneuil Hall on March 25th, less than three weeks after Webster spoke on the Senate floor, he delivered a blistering reply which cast the senator as a traitor to New England, to his conscience, and to the nation's revolutionary tradition. The effectiveness of Parker's argument was in its skillful use of revolutionary symbolism to undermine Webster's association of compromise with patriotism. In grasping "for that 'bad eminence,' the Presidency," he insisted, Webster had betrayed the rights of man and thrown in his lot with the Slave Power's campaign to nationalize slavery. How far would men like Webster and Winthrop go in appeasing their southern friends? Would they hunt down fugitives on April 19th when other citizens were celebrating the anniversary of Lexington and Concord? Would they look on "cheering the slave-hunter" as he chased a "weary fugitive" with "bloodhounds" into Faneuil Hall itself?[13]

This lurid image of Bay State conservatives laughing and cheering as the sacred sites and rituals of revolutionary memory were profaned was characteristic of the speech. Even more stunning was its reversal of Webster's argument that abolitionists were irresponsibly threatening the peace and stability of the Union. In truckling to the Slave Power for political gain, Parker declared, Webster and his friends ensured that southern slavery would not end "as it ended in Massachusetts," but as it ended in "St. Domingo." Slavery would certainly end; it was not possible to "repeal the will of God." But the North's failure to stand up to the political designs of the South meant that "three millions or thirty millions of degraded human beings, degraded by us, must wade through slaughter to their unalienable rights." Far from offering America an alternative to conflict, the counsels of Daniel Webster would lead to the "fire and blood" of the Haitian Revolution.[14]

Parker's invocation of events in Haiti is striking in this context. He employed it mainly as a scare tactic, but it indicates that his interaction with African Americans in Boston had produced a growing awareness of the black revolutionary experience and the possible legitimacy of violent resistance. At times, his rhetoric bore a striking resemblance to that of David Walker, the black radical whose 1829 *Appeal...to the Colored Citizens of the World* invoked both the American and Haitian Revolutions as legitimate models for American slave resistance. In his 1848 "Letter to the American People" on slavery, for example, Parker made it very clear that blacks enjoyed the same natural right to rise up and kill unrepentant oppressors as the American Revolutionaries possessed. Only when "Bunker Hill and Lexington" were "wiped out of the earth" and the "whole history of the Revolution is forgot" could blacks be denied the right to "draw the sword" and "smite at your very life."[15]

Garrisonian abolitionists believed that oppressed people possessed a natural right to take their freedom by force if necessary, but they regarded violence as essentially sinful and counterproductive. Parker's emphatic endorsement of such means, therefore, drew him closer to black abolitionists who increasingly regarded the movement's pacifism as principled inaction. Black minister and activist Samuel Ringgold Ward, himself a former slave, applauded the March 25th speech of "my friend Theodore Parker," and agreed that the fugitive slave law would leave no alternative but "the right of Revolution." Here was the common ground between Parker and black abolitionists that would bear fruit in the coming conflicts over fugitive slaves.[16]

For all their visceral power, however, revolutionary symbols could not motivate sustained action against the Fugitive Slave Act unless they were tied to a larger political and moral analysis that could unite Massachusetts antislavery forces. In his speech to the New England Antislavery Convention in May 1850, therefore, Parker argued that the friends of freedom must put aside their differences and meet the present crisis together. The Fugitive Slave Act, he believed, had rendered old arguments obsolete. The United States was now in an elemental struggle between the national ideal of freedom and the South's sectional ideal of slavery. It was time to create a new party of freedom that would "declare that the nation itself must put an end to slavery." Parker told skeptical Garrisonian friends that political antislavery men like Sumner, Palfrey and Hale truly grasped the fundamental polarities between slavery and freedom, truth and falsehood, conscience and compromise. "These men have spoken very noble words against slavery," he argued, "heroic words in behalf of freedom." If Garrisonians wanted legitimate targets for criticism, Parker offered them the "demagogues of the churches" who supported the fugitive slave bill. Referring to the public displays of affection between Webster and Moses Stuart, he noted that a northern politician must be pretty far gone when he gets a clergyman to "indorse for the Christian character of American slavery." Stuart's attempt to reconcile the Bible and slavery fell under the same condemnation as Webster's quixotic quest to meld freedom and slavery.[17]

Parker's response to Stuart's biblical argument, moreover, reveals how his two decade engagement with biblical criticism could serve blunt and effective political purposes. "If the Bible defends slavery," he declared flatly, "it is not so much better for slavery, but so much the worse for the Bible." Far from defending his faith, Stuart had provided "deists" and "infidels" with an explosive charge against Christianity. No text, not the Constitution and not the Bible, could invalidate the demands of conscience or nullify the decrees of a just and benignant God. However Massachusetts voters felt about Parker's views on either of the nation's sacred texts, they vented their wrath on conservative Whigs who lost control of the state legislature in November 1850.[18]

But the election of Free Soilers and Conscience Whigs in Massachusetts could not stave off the impending chaos which the enforcement of the new Fugitive Slave Law would create. On September 18, 1850, President Fillmore signed the bill into law and federal authorities prepared to execute it across the nation. There was panic among the black population of Boston and at least forty fugitive slaves immediately fled the city. At an October 4th meeting of "Colored Citizens," African American merchant Joshua Smith told every fugitive in the audience "to arm himself with a revolver," and pulled out a knife to demonstrate his own determination to defend himself "to the *hilt*." Fears reached a fever pitch when news reached Boston that a New York City fugitive named James Hamlet had been hustled back to his Maryland owner with the aid of the city's leading citizens. Like their Boston counterparts, New York City's conservative Whig leaders were determined to carry out the law over the objections of the abolitionists.[19]

In Washington, Daniel Webster applauded President Fillmore and all those whose "scruples" about slavery had not outweighed their love of the Union. He had nothing but contempt for his colleague, antislavery Whig Senator William Henry Seward, who had argued that the Fugitive Slave Act violated a "higher law" of freedom. Higher law or conscience politics was to him "merely politics of opinion" and he complained that antislavery Whigs in Massachusetts were "sorely afflicted by three priests, yea four," who were "running into extravagant abolitionism." Conservative Boston lawyer Rufus Choate agreed that no "mere feelings" or individual "sense of right" could stand against the claims of law. Was Parker one of the "priests" that Webster had in mind? Was it Parker's "sense of right" that was disturbing Choate's placid vision of an ordered society?[20]

If so, they had good reason to be concerned, for Parker's understandings of conscience and the higher law went well beyond the version that William Seward had pronounced on the Senate floor. As the bill moved toward final passage in early September, Parker's mood grew increasingly dark. He told John Gorham Palfrey that the nation had fallen on "evil times, which in Boston are getting worse." He was convinced that the "controlling men" of the city were motivated by nothing other than "money and respectability." He was certain that they would comply with the evil law to preserve both. Questions about resistance to the law and the possibility of violence were almost omnipresent in the city.[21]

In this highly charged environment, Parker offered his congregation at the Melodeon the most comprehensive and philosophically sophisticated defense of conscience that ever issued from his pen. He called the sermon "The Function and Place of Conscience in Relation to the Laws of Men." In it he defined conscience as a special faculty of the mind whose function it was to "discover to men the moral law of God." Working from an ontological framework, he told his congregation that the presence of such a faculty in human consciousness presupposed the existence of its object: "absolute justice" or God's moral law. He was willing to concede that human conscience was not "absolutely perfect," that it could not apprehend justice with "infallible certainty." But this was a minor limitation stemming from the fact that human beings were finite creatures who did not possess the full mind of God. But after all, human beings only knew the *physical world* through the relative categories of time, space and causation, and that had been no obstacle to dependable scientific knowledge. To say that conscience was finite in character was no excuse for failing to act upon its dictates. To do otherwise would be to deny the possibility of moral knowledge itself.[22]

In practice, the "relative" perfection of conscience was the only reliable guide to moral action and *all* human institutions and statutes were accountable to its judgments. To those, like Professor Stuart, who believed that conscience required constant instruction from external authority, Parker defended the intuitive nature of moral perception. "We have a transcendental way" to learn the requirements of justice, he argued. "Conscience enables us to...learn the right...intuitively in advance of experiment...from immediate consciousness." To deny the existence of conscience or to deride it as "opinion" or "mere feelings" was to remove the only objective basis upon which moral action could be generated and to replace it with naked power or self-interest. He later labeled this view as "practical atheism."[23]

Parker's sermon went beyond definitions, however, and formulated a philosophy of violent resistance that would soon result in direct action. If the individual conscience was "the last standard of appeal" in matters of justice, he argued, its dictates defined the central "duty" of human life and the best engine of social progress. No institutional obligations, political commitments or personal relationships could outweigh the duty to keep the laws of conscience. Once discerned, duty was absolute and overrode any "special obligations a man takes on himself as a magistrate" or, by implication, as a citizen of a democracy. At the heart of his argument was an attack on the conservative Constitutionalism of Moses Stuart which held that moral objections to slavery could not outweigh the higher ethic of loyalty to a constitutionally-defined Union. To Parker, Stuart's position amounted to moral anarchy. It seemed to say that if a man were born among a nation of pirates, tied to such a community by custom, law and filial loyalty, such relationships would absolve him of any moral duty to oppose piracy! America's piracy, he thundered, consisted not of "forty thieves on Fire

Island," but "twenty millions of men...to enslave every sixth man." "Am I morally bound to keep that compact?" he asked.[24]

Parker told his congregation that their duty was not to uphold or to condemn the Constitution as it was, but rather to determine which of its provisions were consistent with conscience and to "violate" those that were not. If conscientious resistance to the law meant violence, he was ready to take action consistent with his duty, whatever the results might be. As for fugitive slaves, they had every right to use force to defend their lives and their freedoms. "The man who attacks me to reduce me to slavery, in that moment of attack alienates his right to life," he argued. "I would kill him with as little compunction as I would drive a mosquito from my face." If this sounded offensive to the conservative Boston establishment, he asked how many of them worried about the letter of the law when their merchant friends violated statutes against usury. Somehow, he mused sarcastically, "when a man's liberty is concerned, we must keep the law...betray the wanderer and expose the outcast."[25]

Boston conservatives were appalled by Parker's disregard for what they regarded as a Union-saving law. They rejected his claim that conscience absolved citizens of their duties under the Constitution. Among the most vehement of his detractors was Benjamin Curtis, a wealthy Boston lawyer whose support for Webster Whiggery would soon earn him an appointment to the United States Supreme Court. Parker's views on conscience and the law sounded like "insurrection and revolution" to Curtis, and he warned antislavery Whigs against endorsing them. Indicating that Parker's sermon was circulating widely in Boston, Curtis rebuked it publicly during a "Constitutional Meeting" held at Faneuil Hall in late November 1850. With Parker in the audience, he made a speech that was personal, even nasty, in suggesting that minister's attack on the law stemmed from nothing higher than a love of "excitement or notoriety." It seemed to him that Theodore Parker was searching for "new field of promise" because he was "smarting from disappointment." Whether this was a reference to Parker's pariah status among the Brahmin elite is unclear, but he left no doubt that he regarded the agitation against the law not, as an expression of conscience, but rather of "malignant philanthropy" and "bad passions."[26]

Curtis quoted Parker's statement that active slave-hunters forfeited their "right to life," and he angrily told the crowd of respectable citizens that such statements "disgrace our community," and endanger "its peace and security." He wondered aloud if the radical minister "would expect to receive the punishment that would await him, here and hereafter, if he were to do what he recommends to others." Parker shouted back "Do you want an answer to your question sir?" but was ignored. Curtis was not comfortable with the kind of public sparring that Parker had come to embrace, and so he did not respond to this offer of battle. But this was only the opening salvo in a series of clashes between these two men, and it indicates the deep conflict of values in Boston at the outset of controversy over fugitive slaves. For Curtis, conscience was no substitute for the order and security guaranteed by law, but he could offer no solution to the moral dilemma posed by the Fugitive Slave Act. For Parker, law could only produce order and security if it were grounded in those eternal principles of justice that were revealed to human beings though conscience. Both claimed that Faneuil Hall symbolically embodied their values.[27]

Although Henry David Thoreau is often credited with authoring Transcendentalism's greatest manifesto on civil disobedience, Parker's sermon on the function of conscience was much better known at the time. It also went beyond Thoreau's essay in its demands for individual action on behalf of the collective good. Thoreau's 1849 essay, which was originally called "On Resistance to Civil Government," had appeared in Elizabeth Peabody's short-lived periodical *Aesthetic Papers*. Ultimately, it was less concerned with direct action than with principled disengagement from what its author regarded as oppressive or immoral political systems. "It is not a man's duty, as a matter of course, to devote himself to the eradication of any, even the most enormous wrong," Thoreau had written. "But it is his duty to wash his hands of it." In refusing to pay his poll tax in Concord, Thoreau had washed his hands of the Mexican-American War and ensured that as he devoted himself to his "other pursuits and contemplations," he did so without "sitting upon another man's shoulders."[28]

For Parker, however, conscience demanded a far more active conception of duty requiring direct engagement with social wrong. It was not enough for him to go back to writing theology in a city where fugitive slaves were being chased though the streets by municipal authorities acting under color of law. "I will ring the bells and alarm the town," he proclaimed from the pulpit. He was also convinced, perhaps more than Thoreau, that because conscience provided access to a universal moral law, it could be the basis of effective collective as well as individual action. Trusting that there were "manly men enough" in his own congregation to "secure the freedom of every fugitive in Boston" he pledged to "serve as head, as foot, or as hand to any body of serious and earnest men who will go with me." He soon found that many were willing to do so.[29]

The Boston Vigilance Committee

For all the theoretical groundwork Parker had done in his speeches and sermons, fighting the Fugitive Slave Act took on a deeply personal dimension for him. Since his move to Boston, he had had sustained contact with the scarred refugees from southern slavery who trickled into the city each year. Most fugitive slaves who sought spiritual community in Boston attended one the city's black churches, but the presence of so many abolitionists in the Twenty-Eighth Congregational Society, and the reputation of its controversial minister meant that a few attended services at the Melodeon as well. Parker's sermons and letters during this period make numerous references to fugitives visiting his home in Exeter Place.

The most famous of these guests were William and Ellen Craft, a couple who had recently escaped from slavery in Georgia and who attended services at the Melodeon. The spectacular circumstances of the Crafts' escape from slavery in the Deep South made them objects of intense curiosity in the North. Ellen, was very light-skinned, and had posed as an elderly slave owner traveling north. Her husband William accompanied her in the role of her black servant. After several close calls, the Crafts arrived in Philadelphia in December 1848 and then moved to Boston where they took rooms at Lewis Hayden's home in the West End, the center of the city's black community. Parker met them soon after they arrived and they valued his friendship and his message enough to choose him as their pastor. They received endless invitations to tell their spine tingling story of escape and disguise on antislavery platforms in several states.[30]

Parker was enchanted by the Crafts, describing them as "sober and industrious people" and marveling at their daring escape from bondage. He found Ellen's "whiteness" fascinating and he was not above using it as a prop in his public denunciations of the Fugitive Slave Act. "[Ellen] is not so dark as Mr. Webster himself," he had said to the great laughter and applause of a Faneuil Hall crowd. He conjured up an image of Ellen fleeing for her life from slave hunters in order to counter the notion that "freedom is to be dealt out in proportion to the whiteness of the skin." However William or Ellen may have felt about such tactics, it was Parker who they asked to perform their wedding ceremony.[31]

In the meantime, specific steps were necessary to prevent the law and order party in Boston from subjecting Ellen Craft and the city's other fugitives to fearful uncertainty. This meant forging a better working relationship between white activists and the Boston black community. Fortunately, there were a growing number of white abolitionists who agreed with Parker's view of the Fugitive Slave Act. Boston lawyer Richard Henry Dana, and reformers Samuel Gridley Howe and Dr. Henry I. Bowditch, for example, clearly agreed that conscience demanded the direct, not passive resistance to the law. Dr. Bowditch, the son of Harvard College's most famous mathematician and himself an accomplished pulmonary physician, turned down an invitation to dine at a fashionable Boston club in October of 1850 saying "I should be ashamed of myself, and traitor to my highest principles, if I did not spend every leisure hour in plotting how that infamous law...can be defeated." Bowditch accepted Parker's fusion of private judgment and revolutionary memory. "I go, if need be, for open resistance," he wrote. "For my support I appeal to the God to whom our fathers appealed in the dark hours in the Revolution."[32]

Boston blacks, who needed no encouragement from white activists to oppose the Fugitive Slave Act, formulated a resistance ideology of their own which nevertheless bore some similarities to Parker's. On September 30, 1850, former slave Lewis Hayden chaired a meeting of "Colored Citizens" at the May Street Methodist Episcopal Church that condemned the Fugitive Slave Act as a "God-defying and inhuman law." Black citizens pledged to "defend ourselves and each other" from the "bloodhounds in pursuit of human prey" who were soon to appear in the streets of the city. Accounts of the meeting suggest a highly charged atmosphere in which shouts of personal and collective defiance were heard throughout the evening. The presence of several well-known fugitive slaves, including Hayden, Josiah Henson and William and Ellen Craft, clearly helped to unite the group by personifying the threat posed by the law. Displaying their own sensitivity to American Revolutionary memory, Boston's blacks pledged to "do all and dare all, in imitation of Patrick Henry's immortal sentiment, *Liberty or Death*." The following week, these same activists assembled again at the African Baptist Meeting House on Belknap Street. At that gathering they added Crispus Attucks' name to Patrick Henry's in the pantheon of revolutionary heroes, and then called for an October 14th meeting of the city's larger antislavery community at Faneuil Hall.[33]

The growing consensus among black and white abolitionists about the need for organized resistance to the Fugitive Slave Act took practical shape at the Faneuil Hall meeting, an event which some observers claimed was attended by more than 6,000 people. Parker's friend Caroline Dall simply could "not resist" going and she reported that there was "no bluster" at the meeting, only a grim determination to "trample the law under foot." Frederick Douglass was a key speaker that night, thrilling the audience for over an hour with his militant affirmations of the right of self-defense. At one point he warned that opponents of the law should be prepared to "see the streets of Boston running with blood," rather than acquiesce to enforcement. When "men throw off the dignity of manhood and become bloodhounds," he proclaimed, "they should be treated as bloodhounds." In addition to his electrifying persona, Douglass's presence cemented the Vigilance Committee's association with the political antislavery movement. By the fall of 1850, Douglass had rejected Garrisonian dogmas about the proslavery character of the Constitution, and he was forming a new alliance with political antislavery leader Gerrit Smith.[34]

Parker hoped that the new "Committee of Safety and Vigilance" would include both Garrisonians and political activists, but the resolutions he helped to draft at the Faneuil Hall meeting were far closer to Douglass's views than to Garrison's. The law violated the Constitution because it did not carry out the ends for which the Constitution was formed. It "does not tend to form a more perfect Union," nor did it "establish justice, ensure domestic tranquility...or secure the blessings of liberty to the people." Here was an argument for those who sought to ground their opposition to the Fugitive Slave Act within American law and tradition, not against them. The resolutions did not explicitly call for violent resistance, but they did authorize committee members to use "all just means to secure the fugitives and colored inhabitants of Boston and vicinity from any invasion of their rights." Since Parker had told his congregation only two weeks earlier that slave catchers forfeited their right to life in the act of reducing another human being to slavery, it seems likely that many in the audience understood "just means" to include violence. Calculated ambiguity about the use of force, even if it would later come back to haunt the Vigilance Committee, was necessary to keep principled pacifists in the fold.[35]

Parker's resolutions were adopted enthusiastically by the Faneuil Hall meeting and the resulting committee was at least in part a tribute to his role as a neutral broker among antislavery factions. Radicals were well represented, with Garrison, Wendell Phillips, Ellis Gray Loring, and Edmund Quincy all agreeing to support the committee's work. Political abolitionists such as Elizur Wright and Lysander Spooner appear on the membership list as well, as do Free Soilers and Conscience Whigs like Anson Burlingame, Samuel Gridley Howe, and Richard Henry Dana. The committee had a healthy dose of intellectuals and writers as well. A. Bronson Alcott and James Russell Lowell joined, as did Parker's old allies among the reform clergy like John Sargent and John Pierpont. Important members of Parker's congregation at the Melodeon, including Francis Jackson, Charles Ellis, and Robert Apthorp were among the officers of the original committee.[36]

But perhaps most impressive was the biracial character of the group. From the very beginning of the committee's history, black leaders Lewis Hayden, Joshua Smith and Robert Morris served in critical leadership positions on its executive, finance and relief boards. Historian Gary Collison has noted that despite the small number of black Bostonians on the formal membership lists, these black leaders of the group formed an indispensable bond between the wealthy, politically-connected, white members of the Vigilance Committee and the larger black community centered in the city's West End. The records of the committee's finances list countless small reimbursements to black citizens who provided relief or transportation to fugitive slaves. As it had been for years, the daily work of assisting fugitive slaves would be done by the African American community in Boston. Now, however, money, legal defense, and other forms of support would come from energized white activists.[37]

The Vigilance Committee was elected at the mass meeting in Faneuil Hall on October 14th, but the real work of formulating tactics remained. At subsequent planning sessions, the committee increased its number to eighty and divided itself into an executive committee, a legal committee, and a relief committee. With Parker as its chairman, the Executive Committee was given the ongoing task of being "on the watch, and to warn when an attempt is making to arrest a fugitive; and to see that he has knowledge of it." If a defendant were judged to be a fugitive slave by the Commissioner, the executive committee was expected to "alarm the town." The legal committee consisted of all the lawyers in the committee of the whole, and was led by Garrisonian Samuel Sewall with help from Charles M. Ellis and Richard Henry Dana, a well-respected Boston lawyer and author of the popular book *Two Years Before the Mast*. The lawyers' task was to ensure that "all legal delays are made use of" in holding up the proceedings of the Fugitive Slave Court and impeding the successful issue of a certificate of rendition. The relief was composed almost exclusively of black members and it was charged with providing aid and assistance to recently arrived fugitives. Black abolitionist William Nell, who eventually became the general agent of the Boston Vigilance Committee, headed up the relief activities. While each group was given special tasks, the purpose behind them all was to prevent the execution of the law. "The first business of the anti-slavery men is to help the fugitive," Parker wrote after the meeting "We, like Christ are to seek and save that which is lost."[38]

XII
CONTINUAL ALARMS
1850–1851

In agreeing to serve as a leader of the Boston Vigilance Committee, Parker made a crucial decision about the direction of his life. Protecting fugitives became a second, full-time occupation over the next several years. It also sapped the energy of a man whose physical and psychological health was already precarious. During 1850 and 1851, he was engaged almost constantly in what he called "fugitive slave matters" and complained that his theological and pastoral work was "continually interrupted" by meetings and crises. He was frequently ill and also experienced the return of what can only be described as periodic depression. Among the chief causes of his melancholy was undoubtedly the childlessness of his marriage to Lydia. Although their relocation to Boston and the death of Lydia's meddling Aunt Lucy Cabot had given the couple the freedom to redefine their marriage, the improvement in their relationship was not enough to compensate for Parker's disappointed expectations. "How strange that I should have no children, and only get a little sad sort of happiness, but not of the affectional quality," he confided to his private journal during this period. Hinting at the source of the problem, he described himself as "only an *old maid in life*," and confessed that at times "I am deeply sad."[1]

Theodore and Lydia had compensated somewhat for their lack of offspring by becoming the legal guardians of George Colburn Cabot, the illegitimate son of Lydia's deceased brother John L. Cabot. "Georgie" as they called him, was educated at the Brook Farm School and then came to live permanently with the Parkers in 1847 when he was eleven years old. But the obstacles to a full and harmonious relationship between Theodore and Lydia remained, and he lamented that "even religion will not fill the void left by other things which I have not." He was now over forty, bespectacled and nearly bald, and his body had been thinned out by overwork and recurrent illness. To some observers, he now seemed less and less a physical presence than a powerful idea, awkwardly clothed in flesh. The poet Elizabeth Oakes Smith was struck by the way in which his "broad white forehead" and his "clear, young eye" contrasted with his "slightly old-fashioned dress" and "coarse features." She observed that "his brain seemed to dominate his whole person," and as she listened to him speak she could not help but think of Socrates. As his opportunities for private happiness slipped away from him, Parker became more and more determined to make his life an expression of his thought. Only in theology and in the fight against slavery was there any real possibility of leaving a personal legacy.[2]

But these twin commitments existed in significant tension. Since the late 1840s Parker had been planning to write a large work called the "History of the Development of Religion in Man." Though it was never completed, he spent every spare moment mastering a huge body of literature on the history and philosophy of religion. In the early 1850s he developed a detailed outline of the work that indicates the Herculean nature of the task he envisioned. Divided into six parts with as many as eight chapters each, he intended to categorize the universal elements in human religious consciousness and then trace their theological and moral development in the world's major religious traditions. Working from the premise that all manifestations of religion proceed from the idea of God "as a fact of consciousness, intuitively known," he proposed to chart the progressive development of religion toward "pure theism" or Absolute Religion. In the process, he hoped to demonstrate the correspondence between the physical and spiritual laws that governed both the natural world and human history.[3]

He wanted to show, for example, that God's immanent presence, both in the laws of nature and in the consciousness of the human race, had shaped the direction of history even as it left individual human beings free to live in harmony with or in opposition to the moral law. Since he believed that the historic forms of religion influenced and were influenced by social, political, national and intellectual life, the subject matter of his proposed work stretched across a vast array of fields. The Roman priesthood, the philosophy of the Stoics, gender relations among the ancient Hebrews, all was grist for the enormous mill that turned constantly in his mind. For all his belief in intuition, Parker reveled in the compatibility of transcendental lines of argumentation with the most thoroughgoing empiricism. His book on religion would rest upon the *a priori* truths revealed in consciousness, but he would not leave out a single observable fact if he could help it.[4]

It is one of the tragedies of Parker's life that he was not able to see that the intellectual task he had set for himself demanded more time and energy than was physically possible. Younger and healthier colleagues marveled at his stamina, but they shuddered at the terrible toll persistent overwork was taking on him. Rev. Thomas Wentworth Higginson, whose progressive Unitarian church in Worcester was modeled on Parker's Boston society, understood that his mentor was following a self-destructive path. "[Parker's] young companions," he wrote later, "had long assured him that the tendency of his career was not only to kill himself, but them as well." Just a few weeks after Parker's death in 1860, fellow abolitionist Wendell Phillips, whose house on Essex Street was near to Parker's, remarked admiringly on his neighbor's constant devotion to work. "When some engagement brought me home in the small hours of the morning, many and many a time I have looked out and seen that unquenched light burning—that unflagging student at work," he remembered.[5]

Parker sometimes complained privately that the fugitive slave agitation prevented him from an exclusive focus on what he always called his "great work" of theology. His journals frequently mention the "continual streams of people" that demanded his attention. "Suppose I could have given all the attention to theology that I have been forced to pay to politics, slavery, etc.," he wrote in August 1851, "how much I might have done!" Parker sometimes felt that, though he was meant to be a philosopher, the "times call for a stump orator." But these complaints masked a deeper reality. The anti-slavery movement, and especially resistance to the Fugitive Slave Act, engaged his conscience and his self esteem in a way that little else did. The enormous enthusiasm with which he plunged into the work of the Vigilance Committee, and the pleasure that he derived from confronting the allies of slavery, belies his stated preference for the quiet of his study.[6]

William and Ellen Craft

His first opportunity for direct confrontation with slavery came quickly. Members of the Vigilance Committee learned on October 25, 1850, that arrest warrants had been issued that morning for William and Ellen Craft. Willis Hughes, a "gaoler" from Macon, Georgia, and a witness named John Knight had been sent to Boston by Robert Collins, a Georgia slaveholder claiming the Crafts as his property. It had taken the slave hunters more than a week to pry warrants out of the hands of reluctant Boston officials. U.S. District Court Judge Levi Woodbury and U.S. District Attorney George Lunt had refused to implicate themselves in what they knew would be an explosive test of the new law. After days of frustration, however, Hughes and Knight had better luck with Commissioner George Ticknor Curtis who convened a meeting of the city's legal officials and persuaded them to hand down warrants for the arrest of the city's most famous fugitive slaves. Curtis was a Cotton Whig, an admirer of Daniel Webster and a highly successful patent attorney in Boston. Like his brother Benjamin, he was a conservative nationalist, deeply critical of the antislavery movement, and determined to show that the new Fugitive Slave Act could be enforced in Boston.[7]

The delays gave the Vigilance Committee time to consult with the Crafts and then devise strategies to prevent their arrest. Returning home from a lecture engagement late on the afternoon of Friday, the 25th, Parker found a hastily-written note from Samuel Gridley Howe informing him that the Crafts were in imminent danger. He quickly convened a meeting of the executive committee where black abolitionist Joshua Smith told him that at least two other warrants had also been issued for fugitive slaves working at a restaurant near Court Square. "Five or six fellows" were said to have congregated on the street outside and later entered the building and "inquired about their fugitives." Although little was known about the identity or whereabouts of these new targets of the law, Smith told the committee that the Crafts were safe for the time being.[8]

The committee quickly agreed upon short-term measures. To prevent Ellen from being arrested and used as a lever to ensnare her husband, she was taken to the home of attorney Ellis Gray Loring and later moved to Parker's house at Exeter Place. William, who preferred to confront his pursuers, obtained a revolver and barricaded himself inside his furniture-repair shop on Cambridge Street in the West End. The next day Parker theatrically inspected William's weapons and found them "adequate" to fend off the kidnappers. In the meantime, the executive and legal committees devised a strategy of personal and legal harassment of the slave catchers that was designed to chase them out of Boston. Over the next five days, Hughes and Knight were arrested on two counts of slander against the Crafts and no fewer than five other minor offenses which included "smoking in the streets," "swearing in the streets," and "driving fast through the streets." Each of these complaints was brought by a member of the legal committee, and they resulted in mounting bail fees for the two Georgians. The committee also endorsed a policy of personal harassment that took on a more threatening nature. After returning to the South, Hughes and Knight complained bitterly that they had been repeatedly mobbed by small crowds of men shouting, "Slave Hunters, Slave Hunters, there go the Slave Hunters!" As Parker described it to his English friend James Martineau, the Vigilance Committee hoped to keep "the Slave Hunters in a state of disturbance all the time they remain here," and to frighten them "so that they were glad to march out of the city."[9]

By the morning of October 30th, it had become clear that the Boston authorities were unable to locate Ellen Craft and that Marshal Charles Devens would not risk violence in apprehending her husband. The only thing left was to get rid of Hughes and Knight, and Parker decided to take on that job himself. Based on his conversations with William Craft, he had concluded that neither of the two slave hunters were men of any character and could be easily intimidated. Knight, who Parker described as an "imbecile," had already bungled one attempt to lure William into the open, and depended on Hughes for guidance.[10]

On Wednesday morning, Parker went to the lobby of the United States Hotel where the pair were staying and sent up his card requesting an interview. When a reply came back containing a misspelled rebuff claiming that "Mr. Hughes is inguage," Parker knocked on the door and was eventually admitted to the room. He found Hughes and Knight extremely bitter about their treatment in Boston but resigned to the fact that they would not accomplish their mission. This was a change in attitude, for several days before they had bragged that they would never leave Boston "till they got hold of the niggers." Their bravado was wavering under the pressure of harassment. Hughes remarked caustically that he had heard that Parker was a "great moralist" but that his actions did "not look much like it." When Parker asked him what it did look like, Hughes said: "mobs and violence." Parker thought the two men seemed "considerably frightened," and he offered them "safe passage" out of the city only if they would leave immediately. "I told them that I had stood between them and violence once—I would not promise to do it again," he wrote. After five days of continuous persecution, Hughes and Knight took Parker's threat seriously and left the city that same afternoon. [11]

In the days following the departure of the slave hunters, Parker reveled in the role he and the Vigilance Committee had played in thwarting their designs. He was thrilled by his confrontation with the two men and imagined himself a latter-day member of the Sons of Liberty. He read John Adams's diary and was struck by the parallels between Adams' battle with Boston Tories and his own struggle against the northern allies of slavery. Boston seemed to be recapitulating the divisions of its revolutionary past when "most of the men of property were on the side of tyranny," and when "the greater part of [the clergy] sided with power." Rumors in the Boston papers about the possible dispatch of several hundred troops to "dragoon us into keeping the Fugitive Slave Law" brought to his mind the hated Quartering Act, and the revolutionary generation's revulsion against standing armies. As a boy, he had watched the battle of Lexington reenacted by aging veterans of the Revolution. Now he imagined himself waging the same fight against similar enemies in the heart of Boston.[12]

But Parker's revolutionary parallels also contained the sting of bitter irony. In the letter of introduction he sent with the Crafts to James Martineau in Liverpool a few weeks later, he could not help but call attention to the reversal of the revolutionary era's polarities. America was now a land from which freedom loving exiles fled, and Britain was their refuge. "I am now obligated to look to 'the British' for protection for the liberty of my own parishioners," he fumed, people "who have committed no wrong against anyone!" The marriage ceremony which he conducted for William and Ellen before their departure for England contained more evidence of his growing infatuation with the symbols of violent resistance in the name of human liberty. Finding a "California knife" and Bible in the Crafts' rooms, he told William to use the first to "save his wife's liberty, or her life if need be," and the other to "save his soul, and her soul." Lest his actions sound overly paternalistic, Parker reassured one of his parishioners that he would have given the same advice to white men "escaping from slavery in Algiers."[13]

Shadrach and Thomas Sims

In some ways, the circumstances of the Crafts' case were ideal for Parker and the Vigilance Committee. William and Ellen were well-known and respected members of the Boston black community and their cause garnered enormous attention. The Vigilance Committee learned of the warrants before any arrest was made, and they remained in control of the situation from the start. In the case of Shadrach Minkins, a fugitive slave who had escaped from his Norfolk, Virginia, owner in May 1850, it was the Boston authorities who initially seemed in control.

Commissioner Curtis, who was now emerging as the city's best bet for slave hunters seeking legal support, issued a warrant for Minkins's arrest on the evening of Friday, February 14, 1851. Minkins was being pursued by John Caphart, a middle-aged police constable from Norfolk who carried legal documents proving that Virginia slaveholder John Debree was Minkins's rightful owner. Unlike Hughes and Knight, Caphart was tough and experienced. Parker called him a "monster," but recognized that he was unlikely to be easily intimidated. Caphart also received greater support from Boston officials who were now eager to show that they had learned from their failures in the Crafts' case. On Saturday morning, the U.S. Marshal's office sent Assistant Deputy Marshal Patrick Riley and two assistants to the Cornhill Street coffee-house where Minkins worked. They apprehended him and escorted him to Curtis' courtroom where Caphart's Boston lawyer Seth Thomas hoped to conclude the case before resistance could be mounted. But news carried quickly in the city, and the legal wing of the Vigilance Committee learned of the situation just in time to disrupt the proceedings. Led by Richard Henry Dana, Ellis Gray Loring, and black attorney Robert Morris, the friends of the prisoner prepared writs of personal replevin and habeas corpus which they intended to present to the Supreme Court of the Commonwealth. According to Dana, their ultimate strategy was to challenge both the constitutionality of the Fugitive Slave Act and the power of the Commissioner to issue warrants. Though Massachusetts Chief Justice Lemuel Shaw bluntly denied Minkins's habeas petition, Loring and Dana were able to stall the proceedings for seventy-two hours in order to prepare an adequate defense.[14]

The Vigilance Committee and the Boston black community were caught off guard by Minkins's arrest. Parker did not hear about it until court proceedings were about to adjourn at two in the afternoon and he could not reach the Court House until the dramatic events of the afternoon were over. But as he made his way toward Court Square from Exeter Place, "intending to make a rescue, if possible," he heard a shout of celebration coming from the direction of the Court House. A few minutes earlier, Deputy Marshal Riley had ordered the clearing of the Commissioner's court in preparation for moving the defendant back to his cell. The Marshal's precautions were understandable because a large, angry crowd of mostly black Bostonians had made its way inside the building and now outnumbered the police by a large margin.[15]

As the last of the attorneys was leaving through the guarded door, the crowd suddenly forced it open and a party of "fifteen or twenty black men" rushed in and grabbed hold of Minkins and rushed him through the hallway, down a flight of stairs and into the square. Within minutes, a crowd of nearly 200 was seen speeding their way into the West End where Minkins disappeared from view. Later accounts suggest that he was briefly hidden in the attic of a house on Southac Lane, an alley tucked away deep within the Sixth Ward. Within hours, Lewis Hayden and Robert Morris had successfully escorted Minkins across the Charles River into Cambridge and beyond the reach of the authorities. Although he did not witness the drama first hand, Parker exulted in the outcome. Deploying his penchant for ironic biblical references, he noted that "this Shadrach is delivered out of his fiery furnace without the smell of fire on his clothes and now he sings 'God Save the Queen' in token of his delivery out of this republican Babylon."[16]

The resistance in Boston created a stir in Washington where sectional peace was predicated on the successful enforcement of the new law. On February 18th, President Fillmore issued a proclamation condemning the rescue and calling upon "all well-disposed citizens...to aid and assist in quelling this and all other such combinations." In Congress, John C. Calhoun and Henry Clay expressed their horror at what had been done, and they received assurances from the Navy and War Departments that the forces of the United States military could be used to prevent such incidents from occurring again. Daniel Webster spoke for many Massachusetts conservatives when he said that the Shadrach rescue was "strictly speaking, a case of treason" and Union Whigs applauded when Boston officials gave the Marshal's office control of the city police in the event of subsequent incidents.[17]

Following so closely on the heels of the Crafts case, the Shadrach rescue was a terrible embarrassment to Boston's conservative Whigs. To them, "this mob and its results" dishonored the people of Massachusetts and impaired the city's commercial ties with the South. They were also furious at the failure of the legal system to secure any convictions against those responsible for the deed. Eight blacks and two whites, including Robert Morris and Lewis Hayden, were arrested for their participation in the rescue, but determined work by the Vigilance Committee's legal team secured acquittals. When he received the news of Morris's acquittal, Parker was elated. Despite "all the Boston influence and the money of the United States," the conscience of a New England juror could not be unmanned by "judicial tyranny."[18]

The Shadrach rescue was an important turning point in Parker's relationship with black abolitionists in Boston and moved him in the direction of a more bi-racial image of the revolutionary tradition. He now spoke with great admiration for the work of his black colleagues on the Vigilance Committee, calling their action the "most noble deed done in Boston since the destruction of the tea in 1773." He began to imagine the city's black population as a critical part of its resuscitated revolutionary character. Here were men who had followed their conscience, opposed an unjust law, and rescued a fellow human being from the brutal nightmare of slavery without resort to lethal force. He was deeply impressed by Lewis Hayden, who he described as a "careful man" whose discretion and bravery made him an invaluable ally.[19]

But members of the Vigilance Committee had very little time to admire their accomplishments as embarrassed Boston authorities quickly intensified their search for fugitives. By the end of the month the committee was meeting almost every night and took new precautions to prevent spies from overhearing their deliberations. Rumors of impending mass fugitive hunts circulated wildly throughout the city. Terrified former slaves called on committee members constantly and black leaders needed special protection from city and federal authorities. As the police prepared to arrest Lewis Hayden, for example, the former slave became terrified that his wife Harriet would be recaptured while he languished in jail. Parker agreed to hide Harriet at Exeter Place, but said that Hayden would have to wait a day because there was already another fugitive "in the spare chamber." Fortunately, the black community had a remarkable network of informers who could warn of impending arrests. Joshua B. Smith, a prosperous black caterer and member of the executive committee, became the Vigilance Committee's most effective intelligence gatherer during this period. After listening to Smith recount a recent conversation with Boston City Marshal Francis Tukey, Parker concluded that the caterer had "ways of hearing which men know not of."[20]

Among the intelligence gathered by Smith's network of informants was the ominous news that slave hunters in the city now wanted "*only one from Boston, to show the discontented ones at home that it can be done.*" On April 3, 1851 they found their victim when fugitive slave Thomas Sims was arrested on Richmond Street by Boston city police officers disguised as watchmen. Sims was in his early twenties and had escaped from slavery in Savannah, Georgia by concealing himself on a commercial ship reaching Boston in early March. He was discovered by the crew when the vessel arrived in the harbor, was beaten and then confined in a cabin. But Sims was both determined and resourceful. He broke out of his nautical prison in the middle of the night, stole a dinghy attached to the ship, reached the South Boston shore and then disappeared into the city. Unfortunately, his desperate need for money forced him to take the risk of wiring his family in Savannah, an act that alerted his owner to his location in Boston.[21]

A week later, on April 3rd, slave hunter John B. Bacon arrived in the city and secured the services of attorney Seth Thomas who had assisted the "monster" Caphart just a few weeks earlier in the Shadrach case. Based on documents and testimony presented by Bacon and Thomas, Commissioner Curtis dutifully issued a warrant for Sims's arrest and the police began scouring the streets. When the fugitive was caught at about nine in the evening, however, he refused to go quietly. Pulling out a concealed knife, he stabbed Deputy Marshal Asa Butman in the thigh, and then, before he could be dragged inside the Boston Courthouse for trial, screamed to passers by that he was "in the hands of the kidnappers!" Sims knew what he was doing. His use of the word "kidnappers" was a short-hand message that members of the Boston black community and the Vigilance Committee would undoubtedly understand to mean slave hunters. Within minutes, the bell at Faneuil Hall began to ring, announcing a new crisis.[22]

At fifteen minutes before eleven, Parker was reading at home in his "night gown" when the bell began to ring "violently." He threw his clothes on and rushed toward the courthouse determined to prevent a rendition. But he only got as far as Chauncy Place where he found Vigilance Committee members Samuel Sewall and Elizur Wright Jr. remonstrating in the street with Deputy Marshal Patrick Riley. Sewall demanded to know if Sims would be tried that night, and in the heat of the argument he took rough hold of the Deputy Marshal's coat.

Parker said later that Riley was initially "dumbfounded" by the fury of Sewall's address, but then quickly lost his temper. Riley had been bested by the Vigilance Committee in the Shadrach case and he now locked Sewall up in the city watch house. But Parker's night was not over yet. After making sure that no trial was taking place in the Courthouse, he called an emergency meeting of the executive committee at Exeter Place. The mood among the group appears to have been optimistic. "We had a very pleasant meeting of friends and parishioners at our House that evening," Parker wrote a few days later. He confessed that none of them could have dreamed of "the terrible evil that was to befall Sims."[23]

The nightmare began early the next morning. After a six o'clock meeting at the antislavery office at 21 Cornhill Street, Parker arrived at the Courthouse at about nine. There he encountered a scene that he would never forget nor ever tire of recounting in his anti-slavery speeches. To prevent a rescue attempt, Marshal Tukey had directed the construction of chain barriers around the Court House. Doorways and sidewalk approaches were lined with belts of rope and chains making it necessary for judges and lawyers to stoop down under them to get into the building. Court Square was full of people and at least a hundred armed police officers menaced the crowd. To abolitionists the idea of northern justice forced to hunker down under the iniquity of the Southern Slave Power had never been more visibly represented.

The Free Soil newspaper *Commonwealth* printed an engraving of the scene under the caption "Justice in Chains" and commented mournfully that Boston's "Temple of Justice" was now "in chains under the shadow of Faneuil Hall and Bunker Hill." Massachusetts, the editors claimed, was "in the dust before the Slave Hunter." Parker noted in the margins of his copy that while "some of the justices grumbled" about the security measure, "they all went under the chains to their seats." Yet he could not help but be "glad of the symbol" that the scene offered, and he made the most of it several days later at the Melodeon. "One by one the judges bowed and stooped and bent and cringed and curled and crouched down," he told his parishioners. "Think of old, stiff necked Lemuel [Shaw] visibly going under the chains!" If a reawakened revolutionary Boston was to resist the designs of its present day Tories, symbols like this one would be of great value.[24]

The Courthouse looked besieged from the outside, but the scene within was not much better. Sims sat in the dock flanked by two Boston police constables while slave hunter Bacon and his two witnesses "took the stand and testified." At the center of it all sat George T. Curtis, the man who would decide Sims's fate. Where Curtis was concerned, Parker simply lost all moral restraint and lapsed into what can only be described as vulgar invective. Curtis was to Parker what Gov. Thomas Hutchinson had been to John Adams, the embodiment of selfish Toryism and place seeking. He described Curtis as "uncommonly ugly looking" and rejoiced that the commissioner seemed "troubled." In expressing his intense hatred for Curtis, moreover Parker betrayed his own inner demon, one that lurked beneath the surface of his heroic abolitionist self-image. Reaching for the worst insult he could find for the Commissioner, he embraced the lexicon of crude racism. "He looks like a nigger, only he is pale" Parker wrote of Curtis. "He has the same...nose and lips with a retreating forehead."[25]

In his dealings with black men like William Craft, Lewis Hayden, and Joshua Smith, Parker clearly struggled against such offensive racist language. But his easy use of it to describe a white man he despised reveals both how difficult and how close to the surface that struggle was. At the same time, however, his racialized portrait of Curtis was also an outgrowth of the power reversal that seemed to be occurring as Boston fell under the sway of the Slave Power. Saying that the Commissioner looked "like a nigger" was another way to describe the symbolic enslavement of Massachusetts by southern, white men who had brought chains and armed guards to a Boston Courthouse within sight of Faneuil Hall.

As Parker struggled to control his fury at Curtis, Sims's lawyers, including Massachusetts Senator Robert Rantoul, succeeded in delaying the Commissioner's proceedings for a week while they applied for a writ of habeas corpus from Justice Shaw. During this period, Parker kept the executive committee in almost constant session, meeting sometime at the *Liberator* office and other times in his own study at Exeter Place. Following up on their success in the Crafts case, the committee again endorsed legal harassment of the slave hunter. On April 7th, the day that Justice Shaw denied Sims's habeas petition, Bacon was arrested on a charge of conspiracy to kidnap and charged a five thousand dollar bail fee. This time, however, bail was immediately paid by Boston conservatives, and Bacon was kept off the streets to prevent further incidents. Besides the legal strategy, a number of forcible rescue plans were offered throughout the nine days of Sims's imprisonment in the Courthouse. Austin Bearse, a Boston ship captain and Boston Vigilance Committee member, was sent to locate the brig which had been prepared to return Sims to Georgia, and at one point the committee seriously considered an attempt to rescue him at sea. Another plan involved arranging for a mattress to be placed under Sims's window in the courthouse which would allow the prisoner to jump safely from his second-story room. Whether the authorities received warnings, or simply by chance, bars were placed on the window only hours before the proposed escape.[26]

The precautions taken by the supporters of the law presented serious problems for the Boston Vigilance Committee. But even more serious was the indecision of committee members, including Parker, about how far to take their resistance. The calling of nearly five hundred state and federal troops to prevent a repeat of Shadrach's rescue led many Boston abolitionists to conclude that a rescue attempt was too risky and potentially too violent. Worcester minister and Parker protégé, Thomas Wentworth Higginson, argued later that he had been one of a small group of committee members willing to use violence to rescue Sims. He claimed that his plans were thwarted by non-resistants, who opposed violence on principle, and by Free Soilers who wanted to use an exclusively legal strategy even if it meant defeat for Sims and his allies. Richard Henry Dana spoke for the latter group when he said that "moderate counsels" on the committee had worked hard at "keeping the people within bounds."[27]

Where was Parker in this spectrum of views? Surprisingly, given his stated belief in the legitimacy of violent resistance, he was among those who opposed a forcible rescue. But his opposition seems to have been practical rather than ideological. He concluded that such a rescue attempt would fail and expose the weakness of the resistance movement. He also feared that violence would discredit political antislavery forces in Massachusetts who were on the verge of electing Charles Sumner to the Senate. His views became clear on Fast Day, April 10, 1851, while Sims sat in his "prison room" at the Boston Courthouse. To a huge crowd at the Melodeon, he poured his wrath out upon Curtis, Thomas and the rest of Boston's Union-Whig establishment. They were Boston's equivalent of Torquemada the Inquisitor, George Jeffreys the "judicial butcher" of England's bloody assizes, and even "Herod the Wicked." Worse still, they had no excuse for their actions since they lived in an enlightened age, and "within two hours of Plymouth Rock, within a single hour of Concord and Lexington, in sight of Bunker Hill." And yet, despite these crimes against conscience and public morality, Parker counseled his listeners to "resist not now with violence...because it is not time just yet; it would not succeed." Timing was everything and the great mass of the people were not yet ready for the final reckoning with slavery. If the American Revolutionaries had tried to fight for independence in 1765, he reminded them, "they would have failed, and we had not been here today." Sims, it seemed, could not benefit the movement by being violently rescued. But perhaps his suffering could be the beginning of America's political redemption. "The blood of martyrs," he argued, "is the seed of the church."[28]

Some of Parker's admirers, who had been thrilled by his earlier comments about killing slave hunters like mosquitoes, were surprised and disappointed by his conduct in the Sims case. Abolitionist Deborah Weston, who attended a Sims protest meeting at Tremont Temple, had applauded Wendell Phillips's pledge to use "all means that God and nature have put into my hands." But she told her sister Anne that Theodore Parker had "shrunk at the meeting" and had "not stood by Wendell." Weston did not think that Parker was "afraid," but complained that "preaching peace" made no sense as long as Sims languished in his courthouse cell. On the brink of violent resistance, Parker's sense of revolutionary timing had deserted him, and he found it difficult to tell if it was 1775 or 1765. This is not entirely surprising. Dramatic and inspiring as they were, accounts of Captain John Parker's famous stand at Lexington hardly offered solutions to the complex practical problems that confronted the antislavery movement in 1851. At the same time, however, it was critical for abolitionist leaders not to convey indecisiveness or fear, as the alliance between white activists and the black community was predicated on the former group's willingness to join the latter in using force, if necessary, to prevent rendition. Here was an agonizing dilemma for Parker. Was there ever a "perfect" time for direct action? Could the Revolution really serve as a blueprint for meeting the current crisis? As it turned out, the elusive mix of conscientious action and effective planning would have to wait for a future crisis.[29]

Deborah Weston's disapproval of Parker's conduct was echoed by conservatives who recognized an opportunity to accuse him of vacillation. In a pamphlet review of the Fast Day sermon, for example, Orestes Brownson wrote sarcastically that "Mr. Parker plainly counsels resistance to the laws, downright treason, and civil war,—only not just yet." Brownson had no doubt that Parker was, at heart, a "red republican," but accused him of moderating his position temporarily in order to aid his Free Soil allies. This observation was, of course, partly true. Parker was still optimistic about the political process and he understood that ill-considered acts of violence might endanger the fragile antislavery political alliance. Of course it was this very sensitivity to political considerations that endeared him to Free Soilers who believed they were on the brink of victory. Charles Sumner clearly loved the Fast Day sermon, saying that it "stirred me to the bottom of my heart." He wished that Parker "could live a thousand years" and wished the sermon could be read everywhere throughout the land."[30]

As the political meaning of the Sims case became Parker's paramount consideration, his thought turned away from the suffering fugitive himself and focused instead on the symbols his rendition might offer the Free Soil movement. When Curtis's decision against Sims was issued on Friday, April 11, the Boston Vigilance Committee was ready with handbills calling for a mass meeting of "every friend of the slave" to witness "the last sad scene of the State's disgrace...come by the thousands!" Due to last minute legal appeals by Sims's lawyers and the caution of the city police department, however, the convicted fugitive was not removed from the Court House until four o'clock the next morning when only a small crowd of abolitionists and black citizens could be assembled to register their disgust. Sims was escorted though the streets by a tight formation of two-hundred city police officers and volunteers, while a federal "Sims" brigade waited on high alert inside Faneuil Hall in case of a last minute rescue attempt.[31]

Parker waited throughout the night at the *Liberator* office and then followed the procession from the Courthouse to Long Wharf like a mourner at a funeral. He could only cringe, as a terrified, weeping Sims was carried "over the spot where, eighty-one years before, the ground had drunk the blood of Crispus Attucks." Paying close attention to the black Bostonians in the crowd, he noted that when the cortege reached the Boston Massacre site, "the hisses and groans" of the protesters were redoubled. As Sims was taken toward Long Wharf where the brig *Acorn* waited to return him to slavery, Parker shouted "Shame!" at the police, and asked "Where is Liberty?" He hung his head when Sims again burst into tears on the deck of the brig and shouted the words: "And this is Massachusetts Liberty!"[32]

Once the ship was out of sight, he returned to the *Liberator* office with other frustrated abolitionists and listened as Henry Bowditch conceded that "we have naught left us now but to pray." On April 19th, the anniversary of Lexington and Concord, Sims arrived at Savannah and was whipped publicly in the city square. Boiling over with anger and frustration, Parker expressed his outrage to Charles Sumner, whose election to the United States Senate would take place in less than a week. "I wish it was the 19th of April 1775," he wrote. "What a disgrace the city has brought on herself...Boston, Boston, thou that kidnappest men!"[33]

XIII
RACE, POLITICS AND ANTISLAVERY VIOLENCE
1852–1853

The Boston fugitive slave crises made Theodore Parker a celebrity and greatly enhanced his influence in shaping public opinion in the North. Though his reputation as a theological heretic had been firmly established in the 1840s, his leadership of the Vigilance Committee and his thundering denunciations of the Fugitive Slave Act from the pulpit gained him a place alongside Garrison and Phillips in the public mind. His published addresses, sermons, and essays reached a wider and more eager audience than ever before. Western distributors of his work could not keep enough copies of his sermons in stock. Throughout the 1850s he received thousands of letters from men and women all over the United States and Europe who read, and either hated or admired his writings on religion and reform.[1]

Locally, the rising interest in Parker's weekly sermons led the Twenty-Eighth Congregational Society to relocate in the larger and recently-constructed Boston Music Hall in the fall of 1852. Located at Winter Street and Bumstead Place, the Music Hall had been built with funds raised by the Harvard Music Association and it was designed by Boston architect George Snell according to the latest, most precise acoustic principles. At the front of a main hall that was "130 feet long, 78 feet wide and 65 feet high," were seven steps that led up to a stage raised about five feet from the ground. On the stage, the preacher spoke from behind a small table where his sermon manuscript, Bible, and hymn book lay. Visitors remembered that when the seats were filled, Parker's closest friends sat on the steps or even on the stage and formed "a kind of body guard" for the minister. But there was usually room for everyone. With narrow balconies lining each wall, the building had a seating capacity that accommodated 2700 people.[2]

Yet even in such a magnificent venue, Parker remained the central attraction. Travelers who came to the Music Hall to hear him during the 1850s were struck by the contrast between his reputation for deep learning and the simplicity of his appearance and delivery. "He is plain in every way; in look, manner, and dress," wrote a visiting Western newspaper editor. A female observer noted that his clothes were always "slightly old fashioned" reminding her of the "Pilgrim fathers." Having been critical of the intellectual and social conservatism of the Boston Brahmins, Parker was determined to avoid their affectations and carefully cultivated an alternative image. He refused to don clerical vestments, standing before his congregation in a plain lecturer's suit rather than in ministerial gown and collar. Since Parker claimed that his authority as a religious leader came only through his exercise of reason and conscience, he regarded clerical vestments as a relic of more primitive forms of church organization. "He reminds one of a New England or Western farmer, afraid of no pressure and ready for any emergency," wrote one observer.[3]

Despite his rough-hewn exterior, however, Parker's weekly services, in keeping with their theatrical setting, were carefully orchestrated to engage his congregation on intellectual and emotional levels. Beginning each week with a prayer, he would gradually increase the volume of his voice and the intensity of his delivery from meditative whisper to an animated shout. "As he spoke," wrote Louisa May Alcott in her 1873 fictionalized portrait of Parker, "a curious stir went through the crowd at times, like as a great wind sweeps over a cornfield." Bible readings were carefully chosen to exclude passages that shocked reason or outraged conscience, and hymns were sung from what Parker called "the Sam book," an 1846 collection compiled by Unitarian ministers Samuel Longfellow and Samuel Johnson. Observers were fascinated by the transformation that occurred when Parker began to speak. "His lead-like eyes begin to glow with genius, and his bald head begins to shine transparently with thought," wrote one visitor. Black abolitionist William Nell, who went faithfully to the Music Hall each week, was inspired by what he called "the moral and mental feast" he found in the sermons. On one snowy Sunday in February 1853, Nell walked home cold but happy after hearing Parker describe the bad weather as simply "the last smile of departing winter."[4]

Along with benevolent analogies from nature, however, Parker delivered more than his share of fire and brimstone at the Music Hall. Wendell Phillips liked to say that Theodore Parker's nature was to "grapple with the tiger and throttle him" and it is clear that he was not afraid to do his throttling in the pulpit. Emerson reversed the tiger metaphor when he described Parker as having "beautiful fangs" and observed that the assembly at the Music Hall delighted to hear their minister "worry and tear his victims" on Sabbath mornings. But there was a distinctive style to his denunciations. According to Louisa May Alcott, he spoke "not loudly nor vehemently, but with indescribable effect of inward force." He appeared to his hearers as "one indomitable man" who taught them to see that "their golden idols had feet of clay." Parker's preaching celebrated the vast spiritual and moral resources with which God had endowed human nature, but it also poured out scorn and contempt upon those who betrayed their natural birthright. Since he believed that evil was a conditional, not a permanent part of the human character, he was intolerant of it and unloaded the full force of his rhetorical power to condemn it. The result was sometimes overwhelming. Samuel Gridley Howe was almost speechless after hearing one of Parker's jeremiads against Commissioner Curtis and the slave hunters. Howe was "moved to the deepest depths of my soul" by the sermon, but he gasped at the "great storm of wrath and indignation" that clearly boiled within Parker's soul. "Tell me you are not destructive? Ha!" wrote Howe.[5]

Julia Ward Howe also found Parker's "power of denunciation" to be one of his most distinctive qualities as a preacher and she praised his willingness to wield the "two-edged sword of the spirit" against oppression and religious intolerance. But unlike her husband, who complained that Parker's preaching was not spiritual enough, Julia found Parker to be a gentle Jeremiah. She remembered him as a humbler and more deeply spiritual man than he seemed to those who read only his printed sermons. At the Music Hall, she said, Parker rose and stood before his listeners with a "sublime attitude of humility" with his "arms extended" and his "features lit up" in reverence. "Truly, he talked with God, and took us with him into the divine presence," she remembered.[6]

Though Parker's sermons at the Music Hall were popular attractions, he also remained in demand as a lyceum lecturer. He had always done well on the lyceum circuit, but improvements in print distribution and passenger transportation now offered him a much larger audience. The commercial and cultural ties that linked New England with the growing states of the Middle West had created a highway for ideas as well as goods. In states like Illinois, rising, self-educated men like Abraham Lincoln and his law partner William Herndon, were eager to consume Yankee culture as a mark of refinement. It was the attention of men like these that allowed Parker to begin "extending his diocese to the prairies." Commanding twenty-five dollar lecture fees, he spoke as many as a hundred times each winter throughout most of the decade in places as far west as Illinois and Wisconsin. For a man who had always feared that that clerical ostracism would confine him to a career of obscure labor in a small rural parish, this was vindication indeed. In 1859, he estimated liberally that he had spoken to "sixty or a hundred thousand persons in each year" through these lyceum lectures.[7]

Whatever the actual numbers, Parker's northern and western speaking tours were important in spreading his religious and anti-slavery sentiments to a wider audience and exposing him to a broader set of views on the sectional crisis. As he traveled on the "railroad cars and steamboats" or lodged in the "public and private houses," moreover, he found a respite from the cares of his ministry and the disappointments of his private life. Always carrying a stack of books and sheaf of paper, he found that the "motion of the railroad cars gave a pleasing stimulus to thought" and that he was able to "read and write all day long." Yet in those hours of meditation, the smoldering passions of Parker's revolutionary conscience lost none of its intensity. He always returned to Boston ready to "grapple with the tiger and throttle him."[8]

Race, Violence and the Revolutionary Center

Among the "difficult problems" that Parker doubtless contemplated on his western travels was the growing violence resulting from the passage of the Fugitive Slave Act. The years 1851–52 represent the height of the government's attempt to enforce the law and there were nearly 130 fugitive slave cases in the North during that period. For those who hoped that the law would be unenforceable above the Mason-Dixon Line, the record in those cases was dismal. In only eleven of them were accused fugitives rescued or released. It became clear in the aftermath of the Sims case that northern outrage against the law had cooled, and that conservatives like Webster and Stuart had, at least temporarily, won the public debate. Southern slaveholders were not above gloating in such victories. After returning to Georgia with Thomas Sims, for example, James Bacon published letters expressing his gratitude to the "many hundreds of gentlemen who aided us" and singling out the city's merchants for special thanks. The merchants of Boston, Bacon wrote, "were conspicuous in their efforts to serve us" and would have provided security "to the amount of millions of dollars." Bacon assured the southern elite that they could carry on trade with Yankee merchants secure in the knowledge that the law would be carried out to the letter.[9]

Parker, who could believe almost anything of the Boston merchants, could have had no better evidence with which to indict them. But in the final accounting for that year, a close observer could not have missed the fact that in the vast majority of cases where accused fugitives had escaped rendition to the South, they were freed by rescues, some of them violent, rather than through legal means. In this environment, Parker began to regard the choice he had made in the Sims case between politics and violence, 1765 and 1776, as a false one. Perhaps violent confrontations between slavery and freedom themselves contained the seeds of political change. If he had once been content to allow Thomas Sims to become a "crucified redeemer," he soon came to believe that redemption required something more akin to Lexington and Concord than the garden at Gethsemane.

But Parker's endorsement of violence was never absolute, nor was it ever embraced for its own sake. Instead, violence was always linked to the demands of conscience, the collective memory of the American Revolution, and the defense of the nation's core idea of republican liberty. These three concepts formed what might be called the "revolutionary center" of American abolitionist culture during the 1850s. At his best, Parker deployed those concepts with enormous effectiveness and in doing so he moved to the forefront of the movement in the years before the Civil War. Appealing to widely shared values among his fellow activists, he was able to reach out across the lines that divided the antislavery community. The abolitionist critique of slavery, after all, had always been grounded in a shared republican political culture drawing inspiration from the Declaration of Independence as well as the Bible. It balanced evangelical moral intensity with an equally-strong secular tradition in which abolitionists defined themselves as the "heirs" of the American Revolution. It is important to remember that *both* black and white abolitionists carried personal and emotional connections to the events of 1776, ties which bound them to defend the sacrifice of the revolutionary generation through violent action if necessary. These ties created a sense of shared history that at times cut across the lines of race that too often threatened to divide the movement.[10]

Much like Parker, who liked to display his grandfather's muskets from the battle of Lexington, black abolitionists had revolutionary ancestors of their own. In the 1850s, for example, black abolitionist Benjamin Roberts waged war against segregated schools in Boston in the name of his grandfather James Easton, a revolutionary war veteran. Revolutionary memory was as central to the Roberts/Easton family tradition as it was to the Parkers of Lexington. Historians George R. Price and James Brewer Stewart have suggested that the "powerful ties of memory that linked the struggles of the 1840s and 1850s to the 'spirit of 1776' . . . marked a critical convergence of white and black abolitionist ideology." That convergence even extended to pacifistic, white Garrisonians who could not resist using this most hallowed of America's traditions to sustain their movement. After a bloody, but successful slave revolt on the brig *Creole* in 1841, for example, the Massachusetts Anti-Slavery Society praised its leader Madison Washington, citing the same principles by "which we eulogized George Washington and his brave compeers." The Revolution was an irresistible cultural symbol for the dissident, oppositional culture that the abolitionists were creating and it served as the "overarching signifier" for the dramatic events of the 1850s.[11]

Parker's embrace of the revolutionary center in antislavery culture, however, existed in tension with his equally strong tendency to understand American national identity in racial terms. This most troubling aspect of Parker's thought was at least in part a product of a romantic orientation that viewed human history as an outgrowth of innate principles. As a Transcendentalist and student of German intellectual culture, Parker was steeped in the romantic nationalism that emanated from the German universities in the early nineteenth century. Linked as it was to the liberal-democratic revolutions of the 1840s, romantic nationalism appeared to Parker as a liberating force, wielded by reformers and intellectuals in the interests of freedom and self-determination. At the same time, however, romantic nationalists often understood nations as expressions of ethnic, or what they often called "racial," qualities.

The tendency of this tradition to embrace racial chauvinism had a significant impact on Parker. As early as 1843, for instance, he had added the complete works of Johann Gottfried von Herder to his growing library. Among the titles contained in the set were Herder's *Outlines of a Philosophy of Human History* and his *Treatise on the Origin of Language*, both of which developed a theory of nationalism based upon the unique characteristics of particular peoples. Herder agreed that all of humanity was part of a single species, but he emphasized diversity among human groups as evidence of God's creativity. He also pointed to language as the key to the most basic divisions among the human family. In Herder's philosophy, nations were not political contracts between individuals but expressions of cultural, ethnic, religious, and especially linguistic communities. As cultural communities with unique qualities, he argued, nations represented basic divisions of the human race which commanded a natural and irreversible loyalty from the individuals belonging to them. Herder thought of race in much less fixed or biological terms than American proslavery apologists did, but his romantic nationalism rested upon the existence of qualities that were unshakably rooted in the history, culture and worldview of national groups.[12]

German romantic works on language and nationality shaped Parker's thought during the 1840s and they served a vital function in his growing commitment to American national distinctiveness. Despite moving away from fellow Transcendentalists Ralph Waldo Emerson and Margaret Fuller on social issues, he shared their quest to identify and nurture a truly American cultural life. Parker was certain that the United States possessed a unique culture with its own set of exemplars or "representative men." Such figures embodied the peculiar qualities of their nation's "racial" characteristics. "Franklin, the greatest man who ever touched our soil, is most intensely national," he wrote in a sermon on "Great Men." "He could have been born and bred in no other land; that human gold was minted into America coin."[13]

Parker came to believe that the distinctive qualities of nations defined their special role in the providential and progressive development of human history. No nation could embody the full range of human traits necessary to the advancement of the species, but each national community contributed its own qualities to the stream of improvement. In describing this phenomenon, Parker opted for a corporeal image that emphasized interdependence among distinct human groups. "The hand is one, but it is separated into five fingers, to make it pliant and manifold useful," he once told his congregation at the Music Hall. "God makes us diverse in nationality so that we may help each other; the mantel of destiny girdeth us all."[14]

But what were America's distinctive qualities and where did they come from? By the time of the European revolutions of 1848, Parker saw America's core identity in its people's "love of freedom, of man's natural rights" and their "genius for liberty." Such ideas were useful in the midst of the slavery conflict, and they allowed abolitionists and antislavery politicians to define the South's peculiar institution as un-American, a dangerous anomaly requiring final resolution before the nation could take its rightful place in history. But Parker associated those national qualities with the Anglo-Saxon "race," whose aggressive spirit and tenacious libertarianism, he believed, had emerged among the Teutonic peoples of Germany and then moved relentlessly westward reaching America in the seventeenth century. Tracing the history of the Anglo-Saxons as offshoots of the Caucasian race, he found "racial" qualities that explained key elements of the American national experience. First, they were expansionist: "the Anglo-Saxon prefers new and wild lands to old and well-cultivated territories." Second, they were naturally democratic both in politics and religion: "There is a strong love of freedom...ours is the only tongue in which liberty can speak." Third, they were eminently resourceful: "The Anglo-Saxons have eminent practical power to organize things into a mill, or men into a state, and then administer the organization."[15]

The genius of American democracy, he liked to say, was its ability to balance the centrifugal force of individualism with national "unity of action," a centripetal force ensuring that the American "dread of authority" did not lapse into anarchy and thereby compromise the nation's place in history. These characteristics were linked in Parker's mind with essential traits of the Anglo-Saxon race, "that bold, handy, practical people" who shared both a "love of liberty and love of law." In the end, only "African slavery—the great exception in the nation's history" stood in the way of the nation's destiny. "Once that is removed," he believed, "lesser, but kindred evils will easily be done away with." Racked by contradictions that grew more serious over the decade of the 1850s, Parker's racial Anglo-Saxonism was initially an anti-Southern doctrine. The South's peculiar institution was the exception to the nation's most fundamental character. It must end if America was to realize its destiny.[16]

During the 1850s, however, Parker's interest in the racial components of American national uniqueness led him to read more widely in the growing science of ethnology which rooted national qualities in more innate, biological qualities. Most influential on his thought was Johann Friedrich Blumenbach, an eighteenth century German racial theorist who argued, on the basis of physical comparisons, that the human species was divided into Caucasian, Mongolian, American, Ethiopian and Malayan races. Parker agreed with Blumenbach's basic classification, but he suspected that human racial categories might actually be much more numerous and more porous than the young science of ethnology had yet discovered. He understood race less as a fixed biological category than as a set of physical and cultural tendencies grouped around a mean, so he took Blumenbach's five races as only a "provisional" way of describing human differences. They were merely "five baskets which will help us hold mankind and help us handle them."[17]

And yet at the same time, he could not resist the temptation to rank the "races" of the world based on their state of cultural development. "In respect to the power of civilization, the African is at the bottom," he told his friend David Wasson, "the Indian is next." Living in Boston during the early 1850s, moreover, Parker interacted with growing numbers of Irish immigrants whose deep loyalty to Catholicism and support for a proslavery Democratic Party suggested a "racial" explanation. In comparison with Anglo-Saxon, he argued, "the Celtic stock never much favored Protestantism or individual liberty." The Irish population, he believed, was very different from Teutonic peoples and Anglo-Saxons who "have the strongest ethnological instinct for personal freedom." Although he stopped just short of endorsing the political nativism of the Know-Nothing Party in Massachusetts, Parker clearly believed that Irish votes were "in the market" where the "bishops can dispose of them" and where "politicians will make their bid."[18]

On one level, Parker's willingness to classify and rank races in terms of inherent qualities demonstrates that the trajectory of racial thought increasingly "pointed downward" in the antebellum period. Eighteenth century scientists had generally held that human nature was, with small differences, fixed and universal. A document like the Declaration of Independence, despite its authorship by a Virginia slaveholder, had rested upon a universalism that at least rhetorically recognized a basis for human equality. In the nineteenth century, however, scientific investigation focused on the great diversity of human physical and cultural characteristics. The eagerness to classify races in hierarchical ways demonstrates how powerfully European colonialism and the growth of American slavery shaped the context of scientific thought during this period.[19]

At the most extreme end of the racialist spectrum were thinkers like Louis Agassiz, the expatriate Swiss biologist who went as far as to claim that blacks were actually a distinct species of human beings. Agassiz was a formidable figure and a very prominent one in Theodore Parker's Boston. Having arrived there in 1846 after establishing himself as one of the premier naturalists in Europe, Agassiz had taken the city by storm in a series of public lectures to which thousands had clamored for admittance. Remaining in Massachusetts as the head of the newly-founded Lawrence Scientific School, he became America's preeminent scientific star. His views carried enormous weight and while race had not been Agassiz's primary scientific interest before coming to America, that soon changed. In the years after his arrival, he came under the influence of proslavery ethnologist Samuel Morton, a Philadelphia doctor who used his vast collection of skulls from around the world to "prove" that the average cranial capacity of blacks placed them in separately created, permanently inferior species. By 1850, Agassiz had embraced the "polygenetic" view of human origins and in doing so lent the weight of his scientific authority to the proslavery argument. Proslavery apologist Josiah Nott once triumphantly proclaimed that "with Agassiz in the war, the battle is ours."[20]

While recognizing that Parker's racialized understanding of American nationalism breathed some of the same intellectual air as Agassiz, Morton, and Nott, it is equally important to note that he rejected the most important implications of their views. He admired Louis Agassiz's work on natural history, but he was disgusted by the scientist's views on race. In a clever play on Agassiz' well known opposition to the ideas of adaptation and evolution, Parker offered a darkly comic explanation of the scientist's conversion to polygenism. "He comes to America; he is subdued to the temper of our atmosphere; and from a great man of science, he becomes the *Swiss of slavery*." In a speech at the New York Anti-Slavery Society in 1854, he rejected Agassiz's characterization of Africans as "a sort of arithmetic mean proportional between a man and a monkey." How, Parker asked, did this account for "the power of speech, the religious faculty, permanence of affection, self-denial, power to master the earth, and smelt iron ore, as the African has done, and is doing still every year?" Reason and conscience remained universal human attributes and, even if expressed differently and in different degrees, those human attributes precluded the invidious distinctions made by Agassiz and Morton. Races were not fixed in the way that proslavery thinkers argued, but rather they were "provisional" categories with porous boundaries and overlapping characteristics.[21]

Ironically, Parker's rejection of polygenism placed him on the same side as conservative Christians whose insistence upon a literal reading of Genesis precluded any kind of separate creation not mentioned in Scripture. But biblical considerations were not uppermost in Parker's mind here. For all its contradictions, his invocation of racial Anglo-Saxonism was mainly an argument against the slaveholding South and its valorization of slavery as essential to American history and destiny. Anglo-Saxons supplied the nation's core idea of freedom, and that idea was fundamentally at odds with the ideology of slavery. But even as this view helped Parker to define slaveholders and their values as un-American, it also threatened to define the nation in ways that excluded African Americans.

The tension between Parker's embrace of abolitionism's revolutionary center and his affinity for romantic racialism remained a central problem in his activism until the end of his life. At times, as we shall see, it seriously strained his relationship with black abolitionists. But his "provisional" understanding of race also left enough room to at least conditionally embrace an historical bond linking white and black activists to a common revolutionary heritage. For all his celebrations of the Anglo-Saxon "instinct for freedom," he understood that Anglo-Saxons were not the only ones who loved liberty and who would use violence, if necessary, to preserve it. He had been prepared to see Thomas Sims become a martyr to freedom's cause, but he also celebrated the hunted fugitive's willingness to use deadly force against the kidnappers. "He had a most unlucky knife, which knocked at a kidnapper's bosom but could not enter," Parker told his congregation on the first anniversary of the rendition.[22]

Contemporary black resistance also inspired Parker to revisit the history of the American Revolution itself. Black patriot Crispus Attucks began appearing in Parker's antislavery rhetoric alongside white heroes like John Adams and James Otis. Conservative Bostonians were content to allow the memory of Attucks and his unruly, street-wise compatriots to pass into historical oblivion, but Parker joined black abolitionists in refusing to cooperate. Sims, he told his congregation, had been taken "over the spot where, eighty-one years before, the ground had drunk in the African blood of Crispus Attucks, shed by white men on the fifth of March." Parker would later join black abolitionists in Boston in commemorating March 5th as "Crispus Attucks Day" and he supported their efforts to construct a monument to the fallen hero. Throughout the 1850s, Parker was open to re-imagining the American Revolution in biracial terms. With the assistance of the pioneering black historian William Nell, he gathered substantial information about black soldiers who had fought at Bunker Hill. He remembered that as a child in Lexington he had seen engravings of the battle that depicted black patriot Peter Salem shooting British Major John Pitcairn but noted with disgust that more recent representations of the battle had erased all traces of Salem's gallantry. "Now-a-days a white man is put in his place," he complained. "Negroes get few honors."[23]

Parker also rejoiced when white and black activists came together to embrace violent resistance in the name of freedom and conscience, thereby demonstrating their common heritage. He was thrilled when reports reached Boston of the forcible rescue of William "Jerry" Henry from federal authorities in Syracuse, New York. As three thousand angry people milled near the police station where Henry was being held, a group of fifty white and black abolitionists attacked the building with rocks, clubs, axes and a fourteen-foot battering ram which they used to break down the doors leading to the courtroom. The ferocity of the assault terrified the authorities and one of the federal marshals had his arm broken by a rescuer wielding an iron bar. The police quickly fled the building leaving Henry in the hands of rescuers who soon shepherded him across the border into Ontario.[24]

Parker was overjoyed by the rescue and he congratulated the antislavery community in Syracuse for resisting "successfully, openly, at noonday." None of the monuments "at Lexington and Concord" he said, could tell of a "nobler act" than theirs. He needled his friend Rev. Samuel Joseph May, who was a nonresistant, about shedding his pacifist principles in the rush of events. "Yes sir, we knew who broke the Marshal's arm," he teased. "We had intelligence by the underground telegraph that Mr. May was the head and tail of the mob at Syracuse." In his celebration of Henry's rescue, however, Parker's racial nationalism temporarily disappeared and was replaced by images of a biracial resistance movement, modeled on revolutionary patriotism, for which new monuments would have to be built and new heroic stories told.[25]

Parker clearly believed that a willingness to use force in defense of inalienable rights was a crucial element of American life. The fact that he associated that willingness with Anglo-Saxons did not preclude a belief that it was present in other "races" as well. Indeed, Parker sometimes sounded as if violent resistance to oppression was a universal human quality that was triggered by the existence of injustice itself. Rather than insisting that the "instinct for freedom" was an exclusively Anglo-Saxon trait, he often described it as a human quality, linked to conscience, which God had built into human nature to ensure that injustice would always generate opposition. When blacks resisted slavery violently, Parker applauded their actions as evidence that conscience existed in all of the races of mankind and that the southern "idea" of slavery would ultimately be put to flight. Yet at the same time, he placed an unfair and unreasonable burden on African Americans themselves, somehow demanding that they supply the antidote to his own racialist doubts about their fighting spirit.

Black abolitionists, of course, rejected the notion that they had anything to prove to whites and they pushed Parker to re-evaluate his tendency to think in racial terms. Charles Lenox Remond, for example, bluntly demanded that Parker stop referring to him as a "representative of the African race" and asked him to remember that "the hand of slavery is on every white man, as well as upon the humblest black." Black abolitionist John Rock once described Parker as "one of the noblest of Freedom's champions," but felt it necessary to tell him that "the black man is not a coward." He conceded that Parker understood the "character of the Anglo-Saxon race" better than anyone else, but reminded him that "in the Revolution, colored soldiers fought side by side with you in your struggles for liberty." If Parker sometimes abandoned abolitionism's revolutionary center in favor of racial nationalism, it was black activists who worked hardest to pull him back. In doing so, they helped him to keep his faith in the revolutionary tradition and in the universality of human conscience, the very ideas that defined his public life.[26]

Nothing better demonstrates Parker's characteristic mix of support and condescension than his response to the Christiana rebellion of September 1851. On the morning of September 11th, Maryland slaveholder Edward Gorsuch, supported by a posse of federal officials, had surrounded a farmhouse in Christiana, Pennsylvania intent on capturing four African Americans he claimed as his property. Fortunately, the escaped slaves inside were under the protection of a heavily-armed, black militia group led by former slave William Parker who owned the farmhouse and had turned it into a fortress. After Parker's men repelled one assault on the building, a crowd of fifty black citizens arrived armed with clubs and other weapons. Menaced by an angry crowd that vastly outnumbered the nine-man posse that rode with him, Gorsuch arrogantly refused to retreat. Observers claimed that he said "I'll have my property or I'll breakfast in Hell." During the bloody battle that ensued, Gorsuch was clubbed to death, his son was shot, and the federal marshal's men were dispersed and chased into the next county. Here was violent black resistance in which Anglo-Saxons had played no role except as the defeated agents of tyranny and oppression.[27]

After hearing the news, Parker told Samuel May that he "deeply rejoiced" that "Negroes shot down the kidnappers at Christiana." He sincerely hoped that they would do so "in Boston and everywhere else." At the same time, he could not help but interpret the Christiana rebellion in overtly racial terms. He treated it as a kind of proving ground on which African Americans had offered important, but only partial evidence of their own "instinct for freedom." In a public letter to the Pennsylvania Anti-Slavery Society he said he was "glad that some black men have been found *at last* who dared to resist violence with powder and ball." Now he believed that black men could "hold up their heads before those haughty Caucasians and say 'You see that we also can fight.'"[28]

Many abolitionists, black and white, dissented from Parker's racial views, but his support for forcible resistance at Syracuse and Christiana was widely shared within an antislavery movement whose axis was rapidly tilting away from pacifism. More self-consciously biracial, confrontational and violent, abolitionists were increasingly receptive to Parker's description of their struggle against the Slave Power as a continuation of the American Revolution. William Lloyd Garrison himself conceded that the Christiana rebellion was warranted on the grounds of self-defense and that it was "justified by the Declaration of Independence." Pennsylvania non-resistant Oliver Johnson still hoped that "the mild arms of truth and love" would remain the weapons of abolitionists, but younger members of the Pennsylvania Anti-Slavery Society resolved that the Christiana fugitives "were only following the example of Washington and the American heroes of '76." Parker's views received explicit support from Frederick Douglass' whose frustration with non-resistance was increasingly evident after 1850. At a meeting of Garrisonian abolitionists in Rhode Island, Douglass had a heated argument with white activist Samuel Wheeler who had condemned Theodore Parker for applauding the shooting of kidnappers. When Wheeler asked the group to join him in publicly denouncing Parker's "approval of violent resistance to the Fugitive Slave Law," Douglass defended Parker's views as both "consistent and right."[29]

For Douglass, as for many black abolitionists in the 1850s, Parker's dalliances with racialism could be tolerated, at least in the short term, because he was on the right side of the most practical issues of resistance facing African Americans in the North. In contrast to white Garrisonians like Charles Burleigh who too often made infuriating distinctions between "spirited resistance" to the law which they supported, and "physical violence and bloodshed," which they did not, Parker was unequivocal. Whether endorsing Thomas Sims's "unlucky knife" or applauding the "powder and ball" of the Christiana rebels, he had fewer and fewer qualms about forcible resistance to a diabolical Slave Power that had both freedom and conscience in its sights.[30]

XIV
CONSCIENCE, POLITICS AND RELIGION
1853–1854

If Theodore Parker's endorsement of antislavery violence put him in the vanguard of the movement in the 1850s, so too did his embrace of the political antislavery. During the last ten years of his life, he developed a pastoral relationship with several leading antislavery politicians including Charles Sumner, Henry Wilson, and even his former professor, John Gorham Palfrey. He offered support and consolation when their devotion to antislavery principles drew biting criticism from conservatives. But he also doled out mild rebukes when he detected signs of inconsistency or compromise in their positions. Perhaps more importantly, Parker protected antislavery politicians as best he could against intense criticism from Garrisonian abolitionists who still regarded partisan politics as hopelessly compromised. Having established his credentials as a radical activist during the Fugitive Slave crisis of 1850–51, Parker could now scold the Garrisonians for excessive ideological opposition to political activism without endangering his standing as an abolitionist.

Ample evidence suggests that even America's most prominent antislavery politicians valued Parker for playing just this role. William Henry Seward, who was emerging as the nation's most prominent antislavery Whig in 1852, praised him for understanding "two things which Anti-Slavery men are too slow in learning." The first was that a successful movement rested upon the interdependence of moral and political work. The second was that "ill nature and censure, if right and effective, should be bestowed upon the opponents of all Anti-Slavery men and not on Anti-Slavery men whose views or mode of action differ from our own." There were few activists who could move easily across the ideological landscape of American antislavery, but Theodore Parker was one of them. [1]

Given Parker's intense criticism of proslavery politicians in the 1850s, and his acceptance of violent resistance to slavery, it is easy to forget that for most of the decade he remained optimistic about political solutions. He understood that politics was a mix of high and low ideals, but he had a deep faith in the progressive direction of the nation's history. Slavery, like any moral and political evil, was temporary, and would ultimately give way to more permanent ideals of freedom and natural rights. Even if the leaders of the Whig and Democratic Parties failed to keep faith with the idea of freedom, Parker was certain that "the mass of men interested in this idea will be faithful." As the collective conscience of the nation advanced to embrace higher principles, new leaders and new political institutions would emerge to reflect and refine them. "Their progress is steady," he believed, "their development is sure." Like churches, principled democratic political parties could educate the people and organize them for the betterment of the nation. [2]

Yet having spent so much of his earlier career excoriating timid or self-interested ministers for pandering to the selfish prejudices of their congregations, Parker also recognized that political leaders could easily do the same. Only an awakened public conscience could ensure that those who directed the nation's political life represented and advanced the very highest sentiments of the people. As the stakes rose ever higher, his commitment to a robust dissenting discourse culture deepened.

Daniel Webster and the Public Conscience

Daniel Webster was the best example of how political leaders could lose their way and, in the process, derange the conscience of the nation. Parker blamed Webster more than anyone else for the catastrophe of the Sims rendition and the humiliation Boston had suffered as a result. Next to the Curtis brothers, there was no one he loathed as much as "black Dan." Yet what concerned Parker most was the veneration Webster still received in New England. Why did so many in Massachusetts regard him as their *beau ideal* of a statesman? For two years after the 7th of March speech, Webster had traveled the country ridiculing the "higher law," and accusing abolitionists of having "contempt [for] God and His commandments." At one point during his bid for the Whig Party nomination in 1852, he had nearly disowned his state, telling an audience of Virginians that "suppose I displeased all of the people of [Massachusetts]—what of that?" Somehow, Parker complained, the myth of Webster's greatness left him immune from criticism. He had become a pagan idol whose oratorical gifts had tricked the conscience of the region into suspending its collective judgment. As long as conscience remained at bay, progress against slavery would be blocked and the leaders of the Bay State Free Soil movement would face a public mesmerized by the "Godlike Daniel." The deification of Webster, like the divinity of Christ, discouraged the people from using their own innate capacities for discerning moral truth.[3]

The senator's death on October 24, 1852 promised to make this worse as effusions of gratitude and hagiography poured forth from the presses and conservative pulpits of New England. As he had after John Quincy Adams' death in 1848, Parker understood eulogy to be a powerful tool with the potential to affect the political dynamic in Massachusetts. If Webster's admirers succeeded in controlling the public memory of their hero's life through oratory and monuments, they might use his legacy against the antislavery political movement in the upcoming elections. Within a week of Webster's death, therefore, Parker delivered a blistering, and for some at least, a shocking post-mortem condemnation of the Senator. In it he explained that the veneration of Webster was a product of mistaken notions of greatness. Great men possessed qualities in *advance* of their contemporaries and were scorned, even martyred by those who clung to lower ideals. Webster, by contrast, "had little value as a permanent guide" because he had a "dread of taking responsibility in advance of public sentiment." He had been showered with honors in his own lifetime, but would never enjoy the lasting reputation. "No great ideas, no great organizations, will bind him to the coming age."[4]

Truly great men, Parker insisted, were driven by conscience to new heights of moral, intellectual or religious truth. But Webster had "almost no self-reliant independence of character" and it was "his surroundings, not his will that shaped his character." Those who revered Webster for his intellectual power simply failed to understand that "mere cunning" was no standard for greatness. "The power of justice, of love, of holiness, of trust in God, and of obedience to his law—the eternal right," far outweighed intellectual parlor tricks or rhetorical effusions as standards of human greatness. Ranging widely, and sometimes inaccurately, across Webster's long political career, Parker described the senator as little more than a political weather vane. Without conscience to guide him, his political philosophy had shifted from states' rights to nationalism, free trade to protectionism, free soil to proslavery expansionism, all in a vain quest for the presidency. If the people of New England wanted true greatness, they had better not look to Webster who was "pensioned by the capitalists of Boston" and whose "speeches smell of bribes." They should look instead to the men who were leading the nation in its elemental fight against slavery. "Adams, Giddings, Chase, Palfrey, Mann, Hale, Seward, Rantoul, and Sumner," these were the prophetic politicians of the day who would achieve lasting historic fame.[5]

Heaping public scorn on a dead man was a risky move, and in doing it Parker brought the establishment down upon his neck once more. Conservatives were disgusted by the sermon and furious when it appeared as a pamphlet in the spring of 1853. Edward Everett said that Parker's vision of Webster was distorted by a "fly hatched from a maggot" in his brain. George Osborne Stearns, a conservative Whig from Roxbury who wrote under the pseudonym "Junius Americanus," spent eighty-nine, outraged pages defending Webster and lashing Parker for "malignity, meanness, prevarication, indecency, bad metaphor, false logic, false statement, and canting hypocrisy." The heart of the matter for Stearns, as for Parker, was conscience. Convinced that neither the slaves nor

America was ready for emancipation, he demanded that Parker and the abolitionists respect the consciences of those who disagreed with them. "Do you really believe that we are sinning against our reason, our conscience, and our souls
in this matter, and that you only are obeying the "higher law of God?" he asked.
"All we ask is the same freedom of conscience which you yourselves claim."[6]

Having accepted Webster's claim that the Union had been in serious danger
of dissolution in 1850, men like Everett and Stearns insisted that the Fugitive
Slave Act and the other "compromise" measures had been necessary to avert
bloody civil war. If there really was a "higher law" as the antislavery movement
claimed, did it not demand that everything possible be done to avert a catastrophic conflict? Stearns argued that Parker, like all abolitionists, used conscience to oversimplify an issue of immense political and moral complexity.
"Bestridden by one idea; wedded to a single sentiment," the abolitionists would
"set fire to the temple of liberty itself, and, for the safety of a dozen negroes,
blast the welfare of a continent for ages." Moral clarity on the slavery issue was,
for Stearns and other Massachusetts conservatives, a dangerous illusion.[7]

Political antislavery activists reacted differently to the Webster eulogy.
Charles Francis Adams believed that it would be the only "independent and
thorough analysis that will be made" of Webster's life. He told Parker that he
had once been an enthusiastic admirer of the senator's vast "intellectual powers," but was later "repelled by too near observation of his moral deficiencies."
William Seward, who supplied Parker with advice and information for the pamphlet version of the discourse, agreed that Webster had had a mighty intellect,
but no conscience. "I do not think that his 'inner light,' as the Friends say, was
very bright," wrote the New Yorker. But perhaps most gratifying to Parker was
that despite the condemnations that poured in from conservatives, or perhaps
because of them, the discourse found a wide audience outside New England. A
book distributor in the Western Reserve of Ohio ordered extra copies of the
pamphlet and correspondents from the region praised its value in the battle
against what they called "Hunker" politics. One reader from Huron County,
Ohio said that local residents had read the *New York Tribune* accounts of the
discourse and were impatient to get hold of the expanded version. "I am eager to
let you know that said discourse is doing a good work in this part of the country," he wrote. "It has cleared the Hunker Fog from many minds and let in the
sun-light of truth."[8]

Sumner, Mann and Phillips

Parker was gratified by the support he received from admirers of the Webster
eulogy, but his main objective in writing it had been to establish conscience as
the ultimate standard by which to judge political leaders. In the early 1850s, he
thought he saw signs that northern voters were choosing leaders whose fidelity
to conscience on the slavery issue dwarfed Webster's. New York's William
Seward, Ohio's Salmon Chase and Joshua Giddings, Indiana's George Julian,
and New Hampshire's John Hale seemed to represent a shift toward a morally-

committed, antislavery political culture. But there was no one who represented the politics of conscience better than Charles Sumner. In electing Sumner to the Senate in 1851, Parker believed, Massachusetts had chosen the most principled political opponent of slavery in its history. Here was a man whose voice and vote could be counted on to oppose the Slave Power.

What Parker hoped for in Sumner was nothing less than the perfection of politics. Three days after the election he warned the senator-elect that "I expect much of you, that I expect heroism of the most manly kind . . . you are bound more and more to perfect yourself for the sake of the State, to deny yourself for the sake of the State." Parker was adamant that his friend scorn the temptations of preferment and remain faithful to the moral principles that had, so far, marked his career. As he had pointed out in his eulogy of Webster, leadership in important matters meant taking unpopular stands and risking political capital. "All our statesmen build, on the opinion of today, a house that is to be admired tomorrow, and the next day to be torn down with hootings," he warned. "I hope you will build on the Rock of Ages, and look to eternity for your justification." For his part, Sumner promised that he would be a new kind of politician, guided by "everlasting rules of right and wrong which are a law alike to individuals and communities."[9]

With expectations as high as these, Parker was bound to be anxious about Sumner's performance. After taking office, the senator received a constant stream of letters from the Boston minister demanding speeches on the repeal of the Fugitive Slave Act, something he had promised to do as his first act in office. Finding Washington politics difficult to navigate, however, he missed numerous opportunities to take his stand against the hated law. As the months went by, conservative Whigs and Garrisonian abolitionists began accusing Sumner of betraying his constituents. Parker regularly heard Garrisonians alike condemn him as "playing the part of Hamlet," and warned Sumner that that he would be *"dead—dead—dead"* if he didn't speak by the end of the 1852 session. His letters were insistent. "I hope you will speak on this matter of slavery, will speak long, brave, and with the best ability you have," Parker wrote in August of that year. "I am heartily sorry that you have deferred speaking so long."[10]

In his own defense, Sumner explained that Senate procedure made it impossible to speak out on slavery at the time of one's choosing, and he claimed that he was as anxious to have his say as any of his supporters. "I know my heart and I know that sincerely, singly have I striven for the cause," he told Parker. "I claim the confidence of my friends, for I know that I deserve it." Parker was pleased when, on August 26, Sumner delivered his first great senatorial oration against the Fugitive Slave Act. Based on the Free Soil doctrine that slavery must remain a sectional rather than a national institution, Sumner called the Fugitive Slave Act "inconsistent, absurd, and tyrannical." Parker thanked Sumner for the speech the very next day. "Now you have done yourself justice and put yourself out of the reach of attack from friend and foe."[11]

In speaking of the attacks of friends, Parker alluded to the incessant criticism that Sumner and other Free Soilers were receiving from the radical aboli-

tionists. Parker had used the suspicion of the radicals to coax speeches out of
Sumner, but he recognized that the conflict between Free Soilers and radicals
was, in fact, a conflict of conscience. The Garrisonians maintained their belief in
the proslavery character of the Constitution and they denounced those who held
office under its aegis. Free Soilers, however, believed that federal support for
slavery was, in fact, unconstitutional and they were confident that their movement would play a crucial role in slavery's destruction. Throughout the agitation
over the fugitive slave renditions in Boston, these differences had remained sub-
ordinated to the larger goal of resisting the Fugitive Slave Act. But in the absence of immediate crises, deep-seated differences reasserted themselves. By
early 1853 the confrontation which Parker hoped would take place between supporters and opponents of slavery in the halls of Congress instead broke out
among the antislavery ranks in Massachusetts.[12]

The renewal of open conflict between Garrisonians and Free Soilers occurred in the aftermath of the disastrous fall elections in 1852 when the political
antislavery movement suffered setbacks all across the North. In Massachusetts,
the Free Soil-Democratic coalition which had elected Sumner the previous year
was defeated by resurgent Whigs. To critics of the political antislavery movement, defeat clearly demonstrated the bankruptcy of forging alliances with those
whose antislavery principles were less than heartfelt. Bay State Democrats, who
had helped to elect Sumner, had deserted their former Free Soil allies to support
the presidential campaign of New Hampshire's Franklin Pierce, a thoroughly
pro-slavery candidate. Pierce's election ensured that the Fugitive Slave Act
would have an enthusiastic supporter in the nation's chief magistrate. Almost as
depressing for Free Soilers was the fact that their own gubernatorial candidate,
Horace Mann, had received less than thirty percent of the vote and was defeated
by Whig candidate John Clifford. The slavery issue seemed at least temporarily
to have lost its political muscle.[13]

To radicals like Wendell Phillips, the Free Soilers' strategy of coalition had
clearly failed and it had taken too much genuine antislavery sentiment down
with it. In a speech before the Massachusetts Anti-Slavery Society in January of
1853, Phillips singled out Horace Mann for being "too slow" to resolve the contradiction between his antislavery principles and his oath of allegiance to the
Constitution. He charged that there was a dangerous but unstated tendency
among politicians like Mann to acquiesce in the continued existence of southern
slavery. The Free-Soilers' belief that slavery would die once its spread was halt-
ed was nothing more than an evasion of the fundamental moral issue. Strangled
by a proslavery Constitution and a tainted political process riddled with corruption, the political antislavery movement could not accomplish the moral revolution America needed. "Shall we stand courteously silent, and let these men play
out the play, when to our thinking, their plan will slacken the zeal, balk the
hopes, and waste the efforts of the slave's friends?" asked Phillips.[14]

Phillips's attacks on Mann generated an intense personal and ideological
controversy that forced Parker to renew his pastoral relationship with both wings
of the antislavery movement. Mann was extremely sensitive to public criticism

from Garrisonians. He had earned their disapproval earlier when, as Secretary of the Massachusetts Board of Education, he had failed to call for the integration of the state's public schools. He deeply resented Phillips's accusations that he had not been forthright about his constitutional principles. The day after Phillips's speech appeared in print, Mann told Parker that he was "sorry to have such an occasion to expose Mr. Phillips's falsities and meanness," but that Phillips had "a wide streak of devilishness in him, and such a speech shows it is growing wider and blacker." Defending his principles in a terse letter to the *Liberator*, Mann wrote: "We swear to support the Constitution of the United States because in our interpretation of it, it requires us to do nothing in violation of the higher law of God." He was furious at the insinuation that he had compromised his conscience to secure office. Phillips's reply, which was published in the same number of the paper, chided Mann for oversensitivity and denied that the basic question had been answered.[15]

Parker, of course, had no principle at stake in this fight. He believed that conscience spoke clearly about the evils of slavery but felt that differences of experience or understanding permitted diversity in antislavery action. He was agnostic about the inherent meaning of the Constitution, certain that its flaws or errors could be mended as the idea of freedom gained ascendancy in the public mind. That result, however, would only be postponed by needless enmity among the supporters of freedom. He complained to brother minister Samuel May that "our antislavery friends are a little too sharp in their public condemnations of men who aim at the same end, but use different means to achieve it." Parker had no qualms about the use of denunciation in public controversy, but felt that it should be reserved for the enemies of progress, not its friends.[16]

In an attempt to stave off a wholesale breach between two valued allies, he took each of them to task for their "ungenerous" views of the other's motives. "You said things about Horace in your reply that seemed to me needless and a little crude," he told Phillips. But he also admitted that Mann "has the misfortune of being thin skinned . . . I believe he has no skin at all in some spots." He offered to host a peace-making dinner at his house at Exeter Place, not only for the two combatants, but for both wings of the Boston antislavery movement. Phillips agreed to the plan, but Mann would have nothing to do with it, saying that he could not "answer for my digestion in the presence of such a man as facts now demonstrate [Phillips] to be." He complained in his usual high-toned manner that "purposed falsehood and false honesty disturb me through all my organization." Though Parker saw merit in the views of both parties, he was annoyed that personality conflict and ideological rigidity had shattered Boston's brief antislavery unity.[17]

For the next three months, the vitriolic exchanges between Mann and Phillips continued to divide the Boston antislavery community. In March, the editor of the Free Soil *Commonwealth* lashed out at Phillips and at the radicals as a group comparing them with "certain fishes in India that have worms in their heads and always swim against the stream." Despite the "fierce denunciation" and "utter uncharitableness" of the radicals, they argued, the Free-Soilers "can

bear and have borne with patience their vituperation and abuse of our party because we chose to fight slavery under a banner of our own." Parker clearly sympathized with the Free-Soilers in the controversy, but spoke most often from
Garrisonian platforms. On almost every occasion he used such opportunities to
reprimand the radicals for their lack of tolerance and their inability to see the
benefits of confronting slavery through politics. Before the Massachusetts Anti-
Slavery Society, he spoke of the complementary relationship between the moral
and political wings of the movement, and expressed pain at the "injustice" and
"bitterness of speech" radicals sometimes heaped on Sumner, Hale, and Mann
for following "the course which they see best." His ability to upbraid the radicals and yet remain on good terms with them was a unique facet of Parker's role
in the Boston antislavery movement. "I criticize the Garrisonians from their own
platforms, I praise 'em from other platforms," he told Phillips. "They may need
to hear the criticism; others their positive merits." Though he was unsuccessful
in preventing or even ameliorating the breach which the Mann-Phillips controversy had opened, Parker was important in preventing communication between
these groups from breaking down entirely. In the great crisis that was soon to
engulf Boston, such communication would be essential.[18]

For all his criticisms of the Garrisonians, however, Parker had no illusions
about the Free Soil movement. He believed that they possessed the ablest men in
the state and that their principles were far in advance of the two major parties,
but he had grave doubts about their alliance with self-interested, partisan Democrats. After the defeat of the 1853 revised state constitution, a document crafted
by a Free Soil-Democratic coalition, he told a friend that "if this breaks up the
coalition I shall be glad." It was time for principled antislavery leaders to repudiate their dalliance with "Hunker" politicians like Benjamin Hallett and Benjamin Butler, "men who are a curse to any party." Perhaps electoral defeat was
just what the political antislavery movement in Massachusetts needed to refocus
its energy and its principles on the core idea of freedom.[19]

Indeed, Parker was starting to believe that the larger nation was heading for
a similar political crisis. The victory of Franklin Pierce and the national Democratic Party had represented a serious challenge to his optimism about political
life. Calling it a "re-action in favor of despotism," he was certain that "the
Hunkers" would seek to annex slaveholding Cuba, introduce slavery in California, and reignite a proslavery conflict with Mexico. But there was one "good
thing" about this state of affairs, although he admitted that it was a "dangerous
good." The proslavery South's arrogant control over the national government
could never last. It would generate a sectional realignment of political power in
which a final reckoning of the ideas of slavery and freedom would take place.
The South had won a temporary victory, but Parker was certain that "one day
they will be very sorry for this."[20]

Practical Theism and the American Crisis

By 1854, Parker and his huge congregation at the Music Hall had become a fix-
ture on the Boston landscape. A constant thorn in the flesh of the city's elite, the
Twenty-Eighth functioned as a permanent lyceum where dissidents and reformers could find intellectual nourishment and political energy. Parker's sermons
provided an ecumenical, spiritual foundation for the various reform movements
that circulated among its members. He continued to work on his massive history
of religion, but his most productive theological work in the 1850s appeared in
those weekly sermons at the Music Hall. These were enormously sophisticated
productions, philosophically precise and copiously illustrated with examples
from science, literature, and history. But Parker was also an eminently practical
preacher whose prodigious intellectual arsenal was always at the service of his
activist congregation. As moral and political crises engulfed Boston and the nation during this period, he worked to sustain their faith in God's benevolent purpose while offering a searing critique of the anti-human dogmas of what he
called "the popular theology."

The religion that poured forth from the stage at the Music Hall was a religion of human improvement, a practical theism that placed its faith in the consciences of men and women. Its essence was a holy life, a piety expressed as
gratitude to a perfect God and as unbounded love for the human and natural cre-
ations. True religion, he once said, "rises early every morning and works all
day." Parker told his congregation that they had nothing to fear from those who
denied the existence of God, but rather from those who *professed* belief but acted without conscience. Reflecting his immersion in the social and political
struggles of his day, Parker's theology became less a scholarly quest than a new
front in the larger battle for nation's culture.[21]

In 1853, he published a series of ten sermons under the title *Theism, Atheism and the Popular Theology*. It remains the most accessible of his theological
works, and though it contained a scathing indictment of the nation's dominant
religious culture, it also remains the most constructive statement of his own
thought. Most striking was its claim that philosophical atheism was a far less
serious threat to the progress of Christian culture than the "popular theology,"
by which he meant revivalist, neo-Calvinism. Still a careful observer of German
intellectual life, Parker knew of the atheistic writings of Ludwig Andreas Feuerbach, a Hegelian philosopher who had argued that religious feelings were entirely subjective, "having no corresponding objective reality." But Parker was largely untroubled by these ideas. Such "speculative atheism," he believed, had no
foundation in the nature of man which was naturally religious.[22]

Atheism, Parker believed, was a more complex phenomenon than it appeared. Some atheists, he explained, denied the existence of God because they
could not accept common notions of the Deity as vengeful, punishing or irrational. Others who were *called* atheists accepted the idea of a controlling force
in the universe, but objected to the idea of a self-originating God who was the
first cause of existence. Neither version of atheism was a serious problem to

Parker. The first was actually a force for religious progress leading to the development of purer, more rational conceptions of God. The second accepted the
essential qualities of God under a different name. As for those atheists, like Feuerbach, who denied both the name and the qualities of God, Parker insisted that
their view had no explanation for the origins or order of nature, and failed to
provide any sense of meaning for human life. Atheists were no threat because
they asked human beings to deny their nature. "We should cast no scorn at
them," he told the Twenty-Eighth, "we should give them our sympathy."[23]

But if war was not to be waged against speculative atheists, there were still
battles to be fought. The first was against a "popular theology" that clung to low,
irrational ideas of God that justified slavery and other forms of human suffering.
"For one [atheist] who denies a deity, there are a hundred ministers who preach .
. . of a jealous and angry God . . . who will drive the majority of the race to per-
dition, and go on His way rejoicing!" Parker went as far as to say that atheism,
with its denial of any deity was actually preferable to the tormenting God of the
neo-Calvinists. It was better to have no God at all than one who was ready to
condemn "the vast mass of the human family" to "eternal torment." It is not going too far to say that Parker was literally repulsed by much in orthodox Christian theology. So much so that he could not imagine that leading orthodox theologians like Nathaniel Emmons were actually sincere in their worship of the God
they described. Such views were so plainly contrary to the evidence of human
and physical nature that Parker could not see how anyone could "really believe .
. . that man is a worm, that religion is a torment, immortality curse, and God a
fiend."[24]

The answer, of course, was that Parker's characterization of the "popular
theology" was far from objective. No orthodox Protestant would have acknowledged believing that God was a "tormentor" or that "no good comes from human reason." For all his progressive universalism, Parker shared one thing in
common with his opponents in orthodox pulpits. He was a sectarian leader, fully
willing to do public, theological battle in the name of his conscience and his
anti-creedal creed. Like most sectarian leaders, however, Parker failed to recognize himself as such because he equated his own system of thought with the
truth.[25]

But Parker did differ from his orthodox contemporaries in believing that the
truth of his system could be demonstrated exclusively by its ability to alleviate
human suffering, to end slavery, and to establish a just and equitable society. As
preachers of ethics, he argued, the purveyors of the "popular theology" showed
their true colors when they endorsed the Mexican-American War and the Fugitive Slave Act, and failed to support temperance, women's rights and the abolition of slavery. Their theology replaced the natural conscience of human beings
with the Bible, a collection of ancient books whose authors were largely unknown and whose ethical principles reflected the mores of a violent, primitive
state of society.

But the greatest sin of the popular theology, he insisted, was that it led to
"practical atheism." This form of atheism differed from the speculative kind in

that it involved no overt denial of the doctrines of the popular theology. Practical atheists were judged to be "believers" by those around them and thus lived without the stigma that overt profession of atheism would bring. Yet because the popular theology was so contrary to reason and conscience, it discredited the very idea of a moral law or a perfect God. The practical atheist was therefore free to live and act as if no such law, and no such God, existed. In a society made up of practical atheists, the conscience and the higher law of God were replaced by narrow self-interest, the lust for power, and an endless quest for self-aggrandizement. Practical atheism produced a "society of bodies without souls . . . an earth without a heaven, in a world without a God." Ominously, Parker told his congregation that practical atheism was present in America's churches, its political institutions, and in the nation's social life. In Daniel Webster's actions on the 7th of March, 1850, it had gained its most visible champion. The defenders of slavery, in both sections, carried its standard into the battle for the soul of the nation. At root, he argued, the crisis in America was a spiritual one.[26]

And yet in Parker's estimation neither practical atheism nor the sins of the popular theology could ever achieve a permanent victory over reason and conscience. These faculties could be temporarily suppressed, but their permanent place in human consciousness, and in the divine economy of matter and spirit, assured their eventual triumph. "I do not pretend to understand the moral universe; the arc is a long one, my eye reaches but a little way," he once told his congregation. But "from what I see I am sure that it bends toward justice." Since human beings were equipped with power to "divine [justice] by conscience . . . things cannot be mismanaged for long."[27]

In the place of atheism, both speculative and practical, and against the "hateful doctrines" of the popular theology, Parker looked forward to the rise of a "practical theism" that celebrated God's natural gifts of reason and conscience to his children. Such a faith recognized that God had made the world for a "perfect purpose" and had made human nature "adequate to the end which God designed." Unimpeded by the irrational authority of ancient books, and free from the taint of warlike, tribal theologies, the conscience of man would be liberated to enact absolute justice. Reason would recognize that salvation was achieved by "character, by prayer, and by toil." Heading into the greatest crisis of his public life, Parker clung to the aggressively optimistic theology that had become his spiritual battle cry. As proslavery forces prepared to bring deadly force to bear upon opponents of the Fugitive Slave Law in Boston, he still envisioned an America where religious freedom would nurture an Absolute Religion of pure theism and pure morality. "Then what a nation we have!" he proclaimed. "Aye, what a world!"[28]

XV
THE ANTHONY BURNS CRISIS
1854–1855

For all the elegance and logical power of Parker's theological system, its greatest weakness lay in its inability to fully account for the existence of moral evil. Was it really so self-evident, as Parker believed, that the simple "facts of the world" demonstrated "a continual and progressive triumph of the right"? If reason and conscience were truly adequate to the tasks for which they had been created, why did human beings so often fail to use them? Why did so many, even the refined beneficiaries of the nineteenth-century's highest culture, choose to follow their "lower" passions of greed, power, and narrow self-interest? Parker, of course, had answers to these questions, but his theology was far less equipped to handle them than was orthodoxy, with its dogmas of original sin and atonement.[1]

Many of his contemporary critics recognized this problem. Conservative Unitarian Andrew Peabody had once called Parker's theology a "religion of the perfect—of the unfallen," implying that it held people to a standard that human nature could not achieve on its own. His most trenchant critic, however, was Orestes Brownson, the former Transcendentalist turned Catholic theologian. Brownson found Parker's system troubling because it bet everything on the goodness of human nature and allowed for no authority or revelation external to it. If human beings were not as naturally equipped for moral action as Parker thought, if reason and conscience were flawed guides to human action, there was nothing in his system to check or regulate them. The voice within was now, for better or worse, the voice of God. And Brownson was certain that Parker's optimism about human nature was misplaced. It was "contrary to the universal testimony of the race, and the painful experience of mankind," he wrote. Parker's system denied "all imperfection, therefore all evil, and therefore again, all sin."[2]

The problem of moral evil became increasingly acute for Parker in the spring of 1854. The passage of the proslavery Kansas-Nebraska Act and the rendition of the escaped slave Anthony Burns in Boston represented painful setbacks to the idea of freedom. Far from retreating, the Slave Power seemed on the verge of redefining the American nation, of erasing its core idea. In the conduct of Boston officials who assisted the Burns rendition, moreover, Parker found a bewildering and distressing counterpoint to the assumptions about human conscience upon which he had staked so much. This partly explains the anger, sometimes even rage, which appeared in his most famous sermons during the crisis. It also helps to explain why Parker sometimes lost the ability to judge his own thought and action by the light of his belief in inherent human worth. Like many antislavery activists, he began to imagine the possibility that the American crisis over slavery might result in open warfare between the Slave Power and its enemies. If more traditional Christians like John Brown spoke of God's impending wrath against an unrepentant, proslavery nation, Parker began speaking of a second American Revolution that would bury the idea of slavery forever. To count the costs of such a struggle, or to worry too much about the sacrifices it would require, would be to question God's justice and to deny the universal moral duty decreed by an awakened, revolutionary conscience.

Freedom in Retreat

In the five months preceding the Anthony Burns crisis, Parker had carefully followed the debates in Congress over the organization of the Kansas and Nebraska territories. As the legislation took shape in February of 1854, he became convinced that the Missouri Compromise of 1820 would be repealed and that Illinois Senator Stephen A. Douglas' popular sovereignty formula would result in the unlimited extension of slavery. The Slave Power, he concluded, had begun a final campaign for control of the federal government. He warned his congregation that the "Slave Power wants new slave states, that she may have new slave Senators to give her uttermost power in the Senate of the United States." With a victory in the Nebraska bill and the creation of new slave states, the South would demand a slave empire in Latin America, the reinstitution of the African Slave Trade, and the abolition of northern personal liberty laws. With the political balance in Congress shifting toward slavery, he believed that the North would be powerless to stop it.[3]

The proposed legislation was bad enough, but Parker was even more disturbed by the lack of northern resistance to it. "What a wicked business is the Nebraska-Kansas matter," he told a parishioner. "Men 'hate it but know it will pass.'" The idea of calling conventions of northern citizens to protest against the passage of the bill was appealing to Parker and he wrote to nearly every prominent New England Free-Soiler to propose the measure. Only two days before the Nebraska bill passed the Senate he told John Parker Hale that "there should be a convention from all the Free States on the 4th of July to organize against slavery as we have never done before," and predicted pessimistically that "if this is not done we are ruined and the country becomes one great Slave Power." Despite his efforts, the convention idea did not garner much support from the politicians. Charles Francis Adams told him quite bluntly that he did not "believe in empty conventions and wordy resolutions which represent nobody but the speakers and writers."[4]

Parker's frustration with the direction of national politics peaked on Wednesday, May 24th, two days after the Nebraska bill was passed by the House of Representatives. At his home he could hear the massive 113 gun salute organized by Boston's Democrats to commemorate the exact number of votes it had taken for the bill to pass. To a European correspondent he prophesied for the first time that the sectional conflict would end in bloodshed. "We must have dreadful chastisement one day," he wrote. "I suppose it will come from our own towns, from civil war."[5]

As Parker wrote those words, Charles Suttle of Alexandria, Virginia stood before Boston Fugitive Slave Commissioner Edward G. Loring demanding a warrant for the arrest of escaped slave Anthony Burns. Burns had fled from slavery in Richmond, Virginia the previous February by hiding in the hold of a cargo ship bound for Boston. After recovering from the ordeal of three, brutal weeks packed into the ship's hold, he found work in a tailor's shop owned by black leader Coffin Pitts, the Deacon of the Twelfth Baptist Church. But like Thomas Sims before him, Burns could not resist the need to tell his family in Virginia that he was safe. A letter to his brother in Richmond was intercepted by Suttle who quickly set the wheels of rendition in motion. On the evening of Wednesday, May 24th, as Burns walked home along Brattle Street after a day's work at the shop, he was met by Deputy Marshall Asa Butman and a group of four assistants who arrested him under the commissioner's warrant. There was no violent struggle as in the Sims case, and Burns was quickly taken to an "upper room" of the Boston Courthouse where he was held until the Fugitive Slave Court opened the next morning.[6]

Because of the efficiency of the arrest and the fact that Burns was not yet well known in the city, the Boston Vigilance Committee did not hear of the incident until early Thursday morning when the hearing was under way. By the time Parker and his lawyer friends Charles Ellis and Richard Henry Dana reached the Courthouse at 9 a.m., Commissioner Loring was on the verge of issuing the certificate of rendition. Suttle had identified Burns as his slave, and he was about to produce a witness, William Brent, who would confirm his testimony. It was imperative that the hearing be stopped immediately, but neither Dana nor Ellis would speak on Burns's behalf because they had not been authorized to do so by Burns himself. Parker refused to allow a procedural formality to stand in his way, and approached Burns directly while ignoring the obvious disapproval of the guards who sat on either side of the prisoner's box. He pleaded with the fugitive to accept counsel, telling him naively that "it can do you no harm to make a defense." A bit stunned by Parker's blithe assurances, Burns said that if he had to go to back slavery, he wanted to do so "as easy as I can." But Parker was adamant and Burns finally agreed that the lawyers could do as they pleased. With that "slender authorization" from the prisoner, Dana moved for a delay so that Burns could recover from the shock of the arrest. Loring then asked Burns directly if he wanted to defend himself. It is unclear what the prisoner actually said in answer to this question, but Loring interpreted his response as a request for delay. Over the strenuous objections of Suttle's lawyer and U.S. Marshal Watson Freeman, the commissioner declared a two day recess of the proceedings.[7]

With that delay, the Vigilance Committee quickly set about the business of mobilizing resistance. Redeploying the tactics that had been so successful in the Crafts case three years earlier, they filed a ten thousand dollar slander suit against Suttle and Brent. Notices then went up all over the city warning that the "Kidnappers are Here!" and demanding that the "sons of Otis and Hancock, and the 'Brace of Adamses'" prevent any "free citizen of Massachusetts" from being "dragged into slavery WITHOUT TRIAL BY JURY! '76." Many of these same handbills announced that a public protest meeting was to be held on Friday night at Faneuil Hall.[8]

As the tension in the city began to build, Vigilance Committee members noted that, in contrast to the Sims case, public opinion in Boston seemed to have turned against rendition. Richard Henry Dana was delighted to find that "Men who w[oul]d not speak to me in 1850 & 1851, & who were enrolling themselves as special policemen in the Sims affair, stop me in the street and talk treason." Both he and Henry Bowditch attributed the change to the Kansas-Nebraska Act. "There never was…in the history of Northern sentiment such an entire change as has occurred since the passage of the Nebraska bill," wrote Bowditch during the crisis. Some believed that "this precise time was chosen by the Virginians to insult us the more grossly." Talk of violent rescue was all over the city and quickly spread to other parts of the state. Parker disciple and Worcester minister Thomas Wentworth Higginson was told about the Faneuil Hall meeting by Boston merchant Samuel May Jr., who asked the minister to bring as many Worcester antislavery men as he could muster. Perhaps voicing the beliefs of other Vigilance Committee members, May told Higginson that the Boston authorities would not support the enforcement of the law and that strong opposition would succeed in preventing rendition. After receiving May's note, Higginson contacted one of his parishioners, Martin Stowell, who had taken part in the Jerry Henry rescue in Syracuse and secured his promise to bring two hundred well-armed men to Faneuil Hall.[9]

In Boston, Parker kept the executive committee in session all day, but found it difficult to reach agreement on tactics. The diverse consciences that made up the Boston antislavery movement, consciences that Parker had worked so hard to harmonize since 1845, simply would not be channeled in a single direction. Higginson focused on practical tasks like procuring axes to hack open the court house door, but became extremely frustrated when he discovered that some committee members were prepared only to use the weapons of moral force. When the committee heard that Suttle and Brent were about to pass by their meeting place, Higginson noted sarcastically that the pacifists in the room pro-

posed only "that we should go out and gaze at them...as if Southern slavecatch-
ers were to be combated by such weapons."[10]

By all accounts, Vigilance Committee sessions on May 26th were disor-
ganized, tumultuous, and ultimately indecisive. There was "no leader, no head,
and consequently anarchy was the result," wrote one member. But by the late
afternoon, a small faction that included Parker, Phillips, Higginson, and Samuel
Gridley Howe, met separately from the larger group and endorsed a potentially
violent rescue plan. Higginson told them of his friend Stowell, whose two hundred volunteers were on their way to Boston and he received their qualified support for an attack on the court house that would coincide with the Faneuil Hall
meeting the next evening. But these were men whose ardor for the cause was not
enough to compensate for their inexperience in leading a successful assault on a
well-guarded building. Unfortunately for all involved, the exact time of the attack was not decided on and the signal for the speakers to incite the crowd was
never formalized.[11]

When the public meeting finally convened at seven-thirty on Friday evening, Faneuil Hall was overflowing, and there was no chance for last minute
communication between Parker, Phillips, and Higginson. Parker rose to speak
with the crowd already in a state of excitement. Many were shouting for an immediate attack on the Marshal's men in the Court House. To some in the audience, Parker appeared out of place in a meeting where revolutionary action
might occur. "Mr. Parker moved along with stumbling steps and prone looks,"
wrote Charles Emery Stevens two years later. His "dark eyes that looked forth
from behind spectacles" seemed to belong more to a "recluse student" than to an
incendiary speaker. But when he began to speak, the attention of the crowd was
drawn less to his scholarly appearance than to "torrent of bitter invective" which
he heaped upon the friends of slavery.[12]

Parker's speech is a striking example of the interconnections between his
belief in conscience and the revolutionary memories that infused it with such
explosive power. As many observers have noted, his words had little if anything
to do with the suffering of Anthony Burns. Instead they constituted a strident,
even desperate demand that white Massachusetts prove its fidelity to the "higher
law" and to New England's historic, revolutionary identity. The obvious anger
and taunting style of the address, however, betrays a substratum of fear that faith
in conscience and memory might, in the end, be misplaced. Determined to provoke action, he addressed the crowd as "Fellow Subjects of Virginia!" and was
met with a thundering chorus of "No!" He then hammered on the North's failure
to stand up to the demands of the South and begged for some sign that revolutionary principles still lived in the hearts of northern men. "Boston is a suburb of
the city of Alexandria, fellow subjects of Virginia," he taunted. When the crowd
demanded that he retract the insult, he responded that he would only "take that
back when you show me that it is not so." Until then, he told them, "there is no
North; the South goes clear up to the Canada line." Emotions in the hall had
reached a fever pitch, voices from the back of the Hall called out "Fight!" while
people ran chaotically in and out of the building. Parker continued his tirade

citing the anti-Stamp Act demonstrations and the Boston Tea Party as examples of the higher laws of God in action.[13]

Invoking the scenes of revolutionary action moved Parker and the crowd toward a critical moment of decision about the compatibility of conscience and violence. At first, it seemed that Parker was ready to move beyond the indecision he had shown in the Sims case. As the excitement in the hall reached its peak, he called out "I am a clergymen and a man of peace, but there is a means and an end. Liberty is the end and peace is not sometimes the means towards it." Then he asked the crowd directly: "Now I want to ask you what you are going to do." One voice immediately responded "shoot, shoot." But either because he was unprepared for this response or frightened by it, Parker seemed almost at once to lose the soaring confidence that had propelled his speech to that point. He hurriedly declared that he was certain that "there are ways to manage this matter without shooting anybody." Searching for ways to control what was now a potentially murderous crowd, Parker tried to assure them that the slave catchers and their allies in Boston were "cowards, every mother's son of them" and could be intimidated into relinquishing their prey "without shooting a gun." Parker had again reached the brink of revolutionary action only to step back.[14]

Things were now confused inside the hall, with some in the crowd proposing to "pay the slaveholders a visit" at the Revere House where they were staying. Parker stood helplessly at the podium searching in vain for some sign that Higginson and his Worcester men had arrived. Thinking quickly, he proposed that the meeting adjourn until nine o'clock the next morning in Court Square. Exhausted from his oratory and completely unable to control the situation, Parker turned the stage over to Wendell Phillips who renewed the plea for an adjournment with greater success. But just as Phillips began seizing the attention of the crowd, someone shouted from the back of the hall "that a mob of negroes is in Court-Square attempting to rescue Burns!" With that, the crowd spilled out onto the street and headed up the two blocks toward the Court House. Parker walked quickly toward the court house along with Phillips and Henry Bowditch, but was too late to take part in the dramatic scenes that followed.[15]

Because of the confusion over signs and times, the opportunity to coordinate the actions of the Worcester men and the Faneuil Hall crowd was lost. The fact that the Worcester contingent was nothing like two hundred also severely diminished the chances of success. Most importantly the noise of several hundred angry rioters approaching alerted the guards inside the court house that some kind of rescue attempt was imminent. The doors of the building were immediately locked and fifteen police deputies prepared to hold their ground against all comers.

Aware that they needed to act before the authorities could send reinforcements, Higginson, Martin Stowell and Louis Hayden led a small group of Boston blacks and Worcester volunteers to the southwest door and began breaking it down with axes and a large battering ram. Once the door gave way, they pushed their way inside where they encountered a phalanx of deputies who began swinging at their heads with police batons. The ferocity of the police counterat-

tack overwhelmed the would-be rescuers and they soon found themselves
shoved back out into the street. But before the fight ended, the sound of several
gunshots was heard near the door and a chaotic struggle began. In the ensuing
melee, Police Deputy James Batchelder, a young Irish truckman, received a stab
wound in the left groin that severed his femoral artery and he died almost immediately. A gunshot also narrowly missed killing U.S. Marshal Watson Freeman.
The Boston police then descended on Court Square and made over a dozen arrests, mostly of blacks. Mayor J.V. Smith ordered the two companies of the Boston Artillery to restore order in the square, and it quickly became obvious that
the rescue attempt had failed.[16]

Parker's frustration at the aborted rescue, and perhaps his own performance
in Faneuil Hall, was intense and he quickly lost his scruples about the use of
deadly force. When a bruised and bleeding Thomas Wentworth Higginson told
him that black abolitionist Lewis Hayden had just missed shooting Marshal
Freeman, Parker "wrung his hands" in frustration and asked "why did he not hit
him?"[17]

But the possibility for an even greater confrontation was brewing. Early on
the next morning, Freeman cabled Washington and declared his intention to
station two companies of United States troops from nearby Fort Independence
inside the court house. President Pierce was determined to make an example of
Boston and approved Freeman's deployment order, declaring flatly that "the law
must be enforced." As Parker entered the court house that morning, he passed by
soldiers carrying rifles with fixed bayonets. He was shocked by the sight, but
remembered the chains that had surrounded the building during the Sims case
and the soldiers that had volunteered for the return of the fugitive. Inside, he
listened as Richard Dana gave an impassioned and cleverly designed plea for a
further delay in the proceedings. When the request was granted, Parker drew up
a new handbill announcing that the trial would take place on Monday at
10 o'clock. It contained his characteristic mix of sectional memory and moral
intensity. "Come down then sons of the Puritans," read his announcement. "You
should at least be present to witness the sacrifice and you should follow the sad
procession with your tears and prayers, and then go home and take such action
as your manhood and your patriotism may suggest." He had begun to sense the
inevitability of the rendition but hoped that its humiliating circumstances would
galvanize the conscience of the city and the state.[18]

On Sunday, the crowed that assembled in the Music Hall to hear Parker
preach was unprecedented and "a great multitude" was turned away due to lack
of space. He had intended to preach that morning on the Crimean War which
had broken out exactly two months earlier in Europe, and had had no time to
prepare a formal text on the Burns case. The result was a spontaneous address
that used sentences like sharp blades to channel the preacher's raw emotion. A
man had been killed, twelve men were in the Boston jail under suspicion of riot
and murder, soldiers patrolled the streets, and a fugitive from American slavery
sat in chains in the Boston Court House. Reporters, using a new system of pho-
netic shorthand, worked furiously to keep up as Parker boomed out his indict-

ment of the "gentlemen of property and standing" who had kidnapped Thomas Sims, passed the Kansas-Nebraska Act, and imprisoned Anthony Burns in the "baracoon of Boston." On the verge of the greatest humiliation in its long history, Boston could only blame itself for worshipping the "practical atheism" of its leaders. Men like Daniel Webster, Benjamin Curtis, and Caleb Cushing, he thundered, had stood in Faneuil Hall and "howled down the higher law of Almighty God." And yet Boston's shame, he believed, was also the nation's shame. It proved that slavery and freedom were no longer equals on the playing field of American culture. "Slavery is an institution that is in earnest," he told his flock. "Northern freedom is an institution that is not in earnest. It was in earnest in '76 and '83. It had not been in earnest since." But if there was hope, Parker believed that it resided in the "spirit of our fathers—the spirit of justice and liberty in your heart, in my heart, and in the heart of all of us."[19]

And yet hope can hardly be described as the theme of Parker's sermon that Sunday. Instead it was the search for culprits that dominated its rhetoric. Greedy Boston merchants, cynical politicians, and man-stealing judges populated the address and played their part in the degradation of a once-proud city. These were men without conscience, whose profession of religion was nothing more than an outward show, thinly concealing their avarice. In one of its darkest and most revealing moments, moreover, Parker's sermon described the soldiers inside the courthouse as "mostly foreigners—the scum of the earth, none but such enter the armies in a country like ours." He professed not "to blame them for being born where they were and *what they are*," and reminded his congregation that "an accident of birth kept you and me from being among that same scum." At times like these, Parker's ethnic chauvinism bubbled quickly to the surface. Even more startling were his comments about James Batchelder, the murdered Irish truckman who left a widow behind. Lacking any trace of compassion, Parker described Batchelder as "a volunteer" in the service of "gratuitous wickedness." He must have "liked the business of enslaving a man," and would now have to "render an account to God" for his work. The following week, when his sermon reviewed the entire history of the Burns case, he did not even mention the death of Batchelder. He did find time to express outrage that attorney Richard Dana had been "knocked down in the street by one of the Marshal's men." After all, he said, "the blow might easily have been fatal."[20]

Parker might easily explain the actions of foreign "scum" like Batchelder and the soldiers in the court house, but Commissioner Edward Loring was another matter. As Albert von Franck has noted, Parker simply could not account for Loring's behavior. Given the commissioner's education, his widely respected private character, and his track record of philanthropic giving, his conduct in the Burns affair seemed "deeply mysterious." Having placed so much confidence in the power of cultural evolution to clear the way for pure expressions of reason and conscience, Parker was clearly at a loss to explain why a man of such refinement could go "morally insane." To say that Loring had followed Webster in choosing the "lower law" of practical atheism over the higher law of conscience was only to beg the question.[21]

It was this inability to explain or account for moral evil that drove Parker to make the searing denunciations that surprised those who knew him personally. He could find nothing in human nature that could excuse it. Moral wrong in a man like Loring could only be understood as a willful violation of conscience and Parker denounced such sin as sternly as the Calvinists of old. "He knew he was *stealing a man*, born with the same right to life, liberty and the pursuit of happiness as himself." What was more, Loring was a man of reason who must have anticipated the consequences of his actions and yet undertook them anyway. Loring "knew there would be a meeting at Faneuil Hall—gatherings in the street. He knew there would be violence." And so the responsibility for what had happened to Batchelder rested not with Parker or others who had followed the Higher Law, but with a man who had knowingly violated it. Parker finished his sermon with an indictment. "Edward Greeley Loring," he intoned, "I charge you with the death of that man who was murdered last Friday. He was your fellow servant in kidnapping. He dies at your hand. You fired the shot which makes his wife a widow, his child an orphan."[22]

The Burns trial lasted nearly a week during which Parker and the Vigilance Committee stood by as helpless witnesses to an increasingly inevitable outcome. There had been a glimmer of hope on Saturday when Rev. Leonard Grimes found a small group of Boston merchants willing to purchase Burns's freedom. But District Attorney Hallett, acting under orders from Washington, scuttled the sale and pressed on toward a rendition. All week, the Vigilance Committee used broadsides to stoke the public outrage. Some of them, undoubtedly written by Parker himself, appealed directly to the ethnic tensions that divided the city and its politics. The large Irish presence in the federal units keeping order in the city allowed him to characterize the struggle over Burns's rendition as a contest between Anglo-Saxons and Celts. Would Americans, "the sons of the Revolution...submit to have our citizens shot down by a set of VAGABOND IRISH-MEN!" asked one of these sheets. Parker was unable to contain his revulsion at the sight of these men, describing them as "pimps, gamblers," and "the *succubus* of slavery." His earlier refusal to accept conventional distinctions between the deserving and undeserving poor disappeared as the crisis deepened. No victims of poverty or mercantile avarice, the Irishmen in the army were simply "fighters, drunkards, public brawlers...men whom the subtlety of counsel or the charity of the gallows had left unhanged." These were the new Hessians, the mercenaries of practical atheism who possessed no conscience and no instincts for freedom. In a remarkable statement from a man who had built his life upon the universal moral capacities of man, Parker could not help but confess that the whole affair "destroys confidence in humanity."[23]

Some of Parker's anger can be explained by the perceived threats to his own safety that had emerged after the Faneuil Hall meeting. On the evening of Saturday, May 27, rumors circulated that Irish truckmen intended to attack the homes of both Parker and Phillips. The papers reported that "a number of men were seen to approach the dwellings...and to read the name and number carefully and then to proceed." At around nine that evening, Parker rushed to Phillips's house to warn his wife Ann, a housebound invalid, that she should vacate the dwelling immediately. But because the attack never materialized, Parker's critics in Massachusetts used this incident to mock him. One claimed that he had "ingloriously fled his house" and that those revolutionary relics of which he "made great boast of possessing" were carried to safety rather than deployed in self-defense.[24]

But fears of mob violence against abolitionists were hardly fantasies. During the 1830s antislavery meetings had been routinely disrupted and William Lloyd Garrison had narrowly escaped death at the hands of one such mob in 1835. In this case, the death of James Batchelder had heightened class and ethnic tensions in the city and there was reason to assume that his death might be avenged. Late on Monday evening, Parker walked nervously around his house at Exeter Place, undoubtedly alert to any noises that might signify intruders. He listened at the doors of the bedrooms and to make sure that Lydia and Hannah Stevenson were asleep and then went back to his study to write in his journal. He found comfort in his belief in a God who transcended "space, time, and sense, and soul," but he could not help but believe that "a day of retribution" was coming.[25]

Just four days later, on Friday, June 2nd, Commissioner Loring handed down his final decision in the Burns case, a certificate of rendition giving Charles Suttle the right to carry his human property back to Virginia. When the decision was announced, Mayor Smith declared martial law in the city and prepared to transfer Burns from the court house to T Wharf where a steamer bound for Virginia was docked. Military and police officials organized an escort cortege that was unprecedented for both its size and firepower. A mounted detachment of volunteer militia at the front was followed closely by one company of federal infantry and a company of U.S. Marines. Burns himself was enclosed within a "hollow square" of sixty Boston police officers and a second company of marines. At the rear of the procession was yet another Marine company displaying a fully-loaded cannon. The streets were filled with people, and some of the buildings along the short route to the wharf were draped in black cloth, a symbol of mourning for lost liberty.[26]

Despite these symbolic expressions of support for Burns and the abolitionists, the crowd that assembled on the day of the rendition was by no means unified in its response to the previous week's events. Alongside those who came out of a simple curiosity to see Burns for themselves, were many who applauded city officials for carrying out the Fugitive Slave Act and who looked for opportunities to heckle the abolitionist "fanatics" they blamed for the Court House riot. Parker was watching the procession on Court Street with Hannah Stevenson when a man accosted him, screaming "You killed Batchelder" while others pointed to both Parker and Phillips saying "there go the murderers of Batchelder." At least some in the crowd believed that Boston's most famous minister had blood on his hands. And for those who looked for the rebirth of the radical crowds of the revolutionary era, the day was a disappointment indeed.[27]

The final scenes of the rendition were difficult for Parker to assimilate and he experienced a sense of disorientation. The presence of heavily armed soldiers menacing crowds of protesters had been shocking and it seemed to erase the symbols of liberty that defined Boston's identity. Rather than the cradle of liberty, the city had "looked Austrian" or perhaps like "Warsaw". To another packed house at the Music Hall two days after Burns was taken back to Virginia, Parker confessed publicly that the rendition cast doubt upon his whole system of thought. "Last week," he said, "my faith was sorely tried." The conduct of the troops, "the kidnapper's body-guard," was not difficult to explain because "they were tools, not agents." But Commissioner Loring's role, so clearly at odds with his character and his culture, generated a serious anomaly for Parker's faith in the alignment of conscience with the moral law. "As I looked into the commissioner's face...and then thought of the crime he was committing against humanity," he told his parishioners, "I asked myself, can this be true?...Is my philosophy a dream, or are these facts a lie?" And yet commissioner Loring was only the tip of a spear now poised to destroy American liberty, which Parker believed "was never in greater peril than now."[28]

The Slave Power now seemed in full control of the nation, armed with the military power to enforce its will and flush with the "gold of the national treasury" to carry out its larger designs. Perhaps Haiti and Cuba would be added to the nation's slave empire, and then "all the free states" would follow. Quoting a well-publicized boast by proslavery radical Robert Toombs of Georgia, Parker wondered if it was true that "before long the master will sit down at the foot of Bunker Hill monument with his slaves."[29]

On Trial for Conscience's Sake

For many Boston abolitionists, the Burns case was a shocking defeat. Wendell Phillips was so horrified that he began to despair, fearing for the first time in his long activist career that the battle with slavery might be lost. "There is no hope," he told a friend. "In *national* politics we are beaten." Things were getting worse in Boston as well. Conservative law and order advocates had been appalled by the disorder and violence of the Burns crisis and they sought retribution against those who they believed had fomented it. The *Boston Post* called the meeting in Faneuil Hall "treasonable" and its editors blamed Parker and Phillips for the murder of Batchelder.[30]

The Brahmin elite of the city agreed and they made special efforts to punish Parker for his incendiary speeches against Commissioner Loring. At a June 1854 meeting of the corporation that owned the Boston Music Hall, for example, the Commissioner's stepbrother Charles P. Curtis attempted to terminate the Twenty-Eighth Congregational Society's lease on the building. He admitted to the corporation's directors that his motives were essentially personal, saying the society's offensive minister, "had called his brother a murderer." When that attempt failed, another member of the family, Supreme Court Justice Benjamin R. Curtis, convened a federal grand jury in the Circuit Court of Boston for the purpose of securing criminal indictments against Parker and the other Faneuil Hall speakers. He instructed the jury that the speakers at the Faneuil Hall were indictable under the Fugitive Slave Act of 1793, for aiding in the obstruction of a federal marshal in the lawful exercise of his duty. Justice Curtis went on to say that though Parker and Phillips had not been physically present during the attack on the Court House, they had counseled the attempt through their inflammatory speeches.[31]

Here was an opportunity to demonstrate, once and for all, that Theodore Parker's conscience was nothing more than an excuse for lawlessness. When the original grand jury refused to return an indictment against the two, U.S. District Attorney Benjamin Hallett summoned a completely new set of jurors and secured a five-count indictment against Parker, Phillips, Higginson, and five others. Parker was served with an arrest warrant at the end of November and paid a bond of $1500. The trial, he noted with grim pride, was scheduled for March 1, 1855, "the 85th anniversary of the Boston Massacre." A few days after his arrest, he received a note from Charles Sumner encouraging him to think of the impending trial "as a 'call' to a new parish, with B.R. Curtis and B.F. Hallett as 'deacons' and a pulpit higher than the Strasburg steeple."[32]

The possibility of a sensational trial clearly lifted Parker's spirits and renewed his sense of self-worth and importance. As in his theological conflicts, he saw open confrontation as an opportunity to seize public attention and to demonstrate his fidelity to conscience. He was unable to hide his disappointment when the first grand jury refused to indict him. "I fear the grand jury will not indict the F[aneuil] Hall meeting, nor even my poor self," he had told Charles Sumner at the end of June. He confessed that he rather relished the possibility of being "the first man in N[ew] E[ngland] indicated...for a speech against kidnapping." He dreamed of delivering a spectacular courtroom oration that would indict Curtis, Hallett, and other conservatives who supported the Fugitive Slave Act. "I stand now in as important a position as my honored grandfather at the Battle of Lexington," he told Samuel May, "it is freedom of speech which is assailed through me." Though he worried about the effect that his imprisonment might have on his wife, Parker resolved that if he went to jail, "it will be in triumph."[33]

Fortunately for his health, Parker was spared the "triumph" of imprisonment. Neither Phillips nor Higginson was as eager to go to trial as he was. Defense attorneys Charles Ellis and John P. Hale feared that Judge Curtis might not even allow Parker to deliver his oration. When the trial opened on April 3, 1855, Hale moved that the indictment against Parker and Phillips be quashed as insufficient grounds for trial. Justice Curtis, who no longer possessed his earlier zeal for a conviction, granted the motion on technical grounds and was content that Parker, Phillips, and Higginson had at least been threatened with prison. As Parker left the court that day, District Attorney Hallett ominously told him that the abolitionists had "crawled out of a very small hole." Parker replied characteristically that they would "make a much larger one next time."[34]

In the summer of 1855, Parker published what would have been his courtroom oration and it appeared in Boston bookshops as *The Trial of Theodore Parker*. Running to well over two-hundred pages, the book was an elaborate and carefully researched defense of freedom of speech. Speech, after all, was the primary vehicle for the expression of conscience, and Parker lashed the Boston elite, especially Commissioner Loring and the Curtis clan, for attempting to stifle conscience through a craven manipulation of the law. The *Trial of Theodore Parker* was replete with overt personal invective and it adeptly placed the struggle over the Burns rendition within a dualistic framework of classical republican morality. Boston, it seemed, had become another battlefield in the ongoing struggle between liberty and despotism, magisterial prerogative and individual rights. He pilloried Benjamin Curtis as an American "Judge Jeffries", the ultra-royalist "hanging judge" of England's "bloody assizes" who had ruthlessly persecuted the enemies of King James II. By implication, of course, Parker cast himself in the role of Algernon Sydney, the English Revolutionary defender of republican liberty whose vigorous critique of royal usurpation led to his execution for treason. He had quoted Sydney in his Faneuil Hall speech as well, saying "that which is not just is not law, and that which is not law ought not to be obeyed."[35]

Yet even as he drew inspiration from the English republican tradition, he again claimed the American Revolution as his personal inheritance. He reminded his readers that the little monument to the fallen heroes at the battle of Lexington "covered the bones" of his kinfolk. Most importantly, "the tall Captain who marshaled his fellow farmers and mechanics into stern array and spoke such brave and dangerous words as opened the War of Independence...was my father's father."[36]

The *Trial* illustrates the largely unacknowledged impact of the fugitive slave cases on Parker's moral thought. He now graphically described the sectional conflict as a death struggle between slavery and freedom. Moral evil, which had had only a provisional existence in his earlier writings, was now described as an embodied force with a life of its own. "Already a power of iniquity clutches at your children's throat, stabs at their life—at their soul's life." Conscience was no longer simply an element of human consciousness, but a weapon to be deployed against the advancing forces of oppression. "I stand between the living tyrant and his victim; aye betwixt him and expected victims not yet born." Though he did not preach disunion as the Garrisonian abolitionists did, it was not out of love for traditional political arrangements, but a conviction that the second American Revolution could cleanse the existing Union of its sins. As in his battles against theological conservatism and social apathy, Parker believed that slavery could be eradicated through a defining moment of confrontation between conscience and injustice. The final realization of that goal, he now believed, could not be achieved without violent struggle and dramatic sacrifice.[37]

XVI
THE POLITICS OF CONFRONTATION
1856

In the Spring of 1856, Parker lectured almost constantly, going as far west as Cleveland, Ohio. His pace became so hectic in April that he nearly collapsed from exhaustion as he began a speech at the New Bedford lyceum. A dose of sherry and a brisk, half-hour walk in the night air enabled him to finish his talk, but the strain of constant public appearances was taking its toll on the frail minister. He had always pushed himself to the physical limit, but Parker's frenzied pace that spring stemmed from his desire to influence public perceptions of increasingly urgent national events. In politics, the newly-formed Republican Party was gearing up for its first campaign for the presidency against the Democratic incumbent, Franklin Pierce, who Parker had detested since his approval of the use of federal troops in the Burns affair. "President Pierce is drunk every day," he joked to a friend some months before the election. "[H]e is now gone over, it is said, to cups and cups only."[1]

After the Burns crisis and his subsequent indictment, Parker's antislavery militancy assumed a more urgent, breathless tone. The stakes seemed higher than ever, and the forces of freedom appeared powerless to fend off the malevolent designs of the Slave Power. "America has now come to such a pass, that a small step may plunge us into misery," he told a group of New York City abolitionists in May 1856. The "regressive" power of slavery, "lodged chiefly in the South," now had powerful allies in the "progressive" North. Parker's condemnation of these northern friends of slavery dripped with contempt. Some of them were simply "inhuman by birth...organized for cruelty" and "idiotic in the conscience and heart and soul." Others, like President Pierce, were men who had a great lust for money or power, but had "little conscience, little affection, and only enough religion to swear by." Whatever their motives, such traitors to freedom had brought the Slave Power to the very brink "absolute rule over the

United States." The time had come, he insisted, for America to choose freedom over slavery, liberty over despotism. "I think we shall put slavery down," he predicted. "But shall we do it now and without tumult, or by and by with a dreadful revolution, San Domingo massacres, and the ghastly work of war?" Over the last three years of his life in America, Parker returned to this question many times.[2]

The Conflict in Kansas

The militancy of Parker's 1856 speech to the New York abolitionists can in part be explained by the recent acceleration of violence in the Kansas territory. "The battle," he said, "is first for Kansas." Growing out of Illinois Senator Stephen Douglas' popular sovereignty formula, Kansas settlers on opposite sides of the slavery issue began a pitched battle for control of the territorial legislature in the fall of 1855. The eventual admission of Kansas as a free or slave state had important consequences for the sectional balance of power in Washington, and the struggle for control of the territory captured the attention of the nation. But the conflict also had a deep, cultural dimension. The New England Emigrant Aid Company, organized by Worcester businessman Eli Thayer, sent arms and humanitarian assistance to Yankee settlers, while the Pierce administration aided slave-state forces through its appointment of pro-slavery, territorial governors. As pro-slavery forces from Missouri poured across the Kansas border in the spring of 1856, violence increased and atrocities were committed by both sides.[3]

The style and rhetoric of Parker's public lectures on the Kansas struggle reflect his growing sense that the sectional conflict had reached a point where antislavery violence was necessary to defend the North's superior values. Returning to the sectional nationalist themes that had dominated his contributions to the *Massachusetts Quarterly Review*, he described the struggle in Kansas as a microcosm of the battle between northern and southern culture. A free Kansas would "soon fill up with educated and industrious men, each sharing the labor and government of society...aiding the organization of Christianity and democracy." As the heirs of New England's regional culture, the citizens of free territory would enjoy all the economic, political, social, and cultural benefits of northern life. Parker called New England settlers in Kansas "sons of the Puritans," referred to their Sharps rifles as "missionaries," and described the free-state capital at Lawrence as "a New Haven in the wilderness." Were slave state forces to prevail, however, Parker argued that Kansas would not only be stained by the immorality of the peculiar institution, but would also suffer under a slaveholding oligarchy. "One permanent class will monopolize government, money, education, honor and ease," he predicted. "This is the prospect which the northern man will find before him if slavery prevails in the new territory."[4]

Parker was also convinced that the United States government was consciously backing the Slave Power in Kansas. "I take it we are in a Civil War," he told New Hampshire Senator John Hale after the sack of Lawrence by pro-slavery forces. In September, when the Secretary of War, the "famous Disunion nullifier" Jefferson Davis, ordered federal troops to arrest the free-state leader Jim Lane, Parker concluded that the Pierce administration had become an outright tool of the Slave Power. "America is now in a state of revolution," he wrote in his journal. "There is no legal government but only one which pretends to legality and the show and form of law."[5]

As Parker spread his message throughout the North, many of those who had served with him on the Boston Vigilance Committee organized direct resistance to the slave state forces through the recently founded Massachusetts State Kansas Committee. Led by the wealthy abolitionist George Stearns, and a young Concord schoolteacher and Transcendentalist, Franklin Sanborn, the committee also included Thomas Wentworth Higginson and Samuel Gridley Howe who were prominent veterans of the Boston fugitive slave agitation. Sharing Parker's belief in the supremacy of the Higher Law, the Kansas Committee members were committed to supplying free-state forces with arms and ammunition for their battles with Missouri "border ruffians." Within weeks of its formation in June 1856, the Kansas Committee had raised some $12,000 in military supplies for the Kansas war and had plans to raise $30,000 more. Most of the funds were earmarked for the purchase of Sharps rifles, a breach-loading carbine made in Hartford, Connecticut that cost a little over thirty dollars each. Though Parker was not involved with the committee at the outset, Sanborn brought him into the group in January of 1857 when the free-state warrior, John Brown, made his first fundraising trip to Boston.[6]

Parker took an active role in funding antislavery activities in the embattled territory, and at least some of the recipients were former members of the Twenty-Eighth who had emigrated to Kansas the previous year. The group was led by the Boston-born Unitarian minister Ephraim Nute, an American Unitarian Association missionary who began building schools and churches in Lawrence, Kansas in 1855. Nute received very little practical support from the AUA for his work in the territory, but his organizational ability and tenacious commitment to the Free State cause made him a hero to abolitionists. His letters contained graphic descriptions of atrocities committed by the "mean sneaking cowards" among the proslavery "Border Ruffians." Much like a wartime journalist, he spoke of the movements of "the enemy" and described the "mangled bodies" of free-state men who were "butchered" in their homes by proslavery "banditti." Parker read these letters aloud during services at the Music Hall and he peppered his antislavery speeches with the latest outrages committed against Nute's followers in Kansas.[7]

In early September 1856, Parker feared that Nute had been killed. During a string of brutal murders and reprisals the previous month, the missionary's brother in law, William Hopps, had been shot to death and scalped as he traveled on horseback, alone and unarmed, from Leavenworth toward Lawrence, Kansas. News quickly reached the free-state stronghold that the murderer was a proslavery Missourian who was openly bragging of his deeds, saying that that he had gone "out for the scalp of a damned abolitionist, and I have got one." Nute was determined to recover his kinsman's mutilated remains, but found the United

States military forces in the territory unwilling to provide any protection for him or his widowed sister. He complained to the secretary of the AUA that "it was plainly no part of [President] Pierce's purpose that the troops should give protection to the men who he has denounced...as sectional fanatics." Parker agreed, certain that the Democratic President intended to "push slavery in at the point of the bayonet."[8]

Despite the lack of protection from government forces, Nute made a brave but desperate attempt to retrieve Hopps's body. Riding out from Lawrence in a wagon with his sister and several others, he was waylaid by a mounted company of "armed men who announced themselves as 'Border Ruffians'," and was taken to Leavenworth as a prisoner. Hearing nothing from him for more than two weeks, his friends in Massachusetts despaired of his life. At a "Kansas" meeting in Cambridge on September 11th, Parker told a friend sadly that "Mr. Nute is in the hands of the ruffians. We fear that he is hanged." But Nute survived his "harassing captivity" in Leavenworth, and he used graphic stories of his ordeal to raise funds for the free-state cause. In a letter to Parker, which was read publicly at a protest meeting at Faneuil Hall, he described his proslavery captors as violent, amoral barbarians. Though "so sick I could hardly stand," he had been held in a "close, crowded, filthy dungeon" and constantly threatened with death. At one point, he wrote, "I was saved only by a quarrel and a scuffle in which the weapon with which I was to be shot was wrested from the hands of one infuriated ruffian." For Parker, there could be no better illustration of the elemental conflict between slavery and freedom, practical atheism and conscience, than Nute's courageous stand against the Slave Power and its government lackeys.[9]

On a personal level, Nute's experiences represented a course of conduct that the sickly minister would have liked to pursue himself. After Thomas Wentworth Higginson left for the embattled territory as an agent of the Massachusetts Kansas Committee, Parker entertained the idea of joining him. But his precarious health and heavy parish responsibilities convinced him to drop the idea. He had to be content instead with mobilizing the Twenty-Eighth to help save Kansas from slavery. In early September, he organized several clothing drives and collected over a hundred dollars from the women of his church who were committed to the relief of destitute free-state families. During the service on September 20th, he omitted the reading of the "chapter of St. James" in order to read "a new epistle of St. Ephraim Nute" to a packed house at the Music Hall. At the same service, he collected nearly three hundred dollars at the door for "Mr. Nute and his fellow apostles." Though his own fund raising activities were humanitarian in intent, Parker was overjoyed to hear the Massachusetts Kansas Committee had "raised over five thousand dollars in one day...to buy Sharps rifles." "Now the battle between slavery and freedom is for the physical heart of America," he told his friend Sarah Hunt. "But the actual battle is not less for the spiritual heart of America."[10]

The Republicans

Parker applauded the use of force against slavery in Kansas, but he believed that a Republican victory in the fall 1856 election would provide a more effective check on the larger conspiracy to nationalize slavery. Since the party's inception in 1854, he had followed its emergence with great interest and he kept in close touch with Charles Sumner, William Seward, Salmon Chase, Henry Wilson, N.P. Banks, and John Hale as the party's organization and ideology began to take shape. Though the fundamental principle of the Republicans was similar to what the Free Soil Party's position had been, Parker hoped that the intensification of the sectional conflict and northern opposition to the territorial designs of the South would push the Republicans toward more radical positions. "If I was to lay the platform of the new party, I should fall back on the national declaration of self- evident and unalienable rights, and affirm the proposition that man cannot hold property in men," he had told Massachusetts Congressman Nathaniel Banks in October 1855. Through its influence, "the whole people would be educated, and before long a desirable victory would be obtained."[11]

Parker's correspondence with men like Nathaniel Banks, Anson Burlingame, and Henry Wilson demonstrates his close ties with Republicans who had earlier been members of the Massachusetts American Party. A nativist political movement commonly known as the "Know-Nothings," the American Party advocated lengthy waiting periods for immigrants seeking citizenship and identified the newly-arriving Irish Catholics as a threat to American political and cultural life. The Burns crisis had heightened anti-Irish sentiment among the native-born in eastern Massachusetts and the 1854 state elections saw a Know-Nothing victory of colossal proportions. The party captured the Governorship, the entire state congressional delegation, and virtually every seat in the state legislature.

Parker had, of course, contributed to the Know-Nothing surge as his speeches about "foreign scum" and broadsides about "vagabond Irishmen" demonstrate. He shared many of the anti-Irish stereotypes of the period, once describing the Irish as having "bad habits, bad religion, and, worst of all, a bad nature." His romantic nationalism also told him that it "is possible for a nation to take so much foreign blood in its veins and so many foreign ideas in its consciousness that its nationality perishes." And yet it seems clear that much of the support that Bay State Know-Nothings received in the mid-1850s, including Parker's, was actually a mix of nativist bigotry, antislavery sentiment, and anger at the Whig establishment for its role in the Burns affair. Parker ultimately concluded that the American Party was "not in the spirit of Democracy" and that most of its leaders were little more than opportunists. When Free Soiler Henry Wilson was elected to the Senate by a political coalition that included Know-Nothings, Parker reminded him that "Catholics are also men, the foreigners are also men, and the world of America is wide enough...for them all." He was delighted by Wilson's written promise never to "infringe upon the rights of any man, black or white, native or foreign." At the May 1856 meeting of the American Antislavery Society in New York, Parker said that the American Party's real contribution to the nation's political development had been to weaken the Democratic and Whig organizations, paving the way for an antislavery Republican Party. Unlike the Know-Nothing leaders who were largely "artful, crafty, and rather low-minded persons," he believed that the Republicans had "great names and powerful men."[12]

Parker embraced the Republican Party in 1856 because he believed that it would rouse the North for a final confrontation with slavery. Its success would revolutionize the section's values and force the South to choose between the Union and slavery. As he considered this possibility, he was remarkably untroubled that violent conflict might result. "If the North locks horns with the South," he told Sarah Hunt, "I know which [will be] crowded into the ditch." Of far greater concern was the prospect of a disunited, ambivalent northern public willing to acquiesce in the territorial expansion of slavery and the control of the government by proslavery politicians. The Republicans would propel the slavery issue into the public debate and force a final reckoning. He had little doubt that the slaveholding class viewed the Republicans as abolitionists and he predicted that they would secede in the event of a Republican victory. "I expect civil war," he told a friend, "and make my calculations accordingly." Parker's predictions were of course correct, but his timing was four years off.[13]

Parker's hopes for the Republican Party significantly outpaced those of his Garrisonian friends. They pointed out that not a single Republican endorsed federal interference with slavery in the states. The party's antislavery stance, they reasoned, was "technical, not real." But having worked for more than a decade to mediate the conflict between political activists and moral reformers, Parker was not about to concede this point. In a speech before the New York Anti-Slavery Society, he argued that the Republican principle of non-extension was but the temporary, outward manifestation of a deeper animus toward slavery. He insisted that the Republican Party was "a direct force for anti-slavery," and that the antislavery convictions of men like Charles Sumner, Henry Wilson and John Parker Hale were as strong as "our friend Garrison's." Ironically, these sentiments placed him in substantial agreement with pro-slavery southern Democrats who intentionally blurred the very real distinctions between abolitionists and Republicans. The *Richmond Enquirer*, for example, told its readers that the real "allies" of the "Black Republicans" were Garrisonian abolitionists whose real aim was to undermine "religion, female virtue, private property, and distinctions of race."[14]

The problem for even staunch antislavery Republicans was that open association with Garrisonian abolitionism would destroy their ability to win elections. Southern papers made the connection in order to discredit Republicans with conservative voters in both sections. It was critical, therefore, for Republican leaders to maintain a healthy distance between themselves and the radicals. But explaining this position to highly skeptical veterans of the antislavery cause was difficult, to say the least. "Of course this party, as such, will make mistakes," Parker told them. But "let us not be very harsh in criticizing these men, remembering that they are not so well supported from behind as we could all wish they were." Abolitionists could say what they liked, he reminded fellow activists, but "it is not so easy for Mr. Seward and Mr. Chase to say what they like." "They have a position to maintain and they must keep to that position." The point was to allow the Republicans to educate public opinion on slavery and bring it to the point where stronger antislavery action would become politically possible. "They want to do one thing at a time," he said of the Republicans. "I do not find fault with their wishing to do that."[15]

While he preached patience to his abolitionist allies, Parker continued to press his Republican friends to steer their party toward the highest impulses of conscience. In his spring 1856 lyceum lectures, and in his correspondence with Sumner, Hale, and Chase, he preached a strongly antislavery understanding of the Constitution. The document contained enough internal antislavery language to allow a reinterpretation of the whole, and he therefore urged his Republican allies to embrace the unconstitutionality of the Fugitive Slave Act, the legality of Northern personal liberty laws, and the power of Congress to prohibit slavery in the territories. More importantly he believed that the party must ultimately acknowledge federal authority to abolish southern slavery itself on the basis of the guaranty clause of the Constitution. "Since the Constitution guarantees to each State 'a republican form of government,' that claim puts slavery complete-ly in the powers of Congress as it does Popeism, Hereditary Nobility, and He-reditary Monarchy," he told Charles Sumner. He made the same argument to Salmon Chase and concluded that there was no "republican form of government where 280,000 white men own 3,840,000 black men." When Chase, a former Democrat, protested that such an argument tended toward the "subversion of state sovereignties and other consequences dangerous to the rights of the peo-ple," Parker simply advised the Ohio governor not to "foreclose all Federal ac-tion against slavery in the Slave States."[16]

At the end of May 1856, abstract theorizing about political confrontation was suddenly eclipsed by the news that Charles Sumner had been savagely beat-en on the floor of the Senate by a southern congressman. Parker had been on the lecture circuit in the days before the attack and had read newspaper accounts of the Senator's "Crime Against Kansas" delivered on May 18th. He was still re-covering from several weeks of illness and was cheered by Sumner's scathing attack on the government's policy in Kansas. In a letter from Burlington, Ver-mont, he congratulated Sumner on the speech. "God bless you for the brave words you spoke the other day," he wrote. "Send [the speech] to me in full as soon as you can."[17]

But not everyone was so happy with what Sumner had said. The speech pilloried President Pierce and other Democratic leaders whom Sumner blamed for the upsurge of violence in the territory. Elderly Senator Andrew Butler of South Carolina, who supported the pro-slavery government in Kansas, received the most stinging rebuke. Sumner ridiculed him as "a Don Quixote" who had "chosen a mistress to whom he has given his vows...I mean the harlot slavery." Stephen Douglas received his share of abuse, being described as a "noisome, squat and nameless animal." Parker had no difficulty with Sumner's abusive language, having used similar rhetoric against his own enemies in Boston. But Butler's younger cousin, Congressman Preston Brooks of South Carolina, was determined to vindicate his kinsman's honor by thrashing the offensive senator. On May 22nd, Brooks confronted Sumner who was seated at his desk in the Senate chamber. Before Sumner could rise or adequately defend himself, Brooks began pummeling him with a gutta percha cane. Brooks landed more than thirty blows upon Sumner's head and upper body, leaving him unconscious and covered in blood.[18]

Parker was enraged by the attack and eagerly sought details of the assault and news of Sumner's condition from his many correspondents in Washington. Henry Wilson told him that Sumner was recovering, but painted a chilling account of the incident and its aftermath. Had Sumner not been disabled by the first blow, Wilson said, he would have "grappled" with Brooks and then "would have been shot either by Brooks or his *five* friends that stood guard around him." Wilson went on to say that threats of violence were now rampant in the capital. He and other Republicans went "into the Senate and House with revolvers and knives in our pockets." After Massachusetts Republican Anson Burlingame derided Brooks in the House of Representatives, he was challenged to a duel by the belligerent South Carolinian. Burlingame was an expert marksman and readily accepted. Parker learned from Henry Wilson that Brooks failed to appear on the appointed day, but instead sent "a mob of rowdies to insult [him]—spit in his face, etc. and then, if he resisted, to kill him." Burlingame's friends kept him out of the city to prevent his murder.[19]

On the Sunday after the caning, Parker told his parishioners that Kansas and Washington were now battlefields in America's "incipient civil war." The war was being waged, he said, by the forces of American despotism for the larger purpose of nationalizing slavery and crushing democratic dissent. The "American oligarchy intends to destroy all our democratic institutions," he thundered. "Do not think that the blow was struck at Mr. Sumner alone...it was you and me and all of us—a blow at freedom of speech." It was now more essential than ever that people of conscience remain stalwart in their resistance. When the New Hampshire Republican John Hale wrote of his inclination to resign his Senate seat for fear of physical attack, Parker assured him the "the post of honor is the post of danger." Whether in Kansas or Washington, opposing Slave Power now entailed a willingness to make the supreme sacrifice.[20]

Parker's darkening outlook on America's future lifted only with the prospect of a Republican victory in the 1856 election. He placed his hope on the thought that northern outrage over the assault on Sumner would sweep the new party into power. Despite his doubts about Republican nominee, John C. Frémont, he resolved to do everything he could to further the Republican cause. Parker saw himself campaigning less for a party or an individual, than for the eternal ideal for which that party, and its nominee, imperfectly stood. History was made up of such struggles and it was useless, if not irresponsible, to sit on the sidelines while they were fought out by others. Democratic victory meant the defeat of free-state forces in Kansas, the continued enforcement of the Fugitive

Slave Act, and the completion of the Slave Power's bid for dominance in national politics. "Now a simple issue is before the people—extension of slavery or non-extension," he told John Hale after the Republican convention. "[I]f the Nation says extend—then we go to pieces." Having spent most of the summer regaining his strength at his wife's family home at Newton Corner, Parker felt ready to enter a political campaign for the first time in his life.[21]

Campaign and Defeat

In the year leading up to the 1856 elections, Parker lectured more than one hundred times across New England, New York and the Middle West. It was extremely tiring work, and he began to feel every one of his forty-six years. A few weeks before his birthday in August, he told a European friend that strangers now commonly mistook him for a man of sixty at least. "You don't know how bald my head is," he wrote. "My beard is almost white." And yet the stakes in the upcoming election were so high, that he refused to turn down lecture engagements as long as there was still time to educate the public on the key issues. Most often he spoke on the political and cultural future of the nation, with lectures like "Progress of Mankind," "The Condition, Character, and Progress of America," among the most popular titles.[22]

Although he was not a Republican operative, Parker's political thought during this period was consistent with the needs of party building. Rather than focusing exclusively on the moral wrong of slavery, his public discourses emphasized the threat slavery posed to American economic and social development. Historians have credited Parker with exerting moral influence on Republican leaders, but they have overlooked his contribution to the party's ideology. Parker had observed politics long enough to know that the Republicans could only win the presidency by attracting voters who were as yet unmoved by moral arguments. Consequently, he appealed to them on sectional grounds, describing the slavery conflict as a struggle between northern democracy and economic initiative on the one hand, and southern aristocracy and economic parasitism on the other. "Shall slavery spread over all the United States and root out all freedom from the land?" he asked. "Or shall freedom spread her blessed boughs till the whole continent is fed by her fruit?"[23]

The sectional dichotomies he created were stark. The North's population, he argued, was engaged in productive labor, and class differences were mitigated by widespread mobility. No single class dominated wealth and leisure, so there was no attempt to restrict political participation. "As there is no compulsory vicarious work, but each takes part in the labor of all," he argued, "there is no vicarious government, but each takes part in the making of laws and in obedience thereto." In the South, by contrast, slavery created an oligarchic class that dominated wealth, leisure, and political power at the expense of oppressed blacks and poverty-stricken, non-slaveholding whites. While economic progress and political democracy were sweeping the North, "the South had formed a permanently idle and lordly class, who shun labor and monopolize government."

Looking to Europe for comparisons, he insisted that the North matched up favorably with the best that England and France had to offer. But the South reminded him of Russia and Austria, whose economies were moribund because of their reliance on serfdom. In the battle over the territories, the question of which system would dominate America was being decided. "Now is the time to choose between these alternatives, and choose quickly," he warned. With a Republican as president, the North had a chance to avoid the national disaster of another four years of domination by the forces of slavery and reaction[24]

What Parker articulated here was a version of the "free labor ideology" that historians have identified as an important strand of Republican Party thought in the pre-Civil War period. Though the party's ideology was still in the process of evolution in the 1856 campaign, Republicans from diverse political backgrounds used free labor rhetoric to attract voters who were concerned about the effect of slavery on the economic future of America. Based on the view that free labor was vastly superior to slave labor in terms of economic efficiency as well as in its social and political consequences, Republicans argued that the spread of slavery would have catastrophic consequences for the future of the country. Using statistical methods similar to those employed in Parker's 1848 "Letter on Slavery," Republican leaders like Seward, Sumner, Chase, and Banks argued that free labor had produced widespread economic prosperity in the North while slave labor had impoverished all but the planter class in the South. Northern voters were told that a vote against the extension of slavery was a vote for the continued well-being of the nation's social and economic character.[25]

The free labor ideology had many intellectual sources including the Whig economist Henry Carey, but Parker should not be overlooked as a formulator of its principles. In some ways he was a likely candidate for this argument. His theological writings had consistently linked material and moral progress to the transcendent forces that governed the world under divine providence. Moral failures had material consequences and vice versa. "Slavery is the greatest obstacle to the present welfare and future progress of the South itself," he once asserted. "It prevents the mass of the Southern people from the possession of material comfort, use, and beauty." By contrast, the North's commitment to the principle of natural rights had produced unprecedented prosperity. "No people on earth have such material comfort," he said of the North. Physical and spiritual laws mirrored one another and worked together in the divine economy that shaped the moral and material character of human society. Violations of the moral law, such as slavery, had consequences not only for the inward spiritual state of master and slave, but manifested themselves outwardly in social instability and economic stagnation.[26]

Yet in identifying the North with the "idea of freedom" and valorizing its labor system as an engine of prosperity, social progress and ethical development, he risked losing the sharp edge of his earlier critique of capitalism's social consequences. In the 1840s, he had understood slavery as a metaphor for all exploitive human relationships, including the degradation of northern workers by unremitting toil, poverty wages, and unhealthy living conditions. But in his antislavery speeches of the late 1850s, North and South stood as polar opposites, with their labor systems contrasted in ways that deflected criticism from northern industrial capitalism. Indeed, the indictment he now leveled against southern slaveholders borrowed heavily from the language he had once reserved almost exclusively for northern merchants. Parker never fully surrendered his earlier social vision, and he continued to believe that inequality was the cause of crime in "nine persons out of ten," but the fight against the "regressive" Slave Power absorbed and channeled Parker's moral outrage in ways that left little room for other issues. He confessed openly to one correspondent that his zeal for the plight of Boston's "perishing classes" had been "hindered" by the "alarming shape and proportions" of the slavery question. On that issue, he said, "we must turn head and put it down, or turn tail and die."[27]

By October 1856, Parker's excitement about the election had risen to peak levels. "It is the most important crisis in our national history," he told John Hale. "It is Despotism or Democracy which the people vote for." But he was worried that corruption or the skillful deceit of pro-slavery Democrats would deny victory to the Republicans. In Galesburg, Illinois where he had gone on a lecture tour, he heard Stephen Douglas speak for the first time. "He was considerably drunk," Parker observed, and his pro-Buchanan speech was "mere brutality in respect of morals and sophistry for logic." But he could not help but acknowledge that there was "a good deal of rough power in [Douglas's] evil face." The speech itself was "one of the most sophisticated and deceitful speeches I ever listened to." He told Hale that he was glad not to have to square off against such a "low blackguard" as Douglas. "You earn your "Hon." pretty dear this year," he quipped. "Stumping is no joke."[28]

Returning to Massachusetts just before the election, he arrived in time to welcome Charles Sumner home from a recuperative trip to Europe. Cheering crowds came out to greet the martyred senator and to pay homage to his personal sacrifice. Theodore and Lydia traveled to Roxbury to watch the venerable former President of Harvard, Josiah Quincy, "welcome Sumner as he did Lafayette in 1825." On Election Day, Parker stayed home and waited for friends to bring him news of the Massachusetts returns. In the late afternoon, he was elated by Frémont's easy victory in the Bay State, but he became increasingly depressed by the tidings of Democratic successes in Pennsylvania, New Jersey, Indiana, Illinois, and California.[29]

By evening, he realized that the election, which he called "not less crucial for our future…than the 4th of July 1776 was for our past," was clearly lost. The two and a half years since the Burns crisis now seemed like a succession of defeats that promised little redemption. Two weeks after the election, he told his friend Sarah Hunt that he was now "more than ever of the opinion that we must settle this question in the old Anglo-Saxon way—by the sword." The Constitution "written on parchment, and laid up in Washington," had failed to redeem America's democratic promise. Now the time was fast approaching when appeals must be made to another parchment, the one that lay "on the head of a drum."[30]

XVII
THE IDEA THAT BLOOD MUST FLOW
1857–1858

As Parker lost sight of the nation's political future in the wake of Frémont's defeat, the rapid decline of his health made his personal future seem equally dim. Despite his near collapse at the New Bedford lyceum in the spring of 1856, he had refused to moderate his work schedule or reduce his lecture itineraries. He even agreed to preach a Sunday afternoon service each week at a new congregation in Watertown. Rather than dampening his desire for fervent activity, the defeat of the Republicans at the polls in the Fall of 1856 convinced him that the nation desperately needed his help. "I am lecturing all the time," he told Sarah Hunt in December of 1856. "In January and February I shall go several times to New York State having twenty or more applications."[1]

These trips were exhausting and they exposed him to cold, leaky railroad cars filled with passengers in varying degrees of ill health. In early February 1857, he was on his way to lecture in Syracuse when his train was stopped by a torrential rainstorm just east of Albany. Afraid to cross a rising Hudson River, the train conductor left his passengers to spend a damp and freezing night in their compartment. Parker had no food with him except some dried fruit and a bit of "biscuit" which he carried for emergencies. Once in Albany, he "ate a bit of tough beef at an Irish boarding-house" and spent the night sleeping under "damp sheets." Despite a sharp, persistent pain in his right side and the onset of an "incipient fever," he lectured for the next three days in Syracuse, Utica, Troy, and Rochester. Reaching home early in the morning of Sunday, February 15th, he insisted on preaching at the Music Hall and at Watertown. By early March, his health was in a desperate state, and Dr. Henry I. Bowditch, an expert on respiratory illnesses at Massachusetts General Hospital, diagnosed the problem as tuberculosis.[2]

In deference to his doctors, Parker remained largely immobile during the early spring and summer of 1857. He applied wet linen compresses to relieve the pain in his side and took homeopathic medicine to treat the disease itself. Lydia and Hannah Stevenson brought meals to his room and he was strictly forbidden to engage in intellectual activity. When he was ill, Parker complained much less about the discomforts of his infirmity than about a sense of stolen manhood. Dependent upon the women of his house, he described himself as "a spaniel, a turnspit, a poodle, or some other puppy dog." Revealing the ongoing tug of war between husband and wife, Parker said that Lydia could teach the famous horse trainer John Solomon Rarey many things about the "art of man taming." He agreed to take the prescribed doses of cod-liver oil, but rebelled against his enforced invalidism. In April he insisted on preaching at the Music Hall, where several friends, including Emerson, Garrison, and John Sargent had been filling in. Taken to the door of the building by coach, he "crawled into the house and walked as bravely as I could to the pulpit" aided by his wife. Spreading his feet as far apart as possible and bracing himself on the desk, he haltingly delivered a sermon called "Integrity" to an audience of over two thousand.[3]

The physical exertion of preaching had a positive short-term effect on his condition, but the illness continued to eat away at his strength. By the beginning of June, he had lost twenty-five pounds and told Charles Sumner that "I can, with my two hands, clasp round the thickest part of my thigh." Concerned about the deteriorating condition of their minister, the Committee of Standing at the Twenty-Eighth voted to increase his salary from $1600 to $2,500 per year and offered to send him on a six-month vacation to Europe without any obligation to find an interim minister. Characteristically, Parker agreed only to a $400 increase in salary, and refused to take the trip to Europe saying that "this recent illness is a warning which I shall carefully heed." Though he had said this after nearly every previous illness, Parker understood that his current condition was more threatening. "I never came so near the precipice before," he told Sarah Hunt. "I felt a little doubtful...for a while."[4]

Although he remained outwardly optimistic, Parker was convinced that he, very much like his country, had entered a critical period that might very well end in premature death. Looking back over his family's history with tuberculosis, he noted with trepidation that many of his siblings had died of the disease when they were between the ages of forty-four and forty-seven. The causes of tuberculosis were still obscure to physicians, but Parker recognized that his chances for long term survival were slim. "My brothers and sisters die early," he told Rev. William Fish. "[A]ll are dead, save my brother [Isaac] and myself." Though the pain and immobility were burdens enough, Parker was haunted by the fear that his contribution to the collective conscience of America would remain incomplete. "I have much work to do yet," he told Fish. "I have whole continents and islands to clear up, and make into farms and gardens." As the antislavery firebrand John Brown entered his life, Parker's illness, his intense frustration with the political process, and his nagging doubts about the power of conscience to shape the direction of history, almost ensured that his response to old Captain's promises of immediate action would be positive.[5]

The Old Captain

By the time Parker met him in early January 1857, John Brown had become a celebrity and, at least to some in the North, a hero. Several months earlier, in the midst of the escalating civil war in Kansas, Brown had organized a stout defense of the free-state settlement at Osawatomie against a proslavery militia force. The defense ultimately failed and Brown's son Frederick was killed, but the *New York Tribune* carried glowing reports of the Captain's bravery and devotion to the cause of freedom. "Osawatomie" Brown recognized the fundraising potential of his new-found celebrity, and he traveled east in the fall of 1856 to gather money and supplies. His entrée to the society of prominent antislavery activists in Massachusetts came through Franklin B. Sanborn, the secretary of the Massachusetts Kansas Committee and a disciple of Transcendentalism. A young romantic with an eager eye for heroic causes, Sanborn was swept off his feet by the leathery, pistol-toting veteran and he smoothed Brown's way into the parlors of well-connected eastern reformers. Sanborn wasted no time in bringing John Brown to the Music Hall to hear Boston's most famous abolitionist minister who, like Brown, believed that fidelity to conscience did not preclude the taking up of arms.[6]

Parker and Brown were at least on the surface very different. A native of Torrington, Connecticut, Brown had retained the strict Calvinism of his stern and morally demanding father. He accepted the essential sinfulness of man, and his devotion to the "divine authenticity" of the Bible was so great that he achieved "a most unusual memory of its entire contents." But if Brown was in some respects a puritan, his understanding of the Calvinist tradition placed him in what historians have called the "antinomian strain" of piety. Along with the seventeenth-century religious rebel Anne Hutchinson, Brown believed that divine grace and the "spirit of Christ" trumped all "social codes" and freed the individual to act in accordance with God's sovereign will. No institutions, human laws, or earthly forms of authority possessed a binding claim for Brown because he operated within a divine, rather than human moral framework.[7]

In another significant departure from puritan orthodoxy, moreover, Brown possessed a serene assurance of his own place among the elect of God. He confidently pursued his war against slavery as a personal mission against sin and oppression. His place among the elect insured that his own conscience, unlike those who had not been regenerated by grace, was utterly reliable and bore witness to his fidelity to God's will. All of this suggests that while Brown would have rejected the formal theology and biblical criticism of Parker and the Transcendentalists, he possessed similar notions of radical self-trust and accepted the absolute authority of a purified conscience.[8]

If Brown and Parker could find some common ground in their moral individualism, they found even more in their mutual veneration of the American

Revolution. Both had grandfathers who served and died in the American army during the war and both understood the Revolution in radical, egalitarian terms. This connection between the two men became immediately apparent on the evening of January 4, 1857 when Brown attended a reception at Parker's home that also included William Lloyd Garrison. During the evening, a debate of sorts took place between Brown and Garrison, with the latter arguing that non-resistance remained the only principled response to slavery. To Brown, such views seemed liked principled *inaction* and he was ready with quotations from biblical prophets to bolster his case for forcible resistance. As guests gathered around to hear the conversation, Parker came to Brown's defense bringing "a bit of Lexington into the controversy." Exactly what Parker said was not recorded, but it was clear to John Brown that the minister's antislavery identity was deeply connected to the Revolution and its New England monuments.[9]

Brown was a shrewd man, and he understood how to appeal to revolutionary symbols in ways that would resonate with his potential allies. Before returning to Kansas, for example, he left Parker a cleverly constructed "farewell" note that drew upon those symbols in order to solicit support. Saying "farewell to the Plymouth Rocks, Bunker Hill Monuments, Charter Oaks and Uncle Tom's Cabins," Brown complained that his mission to the "'Heaven Exalted' people" of New England had been a failure. This, of course, was an exaggeration as he had already come away with thousands of dollars in cash and supplies. But the note speaks volumes about Brown's ability to size up his potential backers. He had clearly decided that Parker, with his huge congregation of reformers, was an important ally.[10]

Parker's desire to advance the cause of freedom made him receptive to Brown's appeal, but his illness prevented him from doing more than expressing his approval for the aid that others were willing to bestow. By September, however, Brown began sending tantalizing letters to members of the Kansas Committee, hinting that any new funds he received would go toward a scheme involving more than the defense of Kansas against border ruffians. These requests for money were couched in dramatic, secretive language that intrigued the convalescent Parker. They had the flavor of the European romantic revolutionary culture of 1848 in which clandestine planning had figured prominently in democratic movements against reactionary governments. Many of Brown's young followers, including journalists James Redpath and Richard Hinton, were exiles from those conflicts. Having heaped praise on the democratic revolutionaries of Europe, Parker was unlikely to miss even veiled references to their legacy. Brown said that he was "in immediate want of some Five Hundred or One Thousand Dollars for *secret service* and no questions asked." Playing on the pride of the sickly minister, Brown said that he *expected* Parker's influence on his behalf, and wanted "the friends of freedom to prove me herewith." The letter informed Parker that the money should be sent to him directly under the alias Jonas Jones of Tabor, Iowa, or by way of George Stearns of the Kansas Committee.[11]

Despite their continued faith in Brown's integrity, Parker, Higginson, Stearns, and others who received similar requests from him in September of 1857 found it difficult to send additional funds. Along with concerns about the precise details of the "secret service" Brown had in mind, their access to resources was severely curtailed by the economic contraction which had crippled Massachusetts industry. "Great Factories stop their wheels, little industries cease, and thousands of men are out of employment," Parker told a correspondent in Illinois. "Where their bread is to come from I know not." Though he had planned to defy his physicians and give a few lectures in the late fall, the economic situation had forced nearly all eastern lyceums to cancel their applications. As for Brown's need for money, Parker agreed with Thomas Wentworth Higginson, who told Brown that he was "always ready to invest in treason, but at present I have none to invest."[12]

False Revivals

While John Brown's fascinating but ambiguous plans remained on his mind in the fall and winter of 1857, Parker's attention was distracted by the great upsurge of religious enthusiasm sweeping over northern cities that year. Often called the "Prayer Meeting Revival" or the "Businessman's Revival," the Awakening of 1857–58 has been characterized as "the acceptance of mass revivalism by urban businessmen seeking God's help in time of trouble." In New York, Philadelphia, Rochester, and other cities affected by the economic depression, revivalists like Charles Finney made thousands of converts among the urban business classes. Finney and his wife Elizabeth appeared several times at Boston's Park Street Church with great success. It has been estimated that nearly fifty thousand conversions were occurring each week in the spring of 1858, and newspapers like the *New York Tribune* devoted special coverage to the "outpouring of spirit."[13]

What was striking about the culture of this particular revival, however, was its almost complete disconnection from the social issues of the period. Instead, it embraced a "socially conservative revivalism" that emphasized private piety over social reform. According to the most recent study of the revival, participants carefully avoided the issue of slavery because of its divisiveness and its capacity to threaten the Union. Given the role that earlier revivals had played in the emergence of abolitionism, temperance, and other reform movements, the retreat from social justice in the awakening of 1857–58 raised serious doubts about its authenticity. In the midst of the revival, evangelical abolitionist William Goodell argued that the "Christianity that does not prompt to prayer and action for the oppressed, cannot be the Christianity of Christ."[14]

From Parker's perspective, the revivals were an unmitigated disaster and they presented yet another challenge to his progressive view of history. Since the early 1840s, he had been predicting the ultimate victory of Absolute Religion, or pure ethical theism, over the "popular theology" of the sects. His massive, unfinished project on the "Progressive Development of Religion Among the Races of Mankind" was built upon the idea that the immanent divine laws of matter and spirit worked in history to bring human consciousness to it fulfillment in Absolute Religion. "We shall have it," he had said of Absolute Religion in his 1853 book *Theism, Atheism and the Popular Theology*. "For God, when he put this idea into human nature, meant that it would go before the fact—the John the Baptist that heralds the coming of the great Messiah." And yet here was a massive surge of piety among the educated, urban middle classes that emphasized creed over conscience, otherworldly salvation over social justice. Discussions of slavery, the festering blot upon the conscience and character of the nation, were actually prohibited in revival prayer meetings. This was a battle that Theodore Parker, even in his weakened state, could not resist fighting. He preached several well-publicized attacks on the revivals that thrust him, for the last time, into the spotlight of religious controversy.[15]

The major problem with the revivals, as Parker understood them, was their conflation of religion with dogmatic creedalism. Their sole purpose was to "remove unbelief in ecclesiastical doctrines," while fervently denying that a conscience-driven life, separate from doctrinal assent, had any merit. Revivalists taught that a good man who lived a useful and morally responsible life but who refused to accept the "popular theology" was damned, while "a moment's belief in the ecclesiastic theology and the joining of a church will admit a pirate, a kidnapper...to heaven." But Parker went beyond his usual critique of the popular theology in an attempt to cast doubt on the sincerity of the revivalists themselves. He accused them of consciously using the commercial crisis to "make church members" and "enforce belief in the ecclesiastic theology."[16]

A careful observer of newspaper coverage of religion, Parker understood the role of print in setting the "revival machinery in motion" and compared such techniques to the vulgar advertising culture of the marketplace. Generating a revival was done the same way as "getting up a mechanics' fair, a country muster, a cattle show, or a political convention," he complained. Advertisements touting the successful preaching of "The Rev. Mr. Great Talk," likely a Bunyanesque reference to Charles Finney, were placed in the newspapers with accounts of mass conversions. But the conversions themselves, Parker insisted, were actually products of the anxiety generated by the financial contraction, reinforced by the spiritual fear-mongering of the revivalists "If the Black Death raged in New Orleans, the yellow fever in Cincinnati," he argued, "the revival would be immensely greater than now." Fear was the greatest, and Parker believed the only real weapon in the hands of those who demanded assent to the superstitions of the popular theology. "Ceasing to think, they will cease to doubt," he said of the revival converts. "And where they have made a solitude, they will call it the peace of Christ."[17]

Parker's attack on the revivals had both real merit and some weaknesses. On the one hand, he was quite right to call attention to the revivalists' failure to address social wrongs. None of the major denominations of American Protestantism had yet declared slavery a sin or called for its immediate abolition, and leading clergymen gave at least tacit support for its continuation. In Boston itself, Rev. Nehemiah Adams of the Essex Street Congregational Church had written a blatantly proslavery tract entitled *A Southside View of Slavery* in 1854. In their failure to address the issue of slavery, Parker rightly argued, the revivals reinforced the status quo.

But he was not so effective in assessing the theological errors of the revivals. For example, he repeatedly accused awakening preachers of subscribing to traditional Calvinist ideas, including total depravity and infant damnation. One of his stock caricatures was "Dr. Banbaby," a rigid Calvinist who demanded that a father, "with a baby in his arms," accept that "God will damn this child" if it was not immediately baptized. In fact, most American Protestants had modified the idea of innate sinfulness and had rejected the concept of infant damnation outright. It was good polemic to associate such a repugnant idea with his theological adversaries, but Parker sacrificed some of his credibility in doing so. "If Mr. Parker really believes that the Orthodox churches of New England hold the doctrine of infant damnation...when everybody that knows anything about it knows that it is not so, then, perhaps the rest of his belief is worth just the same as this," wrote one pro-revival minister.[18]

Parker's criticisms of revival theology were not always fair, but the movement's leaders in Boston did little to raise his opinion of them. During one of Charles Finney's sojourns in the city, for example, participants in the regular prayer meeting at the Park Street Church began praying that Parker's "evil influence might in some way be set aside." On two occasions Finney attempted to see Parker personally in order to effect his conversion to orthodox Protestantism, but he was turned away by Hannah Stevenson. But the public prayers kept coming. "If he is beyond the reach of the saving grace of the Gospel," went one offensive appeal, "remove him out of the way, and let his influence die with him." Parker was understandably shocked that any Christian group could pray for a sick man's death, but he responded with a dose of his famous sarcasm. "I make no doubt the persons who pray for my death are sincere and honest," he told a woman who had begged him to repent of his views. "I don't envy them their idea of God when they ask him to put a hook in my jaw, so that I cannot speak."[19]

As if the prayers were not enough, Lydia and Hannah Stevenson constantly turned away zealous visitors who wished to pray over the heretical preacher or to "labor" with him for conversion. Sometimes they gained admittance and Parker agreed to hear them out. But he often found that they were "quite ignorant of the very things they tried to teach me." Such visitors claimed that "a divine illumination" compelled them to seek his salvation, but Parker saw no evidence of godliness "in them, in their lives or in their doctrines." Years after Parker died, Charles Finney wrote with vengeful satisfaction that the prayers for his removal had actually worked. After all, the revivalist observed, the heretical minister "was very soon laid aside by illness, became unable to preach, went to Europe for his health, and there died." God had clearly ensured that the "evil influence of his preaching" was "ended" except as "the remembrance of it may influence future generations."[20]

The Virginia Plan

John Brown's deeply religious and sacrificial commitment to social change stood in marked contrast to the privatized piety of the revivals. In February 1858, as the prayer meetings were heating up in Boston, Parker received yet another letter from Brown saying that he had "very nearly perfected arrangements for carrying out an important measure in which *the world* has a deep interest *as well* as Kansas, and only lack $500 to $800 to enable me to do so." Brown said that he had written to George Stearns, Franklin Sanborn, and Thomas Wentworth Higginson, but told Parker that he "was not informed as to how deeply dyed abolitionists" they were. Shrewdly appealing to Parker's belief in the application of conscience to social life, he asked if the minister knew anyone interested in "giving their abolition theories a practical shape."[21]

Ever since his debate with William Lloyd Garrison in the parlor at Exeter Place, Brown had known of the Parker's willingness to accept dramatic, violent action in the name of freedom. He also understood how to present himself in ways likely to attract the support of potential backers. In a letter to Franklin Sanborn that was given to Parker in the spring of 1858, Brown described himself in terms that could only have resonated with a dying activist desperate for signs of principle in American life. Speaking of his new plan as a "rich harvest," Brown told Sanborn and Parker that "God has honored but comparatively a small part of mankind" for such "mighty and soul-satisfying rewards" as were now available to those willing to engage in "active service." In terms that sounded more like Transcendentalism than Brown's own Calvinist religious culture, he expressed his hope that the "promptings of your own spirit" would lead supporters to stand with him. He expected only to "endure hardness," but was certain that "the cause is enough to live for, if not to [die] for." It is hard to imagine how Brown could have found a better way to recruit Theodore Parker to his "cause" than this letter.[22]

The "great harvest" Brown was referring to was, of course, his "Virginia Plan," a dazzlingly bold scheme to invade the Old Dominion and arm slaves with weapons captured from the federal armory at Harpers Ferry. After a lightning strike at the armory, Brown planned to use the Allegheny Mountain range as a defensive base from which to launch attacks on plantations in the Deep South. He had contemplated this idea for several years, but did not reveal the details of it to his supporters until early in 1858, when the situation in Kansas reached a stalemate.

The only person outside the Brown family who did know before then was Hugh Forbes, a British mercenary and self-proclaimed military expert whom Brown had hired to train his band of raiders. Forbes had fought with Giuseppe Garibaldi's Italian nationalist forces during the late 1840s and his dramatic exploits had vaulted him to minor celebrity status on the American lyceum circuit. Although he was willing to accept handsome payment in exchange for military advice and training, Forbes was not very supportive of Brown's idea. Southern slaves, he argued, lacked the fighting spirit of free whites and would not rally to

Brown's support without more preparation and encouragement from whites. Brown disagreed and pointed to the successful slave rebellion in Haiti and the large-scale rebellions in America led by Gabriel Prosser, Denmark Vesey and Nat Turner. Though Forbes himself turned out to be a treacherous ally, his doubts about the role of the slaves in the Virginia Plan were not unique to him. Similar fears, derived from the romantic racialism that was so pervasive in American culture, also existed in the minds of Brown's closest supporters, including Theodore Parker.[23]

Parker learned the substance of Brown's plan from Franklin Sanborn who had met with the Kansas warrior at the Peterboro, New York estate of radical abolitionist Gerrit Smith on February 23rd. Neither Smith nor Sanborn were "quite converted" to the wisdom of Brown's proposal, but they came away from their meeting convinced that the old Captain would try it with or without the support of his eastern backers. Could they allow Brown to throw himself into the fray, risking everything, without any help? Two days later, Sanborn was back in Boston where he contacted Parker, Thomas Wentworth Higginson, Samuel Gridley Howe and George Luther Stearns. Along with Gerrit Smith in New York, this group became the Secret Committee of Six who helped to fund the raid. To the Boston five, Sanborn revealed Brown's intention to invade the South with a small party of raiders who would arm slaves with captured weapons. It is not clear that Harpers Ferry was specifically mentioned or if it was discussed as only one in a range of possible targets. But Parker, who was just then preparing to write a series of sermon essays on "Historic Americans," was immediately intrigued. Yet he wanted to see the old man one more time before he could give his full blessing to the idea.[24]

Brown accepted Parker's invitation to visit Boston, but kept a low profile during his time in the city. He checked into room 126 at the American House Hotel on Hanover Street and instructed Parker to call on him as "Mr. (not Captain) Brown, of New York." Since he had given Sanborn strict instructions to keep his visit a secret, Brown chose not to attend Parker's Sunday evening reception as he had done the year before. Parker was the first of the committeemen to call on Brown and the meeting between the two men went well. According to Sanborn, the minister was "deeply interested in the project," and although he was "not very sanguine of its success," he "wished to see it tried, believing that it must do good even if it failed." The two men renewed their good rapport, and the Captain felt comfortable making specific requests of Parker that went beyond fundraising. On March 7th, Sanborn carried a lengthy letter from Brown asking Parker to write two antislavery addresses that would specifically address the situation in Kansas. Because of illness and overwork, Parker never wrote the addresses, but he did send Brown a copy of George B. McClellan's recently published report on the conduct of European armies during the Crimean War. Brown's mind was increasingly focused on military planning and Parker was happy to help supply him with ideas and advice.[25]

By the time Brown left the city the next day, Parker had also agreed to raise at least $100 dollars for the Virginia plan which he was told would go into effect within the next several months. As the evangelicals prayed for God to remove Parker "and let his influence die with him," the dying heretic thought he had found a way to reignite the nation's revolutionary conscience. His willingness to endorse Brown's plan, even in the face of his own doubts about its chances for success, suggests that his old optimism about the direction of history had not yet been snuffed out by fugitive slave renditions, endless political compromises and cultural backsliding. Now, however, it would require a violent reckoning between slavery and freedom. But in placing his faith in a violent slave rebellion to provoke that final confrontation, Parker faced another set of doubts that had percolated at or near the surface of his activism since the 1840s. Was the revolutionary conscience really a universal human characteristic or was it the property of only some of the "races" of the world? If this had ever been an abstract question in Parker's mind, the plans for the Harpers Ferry raid gave it very practical shape.

Racialism and the Black Abolitionists

The racial attitudes of the Secret Six conspirators have been examined extensively by historians. It has been shown that, with the possible exception of Brown himself, all of them harbored at least some doubts about the capacity of African Americans to seize their freedom violently. Even after agreeing to support Brown, for example, Thomas Wentworth Higginson admitted that he was sometimes frustrated by "the patience of the negro" and worried that their "cheerful submission" to bondage might indicate a lack of fighting spirit. But Parker's attachment to racialist thinking went a step beyond that of his coadjutors. He had linked American national character with Anglo-Saxon racial traits since the 1840s. If anything, his use of racial explanations for America's political and cultural crisis had become more frequent and more offensive in the late 1850s.

As late as January 1858, for example, he told the Massachusetts Anti-Slavery Convention that "the African is the most docile and pliant of all the races of men." While vengeance was "instantial with the Caucasian," the African race was "not much addicted to revenge" and "always prone to mercy." To make his point more strongly, he told the story of a fugitive slave named John, an "entire negro" whom Parker claimed had "told me his adventures." John was brutally disfigured by his master, cheated out of money he had raised to purchase his own freedom, and finally separated from his weeping wife and children. But when John found himself standing over his sleeping master with an axe in his hand, he was unable to strike the fatal blow and was later sold. Parker told his audience that "John's story is also the story of Africa. The stroke of an axe would have settled the matter long ago. But the black man would not strike." Then he pointed in the direction of the Bunker Hill monument. "One day, perhaps, he will do what yonder monument commends."[26]

Part of the context for these remarks was the strong opposition to violent action among Garrisonian abolitionists. If blacks would not seize their freedom on their own, Parker was saying, white activists needed to shed their non-resistant principles and take up the sword on behalf of the oppressed. The time had passed when the great American conflict of the nineteenth century could be settled "without bloodshed" and if "the black man would not strike," liberty-loving Anglo-Saxons should. In the back of Parker's mind, of course, was the hardy Anglo-Saxon Yankee John Brown, whose "instinct for freedom" seemed representative of his race. But Garrison would have none of this and he prayed publicly that abolitionists would reject Parker's "idea that blood must flow." Almost as if he were speaking directly to his sickly friend, Garrison counseled against the sense of desperation that was setting in among some antislavery reformers. "Do not get impatient' do not get exasperated," he pleaded, "do not attempt any new political organization, do not make yourselves familiar with the idea that blood must flow."[27]

But to men like Brown, Higginson and Parker, this sounded like more of the principled inaction for which Garrisonians had been criticized in the past. Non-violence, they now believed, had become a kind of creedal statement that, like other dogmas, prevented the full expression of conscience. Nearing the end of his story about the slave John who would not strike the fatal blow against his brutal, treacherous master, Parker could not resist taking a shot at Garrison's stubborn adherence to pacifism. Were Mr. Garrison in John's place, Parker insisted, "I think his Saxon blood would move swift enough to sweep off his non-resistant creed."[28]

By 1858, Parker's growing attraction to racial Anglo-Saxonism verged on a betrayal of his earlier belief in the universality of conscience and the interracial legacy of the American Revolution. He stood out among his fellow activists for his persistent use of racialist rhetoric, even at antislavery meetings. Many white abolitionists shared his pride in the political, legal and cultural accomplishments of Anglo-Saxons, but most preferred to explain the divergent historical experiences of Africans and Anglo-Saxons as a product of environment rather than essential differences. Charles Burleigh, for example, argued that those who complained about the "docility" of the slaves simply failed to understand their situation. "Give [the Negro] his liberty and as strong a motive to exertion as you have, and see what he can become." Parker's friend Wendell Phillips agreed that "Saxon pluck" had "placed our race in the van of modern civilization", but he was explicit in rejecting Parker's view of blacks. "I do not believe in the argument which my learned friend Theodore Parker has stated in regard...to the *courage* of colored blood," he said in an 1858 speech. The peculiar circumstances of modern history, not racial qualities, had produced the enslavement of Africans in America. An honest look at history, Phillips argued, would show that "there is no race in the world that has not been enslaved at one period." Reminding his friend that even "this very Saxon blood we boast was enslaved five centuries in Europe," Phillips demanded that Parker rethink his understanding of race. Although no advocate of violent means, he could not help but recall that the Haitian Revolution disproved any notions of African docility. "The only race in history that took the sword into their own hands, and cut their chains," he insisted, "is the black race of St. Domingo."[29]

It is tempting to believe that Parker's attachment to racialism was simply an outgrowth of his immersion in the ethnological science of the day. As a passionately engaged intellectual, could he have avoided the pervasive influence of the "racial science" that defined human variation as "a function of nature, sanctioned by God"? The problem with this explanation is that highly-sophisticated, alternative explanations of human physical and cultural variation were available to Parker and he chose to reject them. In 1858, for example, he reviewed a well-regarded work on the history of civilization by the English "scientific" historian Henry Thomas Buckle, which explicitly disavowed racial explanations for cultural difference. In the first volume of his *Introduction to the History of Civilization in England*, Buckle had argued that physical geography was the primary agent in shaping human history. Man's progressive mastery over his natural environment, not his racial instincts, had fostered the development of advanced cultures in some parts of the world. Buckle was, to be sure, a deeply euro-centric thinker. He believed that colder climates, where the battle between man and nature was more severe, had produced more complex cultures, while hot climates allowed human beings to survive without significant innovation. But Buckle ranked cultures, not races, and he explicitly denied that there was any proof of "hereditary talents, vices or virtues." He insisted that "original distinctions of race are altogether hypothetical" and denied that there was any basis for the view that higher intellectual faculties were more likely found in "the infant born in the most civilized part of Europe" than in those "born in the wildest region of a barbarous country." For Buckle, environment was everything.[30]

In many respects, Parker was impressed with Buckle's work. After finishing it in December 1857, he told a European correspondent that it was the most important book written in English since Isaac Newton's *Principia*. And yet if Buckle had made a greater contribution to "the philosophy of human history" than any of his English predecessors, Parker could not help but find fault with his views of race. How could a man "of such a comprehensive mind, and so exceedingly well read" fail to see that the "natural endowment of different races is enormous?" Parker felt that Buckle was right to say that physical geography had shaped human and national cultures, but he had failed to understand the equally important laws of race. After all, Parker argued, "all the great, permanent, and progressive civilizations are Caucasian" as well "all the great works of science, literature, poetry" and "all the liberal governments." An inductive approach to human history could not account for important facts, especially American slavery, without recourse to race. "The obstinate and ferocious Indian will fight, he will not be a slave," Parker wrote. But the "pliant and affectionate African seldom fights, rarely takes vengeance, and is easily sent into slavery." Citing recent work on heredity by the French doctor and biological scientist Prosper Lucas, Parker insisted that the case for the "individual inheritance of qualities" had been "abundantly made out in the case of man."[31]

Parker's attraction to racialism came not by default, then, but by inclination. He sought out works like those of Lucas that confirmed his view of race as an underlying, natural force that shaped the meaning and direction of history. But Parker's increasing reliance on racial theory is also a measure of his flagging faith in the ability of conscience to check the entrenched power of corruption and moral wrong. In a nation whose collective conscience now seemed on the verge of surrendering its core values to an aggressive Slave Power, perhaps the libertarian racial qualities of the dominant Anglo-Saxon race were the only guarantees that liberty would not die a premature death. If conscience could not always be relied upon as the fulcrum of progress, perhaps race could.

And yet in John Brown's Virginia Plan, Parker was endorsing an armed attack on the South whose success depended on the willingness of African Americans to act in ways that his racial theory predicted they either would not or could not do. How could "pliant and affectionate" African Americans make up the rank and file of an insurrection that would destroy southern slavery? Brown's plan could hardly "do much good," as Parker had predicted it would, if rebellious blacks were slaughtered by aggressive Anglo-Saxons. Historian Jeffrey Rossbach has argued that the secret to this paradox was a "theory of violence and assimilation" to which Parker and the other members of the Secret Six subscribed. In sending John Brown to the South, the conspirators were offering the slaves the opportunity to assimilate his virtues and, through participation in the rebellion, claim the spirit of liberty for their own race. This view assumes that the racialism of the conspirators was, like their attitudes toward violence, somewhat ambivalent. Alongside their belief in distinct racial characteristics, they must have remained open to the possibility that African American racial character was malleable enough to be altered by contact with sturdy Anglo-Saxons. As Parker himself once put it, "the negro will take their defense into their own hands, especially if they can find white men to lead them."[32]

While this view has much to recommend it, it does not fully identify the sources of the conspirators' cautious optimism about the fighting spirit of the slaves. An exclusive focus on Brown's white supporters misses the role that black intellectuals played in countering the impact of racialist thought among white reformers. Well aware of the romantic racialism that ran through white abolitionist culture, black activists used every opportunity to refute it. Perhaps the most common response was to undermine the historical case for Anglo-Saxon exceptionalism. In an 1857 speech on the significance of West Indian Emancipation, for example, Frederick Douglass complained of abolitionists who "talk of the proud Anglo-Saxon blood as flippantly as those who profess to believe in the natural inferiority of races." Douglass insisted that recent history had provided more than enough evidence that blacks possessed the same fighting spirit as whites. In Joseph Cinque of the *Amistad* rebellion, and Madison Washington who led the slave uprising on the *Creole*, he found two icons of resistance who were "more worthy to be remembered than the colored man who shot Pitcairn at Bunker Hill."[33]

As Parker's racialism became a regular part of his antislavery addresses, moreover, black abolitionists began responding to him directly. Hearing Parker discourse at length about aggressive Anglo-Saxons and docile Africans at a meeting of the New York Antislavery Society, for example, black leader William Wells Brown could not resist a sarcastic retort. He described the horrible mutilation of a slave who had repeatedly fled his oppressive master and then wondered aloud if perhaps the man "had too much Anglo-Saxon blood in him to be a submissive slave, as Theodore Parker would say."[34]

But it was Dr. John Rock of Boston who most explicitly refuted Parker's racialist arguments. Educated as a physician at the American Medical College in Philadelphia, Rock had moved to Boston in 1852 where he became an important figure in the black community and a popular lyceum lecturer. Though little information remains on the details of his lectures, Rock's most successful public addresses of the 1850s focused on scientific theories of race. His lecture on "The Unity of the Human Races" was delivered to audiences throughout New England and the Western Reserve of Ohio in 1855 and was praised in antislavery circles as the product of "superior scholarship and much careful research." By the time that he took on Parker, Rock had perfected his performances by mixing humor and artistry with intellectual rigor. The lyceum stage was a medium of communication that both men understood quite well.[35]

On the evening of March 5, 1858, Rock, Parker, Phillips and other abolitionists joined members of Boston's black community to celebrate the eighty-seventh anniversary of the Boston Massacre. Called together by black historian William Nell, the gathering was intended in part as a protest against the Supreme Court's denial of black citizenship in the *Dred Scott* decision the previous year. The meeting focused on the role of the black revolutionary martyr Crispus Attucks, and Nell expected his speakers to commemorate the participation of African Americans in preserving American liberty.

Dr. Rock used the occasion as an opportunity to respond directly to Parker's remarks at the Massachusetts Anti-Slavery Convention two months earlier. Rock had attended the convention and was clearly still smarting at Parker's insistence that "the stroke of an axe would have settled the question, but the black man would not fight." Marshalling the same sarcastic wit Parker had often used against his theological opponents, Rock turned the logic of the minister's racialism on its head. "Mr. Parker makes a very low estimate of the courage of his race," Rock mused, "if he means that one, two or three millions of these ignorant and cowardly black slaves could, without means, have brought to their knees five, ten or twenty millions of intelligent, brave white men, backed up by a rich oligarchy." The Anglo-Saxon courage, about which Parker spoke so eloquently, seemed to consist mainly of mob violence and hypocrisy. "A score or two of them can pounce upon a poor Negro, tie and beat him, and then call him a coward because he submits." But, Rock concluded rather archly, "I know of no one who is more familiar with the true character of the Anglo-Saxon race than Mr. Parker."[36]

Rock went out of his way to call Parker a "true and tried friend," but he was determined to refute the accusations of black cowardice that ran though the minister's recent speeches. "When he says 'the black man would not strike," Rock insisted, "I am prepared to say he does us a great injustice." Rock believed that the historical record was very clear about the fighting spirit of African Americans. In the American Revolution, blacks had fought valiantly and, as Nell's *Colored Patriots of the Revolution* had showed, they had played a vital role in the winning of American independence. And yet what had they received for their service to the nation? "They fought for liberty, but they got slavery."[37]

If Parker and Rock agreed on anything, it was the inevitability of armed conflict between North and South. But unlike Parker, Rock was certain that African Americans would be in the thick of it. "Will the black man fight?" he asked. "Of course he will. The black man will never be neutral." The real question for Rock was not the martial character of African Americans, which had been proved over and over again on the battlefields in Haiti and North America. The question was whether the American nation would ever wage a war in which universal liberty, including the emancipation of slaves, was the central goal. Should that day ever come, Rock believed that all the calumnies heaped upon African Americans would be exposed for the lies they were. "150,000 freemen capable of bearing arms, and...slaves wild with enthusiasm caused by the dawn of the glorious opportunity of being able to strike a genuine blow for freedom, will be a power which the white man will be 'bound to respect'." In Rock's vision of a proud, militant black population that was ready to strike a "genuine blow," Parker saw a very different image of the past and future than his racialist imagination had yet conceived.[38]

Parker responded to Rock with a muted reaffirmation of his earlier position. "My friend Dr. Rock has said a great many good things about the African race," he began rather haltingly. "If I cannot agree with all that he said, I am sorry." Having said "a hundred times," that Africans lacked the same fighting sprit as Anglo-Saxons, he refused to retract his basic argument. All he was willing to concede was that "slavery will not be exterminated with one blow," and he expressed his hope that "the black man will do his part." But the force of Rock's argument and his vision of black militancy was an important and very timely element in Parker's endorsement of John Brown's Virginia Plan. On the evening before Parker's confrontation with Rock, Brown had arrived in Boston and taken up temporary residence at the American Hotel. Over the next several days he met with members of the Secret Six and talked over some of the details of his plan to arm the slaves of the South and ignite a slave insurrection. As he agreed to raise money and provide support for Brown, Parker did so with Rock's forceful defense of black miltancy ringing in his ears. Although he never repudiated his racialist assumptions, Parker ultimately chose to embrace his hopes for a biracial struggle against slavery rather than his fears. "No doubt there is a limit to the negro's forbearance," he wrote after hearing of Brown's capture a year-and-a-half later. "San Domingo is not a great way off."[39]

XVIII
PRINCIPLES, PARTIES AND PARTINGS
1858–1859

A final, but important context for understanding Parker's alliance with John Brown was his ultimate disillusionment with the political process. Throughout his career as an antislavery leader, he had refused to accept the Garrisonian view that party politics rested upon a hopelessly corrupt, proslavery system. He had placed his hope in the power of conscience to transform political organizations into forces for great ideals. It was this hope that had led him to form relationships with leading Conscience Whigs in Massachusetts and to support the Republican Party as an expression of the American core idea of freedom. But John Frémont's defeat in 1856 and the subsequent behavior of leading Republican politicians severely dampened his enthusiasm for the new party.

Many Republican leaders interpreted their party's 1856 defeat as an indication that public attention had shifted away from a sole focus on the slavery question. They therefore began speaking out more often on the economic issues that distinguished them from their Democratic opponents. The protective tariff, free homesteads, and a Pacific railroad became major elements of party strategy after 1856. The Panic of 1857 at least temporarily replaced the conflict in Kansas as the nation's most urgent concern. Republican leaders believed that success in 1860 hinged on their ability to attract conservative voters with previous ties to the Whigs, Democrats, or Know-Nothings. Bearing this consideration in mind, even committed antislavery Republicans William Seward and Henry Wilson pointedly distanced themselves from abolitionism and disavowed any intention to interfere with slavery in the South. For a time in 1858, Wilson and Seward even expressed qualified support for Stephen A. Douglas and the popular sovereignty formula.[1]

Given Parker's idealistic view of the political process, these developments came as something of a shock. His optimism about the party dissipated, and he scrambled to regain a sense of moral purity. "I don't know but it would have been more fatal if power had fallen into the hands of the Fremonters," he told parishioner Sarah Hunt. "I have doubts about such men…they are not quite solid enough for my taste." He was particularly concerned with the tenor of Republican politics in the West, where he believed that "a great deal of bad stuff has come over to the Republican Party." Because of their tendency to utilize negrophobia rather than anti-slavery rhetoric or free-labor ideology, Parker felt that the hands of western Republicans "were not quite clean enough to be trusted with power." The party that he had so recently seen as a vehicle for the abolition of slavery, now seemed on the verge of losing its moral underpinnings. "I am sorry to notice the timidity of the Republican men in declaring that it is not their intention *ever* to interfere with slavery in the states," he complained to John Hale. "It is *my intention* as soon as I get the power."[2]

Parker's bristling impatience with the political process in part reflected his horror at the aggressive, proslavery character of James Buchanan's administration. The president's attempt to use "all the administration's resources of patronage and power" to force Congress to accept the pro-slavery Lecompton constitution for Kansas clearly linked him to the Slave Power. Indeed, many northerners saw the president's support for filibustering expeditions in Mexico and Nicaragua as evidence that he was part of a southern conspiracy to set up a slave empire in Latin America. In June 1857, Parker had bleakly predicted to the still-ailing Charles Sumner that Buchanan would force through the admission of Kansas as a slave state, annex both Central America and Cuba, and secretly encourage the resumption of the African slave trade. "Yes Sumner, all these foul things will be carried in four years," he prophesied. Sumner's continued absence from the Senate left Parker without a political leader whose conscience seemed steadfast and reliable. He hoped that his old friend would soon return to Washington and "elevate the tone of Republican Party."[3]

Herndon and Lincoln

Parker poured out his frustration with national politics to William Herndon, a Springfield, Illinois Republican who also happened to be the law partner of the rising Republican politician Abraham Lincoln. Parker had met Herndon while on a lecture tour in 1854, and the two began a correspondence that lasted until Parker's death. "Billy" Herndon was a fascinating figure for many reasons, not the least of which was the bewildering conglomeration of ideas he kept in precarious balance. Born in Virginia, he had a romantic vision of southern life, and he believed that blacks were naturally inferior to whites. But he considered himself an antislavery Republican and believed wholeheartedly that the South was determined to nationalize slavery. As an admirer of New England intellectual life in general, and of Transcendentalism in particular, Herndon was drawn to Parker's moral vision and his religious faith in human improvement. If his letters were often filled with incomprehensible meanderings on the presence of

God in nature, they also provided Parker with practical insights into western politics.[4]

It was to Herndon that Parker expressed his disgust with the 1857 Supreme Court decision in *Dred Scott v. Sandford*. In that case, the southern-dominated court ruled that blacks were not, and could never be United States citizens and that Congress had no power to prevent the spread of slavery into the territories. Calling the decision "a falsification of history and a prostitution of law," Parker was certain that the court's next move would be to declare the unconstitutionality of statutes prohibiting the international slave trade. He was disgusted that Massachusetts Democrats were holding conventions in support of the decision and complained that Rufus Choate, Edward Everett, and other Massachusetts conservatives were counseling adherence to it as a Union-saving measure. Herndon assured him that in Illinois both Republicans and Democrats "repudiate the Court," but Parker was convinced that the Slave Power could only be checked when the Democratic Party was "broken into fragments and ground to powder." This was only possible, however, if the Republicans resisted the temptation to compromise their principles and became a genuinely anti-slavery party. Otherwise, the political battle for freedom would be lost.[5]

Of course Parker also knew of William Herndon's famous law partner in Springfield and he followed Lincoln's rise to the leadership of the Illinois Republican Party with interest. As Lincoln prepared to face Stephen A. Douglas in the 1858 senate race in Illinois, Parker rather naively predicted that he would score an easy victory. Douglas' signature doctrine of popular sovereignty had been discredited by the *Dred Scott* decision and he was at war with the Buchanan administration over Kansas policy. Yet Parker was a bit dubious about the depth of Lincoln's antislavery principles and he pored over the printed transcripts of the debates for signs of wavering. After reading the *New York Tribune* report of the debate at Ottawa in August 1858, for example, he was dismayed by Lincoln's unwillingness to take a bold stand on slavery. Douglas had questioned Lincoln about a series of strongly-worded antislavery resolutions passed by Republican county conventions in 1854. Aware that his antagonist was attempting to paint him as a radical, Lincoln disavowed any connection with the resolutions. He said that he had "nothing to do" with them and declared that he had "no purpose directly or indirectly to interfere with slavery in the states where it exists." Not only did he have "no lawful right to do so," Lincoln said, but "I have no inclination to do so."[6]

Parker found Lincoln's answers troubling in light of recent trends in the Republican Party. Rather than standing up for basic principles, Republican leaders like Lincoln appeared to be running away from them. Having seen Douglas on the stump, he was convinced that the "Little Giant" could only be defeated by a forthright defense of truth and right. "I thought Douglas had the best of it," Parker grumbled to Herndon. "He questioned Mr. Lincoln on the great matter of slavery and put the most radical questions which go to the heart of the matter before the people." Unfortunately, Parker concluded, "Mr. Lincoln did not meet the issue—he made a technical evasion." Such evasions raised doubts about the moral direction of the Republican Party and its effectiveness as an antislavery vehicle.[7]

A seasoned veteran of Illinois politics, Herndon reassured his eastern friend that Lincoln was being as principled as possible in the context of public opinion. "[Lincoln] takes high and elevated grounds for freedom—as high as our people will bear," he reasoned. "What he may do in the future I cannot say." Herndon also cautioned Parker against judging Lincoln solely on the basis of his debate with Douglas—a man Herndon hated with a passion. Douglas, he said, was "the greatest liar in all America," and since the people were generally not "logical enough" to see through him, he was able to "misrepresent Lincoln throughout." Lincoln's disadvantage in debating Douglas, Herndon claimed, was not that he lacked principles, but that he was "too much of a Kentucky gentleman" to sink to Douglas' level as a political brawler. "He will not condescend to lie; he will not bend to exploding; he will not hug shams, and so he labors under a disadvantage in this state.[8]

But after years of defending political antislavery leaders to skeptical Garrisonians, Parker was understandably impatient. He wanted a political leader who would stand on the highest moral principles and he was not yet convinced that Lincoln was such a leader. "Daniel Webster stood on higher anti-slavery ground than Abraham Lincoln now," he complained to Herndon. Webster-style politics was "certainly not the way to fight the battle of freedom." Since he had always conceived of politics as a way to educate public opinion, Parker was annoyed at Lincoln's unwillingness to risk a bold statement of his deepest values. "We must adhere to the principle of right," he told Herndon in September. "If the attempt to lower the platform is made by the Republican leaders then they are beat."[9]

Despite Parker's criticism of Lincoln, the two men actually shared a good deal in common. Their skepticism about traditional, orthodox Christianity had led each of them toward a rational faith in individual and collective improvement. Though it is not clear how much of Parker's writing reached Lincoln's desk, the Springfield lawyer possessed a remarkably similar understanding of religion as a force for social and political progress. Lincoln's friend and political ally Jesse Fell once said that his religious views resembled those of Theodore Parker more than any other author. Historian Gary Wills has also shown that Parker and Lincoln shared a similar political faith. Both understood the principles of the Declaration of Independence as the transcendent ideals which the nation must strive for during its historical existence. They also saw the political crisis of the 1850s in terms of an aggressive Slave Power conspiracy with which there could be no permanent compromise. Lincoln's view that the Union could not "endure permanently half slave and half free," and that it would become "all one thing or all the other," echoed Parker's belief that final clash between the incompatible ideas of slavery and freedom would determine the destiny of America.[10]

But in 1858, the two men were at very different points in their respective life trajectories. Lincoln found himself on the brink of a meteoric rise to political power that required careful attention to the shape and direction of American public opinion. The race- and abolition-baiting that political opponents like Douglas employed against him seemed to require careful "evasions" like the one Parker had complained about in the Ottawa debate. Parker, on the other hand, was nearing the end of his life as a minister and reformer and had little to gain by patience or compromise. As his health deteriorated and the nation seemed lulled into acquiescing in the designs of the Slave Power, he was less interested in excuses and searched anywhere he could for signs of a pure conscience.

Postponement

As Parker awaited Brown's raid into Virginia, he enjoyed a renewed period of optimism about his life. His lungs were still painful and he remained weak, but he had preached at the Music Hall throughout the year without relapsing and had delivered several lectures in the Boston area as well. He was still plagued by zealous revival converts, but he also received letters from religious progressives who thanked him for his courageous stands against the "popular theology." Some, like J.F. McCalmont of Canonsburg, Pennsylvania testified that their random encounters with Parker's writings had answered a deep spiritual longing. McCalmont spoke of the "inexpressible joy" that had gripped him after coming across a volume of Parker's sermons in a local library. For the first time, he wrote, "I found what I thought to be the truth."[11]

Others translated their enthusiasm for Parker's theology into the building of experimental religious institutions. In April 1858, for example, he received a letter from J.H. Turner, a former member of the Twenty-Eighth who, like so many young New Englanders, had moved west in search of land and opportunity. Turner and a small group of like-minded seekers had formed a religious society in Bedford County, Iowa basing itself on Parker's theological and moral principles. Despite being "surrounded by the most bigoted and narrow-minded sectarians," Turner's group was committed to "elevating ourselves and the community around us from the theological bogs which the people have been foundering in for so long." They had hired a minister and were building a church which they hoped would become "a little branch" of the Twenty-Eighth in southwestern Iowa. During the first year of their experiment, the group endured considerable harassment from their orthodox neighbors. Turner described members being "challenged on juries [and] insulted in public assemblies," but he testified that their individual and collective devotion to conscience had produced a "marked change" in the attitude of the surrounding community. Here at least was some good news.[12]

Even as correspondents like McCalmont and Turner lifted his spirits, Parker became increasingly concerned about John Brown's Virginia plan. At his meeting with Brown at the American House Hotel in Boston in early March 1858, Parker had understood that the invasion of Virginia would begin within the next several months. But an unexpected problem emerged that nearly scuttled the entire operation. 'Colonel' Hugh Forbes, the British adventurer whom Brown had hired to drill his men, was threatening to expose the whole enterprise if he were not paid his promised salary. After receiving stinging rebukes from Frank Sanborn and Samuel Gridley Howe in April, Forbes traveled to Washington where he held audiences with several Republican senators including Henry Wilson and John Parker Hale. On May 9, Howe received a letter from Wilson indicating that Forbes had partly divulged Brown's plans and the identity of at least some of his allies. Wilson said that he hoped that whatever arms had been provided to Brown for the defense of Kansas would be removed from his possession without delay. "If they should be used for other purposes as *rumor* says they may be," he warned ominously, "it might be of disadvantage to the men who were induced to contribute to that very foolish movement."[13]

As soon as he received the news of Forbes's treachery, Parker met with Sanborn, Howe, and Stearns and insisted that Brown postpone his raid until the following spring. Forbes's revelations had compromised the committee as well as the plan itself. Gerrit Smith, who visited Boston at the end of May, agreed that "as things stand…it would be madness to attempt to execute" the plan. The only holdouts were Thomas Wentworth Higginson and John Brown himself. Both men believed that Forbes lacked the intelligence to compromise the plan and Higginson was furious at what he regarded as the timidity of his fellow conspirators. He told Parker that it would be "disgraceful for us to be outmaneuvered by such a fellow" as Forbes. But Parker was in closer contact with the politicians Forbes had spoken to, and he believed that the treacherous colonel knew more than enough to ensure the failure of Brown's scheme. Most significantly, Forbes knew that Brown intended to make the attack with limited resources and a very small group of raiders. Should that information be divulged to the authorities and to the public, the terror the conspirators hoped would result from the invasion would be lessened considerably. Parker understood Higginson's desire for action, but he warned his younger colleague that if he knew "all about 'colonel' Forbes," he would "think differently" about the need for postponement. At no point in these discussions did Parker withdraw his support for Brown's larger intentions.[14]

Even as he urged postponement, Parker tried to limit the damage that Forbes's revelations had done to the scheme. This was a very delicate task. It required that he divulge his personal connections with Brown while at the same time discrediting Forbes's warnings about an imminent invasion of the South. In a letter typical of his handling of this issue, he told New Hampshire Senator John Parker Hale that "the charge which Forbes brings against certain men here is wholly unfounded." All that the committee had done was to advise Captain Brown to "go to Kansas and help the present [territorial] election." He assured Hale that Forbes was a man of little character who, unlike John Brown, had squandered the resources he had been given to assist the free-state cause in Kansas. Hale should give no credence to Forbes's allegations, Parker argued, because he was little more than a self-interested publicity seeker trying to inflate his reputation, and fill his pocketbook at John Brown's expense. If he had real information about "any enterprise of anybody," Parker insisted, "he would sell it to the U.S. government." Parker's estimation of Forbes's character was accurate, but he deliberately concealed his own knowledge of the Virginia plan in order to protect himself, his fellow conspirators, and the long-term viability of the plan.[15]

With this duty discharged, Parker and the rest of the committee needed only to convince John Brown and Thomas Wentworth Higginson to hold fire until the following year. Near the end of May, when Smith was in Boston giving a speech to the American Peace Society, the five members in favor of postponement met at the Revere House. They agreed that Brown should go to Kansas for a year so as to remove suspicions that he intended to invade Virginia. The group offered him an immediate grant of $500, with the understanding that as much as $3000 would be raised for the final excursion into the South. The two hundred rifles that George Stearns had purchased for Kansas work would be transferred permanently to Brown and he was then free to conduct his preparations for the invasion without directly involving the committee or its members.

This was the proposal that Brown heard from his backers when he arrived in Boston on May 31, and it is clear that the old Captain was initially unhappy with it. He told a sympathetic Higginson that delay would demoralize the men he had recruited and he grumbled that Smith, Parker and Stearns were "not men of action" and "did not abound in courage." Although historians have tended to agree with Brown's assessment, it seems just as reasonable to conclude that the committeemen wanted Brown's dramatic but extremely risky plan to proceed under the best possible conditions. Despite his complaints, Brown left Boston on June 3 feeling very optimistic about the future. He had a fresh infusion of both weapons and cash, and solemn promises for a good deal more.[16]

Illness and Departure

But the future looked far less rosy for Theodore Parker that summer. Although he had spent several weeks at Lydia's family property in rural Newton Corner, he suffered with a persistent "ugly cough" and muscle loss that nineteenth-century physicians associated with the second of three stages in the development of tuberculosis, or "consumption". Based upon the medical theory that tuberculosis patients could be cured by exercise and exposure to better air, doctors routinely advised patients to embark on lengthy overland trips. Parker's doctor, Henry Bowditch, was convinced that his own father had escaped the disease by just this method and he now encouraged his famous patient to follow suit. In August, Parker took leave of Lydia and went on "a little ride of seven hundred miles" by wagon through Northern New England and the Adirondack mountains. His companion for the voyage was Joseph Lyman, a wealthy parishioner who was so "gentlemanly" and good natured that Hannah Stevenson jokingly called him Parker's "lover". Riding thirty miles a day at a rate of about five miles an hour, Parker tried to relax his body and mind. He took in the natural beauty of his native region and reveled in what he still believed was the "supremacy of the puritan New Englander over all the other peoples of the continent." In a final tour of his beloved Yankee homeland, he regained some of his optimism about the progress of America's "industrial democracy." In the "wealth, comfort, temperance and intelligence" of New England's "little villages" and "by roads," he found renewed hope in the future of his country. But though his trip inspired him, it did little to improve his health. His cough worsened by the fall, and after hearing Joseph Lyman's description of their minister's condition, the leading members of the Twenty-Eighth all but begged him not to resume his normal duties until he had fully recovered.[17]

Parker, however, was still not ready to let go. His congregation had recently established a "Fraternity" course of lectures that would allow its minister, and other well-known literary figures and reformers, to speak on topics relevant to contemporary life and letters. Throughout the previous spring and summer, Parker had prepared a series of meticulously researched lectures on "Historic Americans" which he intended to deliver to the fraternity. He insisted on giving the first of them, a lengthy review of the life of Benjamin Franklin, on October 6th. But by that time, in addition to his cough, he was experiencing severe pain and other symptoms from an anal fistula, which had to be removed surgically. The procedure alleviated the pain, but he was weakened by it and he remained in bed for nearly a month. Feeling stronger and more optimistic by the first week in November, he tried to resume his normal pastoral duties but experienced another setback. Travelling by train to conduct a funeral for a young child who had tragically drowned, he fell as he entered the railroad car and injured the "delicate parts of my body." His doctors feared infection and absolutely forbade movement of any kind. "I haven't walked since the 24th," he told the Irish religious reformer Francis Power Cobbe in mid-December. "I suffer little pain, except for the lack of tone and vigor that comes from such long confinement."[18]

New Year's Day, 1859, found Parker physically weak and in a depressed state of mind. It was the first new year that he could remember being ill, and he now doubted that he would live to see another. "It looks as if this was my last of my New Year's here on earth," he wrote forlornly that evening. Forbidden to go outside in the cold air, he had been confined to his bedroom and he felt "like a prisoner." The world seemed to be closing in on him and he experienced feelings of hopelessness and futility. He would never finish the work he had started and some "abler and better" man would take it up and finish it. Unfortunately, he could find little comfort in a sense of personal accomplishment, predicting that his memory would not long outlive him. "The Twenty-Eighth will soon forget me," he now sadly predicted. "A few Sundays will satisfy their tears."[19]

But in lighter moments, he still hoped for a reprieve from the death sentence that hung over him. He promised friends that henceforth he would be "very cautious and take special pains to live" and repeated any optimistic statements he heard from the doctors. There was, in fact, no time table for the progression of consumption. The final stages of the illness could go on for a year or more including periods when patients seemed to steadily improve before experiencing devastating relapses. As one historian has written, patients had to "live *with* the disease and make life plans without knowing whether they would come to fruition." And so even as he predicted his death on New Year's Day, 1859, Parker was preparing to deliver a sermon at the Music Hall the next morning.[20]

But a week later, on January 9th, Parker suffered a hemorrhage of the lungs and nearly died of asphyxiation, a common cause of death in tuberculosis patients. These were horrible experiences for those who endured them. Often occurring, as Parker's did, in the middle of the night, patients gagged on mouthfuls of blood not knowing when or if the ordeal would stop. Since he had planned to preach that morning at the Music Hall, Parker sent a short note to the congregation explaining his condition and asking them "not to forget the contribution to the poor." As they had a year earlier, the Standing Committee of the Twenty-Eighth voted to extend their minister's salary for a year and encouraged him to take a trip to Europe to improve his condition. In a letter signed by over three-hundred members of the society, Standing Committee Chairman John Manley wrote that "there is a limit to the endurance of even the strongest man, and the frequent warnings which you have received within the past year or two would seem to indicate that Nature will not suffer even the best of her children to transgress her laws." Though they expressed the deepest regret that they would lose his services as their minister, they still hoped that "it is not too late to arrest the progress of the illness and that in some more genial clime than ours you may regain the soundness of health."[21]

Like many nineteenth-century tuberculosis victims, Parker was advised to leave the United States for milder climates abroad. In warmer, more temperate regions of the globe, it was believed, patients could spend more time out of doors where exercise would soothe irritated pulmonary tissues and allow them to heal naturally. Prolonged confinement in the tiny cabins of sailing ships was a risk of such voyages, but most doctors believed that the sea air itself possessed healing powers. On January 23rd, Parker was examined by four physicians, including pulmonary expert Henry Bowditch, who told him that his chances of surviving the disease at all now depended upon taking just such a voyage. Following a route that many New England consumptives traveled before and after him, he was to go first to the Caribbean and ultimately to Italy in search of good health. He told friends that he intended to return to New England just as soon as he had recovered his former vigor, but he understood privately that this would most likely be a one-way voyage. By early February, he had written reams of farewell letters to his friends and fellow activists, made out a will, and prepared to leave America. "I must go off to the West Indies, to Europe and not return," he wrote in his diary.[22]

Though he believed that the odds against his recovery were nine to one, the prospect of a journey abroad had given him a new determination to fight the battle for his health with stubborn resolve. He allowed himself to remember the many times he had stood alone against overwhelming criticism and seemingly insurmountable obstacles. "I have fought ninety-nine against one, yes 999 against one, and conquered," he told himself. Wasn't he the grandson of Captain John Parker? Wasn't he the man whose resolute conscience had braved the wrath of the Boston mercantile and clerical establishment? "I laugh at the odds of nine to one," he wrote boldly on the eve of his departure. "I mean to live and not die." He made the same proclamation to his congregation at the Music Hall a few weeks later. "I know that I am no longer young, and that I stand up to my shoulders in my grave," he said in a farewell letter. "Yet the will to live is exceedingly strong, more vehement than ever before, as I have still much to do." The same fraying optimism that had sustained Parker's hope in John Brown and in the larger power of conscience to drive human progress, remained with him as he contemplated the prospect of death on foreign soil[23]

Along with Lydia, secretary Hannah Stevenson, and his ward George Cabot, Parker left Boston for good on February 3rd. The group traveled to New York City where they boarded the steamer *Karnak* bound for St. Croix in the Virgin Islands. The steamer was to make stops in Cuba, Nassau and other Caribbean ports before reaching its final destination. On board were Samuel Gridley Howe and his wife Julia, who had agreed to accompany the Parkers as far as Cuba. Julia observed Parker very closely and reported that he was seasick for most of the journey. The steamer met some stormy weather on its way south, and Julia remembered that Parker was confined to his berth as the ship was "rolled and tossed about." As the party reached Havana on February 21, the Howes and Parkers prepared to say goodbye. Samuel and Julia both felt that they were seeing their old friend for the last time. "Parker embraced us both..." Julia remembered more than fifty years later. "I still carry in my mind the picture of his serious face, crowned with gray locks and a soft grey hat as he looked over the side of the vessel and waved us a last farewell."[24]

XIX
THE FINAL JOURNEY
1859–1860

Throughout his life as a theologian and reformer, Theodore Parker's belief in conscience as the engine of human progress had sustained him in the midst of conflict, rejection and even physical danger. He had persistently transformed professional ostracism into a renewed sense of personal importance. By this same method, private disappointments became motives for ever greater public achievement. But by the spring of 1859, Parker's declining health and his deepening fears for America presented a significant challenge to his optimism. Now he was an exile, searching for a reprieve against nearly impossible odds. The public activism that had compensated for his truncated domestic life had been left behind in America and others would reap where he had sown. Now there was only a private Theodore Parker whose sphere of activity and circle of companions were narrowing as each day passed.

The bouts with melancholy which had surfaced periodically in his private journal became more frequent during the last year of his life and he found it difficult to take solace in intellectual or political activity. "I have not much instinctive love of life," he wrote his old friend George Ripley in May 1859. "I am ready [to die] at any time and have never had a minute of sadness at the thought of passing." But like many patients suffering consciously with a terminal illness, Parker used his remaining creative energy to construct a coherent and satisfying narrative of his life. He wrote two autobiographical statements, and sent long letters to old friends and allies reflecting on the meaning of his experiences and speculating about the destiny of America. Unwilling to give up on his nation's hopes for recovery, he re-imagined America's future on an elongated time span in which the revolutionary conscience would gradually perform its appointed task. "How many centuries will it take to bring the actual America up to the Ideal of the Declaration of Independence?" he asked his friend Joseph Lyman.

"Dear old Humanity—it never stands still; upward and onward to the eternal word of God!" America had time to realize its ideals, even if Theodore Parker did not.[1]

Theologically at least, Parker had no reason to fear his own death. The immortality of the human soul was perhaps his most dogmatic belief. The continual life of the soul after death needed no proof; it was an "ontological fact" flowing from the existential consciousness of human beings. Although he usually avoided the traditional word "heaven" to describe the afterlife, Parker was certain that the "future state" was made up of conscious souls living in harmonious social relationships. And he always thought in terms of progressive change. The qualities each human being possessed in mortal life would be made perfect in the next one, much as the fully developed flower developed from its previous existence as a bud. "The next life," he assured his congregation, "will be a continual state of progress, the improvement of old powers, the disclosure or accession of new ones." He was also clear that there was no hell. To believe in a permanent state of torment would be to impugn the perfect love of a God who was "the physician" of mankind not his "hangman." There would be a certain amount of suffering for those who had lived "mean, little, vulgar and selfish lives." But perfect suffering was corrective, not punitive and it was designed as "the medicine of sin" not as some form of barbarous vengeance. If Theodore Parker looked back regretfully upon work left unfinished, he had little fear about what awaited him beyond the grave. "I look through the grave to heaven," he once wrote. "I am conscious of eternal life."[2]

A Spring in St. Croix

If death held no terrors for Parker, he could see only "small merit in being willing to die." To wish for it, even in the midst of suffering, "seems almost sinful in a good man," especially when "the world needs him so much here." And so he began his final journey, determined to recover at least some remnant of health. That journey started in the Caribbean, where he spent the winter and spring of 1859 gathering strength for the long voyage to Europe which he planned for the middle of May. After taking leave of the Howes in Cuba, the Parkers boarded the steamer *Ocean Bird* for the week-long voyage to St. Thomas in the Virgin Islands. From there they took a schooner to the village of Frederiksted on the west end of the Danish sugar island of St. Croix.[3]

Frederiksted had long been a refuge for New England consumptives, including the famous Unitarian philanthropist Joseph Tuckerman. Over the years, its ailing residents had worked hard to maintain New England customs in an unfamiliar environment. But the town had an even more special meaning for an abolitionist like Theodore Parker. In 1848, more than 8,000 rebellious slaves had laid siege to the fort in Frederiksted demanding an end to legal servitude. Rather than risk massive bloodshed, the colonial governor had issued a proclamation of emancipation which was ratified two months later by the King of Denmark. Although the rebellion had not been entirely bloodless, determined slave resistance had ended legal slavery without massive destruction or widespread loss of life. In St. Croix, Parker had the opportunity to observe firsthand what might happen if John Brown's Virginia plan succeeded. Here, at least, was something to occupy the mind of a sick abolitionist grieving for the loss of his vigor.[4]

Parker was unwell when he arrived in St. Croix, but the climate of the island and the return of normal patterns of rest and exercise improved his condition. By the end of April, his only symptom was the persistent cough that had been with him since leaving Boston. Rising early each morning to bathe in the ocean, he rode a small pony along the western part of the island carefully observing its plants, animals, and human inhabitants. For the first time in his life, Parker found himself in a society where whites constituted less than fifteen percent of the population and the result was something like culture shock. "Here we live in the midst of colored folk," he reported to a parishioner. "You may walk for an hour and not see a white man." Without a full understanding of the culture of the island's Afro-Caribbean population, however, he judged their work patterns and cultural life very harshly. After very short observation he concluded that they were cruel parents, unfaithful spouses, uncooperative neighbors, and prone to violent quarrels. "I saw a negro man beat his apprentice with a walnut stick about three feet long," he wrote to Wendell Phillips. "Beating is the custom of the place." Echoing his earlier condemnations of the slaveholding South, Parker's Yankee ethnocentrism was on full display in his judgments of the islanders.[5]

Biases aside, these conclusions were significant in shaping the larger debate over the "practicality of emancipation" in the United States. Proslavery apologists had long argued that West Indian emancipation had been a failure due to the innate laziness of the freedpeople. Abolitionists had, of course, rejected this view of history. They used August 1st celebrations to showcase the building of schools, churches and other progressive institutions in the British West Indies. Parker was fully aware of this debate and its implications, and yet he still complained about a lack of initiative among St. Croix's black inhabitants. "I should think the island was populated by lotus eaters," he told a prominent parishioner back in Boston. "Everything goes lazy." Either unaware or unconcerned about the brutally repressive labor laws that bound the island's workers to unfair, long-term contracts, he decried their lack of efficiency. "I saw men and women hoeing in a cane field," he noted rather contemptuously in his journal a few days after arriving on the island. "They were a sight to behold—so slow did they strike." In language that could easily have flowed from the lips of an American proslavery apologist, he concluded that "The Negro is slow here—a loose jointed sort of animal, a great child."[6]

But if his diagnosis of the problems in St. Croix fell back on the racist assumptions that had bedeviled his antislavery activism, he at least considered the possibility that environment, rather than race, was responsible for the island's "lack" of progress. Perhaps the aversion to labor which he observed in both blacks and whites in St. Croix was the consequence of slavery and the result of climate conditions that, as Henry Thomas Buckle had argued, retarded innovation regardless of race. While the climate could not be changed, it was certainly possible that the conditions of free labor might regenerate the social and cultural life of the island. For all his criticism of St. Croix's former slaves, he was fascinated by the efforts of a local Episcopal priest to bring about the "elevation of the colored people," and criticized the island's whites who did not "help the work or much favor it." He told his friend Joseph Lyman that if he had a chance to write something about St. Croix, he would "have nice things to say about the success of emancipation and the refined look of the Negroes." Typical of his thought about race and freedom, Parker's conclusions about the success of emancipation on St. Croix mixed hope for the future with deep ambivalence.[7]

After a few weeks on the island, Parker's letters home began to sound more optimistic. "I am much better than when I left home, I feel strong, can walk with a cane," he told his old friend Charles Ellis in April. "My face is brown and ruddy, my eyes and teeth look well." The return of physical stamina allowed him to begin thinking and writing again. In mid-March, he began to work four or five hours each day on a "philosophico-biographical" letter addressed to the Twenty-Eighth Congregational Society reviewing his career as a minister and reformer. Published in the United States as "Theodore Parker's Experience as a Minister," the letter demonstrates how deeply its author's self-conception was rooted in the idea of conscience. In well over one hundred pages of self-reflection, Parker expressed not a single regret about the course he had taken as a public figure. A deep commitment to truth telling and individual moral integrity, not mere personal ambition, had driven his battles against theological error, social injustice, and ecclesiastical oppression. "One thing I am sure of," he insisted. "I never appealed to a mean motive nor used an argument I did not think both just and true." And yet Parker also made it clear that his conscience had never been a solitary witness or simply a vehicle for "self-culture." Instead it had functioned best in a social context where "inward consciousness...widened and grew richer as I came into practical contact with living men." In social life, Parker said, the inward experience of conscience "turned time into life, and mere thought became character." Not surprisingly given this theme, the letter made only perfunctory references to the Transcendentalists while describing Garrison and the abolitionists as inheritors of the "best in the Puritan founders of New England."[8]

Parker was not fully able to acknowledge the ways in which his idea of conscience had masked deeper desires for intellectual and popular recognition. It is clear from the letter that he still resented Boston's Brahmin elite and their clerical allies for the treatment he had received in the wake of the South Boston Sermon. For those readers too young to remember, he recalled that the "Unitarian periodicals were shut against me, most of my friends fell off, some would not speak to me in the street, and refused to take me by the hand." The personal wounds were still fresh in his mind when he remembered that "in their public meetings they left the sofas or benches when I sat down, and withdrew from me as Jews from a leper." Forgetting the biting, satirical invective he had leveled against the "Pharisees of the pulpit," the "Jesuitical" leaders of the Hollis Street council, and the "money lords" of commerce, he understood himself as simply a martyr to principle. Implicitly comparing himself to more timid or more self-interested ministers like his former mentor Convers Francis, Parker insisted that he had never backed away from his responsibilities to preach the truth, whatever the personal consequences. "I told my opponents the only man who could 'put me down' was myself," he remembered with pride.[9]

But the story Parker wanted to tell did not end with complaints against his persecutors, but rather with a triumph over them that pointed back to the adequacy of natural conscience. That victory came from the simple, fair-minded Americans who had defied their religious leaders and flocked to hear Boston's heretical minister on lyceum platforms across the North. It had turned out that the plain, uncorrupted farmers and mechanics of America were better judges of truth than the well-educated but jaded ministers who served the wealthy churches of Boston. Like the sturdy, hardworking people of post-revolutionary Lexington with whom Parker had grown up, these audiences judged truth for themselves and usually judged right. "When a few hundreds in a mountain town in New England, or in some settlement on the prairie in the West did look me in the face," he maintained, "I saw that the clerical prejudice was stealing out of their mind, and I left them other than I found them." Adopting a democratic style and resorting to a popular medium, Parker had done an end run around his elite detractors and achieved a different kind of success than he had originally intended. Even as it had vaulted him to regional, if not national celebrity, however, Parker insisted on seeing it as a victory for conscience and duty, not for self.[10]

Parker's letter left a profound impression on his congregation and on social reformers who read it in printed form. Revivalists and conservative Unitarians leveled predictable charges of pride against its author, but those who knew him found his letter honest and inspiring. "It is a noble monument to the greatest scholar of our time and one of its very best men also," wrote abolitionist Lydia Maria Child. "The clergy make a great outcry about its 'excessive egotism,' but it seems to me a simple, straightforward account of what his people would want to know." Despite Parker's criticisms of non-resistance in the letter, William Lloyd Garrison was moved by its descriptions of a life-long struggle for unpopular ideas and oppressed humanity. "In time, full justice will be done to the memory of Mr. Parker," he wrote in 1860. "Theological bigots may try to [disparage] it, but it will shine more and more resplendent as time advances." To individuals like Garrison and Child, who had battled social and intellectual orthodoxy for most of their lives, Parker's account of his own personal sacrifices seemed both noble and familiar. "Some speak of him only as a bitter critic and a harsh prophet," wrote Wendell Phillips, "but I thank God for every drop of that bitterness that came like a wholesome rebuke on the dead saltless sea of American life!"[11]

Among Friends in Europe

While the struggles of the past dominated Parker's autobiographical letter, the more pressing battle for recovery dictated the course of his immediate future. Intending to spend the winter in the dry climates of Italy or Egypt, the Parkers departed St. Thomas on May 17th and began the two week sea voyage to England. The main danger on this trip was seasickness. To avoid it, Parker took three drops of chloroform in a glass of water each day and remained "horizontal on the deck" for the first several days of the trip. By this method, both Theodore and Lydia escaped the "misery of continual vomiting, retching and straining" which they had endured on their earlier ocean travels. But the enforced inactivity also deprived him of the exercise that had proved so beneficial during his stay in St. Croix. Soon after arriving in London, he told Charles Sumner that he had lost ten pounds during the voyage and reported that "the cough still continues and gives me more anxiety for it is far worse in England than it was in the West Indies."[12]

Forced to remain in his rooms at Radley's Hotel in Blackfriars, he was at least able to receive visitors, and there were plenty of them. Among the diverse group of Americans who came were William Henry Seward, who Parker believed would be "the next President of the United States," and Ellen Craft, whose visit reminded him of the great battle over fugitive slaves in Boston. Perhaps the most famous Englishman who called was John Bright, the free trade reformer and political radical who led the fight against the hated Corn Laws in the House of Commons. The two men were kindred spirits, having waged ideological war upon the religious and political establishments of their respective nations. With Bright's help, Parker secured a seat in the gallery of the House of Commons where he witnessed a "great debate" one evening in early June. But this was to be his only major outing as his condition continued to worsen in the "smoke and chill" of the English capital. Once his friend Joseph Lyman arrived from Boston, he insisted that the Parkers travel to Paris, where a new team of physicians could examine the ailing minister. It was frustrating to be in the midst of London's rich intellectual and political life without being able to participate in it. Never content to cede control of his life to others, Parker confessed that "to be weak is to be miserable."[13]

On June 12th, when the Parkers arrived in Paris, they found the city buzzing with news of recent military events. Several months earlier, Emperor Napoleon III of France had joined the Italian Kingdom of Piedmont-Sardinia in its war against the mighty Austro-Hungarian Empire. At the battle of Magenta in Austrian-controlled Lombardy, a combined Franco-Piedmontese force had driven the Austrian army to the edges of the province. Carefully following the conflict in the papers, Parker could see few great ideas at work, only power politics and a lust for military glory. He understood that French victories might result in the freedom of the Italian states from autocratic Austrian rule, but he suspected that they were simply exchanging an Austrian "devil" for a French "Beelzebub." It was in America, he still believed, where the immediate future of freedom would be decided.

Reflecting on the European war in a letter to his congregation, he told them that while "you and I may be thankful that our land is not trodden by the hoof of war," seasons of bloody conflict in America might not be far off. The central contradiction at the core of America's national consciousness was a far greater problem than any European nation faced. Democracy in the United States had foes just as powerful as any Austrian army, he insisted. After all, 350,000 slave-holders and an equal number of Hunkers were now "armed...for the defense of this despotism [of slavery], and are deadly hostile to all the institutions of de-mocracy." Americans should not congratulate themselves on their distance from the scenes of war because "the day will come when we also must write our great charter of liberty in blood."[14]

Paris was never to be a final destination for Parker. Lydia, Hannah and he intended to stay only long enough to consult the doctors before joining a group of Boston friends in the Swiss Alps. The medical examination was conducted by Dr. Samuel Bigelow, an American doctor trained in France, and Pierre Charles Alexandre Louis, a recognized expert in the diagnosis and treatment of con-sumption. After taking Parker's "personal and pathological story," Bigelow and Louis listened carefully to his cough and made observations of his "expectora-tion." Their prognosis was quite optimistic, concluding that while there was "some little tubercular disease at the top of the right lung," there was no sign of disintegration in the tubercles. His condition had stabilized and they prescribed moderate exercise, good air, nutritious food, and one-half bottle of red wine per day as a cough suppressant. Lydia, who had begun to doubt the possibility of her husband's recovery, was enormously relieved. Parker celebrated the good news by taking in the sights of Paris with his old friend Charles Sumner who was still in Europe recovering from the attack by Preston Brooks three years earlier. As the two veterans of the antislavery movement rode through the streets of the city, Parker listened to the senator's views on American politics and applauded his intention to return to the leadership of the radical wing of the Republican Party. "America needs *you* more than ever now," he told Sumner a few months later. "I think we shall see the triumph of the Republican Party next year, it will be a step toward the triumph of its principles one day."[15]

At the end of June, Parker was in Montreaux, the beautiful Swiss resort town on the eastern end of Lake Geneva. After the congestion of London and Paris, the mountain air at Montreux was a welcome change. "The place is beau-tiful," he wrote. "A little mite of a town stuck on the side of a mountain—our boardinghouse is just on the edge of the lake." A little while after arriving, how-ever, Parker received an invitation to visit the home of his old friend Edouard Desor, a Swiss naturalist who had come to Boston in the late 1840s to work with the famous Harvard biologist Louis Agassiz. Parker met him in 1847 and the two became "intimate" friends, exchanging affectionate birthday letters each year. After a bitter falling out with the prickly and self-interested Agassiz, Desor left Boston and returned to teaching in Switzerland. Three years before Parker's visit, he had inherited a spacious hunting lodge at Combe Varin, north of Montreaux in the Swiss Canton of Neuchâtel. Each summer, Desor entertained diverse groups of European scientists, philosophers and literary intellectuals. His guests wrote papers, conducted debates, and discussed the leading ideas in the various fields of interest to them. Parker initially went to Combe Varin alone, intending to spend about a week there before returning to Montreaux. But he found the intellectual atmosphere so intoxicating that after a two week visit he "sent for the women" to join him for a longer stay.[16]

Parker found the physical and human circumstances at Neuchâtel extremely beneficial to the state of his health and his sprits. Careful to ensure that his friend did not over exert himself mentally, Desor integrated Parker into the vibrant, *avant garde* intellectual life at the chalet. The guests that summer included two German scientists, Jacob Moleschott and Carl Vogt, who were well known for their belief in scientific materialism and organic evolution.

Basking in this atmosphere of daring, unorthodox scientific thought, Parker produced his last intellectual work, a clever, satirical essay entitled "A Bumblebee's Thoughts." In it, he attacked the simplistic natural theology that still dominated popular scientific thought in England and America. Natural theologians insisted that the physical world was a perfect, static creation ordered by God for the use and benefit of man. Parker now saw this view as an anthropocentric fallacy. A similar, equally fallacious argument, he believed, could be made by almost any other species and, for humorous effect, he chose the Bumblebee. "It is plain that we are the crown of the universe," intones the pompous, scientific Bumblebee-narrator of the essay. How otherwise could one explain the abundance of red clover in the world? "In its deep cup lies the most delicious honey, the nectar of the world." What was more, says the narrator to the great applause of the hive, "that cup is so deep no other insect can reach the sweet treasure at the bottom." But the final proof was in the perfect adaptation of the bee to the plant. "Our proboscis is so constructed that with ease we suck out this exquisite provision which nature furnishes solely for us!" With these facts in view, the Bumblebee concluded, it was plain that the world of matter exists "only for our use." Charles Darwin's *Origin of Species* would reach Parker only a short time before his death, but the Combe Varin essay demonstrates that he was intellectually prepared for its radical revision of traditional scientific thought.[17]

Parker was not a scientific materialist like Moleschott, Vogt, or Darwin, but his interactions with their ideas revived his hopes for some kind of intellectual life. Desor remembered vigorous debates that summer at Combe Varin in which "Mr. Parker was the most animated of all." The mountain air was as stimulating as the conversation and Parker found himself once again able to spend most of his time outside in the dry, warm days of August. He regained the weight he had lost at sea, and eventually reached 158 pounds, the most he had weighed for three decades. The natural beauty of the Vallée de Ponts was irresistible, and he resumed an arduous physical regimen that worried those around him. "When there is fair weather I am out of doors eight or ten hours a day," he wrote. "I work in the woods, chopping, pruning the trees and get a kind of exercise that is most delightful to me." Lydia tried to moderate his activity, but Parker's new-found strength made him unreceptive to the voice of caution. According to De-sor, he insisted on performing ever more strenuous physical tasks which eventu-ally included felling some of the large fir trees that grew near the chalet. "His friends tried to dissuade him of it, but in vain," the scientist wrote a few years later. "All that we could extort from him was a promise to devote one hour a day to this exercise."[18]

The return of physical and mental vitality at Neuchâtel also reawakened Parker's interest in American affairs. Unfortunately, most of the news was trou-bling, raising the same questions about the national conscience that had dogged him since the early 1850s. In early August, he read that the city's most respecta-ble men were planning to erect a monument to the Boston lawyer and former United States Senator Rufus Choate who had died the previous month. Deeply conservative, and tireless in his efforts on behalf of wealthy railroad and mer-cantile interests, Choate was the epitome of the hypocritical Boston elite Parker had battled for so long. A monument to Choate amounted to an endorsement of his archconservative Unionism with its cynical denials of the Higher Law and its endless compromises with the Slave Power. Parker insisted that his recently deceased friend Horace Mann, the pioneering educational reformer and Con-science Whig, was a far better candidate for public honors than a man who had spent a long career "prostrating the purpose of the law." In choosing Choate over Mann, Boston seemed bent upon betraying its conscience and its revolu-tionary heritage. "Mann warred against all [the great evils of America]," he told his parishioner John Manley. "Choate opposed none of them; he befriended the worst of them...yet how he is honored!"[19]

Actually, Choate's likeness never appeared in the State House yard, but Parker may have regretted that it did not. For in its place, the Massachusetts' legislature approved the installation of another monument, Hiram Powers' bronze statue of Daniel Webster. Parker could barely contain his disgust at Ed-ward Everett's glowing tribute to Webster delivered before a great crowd at the State House inaugurating the statue. As always, Parker was sensitive to the pow-er of monuments in shaping political culture, and he could not help but see the implications of what was happening. If Everett and other conservatives were able to rally Massachusetts behind the legacies of Choate and Webster, what hope was there for the overthrow of the Slave Power? Their "practical atheism" would be chiseled into stone and presented to generations of Bay State citizens as models of statesmanship and public virtue. As for the great oratorical skill that Everett was said to possess, Parker regarded it as smoke with no fire, little more than insubstantial puffery. "Everett is a Rhetorician, his trade is to make speeches, and he does this on all occasions except those where a manly regard for justice is required," Parker wrote in September. "When he dies he will leave behind him a great fagot of speeches which every Hunker will buy but which no mortal man can read with any moral profit."[20]

Things only got worse. As he fumed over Boston's veneration of Choate in early August, he was stunned by a letter from James Freemen Clarke informing him that a recent meeting of the Harvard Divinity School Alumni had refused to approve a resolution expressing its "hope and prayer for the return and renewed strength of Theodore Parker." The resolution was introduced by Parker's friends Moncure Conway and James Freeman Clarke, but it met with an icy response from older, more conservative ministers like Ezra Stiles Gannett and Henry Bellows. Though Parker professed that the snub was "not the smallest consequence" to him, he could hardly have been unmoved by it. In contrast to Webster and Choate, who were being honored and memorialized, he was denied even the most basic courtesy from those who had once taken him by the hand. Callous and unnecessary as they were, the actions of the Divinity School Alumni indicate the personal animus which an older generation of Unitarian ministers still felt for Parker. To the very end of his life, he remained unable to understand the personal costs of his revolutionary conscience or to appreciate the threat that others perceived in it. "I have been in battle for twenty years, treated as no American ever was," he complained to James Freeman Clarke. Could it be that his former colleagues really believed "they're in so much danger that a little consumptive minister in Exeter Place would finish them?" It seemed so.[21]

Roman Winter

With these thoughts running through his mind, Parker approached the end of his idyllic summer in Neuchâtel. The weather had turned colder and Edouard Desor advised his American friends to go to Rome where they would find warmer temperatures and affordable lodgings for the winter. Fortunately, it was once again possible to travel to the Eternal City. The decisive French victory at the Battle of Solferino in June meant that the main routes from Switzerland to Rome were reopened to civilian travelers. And so Parker and his friends left Montreaux on October 12th and arrived in Rome six days later after a "horrid" thirty-two hour steamboat ride from Marseille.

Despite the exhaustion of the long journey, Parker was excited to return to a city that had fascinated him on his first trip to Europe. "I mean to live out of doors in all the fine weather," he told Sumner. He intended to keep his mind and body active, "to study the Geology, Botany, and Architecture of the place, and I shall have books for rainy days and winter nights." There were also fascinating people to see in Rome, including a sizable community of American artists, writers and intellectuals. Not far from the Parkers' lodgings in the Via delle Quattro Fontane, for example, was the studio of the Massachusetts-born sculptor William Wetmore Story. There were also breakfasts with American novelists Harriet Beecher Stowe and Nathaniel Hawthorne and conversations with English poets Robert and Elizabeth Barrett Browning. Parker was fascinated by the Brownings, but the ever-timid Lydia said she "lacked the courage to call" on Elizabeth.[22]

Unfortunately, rainy and cold weather frustrated Parker's intentions to preserve the healthy regimen he had followed in Switzerland. He was trapped indoors most of the time and his physical and psychological state declined rapidly.

The return of his persistent cough sometimes left him unable to speak for hours at a time. Given the dramatic improvement in his condition in Switzerland, the weight and appetite loss he experienced in Rome left him bewildered and depressed. Lydia worried that he was too focused on his symptoms and believed that if he "could forget his sickness I think it would do much in helping his recovery." But she could not hide her growing concern. "My wife thinks of nothing but her husband, and her face is a good measure of my condition," Parker wrote in November. "Just now she has a bad face, and it is painful to me to be the source of such anxiety to one so dear."[23]

And then suddenly there came the electrifying news of John Brown's raid on Harpers Ferry. Reading three-week-old newspaper accounts of the raid, and keeping watch for every news telegraph from America, Parker was riveted by what had happened in Virginia. Suddenly, Boston's tributes to Choate and Webster faded into the background as the dying minister contemplated Brown's revolutionary act of conscience and self-sacrifice. "It is not once in many ages we get sight of such a spectacle," he told Joseph Lyman. "[N]o American has such a chance for earthly immortality." Despite his personal role in hatching the plan Parker felt little or no guilt over the raiders who were killed during the assault on Harpers Ferry. Having received erroneous news that twenty-two year old Francis Jackson Merriam had died in the raid, he wrote a letter to the young man's mother that sounded like a wartime condolence. Reminding her that her own ancestors had fought at the battle of Lexington, he insisted that "your son has fallen a *martyr in a cause not less holy* and much more philanthropic...not a drop of his blood is wasted." All historic victories for liberty had been "bought with the blood of men," he argued, and young Merriam had died for the greatest of them.[24]

Neither was he troubled or disappointed that Brown's immediate plan to liberate the slaves had failed so completely. He conceded that by common standards the plan "may not have been wise," but it was "just and righteous" and sought to deliver oppressed people from bondage by the "simplest means." Those who judged success only by immediate results would label the raid "a failure," but Parker believed the raid had revealed real weaknesses in the slaveholders' regime. The panic that had gripped the Upper South after the raid was clear evidence of the deep insecurity of the slaveholders. He was certain that, like Crispus Attucks and the martyrs of the Boston Massacre, Brown and his fallen comrades would galvanize the faltering cause of human liberty. "Brown's little spark was not put out till it had kindled a fire which will burn down more than far sighted men look for," he wrote. "The Northern sky is full of lightning, long treasured up, the thunder rattles all over the Union now." The sacrifice of John Brown and his men would awaken the revolutionary conscience of the North.[25]

In a widely published letter about John Brown addressed to his old friend and fellow Vigilance Committee member Francis Jackson, Parker set down his final thoughts about race, violence, and the American Revolutionary tradition. Combining these concepts had always presented formidable intellectual prob-

lems, and Parker still struggled to hold them in balance. But at this moment, just
a few months before his death, he chose to embrace the possibilities of a new
society in America. Just as Brown had awakened the North to resist the Slave
Power, he now argued, so too would the millions of oppressed slaves strike out
violently against the moral injustice of slavery. How could it be otherwise in a
nation that was forged in a violent revolution against tyranny, which built monuments to revolutionary leaders, and rejoiced in the "War of Independence?"
Although John Rock and other African American abolitionists had certainly not
succeeded in forcing Parker to abandon his racist doubts about blacks' "power
of mind" or "instinct for liberty," they had not rebuked him in vain. In his letter
to Jackson, he now echoed Rock's belief that there were "many a possible San
Domingo" in the American South where angry, resentful slaves were ready to
seize their freedom violently. He conceded that "there already have been several
risings of slaves in this century" and believed that the "future would be even
more terrible."[26]

All of this could occur "with no white man to help," he wrote, but he was
certain that many whites, following the example of John Brown, would heed
their consciences and join the slaves in a final insurrection. They would be the
Lafayettes of the second American Revolution, men of courage and conscience
who would be honored by history for their heroic role in advancing human freedom. The biracial nature of that second revolution would end the doubts of
many, perhaps Parker foremost among them, about the possibility of blacks and
Anglo-Saxons forging a shared libertarian tradition. Under a divine providence
that favored freedom and conscience, even race would be dissolved into a common history of human progress. "Wait a little and things will come round," he
told Jackson. "One day it will be thought not less heroic for a Negro to fight for
his personal liberty, than for a white man to fight for political independence, and
against a tax of three pence a pound on tea."[27]

Parker was both saddened and inspired by Brown's execution. Two weeks
after the Captain was hanged in Virginia, Lydia told a friend back home that she
and Theodore had been deeply "grieved...at the fate of that brave old man."
Even a month later, Parker reported that he was "sleepless and sick" about what
had happened to Brown's "precious manhood." But he could not help but be
struck by the parallels between himself and the martyred activist, a comparison
that reveals a good deal about his final self-assessment. As the children of humble New England farmers and descendants of "Rev[olutionary] Captain[s]," Parker believed that he and Brown shared the values of industry, modesty, simple
piety, and unshakable moral conscience. It was the defense and extension of
those values, he now felt, which had filled their lives with conflict and lethal
struggle. "It is good he came from such a lineage, right out of the heart of New
England, a plain man, with a common education, hardworking and intelligent,"
he wrote not long after Brown's death.[28]

The ambitions for academic distinction and social mobility that had once
filled Parker's youthful horizons were long forgotten and he now remembered
only pursuing a life of hard work and moral commitment. Like Brown, he had

struggled for something more than "those snobs who have nothing but yester-day's money to base their social rank upon." If Brown's martyrdom had come at the hands of Virginia slaveholders, Parker found a counterpart in the northern conservatives who had rejected his own theology, scorned his reformism and forced him into the exhausting life of an itinerant lecturer. At times he wished that his own death might take on the drama and symbolism of Brown's execu-tion on the scaffold. "How often I have wished to be in my old place at my old work!" he told Lyman. "I should have had to *straighten a rope*, for it is not like-ly that I could have kept out of harm's way in Boston." Although he had repeat-edly stepped back from just the kind of revolutionary activism that had landed Brown on the gallows, Parker still longed to suffer dramatically for his con-science and then to live on as a symbol of resolute moral courage. The prospect of a slow death from wasting disease provided little psychic satisfaction for the grandson of Captain John Parker.[29]

Parker tried to keep in contact with members of the Secret Six as the United States Senate began its investigation of the conspiracy, but he was losing ground fast. By early 1860, there was little else besides the company of friends to lift his spirits. He distracted himself by writing a brief account of his early life, but did not get further than his eighth year. In the unusually cold and damp winter, the tubercular cough returned with a vengeance, and he lost the weight he had gained in the summer. "My voice is in so bad a condition that I can hardly talk at all," he wrote in February. "I have lost 15 to 20 pounds of flesh in the months I have been here and am by no means gaining now." Like so many consumption patients nearing the end of life, he became "thin and emaciated" weighing only about 130 pounds. Still, he insisted to friends in Boston that he was "the same man underneath" and remained unwilling to give up hope. By early April, how-ever, the tone of his letters had changed and his closest friends were told to ex-pect the news of his death at any time. "I hate to write sad things, but once in a while one must," he told Joseph Lyman. "So pardon me if I tell you that I think it is pretty near up with me." In his frustration and despair, there seemed little left to Parker but to hope for "a speedy deliverance."[30]

Deliverance came on May 10, 1860, in Florence, where he traveled with Lydia and Edouard Desor in a final attempt to escape the weather in Rome. Ar-riving in Florence after a rough, five-day carriage ride, Parker fell into a state of semi-consciousness which lasted until his death. He was visited by the Irish feminist and ethical writer Frances Power Cobbe, a longtime admirer who had struggled in vain to see him in England. When she entered his room, she found him lying in his bed with his back to the light, visibly trembling and unable to move. In a moment of lucidity, he whispered hoarsely that it was odd that "after all our wishes to meet...that we should meet *thus*." Aware that Cobbe was a longtime admirer, he apologized that she was not really meeting him at all, but only "the wreck of the man I was." Later, in one of his most peaceful moments, he smiled at her and assured her that while he was "not afraid to die," he wanted just a "little longer to finish my work." As the end neared, he began to express great concern about Lydia, whose own health had suffered under the great strain of her husband's illness. Using the pet name he had given her during their first trip to Europe, he said: "lay down your head on the pillow, 'Bearsie,' and sleep; for you have not slept for a very long time." A few days later, he was buried in the small Protestant cemetery in Florence with only a plain stone of grey marble to mark his place.[31]

Francis Power Cobbe reported that the "English" cemetery where the service took place was "exquisitely lovely, a very wilderness of flowers and perfume." Some of the Americans living in the city wished to attend the funeral services of their famous countryman, but Parker had left precise instructions limiting the numbers of mourners to five and spelling out a simple service centered on the reading of the beatitudes. Lydia wept at the gravesite as the coffin, festooned with laurel wreaths, was lowered into the earth. She soon returned to Boston and lived quietly in the house at Exeter Place until her death in 1881. Despite the tensions in her marriage to Theodore, she remained devoted to the preservation of his memory. Parker's will had stipulated that she was to have all his "manuscripts, journals, sermons, letters," and any books that she wished to keep from his huge collection before its donation to the new public library being established in Boston. For the rest of her life, she diligently collected his letters, interviewed childhood acquaintances, and solicited memories from those whose lives Parker had touched.[32]

XX
CONCLUSION

Theodore Parker died with a sense that the great work of his life remained incomplete. "I am conscious that I leave half my work undone," he told George Ripley in 1860. "Much grain lies in my fields." This sense of regret reflected the fragmented nature of his contribution to antebellum intellectual life. Despite his enormous ambition and the self-destructive pace of his mental labors, Parker had not been able to produce the great works of theology and history he had planned, and his place in the American world of letters remained unclear, even to sympathetic contemporaries. Thomas Wentworth Higginson suspected that his older friend had accumulated more information than he had been capable of digesting, and had thus spoiled his potential for original thought. "Learning is not accumulation, but assimilation," he once wrote. "The most priceless knowledge is not worth the smallest impairing of the quality of the thinking." Unlike Higginson, whose family origins had given him direct access to the culture and refinement of elite Boston society, Parker had been forced to use learning and erudition as a means to gain that access. For the youngest son of a poor country farmer whose mastery of books had been the stepping stone to success, knowledge had simply become an addiction that had no cure.[1]

In addition to the problem of unwritten books, Parker's legacy also suffered under the widespread belief that he had been "chiefly a destroyer," one who relentlessly tore down traditional religious understandings while offering little or nothing in their place. Seen from the perspective of traditional Christianity, there is some truth to this view. The Bible, the Church, the divinity of Christ, the concept of innate sinfulness, all came under relentless, unblinking assault in Parker's major theological and critical works. The destructiveness of his approach was also magnified by his use of blunt, sometimes sarcastic language that seemed inappropriate to all but a few of his contemporaries. In his eagerness to sweep away a theology and a religious culture whose imperfections he saw so clearly, Parker did not think deeply enough about the package in which his radical message came. He worked quickly, often in the midst of public controversy, and he sometimes scorned or satirized what others regarded as sacred. Supremely confident that religion and morality could stand without the aid of ancient scriptures or ecclesiastical authorities, he had too little patience with those who were more hesitant to dispense with them. His admirers correctly understood that he was building a new house of faith, but others saw only the wreckage he had made of the old one.[2]

Ironically, Parker's severity upon people or ideas he disliked was partly the product of his optimism about human nature. So eager was he to celebrate the vast potential of the self that he struggled to account for the presence of moral evil and lacked a full appreciation for the complexity of human motivation. Speaking a few weeks after Parker's death, James Freeman Clarke said that all his old friend's mistakes "had their root" in this overly sanguine "doctrine of man." Ascribing "absolute powers to the human will," Parker had not understood that the "presence of evil" was sometimes "caught by contagion" and often obscured moral judgment. Clarke implied that this was the root of the "terrible blows" of "fiery invective" that Parker poured out upon his foes. If moral evil was "self-originated" rather than an "inherited tendency," the actions of men like Edward Loring could be explained only as conscious, and therefore, inexcusable transgressions. The same was true of the slaveholding South. Abraham Lincoln may have resisted easy moral condemnations by conceding that southern slaveholders were "just as we would be in their situation," but Parker would not. His angry and increasingly warlike condemnations of the South proceeded from his belief that slavery was a conscious, not an inherited wrong.[3]

Significant as they are, these criticisms should not obscure Parker's importance in American religious history. In introducing German biblical criticism to American audiences, for example, he undertook truly pioneering work. It would not be until the end of the nineteenth century that the historical-critical techniques Parker had used so effectively in the 1840s came into general use by the major denominations of American Protestantism. A similar, but perhaps more important point can be made about his lifelong dedication to proving the existence of a "religious element" in man. In his insistence that all religions were manifestations of a universal religious impulse, Parker helped to lay the philosophical grounding for the scholarly appreciation and understanding of the world's many religious traditions. Because it pointed to "absolute religion" as the standard against which all religions, even Christianity, should be examined, Parker's work created a framework to compare and analyze the historical, cultural, and theological components of multiple faith traditions. As an early practitioner of the historical-critical approach to the Bible, and as an important forerunner in the emergence of comparative religion, therefore Parker should be seen as a central figure in the rise of American religious modernism.

Theodore Parker would have been proud of these contributions to what he called "religious progress," but it was above all as a man of conscience that he had stood before his contemporaries. In a society permeated by romantic equations of steadfast principle with individual greatness, Parker found the means to connect his own deeply rooted self-conception as a fearless truth-teller with his generation's collective longings for men of authenticity and sincerity. Doubtless there were some who had come to the Music Hall to hear Parker expound his views on the Bible or human nature, but it was the great preacher's well-cultivated persona as man of implacable moral and intellectual courage that attracted the huge crowds. The fairly rapid decline of the Twenty-Eighth Congregational Society after the Civil War, despite the leadership of ministers who shared Parker's theological views, testifies to the role that his dynamic personality had played in holding that diverse community of reformers and religious radicals together.[4]

Together, Parker and his church had worked with the larger reform community to create a democratic, critical public culture in mid-nineteenth century Boston. The essential components of that culture were the fiercely assertive idea of conscience rooted in American Transcendentalism, and the radicalized memories of the American Revolutionary tradition which Parker deployed with such effectiveness. Those who sympathized most deeply with Parker understood that the bitter language he employed was, in some sense, essential to the critical spirit of his larger ministry. Ralph Waldo Emerson, who never spoke as harshly as Parker did, could not help but identify raw sincerity as his old friend's cardinal virtue. "He held nothing back," Emerson said during Parker's memorial service at the Music Hall. "It was his merit, like Luther, Knox, Latimer and John Baptist to speak tart truth." Wendell Phillips agreed, telling the same group of assembled mourners to remember their minister's life as a permanent rebuke of aristocratic, political chameleons like Webster or Choate. Parker stood as a "guidepost and landmark," a "mete-wand to measure the heart and civilization of Boston."[5]

During the Civil War years, Parker remained an important symbol for those who hoped to preserve and extend democratic culture. On July 4, 1862, for example, black abolitionist John Rock brought Parker's memory to bear against those who resisted emancipation and the enlistment of African American troops. "If he was with us now," Rock asked, "would he not make our hearts burn while he exposed, in his inimitable way, the duty of the nation?" The day had come, Rock insisted, for President Lincoln to abandon his conservatism; he must "emancipate the slaves and let them help you fight the rebels." Theodore Parker, Rock believed, "saw this day a little clearer than we saw it, and repeatedly warned us that slavery or this nation itself must go down in blood." Although Rock had once been critical of Parker's racial views, memories of that dispute were now less important than preserving their shared vision of a second American Revolution in which African Americans would fight to destroy slavery. Just as Parker had once summoned the spirit of his grandfather to mobilize Boston against slavery, Rock summoned the spirit of the departed minister to complete the work of freedom. Rock would soon help to create the 54th Massachusetts Volunteer Infantry Regiment, the most famous black unit of the Civil War. The regiment was commanded by Colonel Robert Gould Shaw, the son of Parker's old friends and parishioners Frank and Sarah Shaw of West Roxbury. In a scene that would have thrilled Parker to the core, Shaw led the proud soldiers of the regiment through Boston in May, 1863 to the tune of "John Brown's Body." [6]

Linked though it was to dramatic confrontations with slavery and social wrong, Parker's spirit offered other forms of inspiration as well. Louisa May Alcott, who served as a nurse in the Union Hotel Hospital in Washington D.C. during the winter of 1862–63, regretted that the suffering men under her care had to endure sermons by a neo-Calvinist Chaplain who told them "they were all worms," and that their souls "could only be saved by a diligent perusal of certain tracts." In contrast to the great preacher of the Music Hall, whose sermons had excited and inspired her, Alcott found that her dispirited and weakened patients were exposed to "dry and literal applications" of the Bible, which she regarded as little but the "chaff of divinity." To get through these moments of boredom and disappointment, she erased the incompetent preacher from her mind and in his place imagined "a certain faithful pastor who took all outcasts by the hand," and "comforted the indigent in spirit with the best wisdom of a great and faithful heart." Even amidst the terrible suffering of the war, Alcott believed, the voice of Theodore Parker still spoke a word of solace and hope "from its Italian grave."[7]

NOTES

Introduction

1. "Speech of Theodore Parker at the Faneuil Hall Meetings," reprinted in Charles Emery Stevens, *Anthony Burns: A History* (Boston: John P. Jewett and Company, 1856), 293, 294–295, 291.

2. Early biographies of Parker include John Weiss, *Life and Correspondence of Theodore Parker*, 2 vols (New York: D. Appleton and Company, 1864); Octavius Brooks Frothingham, *Theodore Parker: A Biography* (Boston: James R. Osgood and Company, 1874); and John White Chadwick, *Theodore Parker: Preacher and Reformer* (Cambridge: The Riverside Press, 1900). See also Vernon Louis Parrington, *Main Currents in American Thought, Volume II: The Romantic Revolution in America, 1800–1860* (New York: Harcourt, 1927), 414–425; Henry Steele Commager, *Theodore Parker: Yankee Crusader* (New York: Little Brown and Company, 1936); and Daniel Aaron, *Men of Good Hope: A Story of American Progressives* (New York: Oxford University Press, 1951). Revisionist works on abolitionism that contained at least some discussion of Parker include Aileen S. Kraditor, *Means and Ends in American Abolitionism* (New York: Pantheon, 1969); James Brewer Stewart, *Holy Warriors: The Abolitionists and American Slavery* (New York: Hill and Wang, 1976); Ronald Walters, *The Antislavery Appeal: American Abolitionism After 1830* (New York: W.W. Norton, 1984); and especially Michael Fellman, "Theodore Parker and the Abolitionist Role in the 1850s," *Journal of American History*, 61 (Dec. 1974), 666–84.

3. William Hutchison, *The Transcendentalist Ministers: Church Reform in the New England Renaissance* (Boston: Beacon Press, 1959), 178–187. Perry Miller, ed. *The Transcendentalists: An Anthology* (Cambridge: Harvard University Press, 1950); and Joel Myerson, ed., *Transcendentalism: A Reader* (New York: Oxford University Press, 2000). On Parker's differences from other Transcendentalists, see John E. Dirks, *The Critical Theology of Theodore Parker* (New York: Columbia University Press, 1948); Henry Steele Commager, "The Dilemma of Theodore Parker," *New England Quarterly* 6 (June 1933), 257–277; and Anne C. Rose, *Transcendentalism as a Social Movement, 1839–*

1850 (New Haven, CT: Yale University Press, 1981), x; Phillip Gura, *American Transcendentalism: A History* (New York: Hill and Wang, 2007).

4. Dean Grodzins, *American Heretic: Theodore Parker and Transcendentalism* (Chapel Hill: UNC Press, 2002).

5. See for example, Jim Wallis, *God's Politics: Why the Right Gets It Wrong and the Left Doesn't Get It* (New York: Harper Collins, 2005), 67–71; Phyllis Tickle, *The Great Emergence: How Christianity is Changing and Why* (Grand Rapids, MI: Baker Books, 2008) and Harvey Cox, *The Future of Faith* (New York: HarperOne, 2009), 218–219. The growth of popular interest in issues of Biblical criticism can be seen in the success of works such as Adam Nicolson, *God's Secretaries: The Making of the King James Bible* (New York: Harper Perennial, 2005); Bart Ehrman, *Misquoting Jesus: The Story Behind Who Changed the Bible and Why* (New York: HarperOne, 2007); and Marcus J. Borg and John Dominic Crossan, *The First Paul: Reclaiming the Radical Visionary Behind the Church's Conservative Icon* (New York: HarperOne, 2009).

6. T. Gregory Garvey, *Creating the Culture of Reform in Antebellum America* (Athens, GA: University of Georgia Press, 2006), uses the concept of discursive democracy as developed in the work of philosophers Jurgen Habermas and John Rawls. He suggests that reformers imagined the public square as a place where sincerity or "authentic selfhood can be discovered, articulated, and affirmed through reciprocal recognition." (7) Parker's desire to be, and to be seen as, a man of conscience is a close variant of Garvey's notion of sincerity.

7. Daniel H. Meyer, *The Instructed Conscience: The Shaping of the American National Ethic* (Philadelphia: University of Pennsylvania Press, 1972); and Daniel Walker Howe, *The Unitarian Conscience: Harvard Moral Philosophy, 1805–1861* (Middletown, CT: Weslyan University Press, 1988).

8. Parker's radical ideas of conscience are explored briefly in Elizabeth Clarke, "Speech for the Soul: Religion, Conscience and Free Speech in Antebellum America," in John McLaren and Harold Coward eds., *Religious Conscience, the State and the Law: Historical Contexts and Contemporary Significance* (Albany, NY: SUNY Press, 1999), 62–76.

9. Gura, *American Transcendentalism*, 215.

10. Works dealing with the cultural and political meaning of American Revolutionary memory include J.V. Matthews, "Whig History: The New England Whigs and a Usable Past," *New England Quarterly* 51 (June 1978), 193–208; Blanche Linden-Ward, *Silent City on a Hill: Landscapes of Memory and Boston's Mount Auburn Cemetery* (Columbus, 1989); Michael Kammen, *A Season of Youth: The American Revolution and the Historical Imagination* (New York: Knopf, 1978); Len Travers, *Celebrating the Fourth: Independence and the Rites of Nationalism in the Early Republic* (Amherst, MA: University of Massachusetts Press, 1997); Harlow Sheidley, *Sectional Nationalism: Massachusetts Conservative Leaders and the Transformation of America, 1815–1836* (Boston: Northeastern University Press, 1998); and Alfred F. Young, *The Shoemaker and the Tea Party: Memory and the American Revolution* (Boston: Beacon Press, 1999). See also Paul E. Teed, "The Politics of Sectional Memory: Theodore Parker and the *Massachusetts Quarterly Review*, 1847–1850," *Journal of the Early Republic* 21 (Summer 2001), 331–361 and Teed, "A Brave Man's Child: Theodore Parker and the Memory of the American Revolution," *Historical Journal of Massachusetts* 29 (Summer 2001), 170–191.

11. Parker to Samuel May, September 25, 1852, Theodore Parker Papers, 1826-1862 Microfilm edition, Massachusetts Historical Society, Boston Massachusetts [hereafter

cited as Parker Papers, MHS].

12. For an introduction to Parker's racial views and his relationship to black abolitionists, see my "Racial Nationalism and Its Challengers: Theodore Parker, John Rock
and the Antislavery Movement," *Civil War History* 41 (June 1995), 142–160. See also,
George Fredrickson, *The Black Image in the White Mind: The Debate on Afro-American
Character and Destiny, 1817–1914* (Middletown, CT: Wesleyan University Press, 1987),
119–120; and Richard Slotkin, *The Fatal Environment: The Myth of the Frontier in the
Age of Industrialization* (New York: Atheneum Press, 1985), 230–235.

13. Staughton Lynd, *The Intellectual Origins of American Radicalism*, 2nd edition
(New York: Cambridge University Press, 2009), 54.

Chapter 1

1. Theodore Parker, *The Trial of Theodore Parker* (Boston: n.p.,1855), 220.

2. "Recollections of Mr. Greene," Theodore Parker Papers, Library of Congress,
Washington D.C. [hereafter cited as Parker Papers, LOC]; see also Edward P. Bliss, "The
Old Taverns of Lexington," *Proceedings of the Lexington Historical Society* (Lexington:
Lexington Historical Society, 1900) I: 79–80; David Hacket Fischer, *Paul Revere's Ride*
(New York: Oxford University Press, 1995), 328–329; Charles Hudson, *History of the
Town of Lexington* (Boston: Wiggin and Lunt, 1868), 286; Elias Phinney, *History of the
Battle of Lexington* (Boston: Phelps and Farnham, 1825), 6.

3. Theodore Parker to George Bancroft in Parker Papers, MHS; Hudson, *History of
Lexington*, 286–288

4. Edward Everett, *An Address Delivered at Lexington On the 19th (20th) of April,
1835* (Worcester: Tyler and Seagrave, 1835), 19; Elizabeth Parker, "Captain John
Parker," *Proceedings of the Lexington Historical Society* I: 44; see also, Paul E. Teed,
"'A Brave Man's Child': Theodore Parker and the Memory of the American Revolution,"
Historical Journal of Massachusetts XXIX (Summer, 2001), 170–191.

5. *Trial of Theodore Parker*, 221.

6. For a description of similar economic trends in neighboring Concord, see Robert
Gross, *The Minutemen and Their World* (New York: Hill and Wang, 1976), 171–192.

7. "Recollections of Mr. Greene," in Parker Papers, LOC.

8. Parker, "Autobiographical Fragment," in *The Works of Theodore Parker*, 15 Vols.
Centenary Edition (Boston: American Unitarian Association, 1907–1913): XIII, 9–10
[Hereafter, *Works*]; Figures on the Parker family are found in *Early Massachusetts Records, 1692–1840*, Vol 14 Town of Lexington, Assessor's List. The lists show that, after
his mother's death, John Parker farmed twelve and one-half acres of land and possessed a
small number of domesticated animals. In 1828, the land was valued at $263, and by
1834 it had reached a value of $300; and Parker, "Theodore Parker's Experience as a
Minister," in *Works*, XIII, 293.

9. Hudson, *History of Lexington*, 320–350

10. J. Hastings to Lydia Parker, January 3, 1861, Theodore Parker Papers, LOC;
"Autobiographical Fragment," in *Works*, XIII, 10; on the "moderate" Enlightenment, see
Henry May, *The Enlightenment in America* (New York: Oxford University Press, 1976),
3–104.

11. "Autobiographical Fragment," in *Works*, XIII, 11; J. Hastings to Lydia Parker,
January 3, 1861, Parker Papers, LOC; "Recollections of Mr. Greene," in Parker Papers,
LOC; Parker quoted in Weiss, *Life and Correspondence*, I: 23, 29.

12. "Recollections of Mister Greene," Parker Papers, LOC; Philip Greven, *The*

Protestant Temperament: Patterns of Child-Rearing, Religious Experience, and the Self in Early America (New York: Knopf, 1977), 35. 179.

13. "Autobiographical Fragment," in *Works*, XIII, 15–16.

14. Ibid, 14; and "Anecdotes in the Life of Theodore Parker," Parker Papers, LOC.

15. Parker to George Ripley, September 21, 1854 in Parker Papers, MHS; and "Recollections of Mr. Greene," in Parker Papers, LOC.

16. Hudson, *History of Lexington*, 367–371; "Recollections of Theodore Parker by J. Simons," Parker Papers, LOC; and Parker to Miss White, September 21, 1853, Parker Papers, MHS.

17. "Recollections of the Life of Theodore Parker," Parker Papers, LOC . On Lincoln's youthful reading habits, see Douglas Wilson, *Honor's Voice: The Transformation of Abraham Lincoln* (New York: Vintage, 1998), 54–58. Unlike Parker, Lincoln's reading was actively discouraged by his father.

18. Parker, "Experience as a Minister," 292–293; Parker to Lydia D. Cabot, June 17, 1835, in Weiss, *Life and Correspondence*, I: 75.

19. "Recollections of Mr. Greene," Parker Papers, LOC.

20. Ibid.

21. Parker to D. Huntington, August 24, 1832, Parker Papers, MHS.

22. Parker to Samuel Gridley Howe, March 23, 1860, in Weiss, *Life and Correspondence* I: 50.

23. Parker, "Experience as a Minister," 294; Richard Brown, *Knowledge Is Power: The Diffusion of Information in Early America* (New York: Oxford University Press, 1989), 82–109 discussed the status of lawyers in Massachusetts.

24. Donald M. Scott, *From Office to Profession: The New England Ministry, 1750–1850* (Philadelphia: University of Pennsylvania Press, 1978), 52–75; Peter S. Fields, *The Crisis of the Standing Order: Clerical Intellectuals and Cultural Authority in Massachusetts, 1780–1833* (Amherst, MA: University of Massachusetts Press, 1998), 14–46; and "Experience as a Minister," 293.

25. Elizabeth Palmer Peabody to Maria Chase, April, [n.d.], 1820 in *The Letters of Elizabeth Palmer Peabody: American Renaissance Woman,* edited by Bruce A. Ronda (Middletown, CT: Wesleyan University Press, 1984), 52–53; and Theodore Parker, "William Ellery Channing," in *Works*, VIII, 161–162;

26. William Ellery Channing, "The Christian Ministry," in *The Works of William E. Channing , D.D.* 6 Volumes (Boston, 1867) III: 280–281. [Hereafter, *Works of Channing*]; "Experience as a Minister," 294.

27. William Ellery Channing, "Unitarian Christianity," in *Works of Channing* III, 97–102; On Channing, see Daniel Walker Howe, *The Unitarian Conscience: Harvard Moral Philosophy* (Cambridge: Harvard University Press, 1970), 17–20.

28. Parker, "Experience as a Minister," 296.

29. *Spirit of the Pilgrims*, Vol. I (Boston: Pierce and Williams, 1828), 145. Peter Field, *Crisis of the Standing Order*, 208–235. See also, Lawrence B. Goodheart, and Richard O. Curry, "The Trinitarian Indictment of Unitarianism: The Letters of Elizur Wright Jr., 1826–27," *Journal of the Early Republic* 3 (Fall 1983): 281–296.

30. Parker, "Experience as a Minister," 296; Garvey, *Creating the Culture of Reform*, 52–53.

31. Parker to Columbus Greene, April 2, 1834, Parker Papers, MHS; O.B. Frothingham, *Theodore Parker: A Biography* (Boston: James Osgood and Company, 1874), 30; Weiss, *Life and Correspondence* I: 58.

32. There is no modern biography of Convers Francis. The best information on him

comes from Gary Collison, "A Critical Edition of the Correspondence of Theodore Parker and Converse Francis, 1836–1859 (Unpublished Ph.D. dissertation, Pennsylvania State University, 1979), 1–84; Joel Myerson, "Convers Francis and Emerson," *American Literature* 50 (March 1978): 17–36; and John McAleer, *Ralph Waldo Emerson: Days of Encounter* (Boston: Little, Brown, 1984), 271–280;

33. John Weiss, *Discourse Occasioned by the Death of Convers Francis D.D., Delivered before the First Congregational Society, Watertown, April 19, 1863* (Cambridge: Privately Printed, 1863), 66–67.

34. Mary Crawford, *Famous Families of Massachusetts* (Boston: Little, Brown, and Co., 1930), 189; Julia Ward Howe, *Reminiscences, 1819–1910* (Boston: Houghton, Mifflin, & Co., 1899), 160; Parker to Charles Miller, November 1, 1833, Parker Papers, MHS.

35. Frothingham, *Theodore Parker*, 36; Parker to Lydia Cabot, October 30, 1833 in Weiss, *Life and Correspondence* I: 61.

36. Parker to Lydia Cabot, February 24, 1834 in Weiss, *Life and Correspondence*. I: 65.

Chapter 2

1. Parker, "Experience as a Minister," 287.

2. Gary Collison, "'A True Toleration': Harvard Divinity School Students and Unitarianism, 1830–1859," in *American Unitarianism, 1805–1865*, ed. Conrad Wright (Boston: Northeastern University Press, 1989), 214.

3. Cranch's Divinity School memories of Parker are printed in Frothingham, *Theodore Parker*, 45–46; and Cyrus Bartol is quoted in John White Chadwick, *Theodore Parker: Preacher and Reformer* (Boston: Houghton, Mifflin and Company, 1900), 36.

4. Julia Ward Howe, *Reminiscences*, 162.

5. Gary Collison, "A True Toleration", 209–237; Parker to Columbus Greene, April 28, 1834 in Parker Papers, MHS.

6. Parker to Columbus Greene, April 2, 1834, Parker Papers, MHS.

7. William Ellery Channing, "Evidences of Revealed Religion," in *Works of Channing*, III, 113; Henry Ware's teaching is described in Conrad Wright, "The Early Period," in *The Harvard Divinity School: Its Place in Harvard University and in American Culture*, ed. George H. Williams (Boston: Beacon Press, 1954), 38–41

8. The role of supernatural rationalism in Unitarian thought is analyzed in Howe, *The Unitarian Conscience*, 87.

9. William Ellery Channing, "Unitarian Christianity," in *Works of Channing*, III, 60–61.

10. Conrad Wright, "The Early Period," 46; Unitarian scriptural criticism and its intellectual roots are traced in Jerry Wayne Brown, *The Rise of Biblical Criticism in America, 1800–1870: The New England Scholars* (Middletown, CT: Wesleyan University Press, 1969), 10–27, 60–75 and in Philip Gura, *The Wisdom of Words: Language, Theology and Literature in the New England Renaissance* (Middletown, CT: Wesleyan University Press, 1981), 15–34.

11. Parker, "Experience as a Minister," 301; James Walker quoted in Howe, *Unitarian Conscience*, 54.

12. Henry Ware Jr. quoted in Greven, *Protestant Temperament*, 213. My discussion of Unitarian moral philosophy is drawn from Howe, *Unitarian Conscience*, 45–68, and D.H. Meyer, *The Instructed Conscience*, 35–59; Ware's visits to student rooms are men-

tioned in John Hopkins Morison's letter to the editors of *The Unitarian* reprinted in Kenneth Cameron, *Transcendental Epilogue* (Hartford: Transcendental Books, 1982), 705.

13. Henry Adams quoted in Joel Myerson, "Introduction," in *Transcendentalism: A Reader,* Joel Myerson ed. (New York: Oxford University Press, 2000), xxvii; John Sullivan Dwight to Theodore Parker quoted in George Willis Cook, *John Sullivan Dwight: A Biography* (Boston: Small, Maynard and Company, 1898), 14–15; Parker to Columbus Greene, July 11, 1834, Parker Papers, MHS; Weiss, *Life and Correspondence*, Vol. I, 70.

14. Parker to Columbus Greene, July 11, 1834, Parker Papers. MHS; Parker's manuscript journals during this period have been lost, but the segment on rules quoted above was copied and reprinted in Frothingham, *Theodore Parker*, 48–49; Parker to Lydia Cabot, January 25, 1836 in Weiss, *Life and Correspondence*, I, 84.

15. John Sullivan Dwight to Theodore Parker quoted in Cook, *John Sullivan Dwight,* 15; Kenneth Cameron, *Transcendental Reading Patterns: New Areas for Fresh Explorations* (Hartford: Transcendental Books, 1970), 91.

16. Parker, "A Report on German Theology Read Before the Philanthropic Society in Divinity College, Harvard University," in Cameron, *Transcendental Epilogue*, 714.

17. Frederick Henry Hedge, "Colderidge's Literary Character," in Myerson ed., *Transcendentalism,* 93; and George Ripley, "Herder's Theological Opinions and Services," in *The Transcendentalists: The Classic Anthology* ed. Perry Miller (New York: MJF Books, 1997), 96; and Andrews Norton, "The New School in Literature and Religion," in ibid., 193.

18. Brown, *Rise of Biblical Criticism*, 7; On Paulus, see Albert Schweitzer, *The Quest for the Historical Jesus* (New York: MacMillon, 1966), 48–57. On De Wette, see Thomas Howard, *Religion and the Rise of Historicism: W.M.L. De Wette, Jacob Burckhardt and the Theological Origins of Nineteenth Century Historical Consciousness* (Cambridge: Cambridge University Press, 2006), 23–42.

19. Parker, "A Report on German Theology," 708,714.

20. Weiss, *Life and Correspondence* I: 82; Brooks, *Flowering of New England*, 39–40.

21. Weiss, *Life and Correspondence* I: 82.

22. Ralph Waldo Emerson, "Nature," in Myerson ed. *Transcendentalism*, 157.

23. Parker to William Silsbee, September 16, 1836 in Parker Papers, MHS; For the influences on Emerson during the writing of *Nature*, see Robert D. Richardson, *Emerson: The Mind on Fire* (Berkeley: University of California Press, 1995), 218–234 and *passim.*

24. Weiss, *Life and Correspondence* I: 86; Frothingham, *Theodore Parker*, 65; and Convers Francis to Parker, July 23, 1836 in Collison, "Correspondence of Converse Francis and Theodore Parker," 99.

25. Parker to S.P. Andrews, February 15, 1837, Parker Papers, MHS

26. Parker to William Silsbee, August 21, 1836, Parker Papers, MHS; Parker to Lydia Cabot, n.d. in Weiss, *Life and Correspondence* I: 92.

27. Weiss, *Life and Correspondence* I: 94; Parker to Convers Francis, November 12, 1836 in Collison "Correspondence," 103.

28. Francis Bowen, "Emerson's *Nature*," in Miller ed. *The Transcendentalists*, 174.

29. Ibid.

39. For attendance at the Transcendental club meetings, see Joel Myerson, "A Calendar of Transcendental Club Meetings," *American Literature* 44 (1972): 197–207.

31. Parker's voice is described in Elizabeth Peabody to John Sullivan Dwight, September 20, 1840 in *Letters of Elizabeth Peabody*, 245; Parker to William Silsbee, March 27, 1837, Parker Papers, MHS; Brownson is described in William Hutchinson, *The Tran-*

scendentalist Ministers, 42.

32. Parker to William Silsbee, March 27, 1837, Parker Papers, MHS; Parker to Samuel Andrews, January 3, 1837, in Frothingham, *Theodore Parker,* 82.

33. Parker to Samuel P. Andrews, May 2, 1837. Parker Papers, MHS; Parker to William Silsbee, September 22, 1837, Parker Papers, MHS; Richardson, *Emerson,* 91; Charles G. Mackintosh, *Some Recollections of the Pastors and People of the Second Church of Old Roxbury* (Salem: Newcomb and Gauss: 1901), 43, 46, 54–55.

34. Parker to Silsbee, August 21, 1836. Parker Papers, MHS. Parker to Lydia D. Cabot, February 1837, in Weiss, *Life and Correspondence,* I: 97; The "Rules of Conduct" are reprinted from Parker's journals in Frothingham, *Theodore Parker,* 87.

35. Parker to Lydia D. Cabot, February 1837 [n.d.] Greenfield, in Weiss, *Life and Correspondence,* I: 97; Parker to Lydia D. Cabot, January 25, 1836 in ibid, 84.

36. Parker journal entry, June 21, 1847, in Journal and Commonplace Book, Volume II, [Hereafter cited as JCB], Parker Papers, MHS.

Chapter 3

1. Parker journal entry January, 1838 in Frothingham, *Theodore Parker,* 95.
2. Ibid.
3. Parker, "Spiritual Indifference," in *West Roxbury Sermons by Theodore Parker, 1837–1848* (Boston: American Unitarian Association, 1902), 23.
4. Parker to Convers Francis, February 9, 1839 in Collison, "Correspondence," 130; and Rose, *Transcendentalism,* 38.
5. Charles G. Macintosh, *Some Recollections of the Pastors and People of the Second Church of Old Roxbury* (Salem: Newcomb and Gaus, 1901) 7–8.
6. Parker's journal entries are quoted from transcription in Carol Johnston, "The Journals of Theodore Parker: July–December 1840," (Unpublished Ph.D. dissertation, University of South Carolina, 1980) [Hereafter cited as "Journals]. Johnston was the first to identify domestic conflict as the source of Parker's depression in the late 1830s. A more detailed analysis of the same sources can be found in Dean Grodzins, *American Heretic: Theodore Parker and Transcendentalism* (Chapel Hill: University of North Carolina Press, 2002), 92–102; Johnston, "Journals," xv.
7. Parker to Samuel Andrews, December 12, 1837, Parker Papers, MHS; Johnston, "The Journals of Theodore Parker," xvi.
8. Johnston, "Journals," xix, xx.
9. ; Collison, "Correspondence," 190; Johnston, "Journals," 53.
10. Parker to William Silsbee, June 27, 1837, Parker Papers, MHS; Lorien Foote, *Seeking the One Great Remedy: Francis George Shaw and Nineteenth Century Reform* (Athens, OH: Ohio State University Press, 2003), 37.
11. Macintosh, *Some Recollections of the Pastors and People of the Second Church of Old Roxbury;* Parker to William Silsbee, September 22, 1837, Parker Papers, MHS.
12. Parker to Samuel Andrews, January 26, 1839, Parker Papers, MHS.
13. Frothingham, *Theodore Parker,* 91.
14. Parker to William Silsbee, September 22, 1837, Parker Papers, MHS.
15. De Wette's views are analyzed in detail in Thomas Albert Howard, *Religion and the Rise of Historicism: W.M.L. De Wette, Jacob Burckhardt, and the Theological Origins of Nineteenth-Century Historical Consciousness* (Cambridge, England: Cambridge University Press, 1999), 34–43.
16. Parker, "Experience as a Minister," 315; Parker to Convers Francis, February 28,

1840 in Collison, "Correspondence," 171.

17. Parker, "Relation of the Bible to the Soul," in *Works* IV, 65, 71.

18. Parker to George Ripley, November 19, 1858, Parker Papers, MHS

19. Parker to William Silsbee, September 22, 1837, Parker Papers, MHS. See also, Brown, *Rise of Biblical Criticism*, 165.

20. Parker to George Ellis, May 27, 1838. Parker Papers, MHS; Myerson, "Transcendental Club Meetings," 200–203; Margaret Fuller quoted in Charles Capper, *Margaret Fuller, An American Romantic Life: The Private Years* (New York: Oxford University Press. 1992) 319.

21. Weiss, *Life and Correspondence*, I: 106.

22. Parker to George Ellis, May 27, 1838. Parker Papers, MHS; Collison, "Harvard Divinity School Students," 209–215.

23. Emerson quoted in Johnston, "The Journals of Theodore Parker," xxi; Parker, "Experience as a Minister," in *Works*, XIII, 309

24. Emerson, "Divinity School Address," in Myerson, *Transcendentalism*, 236, 233; Richardson, *Emerson*, 259.

25. Convers Francis to Theodore Parker, March 6, 1839 and Parker to Francis, February 9, 1839 both in Collison, "Correspondence," 129, 134; see also Collison's helpful discussion of the differences between Francis and Parker on the role of ministry in "Correspondence," 70–74.

26. Theodore Parker, "The Relation of the Bible to the Soul," in *Works*, IV, 60-61.

27. Ibid, 67.

28. "Reasons Why A Clergyman Should Not Study The Scriptures Carefully and Critically, A Letter From A Very Young Minister To A Very Old One, And To All Other Whom It May Concern," *Christian Register*, 4 November 1837; "A Word In Reply to W," *Christian Register*, 11 November 1837; Parker to William Silsbee, November 14, 1837. Parker Papers, MHS; *Christian Register*, 11 November 1837.

29. [Theodore Parker], "Palfrey's Lectures on Jewish Scriptures and Antiquities," *Boston Quarterly Review* 1 (July 1838): 269, 297; Parker to William Silsbee, November 27, 1838, Parker Papers, MHS.

30. Parker to William Silsbee, August 10, 1838, Parker Papers, MHS.

31. Parker to Elizabeth Peabody, August 30, 1839, Parker Papers, MHS.

Chapter 4

1. Emerson, "An Address," in *Works of Emerson*, Vol. I, 130, 132; Parker mss. journal entry July 15, 1838, Series One, Theodore Parker Journals, Theodore Parker Papers, Volume I. bMS 101. Andover-Harvard Theological Library, Harvard Divinity School, Cambridge, Massachusetts. [Hereafter cited as Parker Papers, A-HTL]

2. George Ripley, "To Andrews Norton," *Boston Daily Advertiser*, November 9, 1836. A full account of the pamphlet controversy can be found in William Hutchison, *The Transcendentalist Ministers*, 52–98.

3. Emerson, "An Address," 137; Andrews Norton, "The New School in Literature and Philosophy," *Boston Daily Advertiser*, 27, August 1838. See also Cayton, *Emerson's Emergence*, 163–175.

4. Andrews Norton, "The New School in Literature and Philosophy"; see also, Anne C. Rose, *Transcendentalism as a Social Movement, 1830–1850* (New Haven, CT: Yale University Press, 1981), 87–93.

5. Parker to William Silsbee, August 10, 1838, Parker Papers, MHS.

6. Parker to George Ellis, October 15, 1838, Parker Papers, MHS.

7. Parker mss. journal entry, January 10, 1839, Series One, Journals, Vol. I, Parker Papers, A-HTL.

8. Parker to William Silsbee, September 22, 1837, Parker Papers, MHS ; Parker to George Ellis, October 15, 1838. Parker Papers, MHS.

9. Parker to George Ellis, January 3, 1839. Parker Papers, MHS.

10. Ibid; On the Boston Association, see Field, *Crisis of the Standing Order*, 68.

11. Parker to George Ellis, January 3, 1839. Parker Papers, MHS; Weiss, *Life and Correspondence*, I: 102.

12. Elizabeth Peabody quoted in Ronda, *Elizabeth Peabody*, 64.

13. Rose, *Transcendentalism as a Social Movement*, 42; Parker to Convers Francis, March 22, 1839 in Collison, "Correspondence"; On Strauss, see Thomas Howard, *Religion and the Rise of Historicism*, 79–109; on Strauss's reception in America, see Brown, *Rise of Biblical Criticism*, 140–152; Delbanco, *William Ellery Channing*, argues that Channing "could not stay with the written law of God, and he would not allow its transformation into instinct." (86).

14. Parker mss. journal entry, April 19, 1839, Series One, Journals, Vol. I, Parker Papers, A-HTL; on Abner Kneeland, see Philip Gura, *American Transcendentalism: A History* (New York: Hill and Wang), 109–110.

15. Parker manuscript journal entry, n.d., 1839, Series One, Journals, Vol. I, Parker Papers, A-HTL

16. Parker, "Strauss's Life of Jesus," in *The Critical and Miscellaneous Writings of Theodore Parker* (Boston: James Munroe and Company, 1843), 297, 299, 304; see also Johnston, "The Journals of Theodore Parker," xxxviii–ix.

17. Parker to William Silsbee, October 15, 1839, Parker Papers, MHS.

18. See Parker's poem "To A.S." reprinted in Johnston, "Journals," xvii; Parker to William Silsbee, October 15, 1839. Parker Papers, MHS. On Parker's relationship with Anna Shaw, see Johnston, "The Journals of Theodore Parker," xiv–xvii; and Grodzins, *American Heretic*, 177–180.

19. Parker quoted in Frothingham, *Theodore Parker*, 119.

20. Parker mss. journal entry, January 2, 1840, Series One, Journals, Vol. I, Parker Papers, A-HTL.

21. Levi Blodgett [Theodore Parker] "The Previous Question between Mr. Andrews Norton and His Alumni Moved and Handled, in a Letter to All Those Gentlemen," in Myerson ed., *Transcendentalism*, 261–262; See also, Johnston, "Journals," liii–lvi, 162; and Collison, "Correspondence," 16.

22. Blodgett, "Previous Question," 278.

23. Ezra Stiles Gannett, "Mr. Parker and His Views," quoted in William C. Gannett, *Ezra Stiles Gannett* (Boston: Roberts Brothers, 1875), 230; Parker mss. journal entry, November, 1840, Series One, Journals, Vol. I, Parker Papers, A-HTL.

24. Ibid.

Chapter 5

1. Parker mss. journal entry, May, 1840, Series One, Journals, Vol. I, Parker Papers, A-HTL. Parker to Isaac Parker, January 22, 1840. Parker Papers. MHS.

2. Parker to Charles Miller, July 12, 1841, Parker Papers. MHS. Parker to Ezra Stiles

Gannett, June 17, 1841, Ezra Stiles Gannett Papers, Houghton Library, Harvard University [Hereafter cites as HLHU].

3. Parker to Chandler Robbins, January 27, 1843, Parker Papers, MHS.

4. Weiss, *Life and Correspondence,* I: 173.

5. Parker to Caroline Healey, December 3, 1841, Parker Papers. MHS; Parker to Charles Miller, July 12, 1841, Parker Papers. MHS.

6. Theodore Parker, "A Discourse of the Transient and Permanent in Christianity," in Myerson ed., *Transcendentalism*, 344–345, 358.

7. Ibid., 347, 358.

8. Ibid., 358.

9. Ibid.,347, 349.

10. Ibid., 364; Convers Francis to Parker, March 6, 1839 in Collison, "Correspondence," 134.

11. *The South Boston Ordination* (Boston: Saxton and Pierce, 1841), 3; *New York Evangelist*, June 12, 1841, 94; *New York Observer*, June 6, 1841; *The Trumpet and Universalist Magazine*, July 10, 1841, 10; Gura, *American Transcendentalism*, 147.

12. *South Boston Ordination*, 14–15.

13. *Daughter of Boston, The Extraordinary Diary of a Nineteenth Century Woman: Caroline Healey Dall*, Helen R. Deese ed. (Boston: Beacon Press, 2005), 25, 29.

14. Elizabeth Peabody to John Sullivan Dwight, September 20, 1840 in Ronda ed. *Letters of Elizabeth Peabody*, 246.

15. Parker to Elizabeth Peabody, June 26, 1841 in Parker Papers. MHS; Peabody to John S. Dwight, June 10, 1841 in Ronda ed. *Letters of Elizabeth Peabody*, 254; and Peabody to Dwight, June 24, 1841 in Ibid., 259–260; *South Boston Ordination*, 55.

16. Elizabeth Peabody to James Freeman Clarke, n.d. 1841, in Ronda ed. *Letters of Elizabeth Peabody*, 255–256; and Parker to Elizabeth Peabody, June 26, 1841. Parker Papers. MHS.

17. *South Boston Ordination*, 36, "To the Rev. J.H. Fairchild," *Christian Register*, July 10, 1841.

18. Parker, "A Letter to the Editors of the Register touching their strictures on my late discourse," *Christian Register*, July 10, 1841.

19. Hutchison, *The Transcendentalist Ministers*, 113–115; A.P. Peabody, "Mr. Parker's Discourse," *Christian Examiner* 31 (September, 1841), 98, 102, 113, 115.

20. Parker, "Experience as a Minister," 324; Johnston ed., "Journals," lviii.

21. Ralph Waldo Emerson, "The Chardon Street and Bible Conventions," *Dial* III (July, 1842), 100–101, 110.

22. Mayer, *All on Fire*, 301.

23. Johnston, "Journals," 52; Rose, *Transcendentalism as a Social Movement*, 140–143; Parker, "Thoughts on Labor," *Dial* I (April, 1841), 501.

24. Johnson, "Journals," 37, 47, 184–187; Gura, *American Transcendentalism*, 150–151.

25. Wiess, *Life and Correspondence*, I: 135.

26. William Larned, Samuel Brackett, Charles Thayer, and Charles Ellis to Parker, June 21, 1841. Parker Papers. MHS. Charles Mayo Ellis, *An Essay on Transcendentalism* (1842), reprinted (Westport, CT: Greenwood Press, 1954*), xiii;* For a more extended discussion of Ellis's view of Transcendentalism, see Gura, *American Transcendentalism*, 10–12; John White Chadwick, *Theodore Parker: Preacher and Reformer* (New York: Houghton Mifflin, 1900), 105–106.

27. Deese, ed., *Daughter of Boston*, 31–32.

28. Ibid., 31.

29. Parker, *Works*, I, 4; Robert Richardson, Schleiermacher and the Transcendentalists," in *Transient and Permanent*, 121–147; Leon Chai, *Romantic Foundations of the American Renaissance* (Ithaca: Cornell University Press, 1987).

30. Parker, *Works*, I, 37.

31. Parker *Works*, I, 275; E. Brooks Holifield, *Theology in America*, 450.

32. Gary Dorrien, *The Making of American Liberal Theology: Imagining Progressive Religion, 1805–1900* (Louisville: Westminster John Knox Press, 2001), 99; Parker, *Works*, I, 214.

33. Parker, *Works*, I, 283–284; Dorrien, *American Liberal Theology*, 104;

34. William Ellery Channing to Jonathan Phillips, July 4, 1842, Channing Papers, MHS; Convers Francis quoted in Collison, "Correspondence," 23.

35. Parker to Convers Francis, June 24, 1842 in Collison, "Correspondence," 252-253.

Chapter 6

1. J.H. Morison, "Parker's *Discourse*," *Christian Examiner* 32 (July 1842), 354.

2. Parker, "The Pharisees," in *Works*, IV, 119–120.

3. The classic work on Transcendentalists and church reform is William Hutchison, *The Transcendentalist Ministers*, see esp. 22–51; Parker to Convers Francis, June 24, 1842 in Collison, "Correspondence," 251; Emerson, "An Address," in *Works of Emerson*, Vol. I, 140.

4. A. Bronson Alcott, *Conversations with Children on the Gospels*, 2 Vols. (Boston: J. Munroe and Co., 1836–1837) II, 114; George Ripley, "A Letter to the Congregational Society at Purchase Street," Manuscript Copy, 2. MHS; Orestes Brownson, *New Views of Christianity, Society, and the Church* (Boston, n.p.,1836), 5.

5. Parker, Works, IV, 90; For a general discussion of the perfectionist strain in Antebellum religion and reform see Lewis Perry, *Radical Abolitionism: Anarchy and the Government of God in Antislavery Thought* (Ithaca: Cornell University Press, 1973).

6. Mayer, *All on Fire*, 304; Rose, *Transcendentalism as a Social Movement*, 1–37; Gannett, *Unitarian Minister*, 229.

7. Parker to Convers Francis, June, 1842 in Collison, "Correspondence," 252.

8. Jane H. Pease and William H. Pease, "Whose Right Hand of Fellowship? Pew and Pulpit in Shaping Church Practice," in Conrad Wright ed. *American Unitarianism, 1805–1865* (Boston: Massachusetts Historical Society, 1989), 194–195.

9. Dean Grodzins, "Theodore Parker's 'Conference with the Boston Association," January 23, 1843," in *Proceedings of the Unitarian Universalist Historical Society* 23 (1995), 72–73; S.K. Lothrop, *Proceedings of an Ecclesiastical Council in the Case of the Proprietors of the Hollis Street Meetinghouse and the Reverend John Pierpont, Their Pastor* (Boston, 1841), 252, 381.

10. Parker, "The Hollis Street Council," *Dial* III (October 1842), 216, 218.

11. George E. Ellis, "Extract from the Records of the Boston Association of Congregational Ministers of all the Passages Relating to the Rev. Theodore Parker, of West Roxbury—made at his request," March 11, 1847, Parker Papers. MHS; Parker to Chandler Robbins, January 27, 1843, Parker Papers. MHS.

12. My account of, and all quotations from, the meeting is drawn from Dean Grodzins' transcription of Parker's journal entry for January 27, 1843 in "Theodore Parker's Conference," 81–88.

13. Grodzins, "Theodore Parker's Conference," 82–83; See also Collison, "Correspondence," 432.

14. Grodzins, "Theodore Parker's Conference," 85–86.

15. Ibid., 86–87.

16. Ibid., 88; and Parker to Chandler Robbins, January 27, 1843, Parker Papers. MHS.

17. Weiss, *Life and Correspondence* I: 197–198.

18. Ibid.

Chapter 7

1. Emerson quoted in Robert Abzug, *Cosmos Crumbling: American Reform and the Religious Imagination* (New York: Oxford University Press, 1994), 3-4. Parker mss. journal entry, 1840, Series One, Vol. I, 311, Parker Papers, A-HTL.

2. Gura, *American Transcendentalism*, xiv, Emerson quoted, 213.

3. Parker to Convers Francis, December 18, 1840, in Collison, "Correspondence," 203.

4. Parker to Convers Francis, July 17, 1844 in Collison, "Correspondence," 420; Carlyle quoted in Carlos Baker, *Emerson Among the Eccentrics: A Group Portrait* (New York: Viking, 1996), 274.

5. Parker mss. journal entry, July 3, 1844, Journal and Commonplace Book [Hereafter cited as JCB], Vol. I, Parker Papers, MHS.

6. Parker to Convers Francis, January 28, 1844 in Collison, "Correspondence," 332; Parker to Mrs. George North and Anna North, April 8, 1844. Parker Papers. MHS.

7. Parker to Isaac Parker, February 12, 1844. Parker Papers. MHS; Parker to Sarah Clarke, April 28, 1844. Parker Papers. MHS. Parker to Miss Stevenson, October 31, 1843, Autograph File, HLHU.

8. Orestes Brownson, *The Laboring Classes (1840) With Brownson's Defense of the Article on the Laboring Classes.* Facsimile reprint, (Delmar, NY: Scholar's Facsims. & Reprints, 1978), 11; George Ripley quoted in O.B. Frothingham, George Ripley (Boston: Houghton, Mifflin and Company, 1882), 74, 87; see also, Rose *Transcendentalism as a Social Movement*, 109–161.

9. Convers Francis to Parker, January 31, 1844 in Collison, "Correspondence," 344; and Parker to Convers Francis, March 18, 1844 in ibid., 350–351; the concept of romantic reform is developed at length in John L. Thomas, "Romantic Reform in America, 1815-1865," *American Quarterly* 17 (December 1965), 656-681; Richardson, *Emerson: The Mind on Fire*, 363–374, contains a useful section on Fourierism.

10. Parker to Convers Francis, March 18, 1844, in Collison,"Correspondence,"350.

11. Rose, *Transcendentalism as a Social Movement*, 29–30; George Willis Cook, *Unitarianism in America*, 106.

12. Parker to Caroline Dall, December 14, 1844. Parker Papers. MHS; Parker, *Works*, XIII, 77; and *Works*, XIV, 104–105.

13. On the Church of the Disciples, see Hutchison, *Transcendentalist Ministers*, 143–152; Parker, *Works*, IV, 460–461; Chadwick, *Theodore Parker*, 144–145.

14. Frothingham, *Theodore Parker*, 214–215; *Works*, XIV, 107, 109.

15. Parker, *Works*, IV, 43–45, 56.

16. Parker, *Works*, XIII, 348; Donald Scott, "The Popular Lecture and the Creation of a Public in Mid-Nineteenth Century America," *Journal of American History* 66 (March 1980), 791–809.

17. Scrapbook of F.E. Burr, Records of the Connecticut Women's Suffrage Association, Box 6. Connecticut State Library.

18. *Waterbury American*, March 14, 1856; *Hampshire Gazzette*, December 29, 1846 and November 27, 1855; on the changes in public speaking, see Kenneth Cmiel, *Democratic Eloquence: The Fight Over Popular Speech in Nineteenth-Century America* (Berkeley: University of California Press, 1990), 23–93.

19. Parker, "Slavery," JCB, Vol. II, 120, Parker Papers, MHS.

20. Parker, "Democracy and Aristocracy," JCB, Vol. II 19, 33, Parker Papers, MHS

21. Parker, mss. journal entry, December 30, 1844, JCB, Vol. II, Parker Papers, MHS; Weiss, *Life and Correspondence*, I: 108

22. George Ripley quoted in Gura, *American Transcendentalism*, 152.

23. Parker mss journal entry, April 7, 1845, JCB, Vol. II, Parker Papers, MHS; Rose, *Transcendentalism*, 131.

24. Parker mss. journal entry, May 26, 1845, JCB, Vol. II, Parker Papers, MHS; Parker to Convers Francis, March 18, 1844, in Collison, "Correspondence," 350.

25. *Proceedings of the Anti-Sabbath Convention, Held in the Melodeon, March 23rd and 24th* (Boston: Anti-Sabbath Convention, 1848), 148; Hutchison, *Transcendentalist Ministers*, 179–180; Dean Grodzins, "Theodore Parker and the 28th Congregational Society: The Reform Church and the Spirituality of Reformers in Boston, 1845–1859," in Capper and Wright eds., *Transient and Permanent*, 82–85.

26. *Daughter of Boston*, 86–87; Helen Deese, "Tending the 'Sacred Fires': Theodore Parker and Caroline Healey Dall," *Proceedings of the Unitarian Universalist Historical Society* 23 (1995), 27–28.

27. Theodore Parker, "The True Idea of a Christian Church; A Discourse at the Installation of Theodore Parker as Minister of the Twenty-Eighth Congregational Society in Boston, January 4, 1846," in *Speeches, Addresses and Occasional Sermons*, 2 Vols. (New York: W.M. Crosby and H.P. Nichols, 1852) I, 20, 19.

28. Ibid., 38, 33.

29. Ibid., 36; Grodzins, "Theodore Parker and the 28th Congregational Society," 88–89.

Chapter 8

1. For statistics on population growth, composition, and living standards see Peter R. Knights, *The Plain People of Boston, 1830–1860: A Study of City Growth* (New York: Oxford University Press, 1971), 119–126; and Oscar Handlin, *Boston's Immigrants, 1790–1880: A Study in Acculturation* (Cambridge: Harvard University Press, 1941), 106.

2. Thomas O'Connor, *The Athens of America: Boston, 1825–1845* (Boston: University of Massachusetts Press, 2006), 75–76.

3. *The Journals of Charlotte Forten Grimke*, Brenda Stevenson, ed. (New York: Oxford University Press, 1988), 187–188.

4. Ibid.; see also Dean Grodzins, *American Heretic*, 495.

5. Parker, mss. journal entry, n.d. 1846, JCB, Vol. II, 364, Parker Papers, MHS.

6. Parker, "True Idea of a Christian Church," 28.

7. Theodore Parker, "The Dangerous Classes," in *Works*, X, 137.

8. Ibid.

9. Parker, "Dangerous Classes," 144, 177, 151.

10. Ibid.,174. On John Augustus, see Roger Lane, *Policing the City: Boston, 1822–1885* (Boston: Harvard University Press, 1967), 50.

11. Ezra Stiles Ely quoted in Bruce Dorsey, *Reforming Men and Women: Gender in the Antebellum City* (Ithaca: Cornell University Press, 2002), 81.

12. Parker, "A Sermon of the Perishing Classes," in *Works*, X, 113, 114, 107.

13. Parker, "Perishing Classes," 111, 120–121. On the use of statistics by moral reformers, see Patricia Cline Cohen, *A Calculating People: The Spread of Numeracy in Early America* (New York: Routledge, 1999), 219. Parker filled scrapbooks with statistical information gleaned from newspapers and government reports. See Parker scrapbook, 1855–1856 in Parker Papers, American Antiquarian Society, Worcester, Massachusetts.

14. Theodore Parker to Isaac Parker, September 2, 1843, Parker Papers, MHS.

15. Parker, "Perishing Classes," 125.

16. Parker, "Mercantile Classes," in *Works*, X, 11–12.

17. Ibid., 14, 16, 19.

18. Robert F. Dalzell, *Enterprising Elite: The Boston Associates and the World They Made* (Cambridge: Harvard University Press, 1987), 113–163. Ezra Stiles Gannett to Theodore Parker, December 18, 1846, Gannett Papers, HLHU.

19. Parker to Ezra Stiles Gannett, December 19, 1846, Gannett Papers,HLHU.

20. Parker to Robert White, July 31, 1848, Parker Papers, MHS; Parker, "The Perishing Classes," 106; A helpful discussion of Parker's understanding of family, gender and conscience can be found in Richard Grusin, *Transcendentalist Hermeneutics: Institutional Authority and the Higher Criticism of the Bible* (Durham: Duke University Press, 1991), 130–150.

21. Parker, "Low Aims and Lofty," *West Roxbury Sermons*, 193; Parker, "Autobiography," 3; Parker, "Low Aims and Lofty," in *West Roxbury Sermons*, 192–193.

22. Parker, "The Public Function of Woman," in *Works*, IX, 204; and Parker, *Works*, II, 234; On domesticity, see, Nancy F. Cott, *The Bonds of Womanhood: "Woman's Sphere" in New England, 1780–1835* (New Haven: Yale University Press, 1977), 63–100; and Linda Kerber, "Separate Spheres, Female World's, Woman's Place: The Rhetoric of Women's History," *Journal of American History* 75 (June 1988): 9–39.

23. Johnston, "The Journals of Theodore Parker," 60–61; and Helen Deese, ed., *Daughter of Boston*, 242.

24. Parker, "Public Function of Woman," 205, 202; Ednah Dow Cheney, *Reminiscences*, 107–109.

25. Parker, "Public Function of Woman," 196; Parker, *Works*, II, 235–236; Parker, "Prayers," in *Works*, XIII, 207; and Julia Ward Howe, *Reminiscences*, 166.

26. Parker to Caroline Dall, August 4, 1846, Parker Papers, MHS; Cheney, *Reminiscences*, 113; Parker, "Experience as a Minister," 37.

27. Mary Alice Wyman, *Two American Pioneers: Seba Smith and Elizabeth Oakes Smith* (New York: Columbia University Press, 1926), 206; Elizabeth Cazden, *Antoinette Brown Blackwell: A Biography* (New York: Feminist Press, 1993), 26; Howe, *Reminiscences*, 166.

28. Parker, "Public Function of Woman," 178, 180, 201.

29. Parker, "Experience as a Minister," 490; The 'middle class' composition of the Twenty-Eighth Congregational Society is demonstrated in Dean Grodzins, Theodore Parker and the 28th Congregational Society," in *Transient and Permanent*, 99-100; see also Commager, *Theodore Parker*, 180-181.

Chapter 9

1. Parker, "A Sermon of Slavery," in *Works* XI, 5, 11.

2. Maria Weston Chapman to unknown recipient, , n.d. in Antislavery Collection, Boston Public Library [Hereafter cited as BPL]; Parker to George Adams, December 5, 1842 in Parker Papers, MHS. Leonard Levy, *The Law of the Commonwealth and Chief Justice Shaw* (New York: Oxford University Press, 1986), 78–85.

3. Douglas C. Stange, *Patterns of Antislavery Among American Unitarians, 1831–1860* (Rutherford, NJ: Fairleigh Dickinson University Press, 1977), 19–42; and Yacavone, *Samuel Joseph May*, 73–95.

4. William Ellery Channing, "The Abolitionists: A Letter to James G. Birney on the Subject of the Anti-Abolition Mobs in Cincinnati—And the Subsequent Fleeing of that City by the Addressee of the Letter," *Works of Channing*, II, 167.

5. William Ellery Channing, "Slavery," in *Works of Channing*, II, 127, 128, 132.

6. George Ripley quoted in Frothingham, *George Ripley*, 86; Margaret Fuller to Maria Weston Chapman, December 26, 1840, in *The Letters of Margaret Fuller*, Vol. II, Richard N. Hudspeth ed. (Ithaca, 1983), 197; see also Charles Capper, *Margaret Fuller, An American Romantic Life: The Public Years* (New York: Oxford University Press, 2007), 38–39. On "self-culture" versus collective action as a dividing line within Transcendentalism, see Gura, *American Transcendentalism*, xiv, 217–222.

7. Weiss, *Life and Correspondence*, I, 176; and Deese, ed., *Daughter of Boston*, 18.

8. *Liberator*, April 24, 1846, 16; and Parker to Caroline Dall, January 17, 1847, Parker Papers, MHS. Edmund Quincy to Caroline Weston, February 9, 1841, Antislavery Collection, BPL.

9. Parker to Ralph Waldo Emerson, July 8, 1842, MS Am 1280 (2423) *Ralph Waldo Emerson Memorial deposit*, HLHU; and Johnston, "The Journals of Theodore Parker," 59.

10. Ralph Waldo Emerson to Parker, September 8, 1842, in Ralph Waldo Emerson, *The Letters of Ralph Waldo Emerson*, 8 vols. Ralph Rusk and Eleanor Tilton eds. (New York: Columbia University Press, 1939-) III, 86

11. *Liberator*, May 1, 1846; May 8, 1846, and January 4, 1846.

12. Ibid.

13. Parker mss. journal entry, August 1, 1845, JCB, Vol. II, Parker Papers, MHS; *Liberator*, August 8, 1845.

14. *Liberator*, August 8, 1845.

15. Parker, "Education by the Nation's Politics," JCB, Vol. II, 215. Parker Papers MHS; and Parker, Mss. Journal Entry, November 1844, JCB, Vol. II, 9, Parker Papers, MHS.

16. Parker to George Bancroft, November 18, 1845, reprinted in Frothingham, *Theodore Parker*, 382–385. On the opposition of John Quincy Adams and other New England Whigs to annexation, see Howe, *American Whigs*, 66–68.

17. Frothingham, *Theodore Parker*, 382–385.

18. Parker mss. journal entry, July 30, 1845, JCB, Vol. II, Parker Papers, MHS.

19. Robert Fanuzzi, *Abolition's Public Sphere* (Minneapolis: University of Minnesota Press, 2003), xvii. Fanuzzi examines the abolitionists' intentional role of anachronism in constructing their dissenting public culture; Parker mss. jounal entry, August 1, 1845, JCB, Vol. II, Parker Papers, MHS.

20. Bruce Laurie, *Beyond Garrison: Antislavery and Social Reform* (New York: Cambridge University Press, 2005), 2–3. John Quincy Adams quoted in Howe, *American Whigs*, 62.

21. Charles Sumner, "The Wrong of Slavery," *The Works of Charles Sumner*, 2 Vols. (Boston: Lee and Shepard, 1870–83), I, 156.

22. Sumner, "The True Grandeur of Nations," *Works of Sumner*, Vol. I, 125; Parker to Charles Sumner, August 17, 1845, Charles Sumner Papers, Houghton Library, Harvard University.

23. The contemporary argument for the existence of a "slave power" conspiracy is described in detail in Len Richards, *The Slave Power: The Free North and Southern Domination, 1780–1860* (Baton Rouge: Louisiana State University Press, 2000), 1–27 John Gorham Palfrey, *Papers on the Slave Power, First Published in the "Boston Whig"* (Boston: Merrill, Cobb & Co., 1846), 26; Parker to John Gorham Palfrey, December 9, 1847, Parker Papers, MHS; see also, Frank Otto Gatell, *John Gorham Palfrey and the New England Conscience* (Cambridge: Harvard University Press, 1963).

24. Parker, *A Sermon of the Mexican War* (Boston: Coolidge and Wiley, 1848), 36; Parker, "A Sermon of War," in *Works*, IX, 318.

25. Postmortem tributes to Stevenson can be found in *Unity*, July 16, 1877, 8–11; Parker to Hannah Stevenson, February 23, 1846, in Frothingham, *Theodore Parker*, 479–480.

26. Parker, "Lectures for 1846–47," JCB, Vol. II, Parker Papers, MHS.

27. *Liberator*, June 5, 1846.

28. Ibid.

29. Ibid.

30. Parker, "A Sermon of War," *Works*, IX, 296.

31. Ibid., 308–309.

32. Parker, "A Sermon of War," in *Works*, IX, 292.

33. *Liberator*, June 19, 1846; and William Lloyd Garrison to Edmund Quincy, July 19, 1846 in *The Letters of William Lloyd Garrison, Volume III: No Union With Slaveholders, 1841-1849* (Cambridge, MA: Belknap, 1974), 351;. E.A. Hitchcock to Parker, February 27, 1847, Parker Papers. MHS.

34. *Fifteenth annual report, presented to the Massachusetts Anti-Slavery Society, by its Board of Managers, January 27, 1847* (Boston: Massachusetts Antislavery Society, 1847), 67–69.

35. Parker to Hannah Stevenson, September 30, 1846 in Frothingham, *Theodore Parker*, 385; *Address of the Committee Appointed by a Public Meeting Held at Faneuil Hall* (Boston: White and Potter, 1846), 18–21, 34–35.

Chapter 10

1. William Henry Seward to Parker, August 10, 1852, Parker Papers, MHS.

2. *First Annual Report of the American Anti-Slavery Society* (New York: AASS 1834), 66; On the origins of immediatism see David Brion Davis, "The Emergence of Immediatism in British and American Anti-Slavery Thought," *Mississippi Valley Historical Review* 49 (September 1962). On the ideology of the Garrisonians and the sources of factionalism in the anti-slavery movement see, Perry, *Radical Abolitionism*; and Aileen Kraditor, *Means and Ends*. On the contested use of the term "radical" to refer to the Garrisonians, see Caleb McDaniel, "What Counts as Radical Abolitionism? A Reconsideration of Recent Scholarship," (unpublished paper, presented at the 2009 annual meeting of the Organization of American Historians), especially 9–10.

3. The Tappan and Smith wings of the movement are discussed in Friedman, *Gregarious Saints*, 68–126; Aileen Kraditor, "An Interpretation of Factionalism in the Abolitionist Movement," in *The Abolitionists*, Richard Curry ed. (Hinsdale, IL: Dryden Press, 1973), 79.

4. Elizur Wright quoted in Lawrence B. Goodheart, *Abolitionist, Actuary, Atheist: Elizur Wright and the Reform Impulse* (Kent, OH: Kent State University Press, 1990), 111.

5. *Fifteenth Annual Report of the Massachusetts Anti-Slavery Society, January 27, 1847,* reprinted (Westport, CT, 1970), 82.

6. Richard Sewell, *Ballots For Freedom: Anti-Slavery Politics in the United States, 1837–1860* (New York: Oxford University Press, 1976), 152.

7. Parker, "True Idea of a Christian Church," 44. Parker's views on the Constitution are analyzed briefly in Grodzins, "Why Theodore Parker Backed John Brown," in Peggy A. Russo and Paul Finkelman, eds, *Terrible Swift Sword: The Legacy of John Brown,* (Athens, OH: Ohio University Press, 1995), 3–22.

8. Parker, "The True Idea of a Christian Church," 44.

9. *Liberator,* June 16, 1848, and August 17, 1849.

10. Parker, "Letter on Slavery," in *Works,* XI, 118–119.

11. Paul E. Teed, "The Politics of Sectional Memory: Theodore Parker and the Massachusetts Quarterly Review, 1847–1850," *Journal of the Early Republic* (Summer 2001), 301–329. Portions of this article are reprinted here by permission of the University of Pennsylvania Press.

12. Emory Washburn, *North American Review,* 41 (Jan. 1833), 193. The relationship between history and politics among Massachusetts conservatives is analyzed in Sheidley, *Sectional Nationalism,* 118–147; Matthews, "Whig History," 196; Howe, *Political Culture of the American Whigs,* 70–73; and R. Kent Newmyer, *Supreme Court Justice Joseph Story: Statesman of the Old Republic* (Chapel Hill: UNC Press, 1985), 181–95.

13. Parker, "The Mexican War," *MQR* I (Dec. 1847), 53, 54. The quotation is from *Hamlet,* III, ii, 65.

14. Parker, "Mexican War," 49.

15. Theodore Parker, "The Free Soil Movement," *MQR,* 2 (Dec. 1848), 118; Parker, "The Mexican War," 49. On the "conscience" Whigs, see Richard Sewell, *Ballots for Freedom,* 139-142; Kinley J. Brauer, *Cotton versus Conscience: Massachusetts Whig Politics and Southwestern Expansion, 1843–1848* (Lexington, KY: University of Kentucky Press, 1967); F.O. Gattel, *John Gorham Palfrey and the Conscience of New England* (Cambridge, MA: Harvard University Press, 1963); and Martin Duberman, *Charles Francis Adams, 1807–1886* (Boston: Houghton and Mifflin, 1961), 122-124.

16. Parker to John Gorham Palfrey, Dec. 1, 1847, and Parker to Palfrey, Jan. 19, 1848, Palfrey Family Papers, HLHU; Charles Sumner to John Gorham Palfrey, Dec. 10, 1847, in *The Selected Letters of Charles Summer,* 2 vols. Beverley Wilson Palmer ed. (Boston: Northestern University Press, 1990), I, 204. That Palfrey found Parker's articles useful and informative is clearly stated in John Gorham Palfrey to Theodore Parker, Jan. 15, 1848, Parker Papers, MHS.

17. Michael Gilmore, "Eulogy as Symbolic Biography: The Iconography of Revolutionary Leadership. 1776–1826," in Daniel Aaron, ed., *Studies in Biography* (Cambridge, MA: Harvard University Press, 1978), 131–57.

18. On reactions to Adams's death in Congress, see William Lee Miller, *Arguing About Slavery: The Great Battle in the United States Congress* (New York: Vintage, 1996), 458–62; and Charles Summer to Nathan Appleton, Aug. 31, 1848, in Sumner, *Selected Letters,* I, 246.

19. Parker, "Discourse on the Death of John Quincy Adams," *MQR,* 1 (June 1848), 340, 341, 345.

20. Parker, "John Quincy Adams," 367, 370–71.

21. Theodore Parker to friend, Oct. 2, 1848, in Weiss, *Life and Correspondence*, I, 458; James Birney to Theodore Parker, Mar. 27, 1848, in Dwight L. Dumond ed. *Letters of James Gillespie Birney* 2 Vols. (New York: Appleton Century, 1938), II: 1095; Birney to Parker, Oct. 27, 1848, in ibid., 1113.

22. Parker, "Hildreth's History of the United States," *MQR* III (June, 1850), 400–401; *Christian Register*, Mar. 11, 1848, 4; *Christian Examiner*, (Jan. 1848), 153.

23. Parker, "Hildreth's History of the United States," *MQR*, 3 (June 1850), 421; Parker, "The Free Soil Movement," 120; Parker to Samuel May, Aug. 11, 1848, Parker Papers, MHS.

24. *Seventeenth Annual Report, Presented to the Massachusetts Anti-Slavery* Society (Boston: MASS, 1849), 28–29; *Liberator*, May 26, 1848.

25. Parker, "Free Soil Movement," 106, 107, 119.

26. Ibid., 115.

27. Ibid., 114–15, 126.

28. Parker to Robert White, October 20, 1850, Parker Papers, MHS; Parker, "Reply to Webster," in *Works*, XI, 246–247.

Chapter 11

1. Parker to James Martineau, November 11, 1850, Parker Papers, MHS.

2. Ibid.; On James Martineau, see Frank Schulman, *James Martineau: 'This Conscience Intoxicated Unitarian'* (Chicago: Meadville Lombard Press, 2002).

3. The symbolic place of Boston in the antislavery movement is discussed in James Brewer Stewart, "Boston, Abolition, and the Atlantic World, 1820–1861," in Donald Jacobs ed. *Courage and Conscience: Black and White Abolitionists in Boston* (Bloomington, IN: Indiana University Press, 1993), 101–126.

4. A detailed examination of Faneuil Hall as a contested symbol can be found in Fanuzzi, *Abolition's Public Sphere*, 129–165

5. Webster quoted in Varon, *Disunion*, 218.

6. Daniel Webster, "The Constitution and the Union," *The Works of Daniel Webster*, X (New York, 1903), 64.

7. Ibid.

8. Moses Stuart, *Conscience and the Constitution* (Boston: Crocker and Brewster, 1850), 60–61. On the intellectual context, see Meyer, *The Instructed Conscience*, 117–118.

9. Stuart, *Conscience and the Constitution*, 61; see also, Laura L. Mitchell, "'Matters of Justice Between Man and Man': Northern Divines, the Bible and the Fugitive Slave Act of 1850" in *Religion and the Antebellum Debate Over Slavery*, in John R. McKivigan and Mitchell Snay eds., (Athens, GA.: University of Georgia Press, 1998), 142–143, 163.

10. *Boston Daily Advertiser*, April 2, 1850; Levy, *Law of the Commonwealth*, 85–86.

11. Winthrop quoted in Irving Bartlett, *Daniel Webster* (New York: Norton, 1978), 250.

12. *Christian Register*, Boston, March 16, 1850; Charles Sumner to George Sumner, March 18, 1850, *Selected Letters*, I, 288; *The Journals and Miscellaneous Notebooks of Ralph Waldo Emerson* XI, 346; Sewell, *Ballots for Freedom*, 221.

13. Parker, "Reply to Webster," in *Works*, XI, 246.

14. Ibid.

15. Parker, *Letter to the People of the United States Touching the Matter of Slavery*

(Boston: James Munroe and Company, 1848), 107–108.

16. *Liberator*, April 5, 1850.

17. Parker, "The Slave Power," in *Works*, XI, 250–51, 261, 279, 285.

18. Ibid., 272; David Donald, *Charles Sumner and the Coming of the Civil War* (New York: Knopf, 1967), 188–189.

19. Liberator, October 11, 1850.

20. Collison, *Shadrach Minkins*, 77, Webster quoted on 88, and Choate quoted on 247. Varon, *Disunion*, 220–221; and Mayer, *All On Fire*, 412–413.

21. Parker to John Gorham Palfrey, September 9, 1850, Palfrey Papers, Houghton Library, Harvard University.

22. Parker, "The Function of Conscience," in *Works*, XI, 292.

23. Ibid.

24. Parker, "The Function of Conscience," 292–310.

25. Ibid., 305.

26. *Memoirs of Benjamin Robbins Curtis*, Benjamin R. Curtis Jr., ed., (New York: DaCapo Press, 1970) I, 122, 126.

27. Ibid; Parker, *The Trial of Theodore Parker For the Misdemeanor of a Speech in Faneuil Hall Against Kidnapping* (Cambridge: Allen and Farnham, 1855), 188. The confrontation between Parker and Curtis at the Union meeting is also discussed in Grodzins, "'Slave Law' versus 'Lynch Law'," 11–12.

28. Henry David Thoreau, "On Resistance to Civil Government," in Myerson ed., *Transcendentalism*, 552.

29. Parker, "Function of Conscience," 304.

30. The Crafts told their story in an extremely successful narrative entitled *Running a Thousand Miles for Freedom; or the Escape of William and Ellen Craft from Slavery* (London: William Tweedy, 1860).

31. Parker, "Reply to Webster," 246; Parker to James Martineau, November 11, 1850, Parker Papers, MHS.

32. H.I. Bowditch to H.W. Torrey, Oct. 28, 1850, in *The Life and Correspondence of Henry Ingersoll Bowditch*, ed. V.Y. Bowditch (New York: Houghton, Mifflin and Co., 1903), 209.

33. *Liberator*, October 4, 1850; Collison, *Shadrach Minkins*, 78–80; Roy Finkenbine, "Boston's Black Churches: Institutional Centers of the Antislavery Movement," in *Courage and Conscience*, 172, 182.

34. *Daughter of Boston*, 130; *Herald* (Boston), October 15, 1850; Collison, *Shadrach Minkins*, 82.

35. Weiss, *Life and Correspondence*, II, 94.

36. A list of Vigilance Committee members can be found in Austin Bearse, *Reminiscences of Fugitive-Slave Law Days in Boston* (Boston: W. Richardson, 1880), 3–6. On the connections between the Vigilance Committee leadership and Parker's congregation, see Dean Grodzins, "'Slave Law' versus 'Lynch Law' in Boston: Benjamin Robbins Curtis, Theodore Parker, and the Fugitive Slave Crisis in Boston, 1850–1855," *Massachusetts Historical Review* 12 (2010), 4.

37. Collison, *Shadrach Minkins*, 83–85; Francis Jackson, "The Boston Vigilance Committee to Assist Fugitive Slaves, Treasurer's Account Book," Garrison Collection, BPL.

38. Weiss, *Life and Correspondence*, II, 94.

Chapter 12

1. Weiss, *Life and Correspondence*, II, 105
2. Ibid., 105; Grodzins, *American Heretic*, 326–327; Wyman, *Two American Pioneers*, 206.
3. Weiss, *Life and Correspondence*, II, 50–52.
4. Chadwick, *Theodore Parker*, 174–178.
5. Thomas Wentworth Higginson, *Contemporaries* (Cambridge: Riverside Press, 1899), 40;, 422.
6. Weiss, *Life and Correspondence*, II, 94; Parker mss. journal entry, August 24, 1851, Series I, Journals, Vol. III, Parker Papers, A-HTL.
7. Collison, *Shadrach Minkins*, 96–98.
8. Weiss, *Life and Correspondence*, II, 95.
9. Liberator, *November* 1, 1850; Collison, *Shadrach Minkins*, 96–99; Parker to James Martineau, Nov. 11, 1850, Papers Papers, MHS.
10. Weiss, *Life and Correspondence*, II, 97.
11. William Craft, *Running a Thousand Miles for Freedom,* 90; and Weiss, *Life and Correspondence*, II, 97.
12. Weiss, *Life and Correspondence*, II, 98.
13. Parker to James Martineau, November 11, 1850, Parker Papers, MHS; Weiss, *Life and Correspondence*, II, 100.
14. My account of the Shadrach case draws from Collison, *Shadrach Minkins*, 110–133; Parker, "Memoranda of the Troubles in Boston Occasioned by the Infamous Fugitive Slave Act, Kept from Day to Day," entry for March 15, 1851, manuscript 210, Parker Collection, BPL." See also, *Liberator*, Feb. 21, 1851; *The Nineteenth Annual Report Presented to the Massachusetts Anti-Slavery Society*, reprinted (Westport, CT: 1970), 10; and *The Journal of Richard Henry Dana Jr.*, Robert Lucid ed. (Cambridge: Belknap Press, 1968), II, 410–415.
15. Weiss, *Life and Correspondence*, II, 103.
16. *Nineteenth Annual Report*, 11; Parker, "The Boston Kidnapping," in *Works*, V, 196.
17. Millard Fillmore in James D. Richardson, comp., *A Compilation of the Messages and Papers of the Presidents*, Vol. VI (New York, 1897), 2616; *Nineteenth Annual Report*, 11; Garrison and Garrison, *William Lloyd Garrison*, III, 327.
18. Collison, *Shadrach Minkins*, 147–148; Weiss, *Life and Correspondence*, II, 105.
19. Parker, "Memoranda of the Troubles in Boston," entry for March 16, 1851, Parker Collection, BPL; Garrison and Garrison, *William Lloyd Garrison*, III, 323–324.
20. Parker, "Memoranda of the Troubles in Boston" entry for March 15, 1851, Parker Collection, BPL
21. Garrison and Garrison, *William Lloyd Garrison*, III, 323–324; Leonard Levy, "Sims' Case: The Fugitive Slave Case in Boston in 1851," *Journal of Negro History* 35 (January 1950), 43.
22. Higginson, *Cheerful Yesterdays*, 142; *Liberator*, April 11, 1851.
23. Parker, "Memoranda of the Troubles in Boston" entry for April 3, 1851, Parker Collection, BPL; Levy, "Sims Case," 45; Parker to Samuel Joseph May, Sept. 25, 1852, Parker Papers, MHS; *Liberator*, April 11, 1851; and Parker, "The Boston Kidnapping," *Works*, XI, 352.
24. *Commonwealth*, April 5, 1851.
25. Parker, "Memoranda of the Troubles in Boston," entry for April 4, 1851, Parker

Collection, BPL; Parker used the word "nigger" on at least one other occasion to refer to white northerners dominated by the Slave Power. In an 1858 letter he described the conflict with the South as one in which "we must conquer as *men*, or die *niggers*." The emphasis is in the original. See Weiss, *Life and Correspondence*, I, 396.

26. Levy, "Sims Case," 64; Bearse, *Fugitive Slave Days*, 24; Parker, "Memoranda of the Troubles in Boston," entry for April 6, 1851, Parker Collection, BPL; and *Liberator*, April 11, 1851.

27. Higginson, *Cheerful Yesterdays*, 139–140; *The Journal of Richard Henry Dana*, II, 424.

28. Parker, "The Chief Sins of the People," in *Works*, IX, 45.

29. Deborah Weston to Anne Weston, April 16, 1851, Antislavery Collection, BPL.

30. Brownson (review of Parker's sermon); Parker, *Works*, IX, 377.

31. *Liberator*, April 11, 1851; Levy, "Sims Case," 69–70.

32. Parker, "Memoranda of the Troubles in Boston," entry for April 6, 1851, Parker Collection, BPL; Parker, "The Boston Kidnapping," in *Works*, XI, 357.

33. Bowditch, *Life and Correspondence*, 220; *Liberator*, April 18, 1851; Parker to Charles Sumner, April 19, 1851. Parker Papers, MHS.

Chapter 13

1. R. Redington to Parker, October 21, 1853. Parker Papers, MHS.

2. Weiss, *Life and Correspondence*, I, 408; Mary Caroline Crawford, *Romantic Days in Old Boston: The Story of the City and Of Its People During the Nineteenth Century* (Boston: Little, Brown and Company, 1910), 216.

3. *Liberator*, April 23, 1852; Wyman, *Two American Pioneers*, 206.

4. Crawford, *Romantic Days*, 216; Louisa May Alcott, *Work: A Story of Experience* (Penguin Books: New York, 1994), 161; William Nell to Amy Post, March 11, 1853, Post Papers, University of Rochester, accessed through the Black Abolitionist Papers online database.

5. *New York Times*, June 2, 1860; Wendell Phillips, "Theodore Parker," in *Speeches*, 432; Emerson quoted in Carlos Baker, *Emerson Among the Eccentrics: A Group Portrait* (New York: Viking, 1996), 205–206; Alcott, *Work*, 161; and Samuel Gridley Howe to "The Reverend Thunder and Lightning Parker Everywhere," in *The Letters and Journals of Samuel Gridley Howe* (Boston: Dana Estes and Company, 1909), 346–347.

6. Julia Ward Howe, *Reminiscences* (Boston: Houghton and Mifflin, 1899), 167.

7. Parker, "Experience as a Minister," in *Works*, XIII, 349–350.

8. Ibid.

9. Stanley Campbell, *The Slave Catchers: Enforcement of the Fugitive Slave Act, 1850–1860* (UNC Press, 1970), 116, 120–121 and appendix I, tables II and III.

10. The term "revolutionary center" was coined by Ronald P. Formisano, *The Transformation of Political Culture: Massachusetts Parties, 1790s–1840s.* (New York: Oxford University Press, 1983), 57. Daniel McInerney, *The Fortunate Heirs of Freedom: Abolitionism and Republican Thought* (Lincoln, Nebraska: University of Nebraska Press, 1994), 2.

11. George R. Price and James Brewer Stewart, "The Roberts Case, the Easton Family and the Dynamics of the Abolitionist Movement in Massachusetts, 1776–1870" *Massachusetts Historical Review* 4 (2002), 104–106, 116; Stanley Harrold, "Romanticizing Slave Revolt: Madison Washington, the Creole Mutiny and the Abolitionist Celebration of Violent Means," in John R. McKivigan and Stanley Harrold, eds., *Antislavery Vio-*

lence: Sectional, Racial and Cultural Conflict in Antebellum America (Knoxville: University of Tennessee Press, 1999), 100; Von Franck, *Trials of Anthony Burns*, 157.

12. On Herder, see Reginald Horsman, *Race and Manifest Destiny: The Origins of American Racial Anglo-Saxonism* (Cambridge: Harvard University Press, 1981), 27; and Elie Kedourie, *Nationalism*, Fourth Edition (Malden, MA: Wiley-Blackwell), 56-58.

13. Parker, "Great Men," in *Works*, V, 68-69.

14. On the cultural nationalism of the Transcendentalists, see Lawrence Buell, *Literary Transcendentalism: Style and Vision in the American Renaissance* (Ithaca: Cornell University Press, 1973); and Buell, *New England Literary Culture: From Revolution Through Renaissance* (Cambridge: Cambridge University Press, 1986).

15. Parker, "The Progress of America," in *Works*, XII, 198-199.

16. Parker, "The Political Destination of America," in *Works*, XI, 126, 161; Horsman, *Race and Manifest Destiny*, 178-179 deals with Parker's thought in the larger tradition of racial Anglo-Saxonism; see also Paul E. Teed, "Racial Nationalism and Its Challengers: Theodore Parker, John Rock and the Antislavery Movement," *Civil War History* 41 (June 1995), 142-160. Portions of this article are reprinted here by permission of Kent State University Press.

17. Parker to David Wasson, December 12, 1857, Parker Papers, MHS.

18. Ibid.; and Parker, "The Rights of Man in America," in Works, XII, 355, 357; On Blumenbach's classifications, see Horsman, *Race and Manifest Destiny*, 47-48. My analysis of Parker's views of race, politics and violence has benefited from Michael Fellman, "Theodore Parker and the Abolitionist Role in the 1850's," *Journal of American History* 61 (December, 1974), 666-684 and Richard Slotkin, *The Fatal Environment: The Myth of the Frontier in the Age of Industrialization* (New York: Atheneum, 1985), 230-235.

19. Patrick Rael, A Common Nature, "A United Destiny: African American Responses to Racial Science from the Revolution to the Civil War," in Timothy P. McCarthy and John Stauffer eds. *Prophets of Protest: Reconsidering the History of American Abolitionism* (New York: The New Press, 2006), 184.

20. William Stanton, *The Leopard's Spots: Scientific Attitudes Toward Race in America, 1815-1859* (Chicago: University of Chicago Press, 1960), 100-121; Louis Menand, *The Metaphysical Club: A Story of Idea in America* (New York: Farrar, Strauss and Giroux, 2002), 97-116, Josiah Nott quoted on page 110.

21. Parker, "An Antislavery Address," in *Works*, XII, 162-163.

22. Parker, "The Boston Kidnapping," in *Works*, XI, 352.

23. Ibid., 357-358; Parker to George Bancroft, March 16, 1858, Parker Papers, MHS. Although he does not mention Parker, Stephen Kantrowitz, "A Place for 'Colored Patriots': Crispus Attucks Among the Abolitionists," *Massachusetts Historical Review* XI (Spring, 2009), 97-117 shows Attucks' re-emergence as a symbol of black resistance during the Boston Fugitive Slave Act crises.

24. On the rescue of "Jerry" Henry, see Bordewich, *Bound for Canaan*, 333-339; and Samuel May, *Recollections of the Antislavery Conflict* (Boston: Fields, Osgood and Co., 1869), 373-388.

25. Parker to Samuel May, November 27, 1851; Parker to May, September 23, 1853, both in Parker Papers, MHS.

26. On the variety of responses to racial science during the antebellum period, see Rael, "A Common Nature, A United Destiny," 186-195; *National Anti-Slavery Standard*, March 20, 1858; *Liberator*, July 18, 1862; *Liberator*, March 12, 1858.

27. Thomas P. Slaughter, *Bloody Dawn: The Christiana Riot and Racial Violence in*

the Antebellum North (New York: Oxford University Press, 1991), 59–76; Bordevich, *Bound For Canaan*, 325–333.

28. Parker to Samuel May, October 2, 1851, in Parker Papers, MHS; *Liberator*, Oct. 31, 1851 (my italics).

29. On abolitionism's increasingly "aggressive" and biracial character, see Stanley Harrold, *The Rise of Aggressive Abolitionism: Addresses to the Slaves* (Lexington: University Press of Kentucky, 2004), 117–139; *Liberator*, October 31, 1851; *Frederick Douglass' Paper*, November 27, 1851.

30. *Frederick Douglass' Paper*, November 27, 1851.

Chapter 14

1. William H. Seward to Parker, August 10, 1852, Parker Papers, MHS.

2. *Liberator*, August 27, 1852.

3. Bartlett, *Daniel Webster*, 270–274; Parker, *A Discourse Occasioned by the Death of Daniel Webster, Preached at the Melodeon on Sunday, October 31, 1852* (Boston: Benjamin Mussey & Co., 1852), 65–66.

4. Parker, *Daniel Webster*, 85, 86, 93.

5. Ibid., 4, 91.

6. Everett quoted in Parker, *Works*, VII, 440; and Junius Americanus, *A Review of "A Discourse Occasioned by the Death of Daniel Webster Preached at the Melodeon on Sunday, October 31, by Theodore Parker, Minister of the Twenty-Eighth Congregational Society of Boston"* (Boston and Cambridge: James Munroe and Co., 1853), 3, 61–62.

7. Ibid., 74.

8. C.F. Adams to Parker, March 24, 1853; William Seward to Parker, March 23, 1853; R. Redington to Parker October 21, 1853; and Seth Parker to Parker, January 13, 1853, all in Parker Papers, MHS.

9. Parker to Charles Sumner, April 26, 1851, Charles Sumner Papers, HLHU; Sumner quoted in Donald, *Charles Sumner*, 219.

10. Parker to Charles Sumner, August 4, 1852, Charles Sumner Papers, HLHU.

11. Charles Sumner to Parker, August 11, 1852. In *Selected Letters*, 368; Weiss, *Life and Correspondence*, II, 213; Charles Sumner, "Freedom National; Slavery Sectional," *Recent Speeches and Addresses [1851–1855] by Charles Sumner* (Boston: Ticknor and Fields, 1856), 81; Parker to Charles Sumner, August 27, 1852, Charles Sumner Papers, HLHU.

12. William Wiecek, *The Sources of Antislavery Constitutionalism in America, 1760–1848* (Ithaca: Cornell University Press, 1977), chapters 9, 10, 11.

13. Martin Duberman, *Charles Francis Adams, 1807–1886* (Boston: Houghton Mifflin, 1961), 180–186; Jonathan Earle, *Jacksonian Antislavery and the Politics of Free Soil, 1824–1854* (Chapel Hill: UNC Press, 2004), 184–187; and Laurie, *Beyond Garrison*, 216–217.

14. Wendell Phillips, "The Philosophy of the Abolition Movement," in *Speeches*, II, 98–153, 147.

15. Horace Mann to Parker, February 22, 1853, Parker Papers, MHS; *Liberator*, March 4, 1853.

16. Parker to Samuel May, April 5, 1853, Parker Papers, MHS.

17. Parker to Wendell Phillips, March [n.d.], 1853, Wendell Phillips Papers, HLHU; Horace Mann to Parker, April 15, 1853, Parker Papers, MHS

18. *Commonwealth*, March 15, 1853. *Liberator*, February 25, 1853; Parker to

Wendell Phillips, [n.d.], in Folder 6; Wendell Phillips Papers, HLHU.

19. Parker to Charles M. Ellis, November 20, 1853, Parker Papers, MHS.

20. Parker to Hannah Stevenson, June 17, 1852 in Frothingham, *Theodore Parker*, 309–310.

21. Parker to Samuel Joseph May, October 24, 1853, Autograph File, HLHU.

22. On the transcendentalists' reaction to Feuerbach, see Elisabeth Hurth, *Between Faith and Unbelief: American Transcendentalists and the Challenge of Atheism* (Boston: Brill, 2007), 123–148.

23. Parker, *Works*, II, 86.

24. Ibid., 154, 155.

25. Ibid., 142.

26. Ibid, 106.

27. Parker, "Of Justice and the Conscience," in *Works*, III, 64. Dr. Martin Luther King Jr. was fond of this quotation by Parker and slightly reformulated it for use during the Civil Rights Movement. It has reappeared, in King's modified form, on the King Memorial in Washington and on Barack Obama's Oval Office rug.

28. Ibid., 221, 252.

Chapter 15

1. Parker, "Of Justice and the Conscience," in *Works*, III, 64.

2. A.P. Peabody, "Mr. Parker's Discourse," 115; and Orestes Brownson, "Parker's Discourse," *Boston Quarterly Review*, IV (October 1842), 442; see also Commager, *Theodore Parker*, 301.

3. Parker, "The Nebraska Question, Some Thoughts on the New Assault on Freedom in America," *Works*, II, 279.

4. Parker to Charles Ellis, February 12, 1854, Parker Papers, MHS; Parker to John Hale, May 23, 1854, Parker Papers, MHS; Charles F. Adams to Parker, June 4, 1854, Parker Papers, MHS.

5. Weiss, *Life and Correspondence*, II, 157.

6. *Liberator*, June 9, 1854.

7. *The Boston Slave Riot and the Trial of Anthony Burns* (Boston: William V. Spence, 1854), 7; and Von Franck, *Trials of Anthony Burns*, 4–5.

8. Seven handbills from the Burns crisis are reprinted in Weiss, *Life and Correspondence*, II, 133–135.

9. Dana, *Journals*, Vol. II, 628; Bowditch, *Life and Correspondence*, 264; Von Franck, *Trials of Anthony Burns*, 9.

10. Higginson, *Cheerful Yesterdays*, 148–150.

11. Bowditch, *Life and Correspondence*, 265; Von Franck, *Trials of Anthony Burns*, 32.

12. Charles Emery Stevens, *Anthony Burns: A History* (Boston: John P. Jewett and Company, 1856), 39.

13. Stevens, *Anthony Burns*, 289, 291; Von Franck, *Trials of Anthony Burns*, 59; and *Boston Slave Riot*, 9–10.

14. Stevens, *Anthony Burns*, 295; Jeffrey Rossbach makes a similar point in *Ambivalent Conspirators: John Brown, the Secret Six and a Theory of Slave Violence* (Philadelphia: University of Pennsylvania Press, 1982), 30–33.

15. Stevens, *Anthony Burns*, 295; *Boston Slave Riot*, 9

16. *Boston Slave Riot*, 10–12, Higginson, *Cheerful Yesterdays*, 152–160; Richard H.

Dana, *Journals*, II, 629; Von Franck, *Trials of Anthony Burns*, 62–70; and Gordon Barker, *Imperfect Revolution: Anthony Burns and the Landscape of Race in Antebellum America* (Kent, OH: Kent State University Press, 2010), 12–13, 130–131.

17. Higginson, *Cheerful Yesterdays*, 155.

18. Stevens, *Anthony Burns*, 273; Broadsides Relating to the Burns Case, (ms. xbH.90.357), Parker Collection, BPL.

19. Parker's sermon is reprinted in *Boston Slave Riot*, 30–33.

20. *Boston Slave Riot*, 31, 32; Parker, *Works*, XII, 320; Von Franck, *Trials of Anthony Burns*, 110.

21. Von Franck, *Trials of Anthony Burns*, 263.

22. *Boston Slave Riot*, 33.

23. Jane H. and William H. Pease, *The Fugitive Slave Law and Anthony Burns: A Problem in Law Enforcement* (Philadelphia: Lippincott, 1975), 39–41. *Commonwealth*, May 27, 1854; Parker, "The New Crime Against Humanity," in *Works*, XII, 305.

24. *Boston Slave Riot*, 17–18; *Evening Telegraph* (Boston), April 16, 1855.

25. Von Franck, *Trials of Anthony Burns*, 108; Weiss, *Life and Correspondence*, II, 137.

26. Pease and Pease, *Fugitive Slave Law and Anthony Burns*, 48–50.

27. Ednah Dow Cheney, *Reminiscences of Ednah Dow Cheney* (Boston: Lee and Shepherd, 1902), 106; Von Franck, *Trials of Anthony Burns*, 208. On the sizable crowd support for the rendition and anger at the abolitionists, see Gordon Barker, *The Imperfect Revolution*, 58–61.

28. Parker, "The New Crime," 266, 318.

29. Parker, "The New Crime," 320.

30. Wendell Phillips quoted in James B. Stewart, *Wendell Phillips: Liberty's Hero* (Baton Rouge: LSU Press, 1986), 174; *Boston Post*, June 4, 1854.

31. For reactions to the Court House attack, see the *Liberator*, June 9, 1854; David Maginnes, "The Case of the Court House Rioters in the Rendition of Fugitive Slave Anthony Burns, 1854," *Journal of Negro History* LVI (January 1971): 17–31. Theodore Parker, *The Trial of Theodore Parker: for the "Misdemeanor" of a Speech in Faneuil Hall Against Kidnapping* (Boston: [n.p.], 1855), 206.

32. Weiss, *Life and Correspondence*, II, 141-142; and Charles Sumner to Parker, December 12, 1854, in Parker Papers, MHS.

33. Parker to Charles Sumner, June 26, 1854, Charles Sumner Papers, Houghton Library, Harvard University; Parker to Samuel May, December 1, 1854, Parker Papers. MHS; Parker to Thomas Moore Esq., February 16, 1855. Parker Papers, MHS.

34. Theodore Parker, *The Trial of Theodore Parker: for the "Misdemeanor" of a Speech in Faneuil Hall Against Kidnapping* (Boston: [n.p.], 1855), vi; Maginnes, "Court House Rioters," 39.

35. Parker, *The Trial of Theodore Parker*, 202. The personal and ideological differences between Parker and Curtis over the nature of law, and the function of juries are handled in Grodzins, "'Slave Law' versus 'Lynch Law'," 17–26.

36. Parker, *The Trial of Theodore Parker*, 221.

37. Ibid., 3.

Chapter 16

1. Parker, Journal Entry, April 19, 1856. HATL; Parker to Sarah Apthorp, September 19, 1856 in Frothingham, *Theodore Parker*, 437.

2. Parker, "Present Crisis in America Affairs," in *Works* XII, 451, 453–454, 488.

3. Nicole Etcheson, *Bleeding Kansas: Contested Liberty in the Civil War* Era (Lawrence, Kansas: University Press of Kansas, 2004), 77.

4. Theodore Parker, "Present Crisis in American Affairs," in *Works*, XII, 433, 468.

5. Parker to John Hale, May 28, 1856, Parker Papers, MHS; Parker mss. journal entry, September 9, 1856, Series One, Journals, Vol. III, 759.

6. Tilden Edelstein, *Strange Enthusiasm: A Life of Thomas Wentworth Higginson* (New York: Atheneum, 1970), 183–193.

7. Ephraim Nute to Parker, September 14, 1856, Parker Papers, MHS; The only modern work on Nute is the remarkably complete compilation of his letters by William C. Groth and Bobbie Groth, *What One Man Can Do For Freedom: The Documented Life of Unitarian Minister Rev. Ephraim Nute Jr.* (South Milwaukee, Wisconsin: self published, 2007), 249–251.

8. Ibid., 223, 229; Parker to Sarah Hunt, September 4, 1856, in Frothingham, *Theodore Parker*, 436.

9. Groth and Groth, *What One Man Can Do For Freedom*, 249–251, 252–253; Parker to Mrs. Apthorp, September 11, 1856; in Frothingham, *Theodore Parker*, 437..

10. Frothingham, *Theodore Parker*, 438-439.

11. Weiss, *Life and Correspondence*, II, 207–208.

12. Anbinder, *Nativism and Slavery*, 87–101; Parker to James Orton, February 22, 1855, Parker Papers, MHS; Weiss, *Life and Correspondence*, I, 397; Parker, "Present Aspect of the Antislavery Enterprise," in *Works*, XIII, 415; Weiss, *Life and Correspondence*, II, 210–211.

13. Weiss, *Life and Correspondence*, II, 189; Parker to Sarah Hunt, November 4, 1856 in Frothingham, 436.

14. *Annual Report of the Massachusetts Anti-Slavery Society*, 1856, 62; *Richmond Enquirer* quoted in Varon, *Disunion!*, 275; Theodore Parker, "The Present Aspect of the Anti-Slavery Enterprise," in *Works*, XIII, 426-427.

15. Parker, "Present Aspect," in Works, *XIII*, 410–411.

16. Parker to Charles Sumner, January 14, 1856, Charles Sumner Papers, HLHU; Parker to Salmon P. Chase, July 25, 1856, in Weiss, *Life and Correspondence*, II, 227; Chase to Parker, July 17, 1856, Parker Papers,. MHS.

17. Parker to Charles Sumner, May 21, 1856 in Charles Sumner Papers, HLHU.

18. Sumner, "The Crime Against Kansas," *Speeches*, Vol. II, 235; William Gienapp, "The Crime Against Sumner: The Caning of Charles Sumner and the Rise of the Republican Party," *Civil War History* 25 (1979): 218–245.

19, Henry Wilson to Parker, May 25, 1856, Parker Papers, MHS; and Frothingham, 436.

20. Parker, "A New Lesson for the Day," in *Works*, XIV, 241, 244–245, 268; Parker to John Hale, May 23, 1856; and Parker to John Hale, May 28, 1856, both in Parker Papers, MHS.

21. Parker to John Hale, June 19, 1856, Parker Papers, MHS.

22. Parker to Edward Desor, August 9, 1856, in Weiss, *Life and Correspondence,* II, 189. See also Parker, "Lecture Journal" in Parker Papers, MHS.

23. William Gienapp, *The Origins of the Republican Party, 1852–1856* (New York: Oxford University Press, 1987), 354.

24. Parker, "The Present Crisis in American Affairs," in *Works*, XII 437, 449.

25. On the free labor ideology, see the classic work by Eric Foner, *Free Soil, Free Labor, Free Men: The Ideology of the Republican Party Before the Civil War* (New

York: Oxford University Press, 1970), esp. ch. 1, 2.

26. Parker, "Present Crisis," 447, 452.

27. Parker, "Crime and Its Punishment," in *Works*, IX, 340; Weiss, *Life and Correspondence*, I, 396; see also Richard Slotkin, *The Fatal Environment*, 229-233.

28. Parker to John Hale, October 21, 1856, in Parker Papers, MHS.

29. Weiss, *Life and Correspondence*, II, 189–190.

30. Ibid., 191.

Chapter 17

1. Frothingham, *Theodore Parker*, 483–484.

2. Parker to William Fish, July 25, 1857, Parker Papers, MHS.

3. Frothingham, *Theodore Parker*, 491–492, 482.

4. Parker to Charles Sumner, June 2, 1857, Sumner Papers, HLHU; Frothingham, *Theodore Parker*, 492.

5. Parker to William Fish, July 25, 1857; and Parker to Fish, November 11, 1858, Parker Papers, MHS.

6. Robert E. McGlone, *John Brown's War Against Slavery* (Cambridge: Cambridge University Press, 2009), 204–209; Franklin Sanborn, *The Life and Letters of John Brown, Liberator of Kansas and Martyr of Virginia* (Boston: Roberts Brothers, 1885), 17–18.

7. Sanborn, *John Brown*, 15; David Reynolds, *John Brown: Abolitionist* (New York: Knopf, 2005), 16–17.

8. Stauffer, *Black Hearts of Men*, 121–123.

9. Wendell Phillips Garrison and Francis Jackson Garrison, *William Lloyd Garrison, 1805–1879* 4 Vols. (New York: Houghton Mifflin, 1889), 487–488.

10. "Old Brown's Farewell," in Oswald Garrison Villard, *John Brown, 1800–1859* (Boston: Houghton Mifflin, 1911), 288; Reynolds, *John Brown*, 236–237; see also Dean Grodzins, "Why Theodore Parker Backed John Brown: The Political and Social Roots for Abolitionist Violence," in *Terrible Swift Sword*, 3–22.

11. Albert J. Von Franck, "John Brown, James Redpath, and the Idea of Revolution," *Civil War History*, 52 (June 2006), 142–160. John Brown to Parker, September 11, 1857, in Parker Papers, MHS.

12. Parker to Ruth and Stephen Crooker, October 26, 1857, Parker Papers, MHS; Higginson quoted in Edward Renehan, *The Secret Six: The True Tale of the Men who Conspired with John Brown* (Columbia, SC: 1996), 142.

13. Katherine Long, *The Revival of 1857: Interpreting and American Religious Awakening* (New York: Oxford University Press, 1998), 95.

14. Goodell quoted Long, *Revival of 1857*, 93–94; and see also Rossbach, *Ambivalent Conspirators*, 156.

15. Parker, *Works*, II, 252.

16. Parker, "The Revival We Need," in *Works*, IV, 406–407; and Parker, "A False and True Revival of Religion," in ibid., 384–385.

17. Ibid, 385–386, 387.

18. Parker, "Revival of Religion," 382; Long, *Revival of 1857*, 111; William Tarbox, "Theodore Parker and the Twenty-Eighth Congregational Society of Boston," *New Englander* (August, 1858): 687. D.G. Hart, "Divided Between Heart and Mind: The Critical Period for Protestant Thought in America," *Journal of Ecclesiastical History* 38 (April 1987): 254–270.

19. Parker to Mrs. Julia Bridges, April 9, 1858, Parker Papers, MHS.

20. Garth M. Rosell and Richard A.G. Dupuis eds., *The Original Memoirs of Charles G. Finney* (Grand Rapids: Zondervan, 2002), 407–408.

21. John Brown to Parker, February 2, 1858, Parker Papers, MHS.

22. John Brown to F.B. Sanborn, February 24, 1858, in Sanborn, *John Brown*, 444–445.

23. Reynolds, *John Brown*, 240–241.

24. Sanborn, *John Brown*, 447; Rossbach, *Ambivalent Conspirators*, 146–147.

25. Sanborn, *John Brown*, 440; McGlone, *John Brown's War Against Slavery*, 208–209.

26. Higginson quoted in Rossbach, *Ambivalent Conspirators*, 168; and Parker, "The Aspect of Slavery in America," in *Works*, XIV, 274–274.

27. Parker, "The Aspect of Slavery in America," 275; and Garrison and Garrison, *William Lloyd Garrison*, III, 473.

28. Parker, "The Aspect of Slavery in America," 275.

29. Charles Burleigh quoted in Jane Pease and William Pease, "Antislavery Ambivalence: Immediatism, Expediency, Race," *American Quarterly* 17 (Winter 1965), 685; Wendell Phillips, "Toussaint L'Ouverture," in *Speeches, Lectures, and Letters, First Series* (Boston: Lee and Shepherd, 1892), 469; and Phillips, "Crispus Attucks," in *Speeches, Lectures, and Letters, Second* Series (Boston: Lee and Shepherd, 1894), 71, 72.

30. Rael, "A Common Nature, A United Destiny," 184; Parker, "Buckle's History of Civilization," in *Works*, VIII, 412.

31. Parker to Henry Rogers, December 29, 1857, Parker Papers, MHS; Parker, "Buckles' History of Civilization," 412–413; Carlos Lopez Beltran, "In the Cradle of Heredity: French Physicians and *L'Heredite Naturelle* in the Early 19th Century," *Journal of the History of Biology* 37 (2004), 39–72.

32. Rossbach, *Ambivalent Conspirators*, 8–9, 182–194; Parker to Francis Jackson, November 24, 1859, in *Works*, XIV, 428; An argument similar to Rossbach's is made in Slotkin, *Fatal Environment*, 276.

33. Frederick Douglass, *Two Speeches of Frederick Douglass* (Rochester: C.P. Dewey Printer, 1857), 21, 22.

34. William Wells Brown, "Speech," in C. Peter Ripley ed., *The Black Abolitionist Papers* (Chapel Hill: University of North Carolina Press, 1991), 4: 341.

35. *Liberator*, April 11, 1856; George A. Levesque, "Boston's Black Brahmin: Dr. John S. Rock," *Civil War History* 26 (December 1980), 326–46.

36. *Liberator*, March 12, 1858.

37. Ibid.

38. Ibid.; and see Paul E. Teed, "Racial Nationalism and Its Challengers: Theodore Parker, John Rock and the Antislavery Movement," *Civil War History* 41 (June 1995), 142–160. Portions of this article are reprinted here by permission of the Kent State University Press.

39. *Liberator,* March 12, 1858; Parker to Francis Jackson, November 24, 1859, in *Works*, XIV, 429.

Chapter 18

1. Sewell, *Ballots for Freedom*, 292, 344–348.

2. Weiss, *Life and Correspondence*, II, 191; Parker to John Hale, December 19, 1856, Parker Papers, MHS.

3. James M. McPherson, *Ordeal By Fire: The Civil War and Reconstruction*, 2nd ed.

(New York: McGraw-Hill, 1992), 108; Parker to Charles Sumner, June 2, 1857, Charles Sumner Collection, HLHU. Sumner did return briefly in December.

4. David Donald, *Lincoln's Herndon* (New York: A.A. Knopf, 1948) is a fascinating study of Herndon, and contains a brief analysis of his relationship with Parker.

5. Parker to William Herndon, August 9, 1857, William Herndon to Parker, May 14, 1857, both in Parker Papers, MHS.

6. Parker to William Herndon, September 9, 1858, Parker Papers, MHS; Paul Angle ed., *The Complete Lincoln-Douglas Debates of 1858* (Chicago: University of Chicago Press, 1991), 114.

7. Parker to William Herndon, September 9, 1858, Parker Papers, MHS.

8. Herndon to Parker, August 23, 1858; Herndon to Parker, July 24, 1858, Parker Papers, MHS.

9. Parker to Herndon, September 9, 1858, Parker Papers, MHS.

10. Gary Wills, *Lincoln at Gettysburg: The Words That Remade America* (New York: Touchstone, 1992), 105–120. Wills argues that Lincoln borrowed his famous description of democracy as "government of the people, by the people, and for the people" from Parker's 1848 "Sermon of Merchants." In that sermon, he calls democracy a government "of all, by all, and for all." See Parker, "Sermon of Merchants," in *Works*, X, 41.

11. J.F. McCalmont to Parker, June 5, 1858, Parker Papers, MHS.

12. J.H. Turner to Parker, April 22, 1858; and Turner to Parker, September 19, 1858, both in Parker Papers, MHS.

13. Henry Wilson to Samuel Gridley Howe, May 14, 1858 in Howe, *Letters and Journals*, II, 356.

14. Franklin Sanborn, "The John Brown Campaign," in Parker, *Works*, XIV, 411–412; Parker to T.W. Higginson, May 10, 1858, Assorted Letters, Parker Collection, BPL.

15. Parker to John P. Hale, May 11, 1858; Parker to John P. Hale, May 12, 1858 both in Parker Papers, MHS.

16. Higginson memorandum in Villard, *John Brown*, 340; Oates, *To Purge This Land With Blood*, 250–251; and Rossbach, *Ambivalent Conspirators*, 172–176.

17. Shiela Rothman, *Living in the Shadow of Death: Tuberculosis and the Social Experience of Illness in American History* (New York: Basic Books, 1994), 16, 20–21; Parker to George Ripley, November 1, 1858 in Parker Parkers, MHS; and Parker to Salmon Chase, August 30, 1858 in Weiss, *Life and Correspondence*, II, 230–231; Frothingham, *Theodore Parker*, 497–498.

18. Chadwick, *Theodore Parker*, 350. Frothingham, *Theodore Parker*, 502; Parker to Francis Cobbe, December 14, 1858 in Weiss, *Life and Corrrespondence*, II, 254–255.

19. Weiss, *Life and Correspondence*, II, 256.

20. Parker to Francis Cobbe, December 14, 1858 in ibid., 255; and Rothman, *Living in the Shadow of Death*, 17.

21. Weiss, *Life and Correspondence*, II, 257, 262.

22. Rothman, *Living in the Shadow of Death*, 19, 31–33; Thomas Dormandy, *The White Death: A History of Tuberculosis* (New York: New York University Press, 2000), 105–116; Weiss, *Life and Correspondence*, II, 265.

23. Weiss, *Life and Correspondence*, II, 265; Parker, "Experience as a Minister," in *Works*, XIII, 288–289.

24. Julia Ward Howe, *Reminiscences*, 233.

Chapter 19

1. Parker to George Ripley, May 13, 1859; Parker to Joseph Lyman, October 14, 1859, both in Parker Papers, MHS.
2. Parker, "Of Immortal Life," in *Works*, III, 335, 344.
3. Parker, "Of Immortal Life," 346.
4. Rothman, *Living in the Shadow of Death*, 33–35, 68; Neville A.T. Hall, *Slave Society in the Danish West Indies: St. Thomas, St. John, and St. Croix* (Mona, Jamaica: University of the West Indies Press, 1992), 208.
5. Weiss, *Life and Correspondence*, II, 286–287; Parker to Wendell Phillips, May 14, 1859, Phillips Collection, HLHU
6. Julie Roy Jeffrey, "'No Occurrence in Human History is More Deserving of Commemoration Than This'": Abolitionist Celebrations of Freedom," in *Prophets of Protest*, 212; Parker journal entry, March 10, 1859, in Weiss, *Life and Correspondence*, II, 278; and Parker to Eliza Apthorp, March, 1859 in ibid., 285; A comparison between Parker's racial views and those of proslavery intellectual George Fitzhugh can be found in Richard Slotkin, *The Fatal Environment*, 230–235.
7. Weiss, *Life and Correspondence*, II, 278, 282; Parker to Joseph Lyman, April 23, 1859, Parker Papers, MHS.
8. Parker to Charles Ellis, April 22, 1859, Parker Papers, MHS; Parker, "Experience as a Minister," in *Works*, XIII, 401, 306, 308.
9. Ibid., 324, 325.
10. Ibid., 350.
11. Lydia Maria Child to Francis Jackson, November 4, 1859 in *Collected Correspondence of Lydia Maria Child* ed. Patricia G. Holland and Milton Meltzer. Millwood, N.Y.: Kraus Microfilm, 1980; William Lloyd Garrison to Lydia Parker, July 20, 1860, in *The Letters of William Lloyd Garrison*, IV, 677; Wendell Phillips, "Theodore Parker," in *Speeches, Lectures and Letters*, Second Series, 434.
12. Parker to Dr. Cabot, June 16, 1869 in Weiss, *Life and Correspondence*, II, 296; Parker to Francis Power Cobbe, June 11, 1859 in ibid., 292–293; Parker to Charles Sumner, June 2, 1859, Parker Papers, MHS.
13. Parker to Miss Mary Carpenter, June 23, 1859, Parker Papers, MHS.
14. For a brief account of the Franco-Austrian War, see A.J.P. Taylor, *The Struggle for Mastery in Europe, 1848–1918* (New York: Oxford University Press, 1980), 111–115; Parker to The Twenty–Eighth Congregational Society, June 25, 1859, in Weiss, *Life and Correspondence*, II, 301.
15. Parker to Dr. Cabot, June 16, 1859 in Weiss, *Life and Correspondence*, II, 296; Parker to Charles Sumner, October 11, 1859 in ibid, 369; On Dr. Louis, see Dormandy, *The White Death*, 110.
16. Parker to Caroline Thayer, July 8, 1859, Parker Papers, MHS; J.P. Lesly, "Obituary Notice of Edouard Desor," *Proceedings of the American Philosophical Society* 20 (May, 1882), 519–527.
17. Parker, "A Bumblebee's Thoughts," in *Works*, IV, 436.
18. Edward Desor quoted in Weiss, *Life and Correspondence*, II, 319; Parker to Caroline Thayer, August 16, 1859., Parker Papers, MHS; Chadwick, *Theodore Parker*, 363.
19. Parker to Charles Sumner, August 31, 1859; and Parker to Caroline Thayer, August 16, 1859, both in Parker Papers, MHS; Parker to John Manley, September 3, 1859, in Weiss, *Life and Correspondence*, II, 349.

20. Parker to Charles M. Ellis, September 22, 1859. MHS.

21. The resolution is printed in Moncure Daniel Conway, *Autobiography, Memoirs and Experiences of Moncure Daniel Conway*, 2 Vols. (Boston: Houghton, Mifflin and Co., 1904), II, 262; Parker to James Freeman Clarke, August 12, 1859 in Weiss, *Life and Correspondence*, II, 337.

22. Parker to Charles Sumner, October 11, 1859, Parker Papers, MHS; Lydia Parker to the Goddards, December 17, 1859 in Assorted Letters, Parker Collection, BP L; Frothingham, *Theodore Parker*, 320.

23. Lydia Parker to the Goddards, December 17, 1859 in Assorted Letters, Parker Collection, BPL; Parker to Matilda Goddard, November 11, 1859, Parker Papers, MHS.

24. Parker to Joseph Lyman, January 13, 1860 and Parker to Eliza Eddy, November 19, 1859, in Parker Papers, MHS.

25. Weiss, *Life and Correspondence*, II, 396.

26. Parker to Francis Jackson, November 24, 1859 in *Works*, XIV, 428, 431.

27. Ibid., 430, 431.

28. Lydia Parker to the Goddards, December 17, 1859 in Assorted Letters, Parker Collection, BPL; Parker to Joseph Lyman, January 13, 1860, Parker Papers, MHS.

29. Parker to Joseph Lyman, January 13, 1860 in ibid.

30. Parker to Mary Drew, March 17, 1860 and Parker to Joseph Lyman, April 4, 1860, both in Parker Papers, MHS.

31. Francis Power Cobbe, *The Life of Frances Power Cobbe, As Told By Herself* (London: Swann Sonnenschein and Co., 1904), 372; and Weiss, *Life and Correspondence*, Vol. II, 439.

32. Cobbe, *Life of Francis Power Cobbe*, II, 12; "Will and Testament of Theodore Parker," Miscellany File, Parker Papers, LOC.

Conclusion

1. Parker to George Ripley, February 28, 1860, Parker Papers, MHS; Higginson, *Contemporaries*, 46.

2. *Tributes to Theodore Parker, Comprising the Exercises at the Music Hall with the Proceedings of the New England Antislavery Convention at the Melodeon May 31, and the Resolutions of the Fraternity and the Twenty-Eighth Congregational Society* (Boston: Parker Fraternity, 1860), 32.

3. James Freeman Clarke, *Memorial and Biographical Sketches* (Boston: Houghton, Osgood and Company, 1878), 123, 125; The quote comes from Lincoln's speech at Peoria in 1854 and is reprinted in part in Davis and Wilson eds., *The Lincoln-Douglas Debates*, 18.

4. The Twenty-Eighth Congregational Society left the Music Hall in 1863 and relocated temporarily to its earlier home at the Melodeon. After several years in the much smaller Parker Fraternity space, the congregation raised money for the construction of the Parker Memorial Meeting House on Berkeley Street. In 1889, the congregation effectively disbanded, transferring its property to the Benevolent Fraternity of the Churches of Boston. See *Dedicatory Services of the Parker Memorial Meeting House by the Twenty-Eighth Congregational Society of Boston, Sunday, September 21 1873* (Boston: Cochrane and Samson: 1873), 14; and *The Unitarian: A Magazine of Liberal Theology*, IV (March 1889), 129.

5. *Tributes to Theodore Parker, Comprising the Exercises at the Music Hall with*

*the Proceedings of the New England Antislavery Convention at the Melodeon May 31,
and the Resolutions of the Fraternity and the Twenty-Eighth Congregational Society*
(Boston: Parker Fraternity, 1860), 16–17, 25.

6. *Liberator*, July 18, 1862.

7. Louisa May Alcott, *Hospital Sketches* (originally published in 1863, reprinted
Boston: Bedford St. Martins, 2004), 73, 109–110. Alcott secured the appointment at the
Hospital in part through the efforts of Hannah Stevenson who used her contacts in Wash-
ington to assist her young friend.

BIBLIOGRAPHY

MANUSCRIPT COLLECTIONS

American Antiquarian Society (AAS)
        Theodore Parker Papers (Scrapbook, 1855-56)
Andover-Harvard Theological Library (A-HTL)
        Theodore Parker Papers
Boston Public Library (BPL)
        Antislavery Manuscripts Collection
        Theodore Parker Collection
Connecticut State Library
        Records of the Connecticut Women's Suffrage Association
Houghton Library, Harvard University (HLHU)
        Autograph File
        Palfrey Family Papers
        Charles Sumner Papers
        Emerson Family Papers
        Ezra Stiles Gannett Papers
        Wendell Phillips Papers
Library of Congress (LOC)
        Theodore Parker Papers
Massachusetts Historical Society (MHS)
        William Ellery Channing Papers
        Theodore Parker Papers

NEWSPAPERS AND PERIODICALS

Boston Daily Advertiser
Boston Post
Boston Quarterly Review
Christian Examiner
Christian Register

NEWSPAPERS AND PERIODICALS (cont.)

Commonwealth (Boston)
The Dial
Evening Telegraph (Boston)
Frederick Douglass' Paper
Hampshire Gazette
The Liberator
Massachusetts Quarterly Review
National Anti-Slavery Standard
New York Evangelist
North American Review
Spirit of the Pilgrims
The Trumpet and Universalist Magazine
Unity
Waterbury American
Western Messenger

PUBLISHED PRIMARY SOURCES

Alcott, A. Bronson. *Conversations with Children on the Gospels*, 2 Vols. Boston: J. Munroe and Co., 1836–1837.

Alcott, Louisa May. *Work: A Story of Experience*. Penguin Books: New York, 1994.

Americanus, Junius. *A Review of "A Discourse Occasioned by the Death of Daniel Webster Preached at the Melodeon on Sunday, October 31, by Theodore Parker, Minister of the Twenty-Eighth Congregational Society of Boston."* Boston and Cambridge: James Munroe and Company, 1853.

Address of the Committee Appointed by a Public Meeting Held at Faneuil Hall, September 24, 1846, for the purpose of considering the recent case of kidnapping from our soil, and of taking measures to prevent the recurrence of similar outrages: with an appendix. Boston: White and Potter Printers, 1846.

Angle, Paul ed. *The Complete Lincoln-Douglas Debates of 1858*. Chicago: University of Chicago Press, 1991.

Bearse, Austin. *Reminiscences of Fugitive-Slave Law Days in Boston*. Boston: W. Richardson, 1880.

The Boston Slave Riot and the Trial of Anthony Burns. Boston: William V. Spence, 1854.

Bowditch, Vincent Y. *The Life and Correspondence of Henry Ingersoll Bowditch*. 2 Vols. New York: Houghton, Mifflin and Co., 1902.

Brownson, Orestes. *The Laboring Classes (1840) With Brownson's Defense of the Article on the Laboring Classes*. Facsimile reprint. Delmar, NY: Scholar's Facisms. & Reprints, 1978.

———. *New Views of Christianity, Society, and the Church*. Boston: James Munroe, 1836.

Channing, William Ellery. *The Works of William Ellery Channing, D.D.* 6 vols. Boston: American Unitarian Association, 1867.

Cheney, Ednah Dow. *Reminiscences of Ednah Dow Cheney*. Boston: Lee and Shepherd, 1902.

Cobbe, Francis Power. *The Life of Frances Power Cobbe, As Told By Herself*. London: Swann Sonnenschein and Co., 1904.

Conway, Moncure Daniel. *Autobiography, Memoirs and Experiences of Moncure Daniel Conway.* 2 vols. Boston: Houghton, Mifflin and Co., 1904.

Craft, William. *Running a Thousand Miles for Freedom; or the Escape of William and Ellen Craft from Slavery.* London: William Tweedy, 1860.

Crawford, Mary Caroline. *Romantic Days in Old Boston: The Story of the City and Of Its People During the Nineteenth Century* Boston: Little, Brown and Company, 1910.

Curtis, Benjamin R. Jr., ed.. *Memoirs of Benjamin Robbins Curtis,* 2 vols. Reprinted. New York: DaCapo Press, 1970.

Dall, Caroline Healey, *Daughter of Boston, The Extraordinary Diary of a Nineteenth Century Woman: Caroline Healey Dall.* Edited by Helen Deese. Boston: Beacon Press, 2007.

Dana, Richard H. *The Journal of Richard Henry Dana Jr.* Edited by Robert Lucid. Cambridge: Belknap Press, 1968.

Early Massachusetts Records, 1692–1840. Microform collection. Boston: Early Massachusetts Records, 1971.

Ellis, Charles Mayo. *An Essay on Transcendentalism* (1842), reprinted Westport, CT: Greenwood Press, 1954.

Emerson, Ralph Waldo. *The Journals and Miscellaneous Notebooks of Ralph Waldo Emerson.* 16 vols. Edited by Ralph H. Orth et. al. Cambridge, Mass.: Harvard University Press, 1960-82.

Everett, Edward. *An Address Delivered at Lexington On the 19th (20th) of April, 1835.* Worcester: Tyler and Seagrave, 1835.

Fifteenth annual report, presented to the Massachusetts Anti-Slavery Society by its Board of Managers, January 27, 1847. Boston: Massachusetts Antislavery Society, 1847.

Fuller, Margaret. *The Letters of Margaret Fuller.* 5 Volumes. Edited by Richard N. Hudspeth. Ithaca: Cornell University Press, 1983-1988.

Garrison, William Lloyd. *The Letters of William Lloyd Garrison.* 6 vols. Edited by William Merrill et. al. Cambridge, MA: Harvard University Press, 1971-1981.

Grimke, Charlotte Forten. *The Journals of Charlotte Forten Grimke.* Edited by Brenda Stevenson. New York: Oxford University Press, 1988.

Groth, William C., and Groth, Bobbie. *What One Man Can Do For Freedom: The Documented Life of Unitarian Minister Rev. Ephraim Nute Jr.* South Milwaukee, Wisconsin: self published, 2007.

Higginson, Thomas W. *Contemporaries* Cambridge: Riverside Press, 1899.

Howe, Julia Ward. *Reminiscences, 1819–1910.* Boston: Houghton, Mifflin, & Co., 1899.

Howe, Samuel Gridley. *The Letters and Journals of Samuel Gridley Howe.* Boston: Dana Estes and Company, 1909.

Lothrop, Samuel K. *Proceedings of an Ecclesiastical Council in the Case of the Proprietors of the Hollis Street Meetinghouse and the Reverend John Pierpont, Their Pastor.* Boston: W.W. Clapp and Son, 1841.

Mackintosh, Charles G. *Some Recollections of the Pastors and People of the Second Church of Old Roxbury.* Salem: Newcomb and Gauss, 1901.

May, Samuel. *Recollections of the Antislavery Conflict.* Boston: Fields, Osgood and Co., 1869.

The Nineteenth Annual Report Presented to the Massachusetts Anti-Slavery Society, reprinted Westport, CT: 1970.

Palfrey, John Gorham. *Papers on the Slave Power, First Published in the "Boston Whig".* Boston: Merrill, Cobb & Co., 1846.

Parker, Theodore. *Additional Speeches, Addresses, and Occasional Sermons.* 2 vols. Boston: Little, Brown and Co., 1855.

———. *A Critical and Historical Introduction to the Canonical Scriptures of the Old Testament From the German of Wilhelm Martin Leberecht DeWette: Translated and Enlarged*, 2 vols. Boston: Charles C. Little and James Brown, 1843.

———. *The Critical and Miscellaneous Writings of Theodore Parker*. Boston: James Munroe and Company, 1843.

———. *A Discourse Occasioned by the Death of Daniel Webster, Preached at the Melodeon on Sunday, October 31, 1852.* Boston: Benjamin Mussey & Co., 1852.

———. *Letter to the People of the United States Touching the Matter of Slavery*. Boston: James Munroe and Company, 1848.

———. *Speeches, Addresses and Occasional Sermons*, 3 Vols. Boston: Horace Fuller, 1855.

———. *Ten Sermons of Religion*. Boston: Crosby, Nichols and Company, 1853.

———. *The Trial of Theodore Parker for the "Misdemeanor" of a Speech in Faneuil Hall Against Kidnapping*. Boston: n.p, 1855.

———. *The Works of Theodore Parker*, 15 Vols. Centenary Edition. Boston: American Unitarian Association, 1907-1913.

———. *West Roxbury Sermons by Theodore Parker, 1837-1848*. Boston: American Unitarian Association, 1902.

Parker, Theodore. *Genealogy and Biographical Notes of John Parker of Lexington and His Descendents*. Worcester, Mass.: Charles Hamilton, 1893.

Phillips, Wendell. *Speeches, Lectures, and Letters, First Series*. Boston: Lee and Shepherd, 1892.

———. *Speeches, Lectures, and Letters, Second* Series. Boston: Lee and Shepherd, 1894.

Phinney, Elias. *History of the Battle of Lexington*. Boston: Phelps and Farnham, 1825.

Proceedings of the Anti-Sabbath Convention, Held in the Melodeon, March 23rd and 24th. Boston: Anti-Sabbath Convention, 1848.

Richardson, James D. comp. *A Compilation of the Messages and Papers of the Presidents*, Vol. VI. New York, 1897.

Ripley, C. Peter, ed., *The Black Abolitionist Papers* (Chapel Hill: University of North Carolina Press, 1991.

Ronda, Bruce A., ed. *Letters of Elizabeth Peabody*: American Renaissance Woman. Middletown, CT: Weslyan University Press, 1984.

Rosell Garth M., and Dupuis, Richard A.G., eds, *The Original Memoirs of Charles G. Finney*. Grand Rapids, MI: Zondervan, 2002.

Seventeenth Annual Report, Presented to the Massachusetts Anti-Slavery Society. Boston: Massachusetts Antislavery Society, 1849.

The South-Boston Unitarian Ordination. Boston: Saxton and Pierce, 1841.

Stuart, Moses. *Conscience and the Constitution*. Boston: Crocker and Brewster, 1850.

Sumner, Charles. *The Selected Letters of Charles Summer*. 2 vols. Edited by Beverly Wilson Palmer. Boston: Northeastern University Press, 1990.

———. *The Works of Charles Sumner*, 15 Vols. Boston: Lee and Shepard, 1870–83.

Ware, Henry Jr. *On the Formation of a Christian Character* (Boston: Carter, Hendee and Babcock, 1831.

Webster, Daniel. *The Writings and Speeches of Daniel Webster*. 18 Volumes. Boston: Little, Brown Co., 1903.

Weiss, John. *Discourse Occasioned by the Death of Convers Francis D.D., Delivered before the First Congregational Society, Watertown, April 19, 1863*. Cambridge: Privately Printed, 1863.

SECONDARY SOURCES

Aaron, Daniel. *Men of Good Hope: A Story of American Progressives.* New York: Oxford University Press, 1951.
———, ed. *Studies in Biography.* Cambridge, MA: Harvard University Press, 1978.
Anbinder, Tyler. *Nativism and Slavery: The Northern Know Nothings and the Politics of the 1850s.* New York: Oxford University Press, 1994,
Baker, Carlos. *Emerson Among the Eccentrics: A Group Portrait.* New York: Viking, 1996.
Barker, Gordon S. *The Imperfect Revolution: Anthony Burns and the Landscape of Race in Antebellum America.* Kent, OH: Kent State University Press, 2010.
Bartlett, Irving. *Daniel Webster.* New York: Norton, 1978.
Bauer, Kinley J. *Cotton versus Conscience: Massachusetts Whig Politics and Southwestern Expansion, 1843-1848.* Lexington, KY: University of Kentucky Press, 1967.
Beltran, Carlos Lopez. "In the Cradle of Heredity: French Physicians and *L'Heredite Naturelle* in the Early 19th Century." *Journal of the History of Biology* 37 (2004), 39-72
Bordevich, Fergus. *Bound for Canaan: The Epic Story of the Underground Railroad, America's First Civil Rights Movement.* New York: Amistad, 2006.
Borg, Marcus J.,and Crossan, John Dominic. *The First Paul: Reclaiming the Radical Visionary Behind the Church's Conservative Icon.* New York: HarperOne, 2009.
Brooks, Van Wyck. *Flowering of New England,* 1815-1865. London: J.M. Dent and Sons, 1952.
Brown, Jerry Wayne. *The Rise of Biblical Criticism in America, 1800–1870: The New England Scholars.* Middletown, CT: Wesleyan University Press, 1969.
Brown, Richard. *Knowledge Is Power: The Diffusion of Information in Early America.* New York: Oxford University Press, 1989.
Buell, Lawrence. *Literary Transcendentalism: Style and Vision in the American Renaissance.* Ithaca: Cornell University Press, 1973.
———. *New England Literary Culture: From Revolution Through Renaissance* (Cambridge: Cambridge University Press, 1986)
Cameron, Kenneth. *Transcendental Epilogue.* Hartford: Transcendental Books, 1982.
———. *Transcendental Reading Patterns: New Areas for Fresh Explorations.* Hartford: Transcendental Books, 1970.
Campbell, Stanley. *The Slave Catchers: Enforcement of the Fugitive Slave Act, 1850-1860.* Chapel Hill: University of North Carolina Press, 1970.
Capper, Charles. *Margaret Fuller, An American Romantic Life: The Private Years* New York: Oxford University Press. 1992.
Capper, Charles, and Wright, Conrad Edick, eds. *Transient and Permanent: The Transcendentalist Movement and Its Contexts.* Boston: Massachusetts Historical Society, 1999.
Cayton, Mary K. *Emerson's Emergence: Self and Society in the Transformation of New England, 1800-1845.* Chapel Hill: University of North Carolina Press, 1992
Cazden, Elizabeth. *Antoinette Brown Blackwell: A Biography.* New York: Feminist Press, 1993.
Chadwick, John White. *Theodore Parker: Preacher and Reformer.* Cambridge: The Riverside Press, 1900.
Chai, Leon. *Romantic Foundations of the American Renaissance.* Ithaca: Cornell University Press, 1987.

278   Bibliography

Cmiel, Kenneth. *Democratic Eloquence: The Fight Over Popular Speech in Nineteenth-Century America*. Berkeley: University of California Press, 1990.

Cohen, Patricia Cline. *A Calculating People: The Spread of Numeracy in Early America*. New York: Routledge, 1999.

Commager, Henry Steele. "The Dilemma of Theodore Parker," *New England Quarterly* 6 (June 1933): 257-277.

———. *Theodore Parker: Yankee Crusader* New York: Little Brown and Company, 1936.

Collison, Gary. "A Calendar of the Letters of Theodore Parker." *Studies in the American Renaissance*. (1979): 317-408.

———. "A Calendar of the Letters of Theodore Parker." *Studies in the American Renaissance*. (1980): 159-229.

———. *Shadrach Minkins: From Fugitive Slave to Citizen*. Cambridge: Harvard University Press, 1998.

Cook, George Willis. *John Sullivan Dwight: A Biography* Boston: Small, Maynard and Company, 1898.

Cott, Nancy F. *The Bonds of Womanhood: "Woman's Sphere" in New England, 1780-1835*. New Haven: Yale University Press, 1977.

Cox, Harvey. *The Future of Faith*. New York: HarperOne, 2009.

Crawford, Mary. *Famous Families of Massachusetts*. Boston: Little, Brown, and Co., 1930.

Curry, Richard O., ed. *The Abolitionists*, Hinsdale, IL: Dryden Press, 1973.

Dalzell, Robert F. *Enterprising Elite: The Boston Associates and the World They Made*. Cambridge: Harvard University Press, 1987.

Davis, David Brion ed. *Ante-Bellum Reform*. New York: Harper and Row, 1967.

———. "The Emergence of Immediatism in British and American Anti-Slavery Thought." *Mississippi Valley Historical Review* 49 (September 1962): 209-230.

Deese, Helen. "Tending the 'Sacred Fires': Theodore Parker and Caroline Healey Dall," *Proceedings of the Unitarian Universalist Historical Society* 23 (1995): 22-38.

Delbanco, Andrew. *William Ellery Channing: An Essay on the Liberal Spirit in America*. Cambridge, MA: Harvard University Press, 1981.

Dirks, John E. *The Critical Theology of Theodore Parker*. New York: Columbia University Press, 1948.

Donald, David. *Charles Sumner and the Coming of the Civil War*. New York: Knopf, 1967.

———. *Lincoln's Herndon*. New York: A.A. Knopf, 1948.

Dormandy, Thomas. *The White Death: A History of Tuberculosis*. New York: New York University Press, 2000.

Dorrien, Gary. *The Making of American Liberal Theology: Imagining Progressive Religion, 1805-1900*. Louisville, KY: Westminster John Knox Press, 2001.

Dorsey, Bruce. *Reforming Men and Women: Gender in the Antebellum City*. Ithaca: Cornell University Press, 2002.

Duberman, Martin. *Charles Francis Adams, 1807-1886*. Boston: Houghton Mifflin Co., 1961.

Earle, Jonathan. *Jacksonian Antislavery and the Politics of Free Soil, 1824-1854*. Chapel Hill: University of North Carolina Press, 2004.

Edelstein, Tilden. *Strange Enthusiasm: A Life of Thomas Wentworth Higginson*. New York: Atheneum, 1970.

Ehrman, Bart. *Misquoting Jesus: The Story Behind Who Changed the Bible and Why*. New York: HarperOne, 2007.

Etcheson, Nicole. *Bleeding Kansas: Contested Liberty in the Civil War Era.* Lawrence, KS: University Press of Kansas, 2004),

Fanuzzi, Robert. *Abolition's Public Sphere.* Minneapolis: University of Minnesota Press, 2003.

Fellman, Michael. "Theodore Parker and the Abolitionist Role in the 1850s." *Journal of American History,* 61 (December. 1974): 666-84.

Fields, Peter S. *The Crisis of the Standing Order: Clerical Intellectuals and Cultural Authority in Massachusetts, 1780-1833.* Amherst, MA: University of Massachusetts Press, 1998.

Fischer, David Hackett. *Paul Revere's Ride.* New York: Oxford University Press, 1995.

Foner, Eric. *Free Soil, Free Labor, Free Men: The Ideology of the Republican Party Before the Civil War.* New York: Oxford University Press, 1970.

Foote, Lorien. *Seeking the One Great Remedy: Francis George Shaw and Nineteenth Century Reform.* Athens, OH: Ohio State University Press, 2003.

Formisano, Ronald P. *The Transformation of Political Culture: Massachusetts Parties, 1790s-1840s.* New York: Oxford University Press, 1983.

Fredrickson, George. *The Black Image in the White Mind: The Debate on Afro-American Character and Destiny, 1817-1914.* Middletown, CT: Weslyan University Press, 1987.

Friedman, Lawrence. *Gregarious Saints: Self and Community in Antebellum American Abolitionism, 1830-1870.* New York: Cambridge University Press, 1982.

Frothingham, Octavius B. *Theodore Parker: A Biography.* Boston: James R. Osgood and Company, 1874.

Gannet, William C. *Ezra Stiles Gannett.* Boston: Roberts Brothers, 1875.

Garrison, Wendell Phillips and Garrison, Francis Jackson. *William Lloyd Garrison, 1805-1879.* 4 vols. New York: Houghton Mifflin, 1889.

Garvey, T. Gregory. *Creating the Culture of Reform in Antebellum America.* Athens, GA: University of Georgia Press, 2006.

Gatell, Frank Otto. *John Gorham Palfrey and the New England Conscience.* Cambridge: Harvard University Press, 1963.

Gienapp, William. "The Crime Against Sumner: The Caning of Charles Sumner and the Rise of the Republican Party." *Civil War History* 25 (September 1979): 218–245.

———. *The Origins of the Republican Party, 1852–1856* (New York: Oxford University Press, 1987.

Goodheart, Lawrence B. *Abolitionist, Actuary, Atheist: Elizur Wright and the Reform Impulse.* Kent, OH: Kent State University Press, 1990.

Goodheart, Lawrence B., and Curry, Richard O. "The Trinitarian Indictment of Unitarianism: The Letters of Elizur Wright Jr., 1826–27." *Journal of the Early Republic* 3 (Fall 1983): 281–296.

Greven, Philip. *The Protestant Temperament: Patterns of Child-Rearing, Religious Experience, and the Self in Early America* New York: Knopf, 1977.

Grodzins. Dean. *American Heretic: Theodore Parker and Transcendentalism.* Chapel Hill: UNC Press, 2002.

———. "'Slave Law' versus 'Lynch Law' in Boston: Benjamin Robbins Curtis, Theodore Parker and the Fugitive Slave Crisis, 1850-1855. *Massachusetts Historical Review* 12 (2010): 1-33.

———. "Theodore Parker's 'Conference with the Boston Association," January 23, 1843." *Proceedings of the Unitarian Universalist Historical Society* 23 (1995), 72-73.

Grodzins, Dean, and Myerson, Joel. "The Preaching Record of Theodore Parker." *Studies in the American Renaissance* (1994): 55-122.

Gross, Robert. *The Minutemen and Their World.* New York: Hill and Wang, 1976.

Grusin, Richard. *Transcendentalist Hermeneutics: Institutional Authority and the Higher Criticism of the Bible.* Durham: Duke University Press, 1991.

Gura, Phillip. *American Transcendentalism: A History.* New York: Hill and Wang, 2007.

———. *The Wisdom of Words: Language, Theology and Literature in the New England Renaissance.* Middletown, CT: Wesleyan University Press, 1981.

Hall, Neville A.T. *Slave Society in the Danish West Indies: St. Thomas, St. John, and St. Croix.* Mona, Jamaica: University of the West Indies Press, 1992.

Oscar Handlin, *Boston's Immigrants, 1790–1880: A Study in Acculturation* Cambridge: Harvard University Press, 1941.

Hart, D.G. "Divided Between Heart and Mind: The Critical Period for Protestant Thought in America." *Journal of Ecclesiastical History* 38 (April 1987): 254–270.

Harrold, Stanley. *The Rise of Aggressive Abolitionism: Addresses to the Slaves.* Lexington: University Press of Kentucky, 2004.

Reginald Horsman, *Race and Manifest Destiny: The Origins of American Racial Anglo-Saxonism.* Cambridge, MA: Harvard University Press, 1981.

Howard, Thomas. *Religion and the Rise of Historicism: W.M.L. DeWette, Jacob Burckhardt and the Theological Origins of Nineteenth Century Historical Consciousness.* Cambridge: Cambridge University Press, 2006.

Howe, Daniel Walker. *The Unitarian Conscience: Harvard Moral Philosophy, 1805-1861.* Middletown, CT: Weslyan University Press, 1988.

Hudson, Charles. *History of the Town of Lexington.* Boston: Wiggin and Lunt, 1868.

Hurth, Elisabeth. *Between Faith and Unbelief: American Transcendentalists and the Challenge of Atheism.* Boston: Brill, 2007.

Hutchison, William. *The Transcendentalist Ministers: Church Reform in the New England Renaissance.* Boston: Beacon Press, 1959.

Jacobs, Donald ed. *Courage and Conscience: Black and White Abolitionists in Boston.* Bloomington, IN: 1993.

Kammen, Michael. *A Season of Youth: The American Revolution and the Historical Imagination.* New York: Knopf, 1978.

Kantrowitz, Stephen. "A Place for 'Colored Patriots': Crispus Attucks Among the Abolitionists," *Massachusetts Historical Review* 11 (2009): 96-117.

Kerber, Linda. "Separate Spheres, Female World's, Woman's Place: The Rhetoric of Women's History," *Journal of American History* 75 (June 1988): 9–39.

Knights, Peter R. *The Plain People of Boston, 1830–1860: A Study of City Growth.* New York: Oxford University Press, 1971.

Kraditor, Aileen S. *Means and Ends in American Abolitionism.* New York: Pantheon, 1969.

Lane, Roger. *Policing the City: Boston, 1822-1885.* Boston: Harvard University Press, 1967.

Laurie, Bruce. *Beyond Garrison: Antislavery and Social Reform.* New York: Cambridge University Press, 2005.

Levesque, George A. "Boston's Black Brahmin: Dr. John S. Rock." *Civil War History* 26 (December 1980): 326-46.

Levy, Leonard. *The Law of the Commonwealth and Chief Justice Shaw.* New York: Oxford University Press, 1986.

———. "Sims' Case: The Fugitive Slave Law in Boston in 1851." *Journal of Negro History* 35 (January 1950): 39-74

Linden-Ward, Blanche. *Silent City on a Hill: Landscapes of Memory and Boston's Mount Auburn Cemetery.* Columbus, OH: Ohio State University Press, 1989.

Long, Katherine. *The Revival of 1857: Interpreting and American Religious Awakening.* New York: Oxford University Press, 1998.

Lynd, Staughton, *The Intellectual Origins of American Radicalism,* 2nd edition. New York: Cambridge University Press, 2009.

Maginnes, David. "The Case of the Court House Rioters in the Rendition of Fugitive Slave Anthony Burns, 1854," *Journal of Negro History* LVI (January 1971): 17–31

Matthews, J.V. "Whig History: The New England Whigs and a Usable Past," *New England Quarterly* 51 (June 1978): 193-208

May, Henry. *The Enlightenment in America.* New York: Oxford University Press, 1976.

Mayer, Henry. *All on Fire: William Lloyd Garrison and the Abolition of Slavery.* New York: W.W. Norton and Co,, 2008.

McAleer, John. *Ralph Waldo Emerson: Days of Encounter.* Boston: Little, Brown, 1984.

McCarthy, Timothy P. and Stauffer, John eds. *Prophets of Protest: Reconsidering the History of American Abolitionism.* New York: The New Press, 2006.

McGlone. Robert E. *John Brown's War Against Slavery.* Cambridge: Cambridge University Press, 2009.

McInerney, Daniel. *The Fortunate Heirs of Freedom: Abolitionism and Republican Thought.* Lincoln, Nebraska: University of Nebraska Press, 1994.

McKivigan, John R., and Harrold, Stanley eds. *Antislavery Violence: Sectional, Racial and Cultural Conflict in Antebellum America.* Knoxville: University of Tennessee Press, 1999.

McKivigan, John R., and Snay, Mitchell eds. *Religion and the Antebellum Debate Over Slavery.* Athens, Ga.: University of Georgia Press, 1998.

McLaren, John, and Coward, Harold, eds. *Religious Conscience, the State and the Law: Historical Contexts and Contemporary Significance.* Albany, NY: SUNY Press, 1999.

Menand, Louis. *The Metaphysical Club: A Story of Idea in America* (New York: Farrar, Strauss and Giroux, 2002)

Meyer, Daniel H. *The Instructed Conscience: The Shaping of the American National Ethic.* Philadelphia: University of Pennsylvania Press, 1972.

Miller, Perry. "Theodore Parker: Apostasy within Liberalism." *The Harvard Theological Review* 54 (October 1961): 275-295.

———, ed. *The Transcendentalists: An Anthology* Cambridge: Harvard University Press, 1950.

Miller, William Lee. *Arguing About Slavery: John Quincy Adams and the Great Battle in the United States Congress.* New York: Vintage, 1996.

Myerson, Joel. "A Calendar of Transcendental Club Meetings," *American Literature* 44 (May 1972): 197-207.

———. "Convers Francis and Emerson," *American Literature* 50 (March 1978): 17-36.

———, ed. *Transcendentalism: A Reader.* New York: Oxford University Press, 2000.

Newmyer, R. Kent. *Supreme Court Justice Joseph Story: Statesman of the Old Republic.* Chapel Hill: University of North Carolina Press, 1985.

Nicolson, Adam. *God's Secretaries: The Making of the King James Bible.* New York: Harper Perennial, 2005.

Oates, Stephen. *To Purge This Land With Blood: A Biography of John Brown.* 2nd edition. Amherst, MA: University of Massachusetts Press, 1984.

O'Connor, Thomas. *The Athens of America: Boston, 1825-1845.* Boston: University of Massachusetts Press, 2006.

Parrington, Vernon L. *Main Currents in American Thought, Volume II: The Romantic Revolution in America, 1800-1860*. New York: Harcourt, 1927.

Pease, Jane H., and Pease, William H. *The Fugitive Slave Law and Anthony Burns: A Problem in Law Enforcement*. Philadelphia: Lippincott, 1975.

———. "Antislavery Ambivalence: Immediatism, Expediency, Race." *American Quarterly* 17 (December 1965): 682-695.

Perry, Lewis. *Radical Abolitionism: Anarchy and the Government of God in Antislavery Thought*. Ithaca: Carnell University Press, 1973.

Price, George R., and Stewart, James B. "The Roberts Case, the Easton Family and the Dynamics of the Abolitionist Movement in Massachusetts, 1776-1870." *Massachusetts Historical Review* 4 (2002): 89-115.

Proceedings of the Lexington Historical Society. 4 Vols. Lexington, MA: The Society, 1886-1910.

Reynolds, David. *John Brown: Abolitionist*. New York: Knopf, 2005.

Richards, Len. *The Slave Power: The Free North and Southern Domination, 1780-1860*. Baton Rouge: Louisiana State University Press, 2000.

Robert D. Richardson, *Emerson: The Mind on Fire*. Berkeley: University of California Press, 1995.

Ronda, Bruce A. *Elizabeth Palmer Peabody: A Reformer on Her Own Terms*. Cambridge, MA: Harvard University Press, 1984.

Rose, Anne C. *Transcendentalism as a Social Movement, 1839-1850*. New Haven, CT: Yale University Press, 1981.

Rossbach, Jeffrey. *Ambivalent Conspirators: John Brown, the Secret Six and a Theory of Slave Violence*. Philadelphia: University of Pennsylvania Press, 1982.

Russo, Peggy A., and Finkelman, Paul, eds. *Terrible Swift Sword: The Legacy of John Brown*. Athens, OH: Ohio University Press, 1995.

Rothman, Shiela. *Living in the Shadow of Death: Tuberculosis and the Social Experience of Illness in American History*. New York: Basic Books, 1994.

Sanborn, Franklin. *The Life and Letters of John Brown, Liberator of Kansas and Martyr of Virginia*. Boston: Roberts Brothers, 1885.

Schulman, Frank. *James Martineau: 'This Conscience Intoxicated Unitarian'*. Chicago: Meadville Lombard Press, 2002.

Scott, Donald M. *From Office to Profession: The New England Ministry, 1750–1850*. Philadelphia: University of Pennsylvania Press, 1978.

———. "The Popular Lecture and the Creation of a Public in Mid-Nineteenth Century America," *Journal of American History* 66 (March 1980): 791-809.

Sewell, Richard. *Ballots For Freedom: Anti-Slavery Politics in the United States, 1837–1860*. New York: Oxford University Press, 1976.

Sheidley, Harlow. *Sectional Nationalism: Massachusetts Conservative Leaders and the Transformation of America, 1815-1836*. Boston: Northeastern University Press, 1998.

Slaughter, Thomas P. *Bloody Dawn: The Christiana Riot and Racial Violence in the Antebellum North*. New York: Oxford University Press, 1991.

Slotkin, Richard. *The Fatal Environment: The Myth of the Frontier in the Age of Industrialization*. New York: Antheneum, 1985.

Stange, Douglas C. *Patterns of Antislavery Among American Unitarians, 1831–1860*. Rutherford, NJ: Fairleigh Dickinson University Press, 1977.

Stanton, William. *The Leopard's Spots: Scientific Attitudes Toward Race in America, 1815-1859*. Chicago: University of Chicago Press, 1960.

Stauffer, John. *The Black Hearts of Men: Radical Abolitionists and the Transformation of*

Race. Cambridge, MA: Harvard University Press, 2002.

Stevens, Charles Emery. *Anthony Burns: A History*. Boston: John P. Jewett and Company, 1856.

Stewart, James B. *Holy Warriors: The Abolitionists and American Slavery*. New York: Hill and Wang, 1976.

———. *Wendell Phillips: Liberty's Hero* (Baton Rouge: LSU Press, 1986).

Teed, Paul E. "A Brave Man's Child: Theodore Parker and the Memory of the American Revolution." *Historical Journal of Massachusetts* 29 (Summer 2001), 170-191.

———. "The Politics of Sectional Memory: Theodore Parker and the *Massachusetts Quarterly Review*, 1847-1850." *Journal of the Early Republic* 21 (Summer 2001): 301-329.

———. "Racial Nationalism and Its Challengers: Theodore Parker, John Rock and the Antislavery Movement." *Civil War History* 41 (June 1995): 142-160.

Tickle, Phyllis. *The Great Emergence: How Christianity is Changing and Why*. Grand Rapids, MI: Baker Books, 2008.

Travers, Len. *Celebrating the Fourth: Independence and the Rites of Nationalism in the Early Republic*. Amherst, MA: University of Massachusetts Press, 1997.

Varon, Elizabeth R. *Disunion: The Coming of the Civil War, 1789-1859*. Chapel Hill: University of North Carolina Press, 2008.

Villard, Oswald Garrison. *John Brown, 1800-1859*. Boston: Houghton Mifflin, 1911.

Von Franck, Albert J. "John Brown, James Redpath, and the Idea of Revolution," *Civil War History* 52 (June 2006), 142-160.

———. *Trials of Anthony Burns: Freedom and Slavery in Emerson's Boston*. Cambridge, MA: Harvard University Press, 1998.

Wallis, Jim. *God's Politics: Why the Right Gets It Wrong and the Left Doesn't Get It*. New York: Harper Collins, 2005.

Walters, Ronald. *The Antislavery Appeal: American Abolitionism After 1830*. New York: W.W. Norton, 1984

Wiecek. William. *The Sources of Antislavery Constitutionalism in America, 1760-1848*. Ithaca: Cornell University Press, 1977.

Weiss, John. *The Life and Correspondence of Theodore Parker*, 2 Vols. New York: D. Appleton and Company, 1864.

Williams, George H., ed. *The Harvard Divinity School: Its Place in Harvard University and in American Culture*. Boston: Beacon Press, 1954.

Wills, Gary. *Lincoln at Gettysburg: The Words That Remade America*. New York: Touchstone, 1992.

Wilson, Douglas. *Honor's Voice: The Transformation of Abraham Lincoln*. New York: Vintage, 1998.

Wright, Conrad. *The Beginnings of Unitarianism in America*. Boston: Beacon Press, 1966.

Wright, Conrad Edick, ed. *American Unitarianism, 1805–1865*. Boston: Northeastern University Press, 1989.

Wyman, Mary Alice. *Two American Pioneers: Seba Smith and Elizabeth Oakes Smith*. New York: Columbia University Press, 1926.

Yacavone, Donald. *Samuel Joseph May and the Dilemmas of the Liberal Persuasion*. Philadelphia: Temple University Press, 1991.

Young, Alfred F. *The Shoemaker and the Tea Party: Memory and the American Revolution* Boston: Beacon Press, 1999.

DISSERTATIONS AND UNPUBLISHED WORK

Collison, Gary. "A Critical Edition of the Correspondence of Theodore Parker and Converse Francis, 1836-1859." Ph.D. dissertation, Pennsylvania State University, 1979.

Johnston, Carol. "The Journals of Theodore Parker: July-December 1840," Ph.D. dissertation, University of South Carolina, 1980.

McDaniel, Caleb. "What Counts as Radical Abolitionism? A Reconsideration of Recent Scholarship," unpublished paper, presented at the 2009 annual meeting of the Organization of American Historians.

Teed, Paul E. `A Very Excellent Fanatic, a Very Good Infidel and a First-Rate Traitor': Theodore Parker and the Search for Perfection in Antebellum America." Ph.D. dissertation, University of Connecticut, 1994.

INDEX

Aaron, Daniel, xi
Adams, Charles Francis, 102, 162
Adams, George, 96
Adams, Henry, 19
Adams, John Quincy, 106
    Congressional gag rule, 27
    Parker's Eulogy for, 113-115
Adams, Nehemiah, 203
Agassiz, Louis, 154, 229
Alcott, Amos Bronson, iv, 25, 35, 98, 131
Alcott, Louisa May, 148, 240
American Party, 189-192
American Revolution,
    Abolitionism and, 112
    African Americans and, xvii, 126,
    132, 209, 213
    J.Q. Adams as link, 103
    John Brown and, 201
    Memory of, xvi, xvii, 1, 103, 106,
    109, 122, 185, 241
    Parker's commitment to, xvi
    Race, Violence and, 152-160, 236-
237
Appleton, William, Boston   merchant,
122
Apthorp, Robert, 131
Attucks, Crispus, xvi, 132, 146, 157, 212,
235

Bacon, James, 142-143, 152
Bacon, John B., 140
Baker versus *Fales*, 10

Bancroft, George, 100
Banks, Nathanial (Massachusetts
    Congressman), 189
Banks, W. P., 189
Batchelder, James, 177-182
Battle of Lexington, 2, 103, 139, 153,
184, 185, 235
Beecher, Rev. Lyman, 11
Bellows, Henry, 41, 45,232
Bigelow, Samuel, 229
Birney, James, 109, 114
Blodgett, Levi. *See* Theodore Parker
Blumenbach, Johann Friedrich , 153
"Border Ruffians," 187, 190, 200
Boston Daily Advertiser, 122
Boston Daily Whig, 102
Bowditch, Dr. Henry I., 144, 174,
219,221
Bowen, Francis, 24
Briggs, George,
    Whig governor of Massachusetts,
    104
Bright, John, 228
Brooks, Preston, 192,229
Brown, Antoinette , 91-92
Brown, John, xi, xvii, 96, 172, 198, 200,
207, 109, 211, 214, 217, 222, 225, 233-
234, 240
Brown, John *(continued)*
    Forbes lacks intelligence to
    compromise the plan, 220

Like Parker believed that fidelity to conscience did not preclude taking up of arms, 201
Osawatomie, 201
Similar notions to Parker on radical self trust and authority of conscience, 201
Virginia Plan to arm slaves with weapons from the Harper Ferry arsenal, 206
Brown, William Wells, 210
Browning, Robert and Elizabeth, 232
Brownson, Orestes, 25, 37, 55, 64,79, 144, 172
Buchanan, James (US President), 214
Buckle, Henry Thomas, 208, 226-227
Buren, Martin van, 115
Burleigh, Charles, 158, 207
Burlingame, Anson, 131, 189, 192
Burns, Anthony, ix, 172-183
Butler, Andrew, 191-192
Butler, Benjamin, 166
Butman, Asa, 140, 173

Cabot, Frederick, 99
  Helped found *Latimer Journal*, 95
Cabot, George, 134, 222
Cabot, Lydia Dodge, 12, 23, 27, 30, 200, 221, 224, 231, 235, 236, 238
  Influence of Lucy Cabot, 30-31
  Lack of children, 31
  Parker fell in love with, 12-13
  Parker married, 26
  Turned away zealous visitors who wanted to pray over Parker, 203
  Travel to Europe with Parker, 69
Caphart, John, 138
Carey, Henry, 194
Carlyle, Thomas, 73
Chapman, Maria Weston, 96, 99
Channing, William Ellery, 9-10, 17, 41-44, 56, 60, 97
Chase, Salmon, 162, 189, 191
Child, Lydia Maria, 227
Christian Register, 37, 50, 54, 55, 115, 123
Christian Union Convention, 57
Choate, Rufus, xv, 122, 125, 215, 231.
Cinque, Joseph, 209

Clarke, James Freeman, 54, 231, 232, 238,
Cobb, Reverend Sylvanus, 99
Cobbe, Frances Power, 220, 235
Collins, Robert, 135
Collison, Gary (historian), 131
Commager, Henry Steele, xi
Comte, August, 59, 85
Conscience, xiii-xv
  Bible and, 36-37
  Channing's view of , 41
  Childhood development, 5-6
  Conservative views, 120-122
  Critique of clergy and, 64-67
  Divinity School curriculum and, 19-20
  Gender, 89-90
  Parker' public persona, 58-59
  Politics, 160-162
  Race, 206-208
  Revolutionary version, 123-128
  Social conscience, 71-72, 79, 86-88
  Twenty-Eighth Congregational Society, 81-82
  Vocational concept, 8-9, 49-50
  Violence, 207-208
Conway, Moncure, 232
Craft, William and Ellen, 128-129, 228
  Attempted arrest of, 135-137
Cranch, Christopher Pearse,16
Curtis, Benjamin R., 127, 183
Curtis, George Ticknor, 135

Dall, Caroline Healey, 50, 53, 58, 81, 91, 100, 132
Dall, Charles, 81
Dana, Richard Henry, 129, 131, 138
Davis, Jefferson, 187
De Wette, Wilhelm, 21, 33-34, 37, 41, 69, 73, 106
Desor, Edouard, 229- 231
"Doctrine of Inspiration," 45
Dorrien, Gary, 60
Devens, Marshal Charles, 136
Douglas, Stephen A., 186, 191, 195
Douglass, Frederick, 130, 158, 209
Dred Scott v. Sandford, 215
Driver, Thomas, 50
Dunham, Z.B.C., 50

Dwight, John Sullivan, 19, 20, 34, 35

Ellis, Charles Mayo, 58, 133
Emerson, Ralph Waldo, xi, xiv-xv 22-24,
39-41, 56, 64, 71-72, 78, 97-98, 111, 123,
148, 152, 198, 239.
Emmons, Nathaniel, 168
Everett, Edward, xvi, 111, 113, 115, 161,
162, 215, 231,

Fairchild, John H., 50
Fell, Jesse, 216
Feuerbach, Ludwig Andreas, 167
Finney, Charles, revivalist, 201-203
Fillmore, President Millard, 125
Flint, John, 81
Follen, Reverend Karl, 41, 97.
Folsom, Abby, 56, 91
Forbes, Hugh, 204-205, 217-218
Fourier, Charles, 57, 74
Francis (of Watertown), Reverend
Convers, 11, 22, 23, 24, 27, 30, 35-36, 43,
45, 52, 61, 72-73, 227
Frederiksted, St. Croix, 224
Free labor ideology, 194-195
Frothingham, Nathaniel, 67, 77
Fugitive Slave Act, speech against, 119-
120
Fuller, Margaret, xi, 35, 72, 90, 91, 97,
152

Gannett, Ezra Stiles, 46, 65, 67, 88, 232
Garrison, William Lloyd, 56, 65, 96, 99,
105, 108-109, 122, 157, 180, 200, 207,
226
Gibbon, Edward, 20, 55
Giddings, Joshua, 161
Goddard, Matilda, 90
Goddell, William, 201
Grimke, Charlotte Forten, 84
Grodzins, Dean, (historian) xii, 81
Gura, Phillip, xii

Hale, John P., 115, 172, 182, 186, 189,
192, 195, 218
Hallett, Benjamin, 166, 179, 182
Hamlet, James, 125
Harrington, Jonathan, 101
Hawthorne, Nathaniel, 232

Hayden, Lewis, 129, 131, 138-139
Healey, Mark, 81
Hedge, Frederick Hedge, 21, 22
Henry, William "Jerry", 156
Henson, Josiah, 130
Herder, Johann Gottfried von, 151-152
Higginson, Reverend Thomas Wentworth,
134, 174-175, 177, 182, 187, 188, 201,
205, 218
Hitchcock, Major Ethan Allen, 105-106
Hollis Street Council, 65-66
Hopps, William, 187-188
Howe, Julia Ward, 12, 92, 149
Howe, Samuel Gridley, 106, 110, 129,
131, 135, 149, 205, 217, 222
Hume, David, 55
Hunker politics, 162
Hunt, Sarah, 188, 190, 195, 197
Hutchison, William, xii

Jackson, Francis, 109-110, 131, 233-234
Johnson, Oliver, 157
Julian, George, 162

Kansas Nebraska Act, 172
Kant, Immanuel, 12, 21, 25
Kneeland, Abner, 43, 53

Lane, Jim, 187
Latimer, George, 95, 106
Latimer Journal, 95
Liberty Party, 80, 108-109, 114
Lincoln. Abraham, 7, 149, 214-217, 238
Loring, Edward Greeley, 122, 178-179,
238
Loring, Ellis Grey, 131, 136, 138
Lothrop, Samuel K., 50, 53, 55
Louis, Pierre Charles Alexandre, 229
Lowell, James Russell, 131
Lucas, Prosper, 208-209
Lunt, George, 135
Lyman, Joseph, 219, 220, 223, 226, 228,
233

Manley, John, 221
Mann, Horace, 164-166
Martineau, James, 119, 136
Massachusetts Anti Slavery Society, 151

Massachusetts Quarterly Review, 108, 110-117

May, Samuel Joseph, 96, 116, 157, 165, 182

McCalmont, J. F., 217

Merriam, Francis Jackson, 233

Mexican-American war, 103-106

Miller, Perry, xii

Minkins, Shadrach, 137-139

Moleschott, Jacob, 230

Morison, John H., 63

Morris, Robert, 131, 138, 139

Nell, William, xv, 131, 148, 155, 210, 211

New England Emigrant Aid Society, 186

North American Review, 55, 111

Norton, Rev. Andrews, 18, 22, 24, 40, 46

Nute, Ephraim, 187-188

Otis, James, 155

Paine, Thomas, 55

Palfrey, John Gorham, 15, 18, 37-38, 41, 112-113, 122, 124

Palmer, Joseph, 57

Parker, Theodore ,

    American Republic is the child of rebellion [but] the national lullaby was treason, xvi

    Anonymous review of John Gorham Palfrey on the Old Testament 37

    Anti-Slavery friends are too sharp in their public condemnation of men who aim at the same end but use different means to achieve it, 165

    Pseudonym "Levi Blodgett," 46, 56

    Brown asked for money from, 200

    Children, lack of, 84, 133

    Civil disobedience as demands for individual action on behalf of the collective good, 138

    Concrete reality shaped by religion, morality, economic liberalism and republican tradition had become an end in itself rather than the beginning of a fairer more just society, xvii

    Discourse in Matters pertaining to Religion, 59-61

    Dramatic conflicts of conscience reinforced by American revolutionary memory, xv

    Family as only social institution where "spirit of Christianity" was consistently practiced, 89

    Fugitive Slave Act enforcement would profane relics of revolutionary heroism, xvi

    "History of the Development of Religion in Man," intending to write, 134

    Insistence biblical precepts yield to authority of conscience seems more germane, xiii

    Member of Secret Committee of Six, 205

    Obtained the pastorate at Spring Street in West Roxbury, 26

    Pernicious social inequality and not moral failure created pauperism and vice, 86

    Poverty as root cause of intemperance, 87

    Received financial assistance from the Divinity School "beneficence fund," 16

    "The Transient and Permanent in Christianity," xii, 51-53

    Parker intervention in controversy between Reverend John Pierpont and congregation, 65-66

    Parker on hypocrisy as the reason for Unitarian stampede to disown views they entertained privately, 68

    Parker shared with Lincoln a rational faith in individual and collective improvement but were at very different stages in their political careers, 216

    Parker's critique of wealth and its deadening impact on the Church, 65

Parkman, Dr. Francis, 41, 45, 67

Parrington, Vernon, ix

Paulus, Heinrich, 21

Peabody, Andrew, 55, 172

Peabody, Elizabeth Palmer, 35, 38, 42-43, 54, 98, 128

Phillips, Wendell, 84, 106, 131, 135, 143, 148, 164-165, 176, 181, 207, 225, 227, 239

Pierce, Franklin, President, 164, 166, 185

Pierpont, John, 65-66, 81, 87

Pitts, Coffin, 173

"Popular Theology," 167-169

"Practical Atheism" xiv, 168-169, 178, 188

Prayer Meeting Revival, 201

Prosser, Gabriel, 205

Putnam, George, 35

Quincy, Edmund, 98, 99, 131

Quincy, Josiah, 195

Race, xv, 85-86, 150-158

Racialism, 206-211

Rantoul, Robert, 142, 161

Reid, Thomas, 18-19

Remond, Charles Lennox, 156-157

Republican Party
    Parker's disillusionment with, 213-214
    Parker's hopes for, 189-193

Revolutionary center of American Abolitionist culture, 150-151

Riley, Patrick, 138

Ripley, George, 21, 25, 27, 35, 40, 44, 57, 67, 74, 80, 97, 224

Ripley, Sophia, 71

Robbins, Chandler, 35, 69

Roberts, Benjamin, 151

Rock, Dr. John, 156, 210-211, 239

Rose, Ann (historian), xii

Russell, George Robert, 26

Sanborn, Franklin B., 187, 204, 205, 217

Sargent, John, 75-76

"Sam Book," 148

Sewall, Samuel, 133

Seward, William Henry, 159, 161, 162, 189, 191, 213, 228

Shackford, Charles, 50

Shaw, Anna Blake, 45

Shaw, Francis, 31-32, 240

Shaw, Robert Gould, 240

Silsbee, William, 24, 37

Sims, Thomas, 140-145

Slavery, x, xi, 34, 71
    Extension of, 105
    Parker's definition of, 79
    Parker predicts violent end of, 233-235
    Polarity with freedom, 124, 150, 166, 178, 183, 188, 216
    St. Croix, 224-225
    Transcendentalism and, 96-98

Smith, Elizabeth Oakes (poet), 91, 134

Smith, Gerrit, 108, 205, 218

Smith, Joshua, 125, 131, 135-136

Sparks, Jared, 111

Stearns, George Luther, 205, 219

Stearns, George Osborne ("Junius Americanus"), 161

Stetson, Caleb, 35, 54

Stevenson, Hannah, 103, 180, 198, 203, 219, 222

Spooner, Lysander, 131

Stewart, Dugald, 18-19

Story, Joseph, 9

Story, William Wetmore, 232

Stowe, Harriet Beecher, 232

Strauss, David, 34
    Channing's view of, 43
    Life of Jesus, 34, 43
    Parker's review of, 43-44

Stuart, Reverend Moses, 121-122

Sumner, Charles, 102, 105, 106, 113, 143, 144, 162-163
    Attacked on the floor of the Senate, 191-193
    Compared Webster to Judas Iscariot, 123
    Return from Europe, 195

Supernatural Rationalism, 17-18

Suttle, Charles, 173

Tappan, Arthur and Lewis, 108

Theism, Atheism and the Popular Theology, 167-169

"Theodore Parker's Experience as a Minister," 226-227

Thoreau, Henry David, 32, 72, 128

Toombs, Robert, 181

Transcendentalism, x, xii
    Ambivalence about abolitionism, 96-100

Conflicts among Unitarians over, 41-42

Divisions over meaning of
conscience, 70-72
Origins of, 23-27
Spiritual vitality and, 29-30
William Herndon and., 214-215
Trial of Theodore Parker, 182-183
Tuckerman, Joseph, 224
Turner, J.H., 217
Turner, Nat, 205
Twenty-Eighth Congregational Society,
xii

Decline of, 239
Formation of, 80-82
Fraternity lectures, 220
Mobilized for Kansas relief, 188
Permanent Lyceum, 167
Promoted by abolitionists, 99
Relocates to Music Hall, 91-92
Women in, 91-92

Very, Jones, 56
Vesey, Denmark, 205
Vigilance Committee (Boston)
Anthony Burns, 175-178, 179
Formation, 128-132
Violence, 142-145
Race and, 150-159, 233-235
Vogt, Charles, 230

Walker, David, 124
Walker, James, 19
Ward, Samuel Ringgold, 124
Ware, Henry Junior, 13, 15, 19
Ware, Henry Senior, 17, 27
Washburn, Emory, 111
Washington, Madison, 151, 209
Waterston, Robert C., 67
Webster, Daniel, 114, 121, 124, 125, 231,
234
Parker's eulogy of, 160-162
Power of conscience overrated, 121
West End, center of Boston black
community, 129
Weston, Deborah, abolitionist, 143
Wheeler, Samuel, 158
White, Robert, Shaker leader, 89
White, William Hoar, 6

Whiting, Nathaniel, 56
Wills, Gary (historian), 216
Wilmot Proviso, 109
Wilson, Henry, 159, 189, 190, 192, 213,
218
Winthrop, Robert C., 112, 113, 123
Woodbury, Levi, 135
Wright, Elizur, 108, 109, 131, 140